KV-512-073

CONFLICT AND HARMONY

a source-book of
Man in his Environment

compiled and edited by

GRACE E. KING

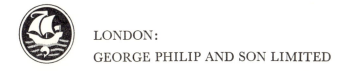

LONDON:
GEORGE PHILIP AND SON LIMITED

*The late Grace E. King, B.A., was Principal
Lecturer in Geography, Cavendish Square Graduate
College of Education, London.*

Printed in Great Britain by the
Garden City Press Limited,
Letchworth, Hertfordshire

SBN 540 00953 9

Foreword

The teaching of geography can result in two radically opposed attitudes among schoolchildren. Some find the subject a wearisome collection of facts presenting a 'load on the memory rather than a light in the mind'. Others are stimulated by the teaching they have received and find their curiosity about other lands and about geographical phenomena to be developing. The root cause of these differences in attitude lies in the way the subject has been presented to the pupils. On the one hand a catalogue of perhaps accurate but uninspiring facts; on the other an exciting adventure into new ideas and new areas, in which the bare bones of factual information have been richly adorned with aural and visual experiences which make an impact on the young mind. Hence the current tendency to encourage the use of audio-visual aids in education, from the language laboratory to the sound film projector, all of which enrichen the experience of the learners.

The written word, however, may be just as effective as the visual image in stimulating the geographical imagination. The literature of travel and of fiction based on personal experience is full of vivid descriptions which can bring to life either an area which had appeared as no more than a name on a map, or a natural phenomenon which when described in scientific language seemed dull and uninspiring. Consider for example this description of the breaking of the monsoon. 'The skies seem literally to break open. The sound is like the crashing of cymbals in an orchestra, with an undernote of drumbeats. The rain comes down in sheets and splashes back in fountains from the hard earth . . . In the morning everything looks fresh and washed. The dust is gone from the leaves. The land looks live again.' Whatever may be the scientific explanation for the sudden change from a hot dry season to a wet season in India, the impact of the above description of the phenomenon is vivid and lends reality to it which it would be difficult to obtain other than by visiting India at the appropriate time. Further, the phrase 'The land looks live again' with its poetic undertones sums up the importance of the phenomenon for the Indian peasant farmer. Unfortunately such descriptive passages are scattered throughout a vast literature and the teacher wishing to avail himself of these needs must spend many hours searching for them and copying those passages he is likely to use with a class.

iii

Mrs Grace King has therefore rendered a signal service to all teachers in compiling this anthology, with commendable care and patience over the years. She first spoke to me of this project at a time when she was lecturing in geography at Cavendish Square Graduate College of Education, and actively engaged in promoting the teaching of her subject.

It is my deep regret that her premature death has robbed her of the opportunity to see her work come to fruition. We are nevertheless fortunate in that her husband, Mr. H. J. King, has been able to see the book through the press so that this very useful anthology is now available to all those, whether in primary or secondary schools, who have the urge to awaken children's curiosity about the world they live in.

NORMAN J. GRAVES

Head of the Department of Geography
University of London Institute of Education

Preface

No doubt many teachers of all subjects keep note of passages that have enlightened them and are constantly looking for fresh material; to them this book may prove valuable, and to others—particularly those just entering the profession—it may form a useful starter and suggest the sheer volume of literary material that is to be had for the seeking, the variety of sources from which it may be obtained and some ways in which it may be used. A source-book of this kind cannot assume to touch more than a fringe. Search, of course, takes time and requires access to a large number of books. It is hoped that this collection will not only prove a time-saver but encourage some to emulate the much-loved school-master in Paustovsky's *Story of a Life*:

> Giving us a lecture on Gogol, Selikhanovich conjured up the Rome of Gogol's time, its hills and its ruins, its painters and its carnivals, its very air and the colours of its sky. Its outstanding figures appeared before us, quickened by a magic which he made us feel to be available to all of us since it was only the magic of a passionate and imaginative scholarship.
>
> Being taught literature by Selikhanovich was a breathtaking journey through time and space. We visited the armouries of Tula and the Cossack outposts on the road to Daghestan; we felt the very drizzle of the 'autumn in Boldino'; we moved from the debtors' prisons of Dickensian England to the market places of Paris, and from Chopin's sick bed in the ancient monastery on the island of Majorca to the unpeopled valleys of Tasmania where the sea winds rustled through the fields of maize.

In quoting this passage it is not the intention to suggest that everything must be done for children and young people; the emphasis today is on learning, on education rather than on teaching.

The above was found among Grace King's notes. Had she lived to see her book published she would no doubt have wanted to say more about imaginative teaching. All through her teaching life she had laid stress on the need, particularly for geography teachers, to stir the imagination of their pupils.

The idea of this source-book had been in her mind for many years and it has been due largely to the help and encouragement of Miss Emmeline Garnett, Warden of Wreake Valley College, Leicestershire, and formerly Senior Lecturer in English at Cavendish Square Graduate College of Education, London, that it has finally come to fruition. A large number of extracts had been collected over the years and it was Miss Garnett who provided the final spur to publication as well as contributing a number of passages herself. Thanks are also due to various friends who furnished accounts of their experiences and to Dr. N. J. Graves for his interest in the project and his kindness in contributing the Foreword.

H. J. KING

Contents

3 Coming to terms with environment

4 The less fortunate ones

5 Pioneers and adventurers

6 Spoliation of environment: what now?

7 We don't all think alike

xi

8 Labour on the land

9 Labour in industry

xiv

1

Conflict with Nature: Climate

The object of this section is to present statements of the natural hazards of living and working in some of the more exacting climatic conditions which in one form or another are endured by the vast majority of people on earth, presenting problems and restrictions to those exposed to them.

The technology of artificial environment and mechanised transport are enabling affluent societies to establish communities in difficult climatic conditions, whether for economic or strategic reasons; individuals take opportunities, and it is in some of these areas with 'difficult' climatic conditions that the biggest economic and social changes must be expected. Even so, Man can be held to ransom by the efficiency of his machines.

1 Winter the great waster

U.S.S.R., circa 1960

And still in fifty thousand Soviet villages and in Soviet cities under the wail of factory sirens and the hoot of American-style locomotives Winter is the great waster and consumer, wearying body and soul for more than half the year ... Slipping and stumbling one goes, and the winter eats up armies of labour to keep city roads usable. In the most important avenues bulldozers attack the snow at once, pushing it into great heaps to slip down the sewer manholes which are left open and unguarded. In lesser streets and yards the house porters, or *dvorniks*, stack up banks of snow until by the end of winter there is barely room for a car to pass. If no more snow falls for a long time, drab bands of sweepers attack the city ice with pick and shovel and pneumatic drill. The points at tram and railway junctions must be kept clear day and night and this work, like so much unskilled work in Russia, is done by women. Muffled in padded clothes and grasping iron stakes in their clumsy gauntlets, they stand bowed and patient witnesses to the incubus of winter.

In the worst weather it is so cold that it seems to burn. You launch yourself out of double doors into the street and you gasp. You narrow your shrinking nostrils to give your lungs a chance to get acclimatised, but you gasp again and go on gasping. Ears are well covered against frostbite, but eyebrows and moustache grow icicles in bunches, and sweat runs from under your fur cap and freezes on your temples. Presently a tickle and the longer hairs of your nostrils have become rigid with ice. Another moment surely, and the whole nostril will freeze over : in a panic you warm your nose with your glove, but the nostrils do not freeze and you go on warming your nose and stinging cheeks with your gloves and you go on gasping ... nothing will keep frostbite from your feet except the clumsy felt boots called *valenki*. These are simply right-angled tubes of felt closed at one end, and you must wear them several sizes too big, after you have first wrapped your feet and legs in strips of cloth rather like puttees. For short journeys goloshes pulled over shoes will do, and some people stretch outsize goloshes over the feet of their *valenki*, not to keep out the wet, except for a short period in spring and autumn, but to keep out the cold.

During the winter it is far too cold for the snow to be melted by any human warmth inside a felt boot; if you stand still the cold slowly freezes you through felt and rags, more quickly through goloshes, and quickest of all through leather ... So a bundle on two bundled legs, one must go shuffling and stumping through the city winter, scheming to avoid waiting in the open air, banging in and out of double swinging doors and treble swinging doors, leaving everywhere a trail of steaming breath and sweat, queueing always to park your coat, hat, scarf, gloves and goloshes and queueing half an hour to get them out again. It is a very indoor life behind the double windows gummed all round with paper, and an Englishman soon suppresses his desire for more fresh air or lighter clothing. Sometimes the outer air can be allowed into rooms for a little while through the *fortushka*, the little inset double window, but the foreigner, tempted by a milder spell, who re-opens his whole inner window will not only get a room which may take a day to heat up again but an outer window which will stay frosted over by his own rash breath for the rest of the season.

... But in the villages—and quite half of the Soviet Union live in villages—life in winter is more its grim and ancient self. The open country is an icy white desolation ... Inside a good *izba* (log hut) it is stifling. Every chink is stopped with rags or moss, and the living space between the rough wooden ceiling and raised floor is even less than one would expect. The long wandering flue often smokes, and the accumulated breath of a large family, of smoke and heavy clothing, bed, cooking, stored food, dog, cat and cockroaches takes a little getting used to. At least one can be grateful that the peasants no longer shelter farm animals inside the *izba* too. Everything centres round the stove, but few huts can afford the upright tiled Dutch stove; in most of them the fire is contained in the *pechka*, a home-made thing of brick or clay which may be no taller than a couple of bookshelves and little wider, but which serves as fire, oven, drying table, bench and even bed. And still without a tall stove it is never warm enough in the worst weather, inside the *izba* or the double-windowed cells of town flats, or the leaking little frame houses in the suburbs. To come through many thicknesses of doors and curtains into such a fug, to be stuffed into such a little choked and steaming chamber and still be cold—it gives some inkling of the impotence and despair generated through centuries by the Russian winter.

from : Wright Miller, *Russians as People*

2 Droving in a cold spell

British Columbia, Canada, nineteen-thirties

It was clear and sunny when we left, and we had no premonition of what was going to happen. The first morning on the trail we crawled out of the soogans* in a white shimmering world. Lakes and timber

* Sleeping bags

thundered and boomed beneath a cold half light, with the temperature at sixty below zero. By eight o'clock our frosted shivering outfit, almost obscured in a blanket of rising blue steam, moved methodically west towards a gap in the Coast Range and distant Bella Coola . . .

I shall never forget the second night out. Both of us were sleepy— a bad sign. We dragged windfalls and down timber into camp with our saddle horses at first, but the cold became so unbearable that we were forced to keep moving on our feet to keep from freezing; and from then on and during the entire night, one of us constantly dragged in windfalls and roots by hand to the fires.

We kept fires burning about thirty feet apart, and between them we kept horses tied to trees. The man that wasn't dragging in windfalls kept himself and the horses alive by leading alternately two horses at a time up and down the trail. This kept the blood circulating. We couldn't turn the horses loose, for they were ready to break back for home.

The cattle walked steadily all night around bundles of hay, their hoofs making a brittle crackling sound on the crusted snow. These suffering animals wouldn't stop long at a bundle of hay, but would snatch a mouthful or two and continue to walk. I think this is nature's way of keeping these animals from freezing solid. Their instinct is to keep moving. Coyote and Slats were left with their saddles on, the cinchas* loose, and Alfred's only two horse blankets covering saddle and animal.

Here—in this camp—with death hovering close, no little detail of survival could be overlooked. It was necessary to be constantly alert. We took every precaution that Alfred, experienced in this game, was wise to. Later we discovered that on this night thermometers in the Anahim district had dipped to sixty-six below zero, and at Redstone in the Chilcotin to seventy-four below.

My first impressions of sixty-six below were startling. What I had read and pictured in my mind was reversed in actuality. Since this first experience I have learned that forests, lakes and sky react differently and in accordance with the speed of the falling of the mercury, the length of the cold wave and the humidity of the atmosphere.

For instance, I had heard and visualised, and have since witnessed, a silent land gripped in intense cold, but during this almost-record cold snap, the thermometer had dropped from ten above zero with probably a high degree of humidity, to sixty-six below zero in about fourteen hours. The sudden expansion of the trees, rocks, lakes and atmosphere produced a weird and fantastic effect.

On this day, instead of traversing a silent brilliant land, we found ourselves in the midst of a volley of explosions and gun-like reports.

*Saddle girths

The lakes, woods and rocks, suddenly being forced to freezing point, and filled as they were with a certain amount of moisture, simply were all bursting at once. The air was alive with a very fine frost, and although the sun shone out of a clear sky, it threw a strange dulled yellowish light over the land.

from : Richmond P. Hobson Jnr., *Grass Beyond the Mountains*

3 The long winter

Manitoba, Canada, 1945

No one has turned over a garden here yet. Not a thing planted. Not a leaf on the trees. The evergreens look fresh—that's all. The cows are being fed on hay. Which reminds me that I have got to get some more to see us through this winter—and it is now May! It would help a lot if we could turn the cows out to grass—but there isn't any grass. That must seem strange to you, accustomed to the lush green grass of the English countryside. Two months from now it will be possible to walk through grass—or rather hay—wild hay—that you cannot see over because it will grow six feet high. But today, there is no grass. Everything is grey, with here and there a blade of green trying hard to come through. When the sun comes out strong everything will break into life and will grow horribly fast. So fast indeed that it is impossible to keep things in check and looking tidy. Then, if it doesn't rain, all the moisture in the ground will be used up, and after that everything will begin to parch. What a gamble farming is in this country! A protracted spring such as we are having can hold things up more than one can hope to insure against.

It will be quite interesting to see when the trees will get their leaves. At the present rate of going I don't expect it will be till the beginning of June.

from : Letter from Jack Jones, Great Falls, Manitoba

4 Car breakdown in the desert

Sahara, nineteen-fifties

With a sickening feeling we stuck, every wheel held fast by the fine powdery sand. Buried so low that even the rear axle and petrol tank were partly covered.

Gone now was the slight breeze of air caused by the forward movement of the car, standing stationary there under that relentless sun the interior was unbearable. Quickly I jumped out, almost in a daze now, and the sun struck my bare flesh like the flame of a blowlamp. Not even at the side of the car was there any shade, it was just noon and the sun was dead overhead. Falling on my knees I scraped with my bare hands at the sand under the running board. In a desperate frenzy I tore it away, cursing as it fell back into the little trench I was trying to form. At last, after what seemed to be hours of work, there was enough space between the car and the ground to enable me to roll under. There, exhausted, I lay, panting for breath, pouring sweat from every pore and my whole body trembling from fatigue...

I looked around me at the surrounding country. Over to my right about a mile away was a large hill, and between me and the hill was a patch of vegetation. Over to my left there was a sea of sand dunes stretching away out of sight. Ahead and behind the desert stretched level, right to the distant horizon. There was no more to see than if I'd been alone on a raft in the middle of the Atlantic. I had a strange feeling that this part of the earth was mine, that I owned it.

It was difficult to imagine that any one would ever come this way, so desolate was the spot... How slowly the time passed, it was about two-thirty now, another hour and a half before it would start to cool off. Had my watch stopped? No, it was still going, that's strange! There didn't seem to be the terrific glare on the sand as I looked out and then I noticed that it wasn't quite so hot lying there. What was happening? I rolled out and stood up. In the whole of that vast blue sky there was one large cloud and at this moment it was completely blotting out the sun. For the first time I was able to stand out there in the open and look at the car.

Walking ahead for some twenty paces I stabbed my heels into the sand, it was soft, very soft. I felt better now, the two hours' rest had done me good. I had, for the first time since leaving Algiers, been able to relax.

Was there anything I could do? The more I studied the situation the more hopeless it looked. Could one man ever get this car to move again? There was only one way to find out, I must have one final try.

Getting out the shovel, I cleared the sand away from the front wheels and axle. Under the car it was impossible to use the shovel, so I lay on my back and with my hands and arms scraped the sand away. It was hot work and took a long time but eventually the underneath of the car was clear; a patch of sand the size of the car and about twelve inches deep had been removed. Next thing to be considered was weight. It would never be any good trying to move the car heavily loaded as it was.

Opening all the doors, I started to drag out every moveable object. It was now that I realised how weak I was. My suitcase, which I could normally throw about, was more than I could move now. Getting in the back seat I pushed it out, followed by everything else ... Next I sorted out the few items that must be taken along. First the water and food, my shotgun and twelve cartridges, the spare wheel, jack and wheel brace and one electric torch. That was all. The rest of the goods I dragged a few paces away from the car and just left them scattered about. There was only one more thing which could be done to help. I went round every tyre and let out the air until about 10 pounds was left in. They looked almost flat, but not quite on the rims. She was ready now, there was nothing else that could be done. Everything which had been thrown out would, of course, have to be abandoned, if it did move there would be no stopping. If it moved and then buried itself again a few feet on, the only thing would be to give up and wait.

I got in and pressed the starter, at the first touch the engine started. As I let in the clutch she moved; hardly daring to breathe I accelerated away in bottom gear. We were out and on the move again.

from : Ralph Sleigh, *Savage Sahara*

5 A hot day in winter

Paraguay

One day comes that common South American phenomenon, reversal of the seasons. A too early summer stays unwelcomed. Day after day a windless, visionless vacuum. The long tricolours on Government House and Customs House float with slow, oily convulsions on the thick, humid air. In the streets the people sag. Politics displaced by the one question. No position relaxes, no clothes are comfortable. No drink cold enough, no shower refreshing. Each night a hopeless rearguard action against mosquito squadrons ... close the windows and be asphyxiated, or open them and be bloodsucked ... It is August, the northern January, but these days, their temperatures fingering the

7

100's have been filched from summer's index; procure strange sunrises: an orange-red disc throbbing over the swamps, casting no shadow, terrifyingly near, as it might be to some other world on which one has found oneself. Hot tongues of furnace winds lick into the house. Foliage and vegetation lift in tortured response. The slow baking earth begins at last to open. Sunset a crimson Chinese lantern held in a palm tree by the talons of a heraldic black vulture.

from : Gordon Meyer, *The River and the People*

6 Damp heat and tropical fatigue

Malaysia, nineteen-sixties

There is no doubt that efficiency is affected by climate, and that a cool and dry climate which is not too cold and too dry, is more conducive to efficiency than a hot damp one. The difference is most impressive for anyone moving from a temperate to a tropical climate, but the effect of comparatively local movements can be impressive too. For example, industrialists who have moved their factories only 75 miles from Bombay to the new industrial area outside Poona, have noted the improved output of their workers who have moved with them, because Poona has a greater diurnal range and is also cooler generally from June to December than Bombay. It is 1,500 feet higher.

Singapore and Malaysia provide an excellent case study of the effects of climate. My impression on arrival was how bearable the climate was because it wasn't astronomically hot. But it is very humid and it is only with the passing of time that one realises that the monotony of steady heat and humidity can be very trying. One can get up at five o'clock and be soaked with perspiration by half past five. Rainfall of just under 100 inches a year is far from the world's heaviest, but in Singapore it rains every day and the same amount of rain seems to fall every month of the year. The sun rises and sets at almost the same time every day of the year and the thermometer hits 87°F so regularly that it is said that a temperature of only 10°F above that has ever been recorded. The temperature at night is equally steady, and the diurnal range is very low, less than 15°F.

In Taiping, inland from Penang, it even seemed to me to rain at the same time every day, the convection currents and steep hill behind the town being what and where they are.

The absence of seasons is very debilitating, and I well remember how pleasant it was, after a few years of Malaysia to move to Ceylon, where, in the north at least, there are seasonal differences; they would be imperceptible to a new arrival from the west but were wonderful when coming from further east.

In this climate one becomes sensitive to minor climatic differences; after the hot nights of Singapore and Penang, one appreciates the less hot nights of Kuala Lumpur, where the temperature gets down to 72°F. This comparatively pleasant situation is due to being surrounded by trees, which have a marked effect on climate. Ipoh, only 150 miles north of Kuala Lumpur and as far inland, is hotter because so much jungle has been cleared for tin mining.

Malaysia's developing electricity supplies make for widespread air conditioning for those who can afford it. Nationals are as much affected by the enervation of the climate as expatriates and they site their houses to take maximum advantage of prevailing breezes and so on, but they naturally are more relaxed about it, knowing nothing of any more bracing climate. They don't fret when they wilt.

A special contribution by Ralph Wyeth

7 Continental summer

Canada, nineteen-thirties

The heat not only covered the Great Plains, it fastened a deathly grip on Ontario and the Great Lakes as well.

No one who lived in southern Ontario that summer could have failed to understand what life was like on the Prairies. From Windsor to Belleville, for a solid week in July, it was 100 above or hotter every day, and in Toronto it reached 105 on three successive days. During that awful ten days, 500 died in Ontario alone from heat prostration . . .

What made the heat intolerable was the way the wave built. Every day was hotter than the previous day, with heavier haze and more dust. At the end of the first week in July, people were taking pillows into the down-town parks in Winnipeg and Regina in an effort to get some rest. In the down-town tenements beds were deserted as the inhabitants stretched out on floors, on verandahs and on lawns. But there was no escape. Swarms of mosquitoes and crickets made sleeping out of doors almost impossible in Winnipeg. . . . The Manitoba peak was reached on July 11 when the temperature reached 108 in Winnipeg, 110 in Brandon and 110 at Morden. During the third week in July it went over 100 every day everywhere in the south country of Saskatchewan and Alberta.

from : James H. Gray, *The Winter Years*

8 High summer

Patagonia

Gradually the tempo of the year increased from the brief green blush of spring to the fierce burning climax of high summer.

From then on, under an arrogant sun streaming out of cloudless blue which arched from flat horizon to mountain rim, the long tussocky grass and low bush foliage would grow more parched day by day. The landscape, bleached of its youthful colours, was transformed in a few weeks to a sun-scorched waste as the heat continued to suck all moisture from the earth. It took on a kind of pallor as though the very life-blood was being drained from it.

League after league, the plain unrolled like a carpet to the shimmering horizon, sterile and seemingly without life. It was as though spring had never been.

From the blistering canyons the mountains climbed skywards, wrapped in a day-long quiver of heat-haze, as if their hoary heads sought the coolness of the upper air. The only relief to the eye was the thin ribbon of green where the stream still ran through the fretted creases. But by midsummer, even the stream flowed more sluggishly as each week it receded further from the heat-cracked bank . . .

There were two kinds of summer weather, both of which my mother hated. One was the day that dawned with a pleasantly cool breeze which would soon be burnt up by the relentless sun. Ravished under a torrid sky, which by noon would be bleached almost white, the land would swoon. Every living creature panted in the motionless air, craving the balm of nightfall.

The other kind of summer day would be ushered in on the wings of a Turneresque sunrise. Not a single dust devil would disturb the glowing early hours; the newly washed laundry would hang dry on the bushes; the air would be like a delightful June day in England. Then precisely at 10 a.m. a little breeze, born of nowhere, would suddenly fan the cheek. From a whisper it would grow to a flurry, increasing rapidly to a hot pitiless blast that whirled the white dust in obliterating clouds along the track, smote the mallin grass into flat swathes and drove both man and beast to irritated distraction. Punctually at 4 p.m. this wind would drop; it was uncanny, almost as if a gigantic pair of bellows had been switched off, leaving a perfect summer evening, mild and blissfully cool.

from : Mollie Robertson, *The Sand, the Wind and the Sierras*

9 Heat in the Karoo

South Africa

The summer heat of this wide upland world can today scarcely be imagined by those even a hundred miles to the south. My first memories are of heat like the heat of blazing ovens; of shutters, and sunbeams making a hot bright path through a chink in a dark blind, of soil too hot to walk on barefoot and rocks too hot to touch. Heat, I suppose, is the most positive and formidable thing on the Karoo, and the beginning and sometimes the end of many a Karoo story ...

I watch our dogs running from one spot of shade to another in the veld and think of all the dogs of all the travellers and trekkers who crossed the Karoo. Every traveller had several and these suffered terribly unless their masters were humane enough to lift them into the over-crowded wagons. With the ground as hot as the side of a wood-stove, they would rush along the track from bush to bush to find even the miserable shade cast by a bush too small to defend them from the scorching sun ... Many a dog was crushed to death as it tried to keep in the shade of a moving wagon.

from : Eve Palmer, *The Plains of Camdeboo*

10 Sicilian summer

Sicily

This landscape which knows no mean between sensuous sag and hellish drought; which is never petty, never ordinary, never relaxed, as should be a country made for rational beings to live in; this country of ours in which the inferno round Randazzo is a few miles from the beauty of Taormina Bay; this climate which inflicts us with six feverish months ... May, June, July, August, September, October; six times thirty days of sun sheer down on our heads; this summer of ours which is as long and glum as a Russian winter and against which we struggle with less success. You don't know it yet, but fires could be said to snow down on us as on the accursed cities of the Bible. If a Sicilian worked hard in any of these months he would expend energy enough for three. Then water is either lacking altogether or has to be carried from so far that every drop is paid for by a drop of sweat; and when the rains come they are always tempestuous and set dry torrents to frenzy, drown beasts and men on the very spot where two weeks before both had been dying of thirst.

from : Giuseppe di Lampedusa, *The Leopard*

11 Hot weather in East Harlem

New York, U.S.A., nineteen-fifties

On the third really hot day in May 1954, Billy, a mischievous thirteen-year-old, decides the time has come to start one of East Harlem's traditional summer sports. In his bright scarlet T-shirt and old blue jeans he gets a wrench from a friend on 100th Street and advances on the nearest fire hydrant.

The atmosphere is heavy, for the concrete has held the heat through the night, and all those who can have left their stifling apartments for the almost stifling street.

The sight of the boy with the wrench causes a general stir on every doorstep, and as he approaches the hydrant on the sidewalk, he is joined by a dozen bright-eyed youngsters who begin to jump and cheer and clap as he struggles to open the outlet wide. First a trickle, then a spurt, and then a rush of water comes forcing itself out over the street at six hundred gallons a minute. In a moment the difference is felt even in the houses, for the temperature drops as the water spreads across the street.

About a hundred boys and girls of every colour and shape and size come rushing from all directions to paddle and leap and fight in the flood. A twelve-year-old has knocked both ends out of a tin can and fits it over the hydrant's outlet, directing the jet down on to the ground. Now he slowly points the can higher and higher until, amid excited screams, the strong jet is hitting the opposite tenement, and just as it is about to pour in through the open windows, shouts and threats of vengeance persuade him to play the jet along the street where it cascades down from a height of twenty feet on to children in their summer underwear who dart in and out of the gushing fountain or sit down, beaming joyfully beneath it.

Suddenly the jet player looks eagerly up the street. This is what he has been waiting for. The children (including a well-dressed boy, dancing in the downpour beneath an umbrella) clear as if by magic off the street. The car approaches, sounding its horn uncertainly. All the children are shouting and screaming, while their laughing parents gather on the doorstep or crowd the tenement windows. The driver of the car is stepping on the accelerator and winding up his window at the same time, but the force of a direct hit on the glass sends a triumphant jet through the closing half-inch gap. Cheer on cheer from the overjoyed enthusiasts follow the car down the flooded street, but before the echo of applause has died, a youngster comes rollerskating into the water and speeds back and forth, raising waves on either side of his path and laughing and shouting to his delighted friends before he slips and falls headlong in the flood and the whole street rocks with laughter.

from : Bruce Kenrick, *Come Out The Wilderness*

12 In the desert at night

Sahara, nineteen-forties

In this air devoid of moisture the soil is swift to give off its temperature. It was already very cold. I stood up and stamped about. But soon a violent fit of trembling came over me. My dehydrated blood was moving sluggishly and I was pierced by a freezing chill which was not merely the chill of night. My teeth were chattering and my whole body had begun to twitch. My hand shook so that I could not hold an electric torch. I who had never been sensitive to cold was about to die of cold. What a strange effect thirst can have! ...

I dug a pit in the sand, lay down in it, and flung handfuls of sand over me until all but my face was buried in it.

Prévot was able to collect a few twigs, and he lit a fire which soon burnt itself out. He wouldn't bury himself in the sand, but preferred to stamp round and round in a circle. That was foolish.

My throat stayed shut, and though I knew that was a bad sign, I felt better. I felt calm. I felt a peace that was beyond all hope ...

Do not blame me if the human body cannot go three days without water. I should never have believed that man was so truly the prisoner of the springs and freshets. I had no notion that our self-sufficiency was so circumscribed. We take it for granted that a man is able to stride straight out into the world. We believe that man is free. We never see the cord that binds him to wells and fountains, that umbilical cord by which he is tied to the womb of the world. Let man take but one step too many—and the cord snaps.

from : Antoine de Saint-Exupéry, *Wind, Sand and Stars*

13 Advice to an airman wrecked in a desert

Hot deserts

In hot deserts you need about a gallon of water per day. If you follow the rules and walk in the 'cool' desert night, you can get about 20 miles for that daily gallon. If you do your walking in daytime heat,

13

you'll be lucky to get 10 miles to the gallon. Whether you sit out your desert survival or walk out, you'll need water, at least three to four quarts a day.

The only way to conserve your water is to ration your sweat. Drink your water as you need it, but keep heat out of your body. That can be done if you wear a shirt or similar light garment, white or light-coloured if at all possible, in addition to the usual trousers, hat and shoes. Clothing helps ration your sweat by not letting it evaporate so fast that you get only part of its cooling effect. Light-coloured clothing also reflects or turns away the heat of the sun and keeps out the hot desert air.

Stay in the shade as much as possible during the day. Desert natives have tents open on all sides to allow free circulation of air during the daytime. If possible, sit up a few inches off the ground, rather than lying down. It is 30 to 45 degrees [Fahrenheit] cooler a foot above the ground than on the ground itself. That difference can save you a lot of sweat.

Slow motion is better than speed in hot deserts. Slow and steady, slow and easy are desert working rhythms. If you must move about in the heat, you'll last longer on less water if you take it easy. Remember the Arab. He is not merely surviving in the desert; he *lives* there —and apparently likes it. He isn't lazy; he's just living in slow motion, the way the desert makes him live.

from : Nesbitt, Pond and Allen, *The Survival Book*

14 Heat trap in the mountains

Kashmir, nineteen-sixties

We left Goner at 5.30 a.m. and arrived here at 4.30 p.m. having only covered twenty-eight miles, yet I came into the shade of this nullah* in a state of total collapse ... By 7 a.m. the sun was so hot that I was saturated through with sweat and as we only came to one nullah, for wetting, cooling and refilling the waterbottle, dehydration became my fear. I found shade once, under a rock, and slept very soundly from 1.40 to 2.50 p.m., although lying on sharp flints. After that the real trouble began and by 3 p.m. I was seriously worried; I had stopped sweating, which is a danger signal, and my mouth was so dry that my tongue felt like an immovable bit of stiff leather. By 3.30 I was shivering with cold though the heat was so intense that I did not

* Watercourse ravine

dare touch any metal part of Roz.* After that I just kept going but don't remember one bit of the road—only that the green trees of Chilas were visible in the distance. I had just enough sense left, on getting to the nullah, not to drink gallons, but to lie under a willow and take mouthfuls at a time until gradually I began to sweat again and get warm. Then I rolled into the water and lay there for a few minutes with it rushing deliciously over me ...

The horror of today's trek really was extreme with heat visibly flowing towards me in malevolent waves off the mountainsides and the dreadful desert stench of burning sand—which still persists here—nauseating me; the terrifying dehydration of mouth and nostrils and eyes until my eyelids could barely move and a sort of staring blindness came on, with the ghastly sensation of scorching air filling my lungs, and the overpowering drug-like effect of the wild thyme and sage, that grow thickly over the last few miles, being 'distilled' by the sun; and above all the despair of coming round corners and over hilltops time and time again, hoping to see water—and never seeing it ... The irony of it all was that all day the vast, swirling Indus flowed beside me, inaccessible [1,000 feet below in its deep gorge].

from : Dervla Murphy, *Full Tilt*

15 Drought years

Queensland, Australia

He had seen only one bad drought, and even though he had been only nine at the time he would always remember it. At a little town in western Queensland, five years without rain, and the vast plain on which it stood turning to a thin powder, creeping on the town like a slow brown sea, the waves trailing a faint dry spume in the wind that came out of the Centre like the final kiss of death. Dried-up people, and everyone drinking beer because it wasn't as precious as fresh water and tasted better than bore water. The cattle lying dead in the paddocks, washed by the creeping dust, and only the crows happy.

Then the change of colour low in the sky that none of the towns-folk noticed because they had long ago given up looking for it. The clouds coming fast over the horizon, at first indistinguishable from the dust, then suddenly the black sky and the silver lances of the rain driving hard into the earth. And the panic and the fear: that was what he remembered most. The children under five, the ones who had

*The author's cycle

never seen rain, running screaming into the houses, shutting their ears against the drumming on the roof, burying their faces against their mothers' skirts, waiting for the end of the world; and the mothers unable to give comfort, for their minds and their praying lips were giving thanks. And the men standing in the rain, their faces flung back and their mouths open, drunker than they could ever get on beer. He didn't want to see another drought like that one.

from : John Cleary, *The Sundowners*

16 The dust bowl

Oklahoma, U.S.A., nineteen-thirties

A gentle wind followed the rain clouds, driving them on northward, a wind that softly lashed the drying corn. A day went by and the wind increased, steady, unbroken by gusts. The dust from the roads fluffed up and spread out and fell on the weeds beside the fields, and fell into the fields a little way. Now the wind grew strong and hard and it worked at the rain crust in the corn-fields. Little by little the sky was darkened by the mixing dust, and the wind fell over the earth, loosened the dust, and carried it away. The wind grew stronger. The rain crust broke and the dust lifted up and out of the fields and drove grey plumes into the air like sluggish smoke. The corn threshed the wind and made a dry, rushing sound. The finest dust did not settle back to earth now, but disappeared into the darkening sky.

The wind grew stronger, whisked under stones, carried up straws and old leaves, and even little clods, marking its course as it sailed across the fields. The air and the sky darkened and through them the sun shone redly, and there was a raw sting in the air. During the night the wind raced faster over the land, dug cunningly among the rootlets of the corn, and the corn fought the wind with its weakened leaves until the roots were freed by the prying wind and then each stalk settled wearily sideways towards the earth and pointed in the direction of the wind.

The dawn came, but no day. In the grey sky a red sun appeared, a dim red circle that gave a little light, like dusk, and as that day advanced, the dusk slipped back toward darkness, and the wind cried and whimpered over the fallen corn.

Men and women huddled in their houses, and they tied handker-chiefs over their noses when they went out, and wore goggles to protect their eyes.

When the night came again it was black night, for the stars could

16

not pierce the dust to get down, and the window lights could not even spread beyond their own yards. Now the dust was evenly mixed with the air, an emulsion of dust and air. Houses were shut tight, and cloth wedged around doors and windows, but the dust came in so thinly that it could not be seen in the air, and it settled like pollen on the chairs and tables, on the dishes. The people brushed it from their shoulders. Little lines of dust lay at the door sills.

In the middle of that night the wind passed on and left the land quiet. The dust-filled air muffled sound more completely than fog does. The people, lying in their beds, heard the wind stop. They awakened when the rushing wind was gone. They lay quietly and listened deep into the stillness. Then the roosters crowed, and their voices were muffled, and the people stirred restlessly in their beds and wanted the morning. They knew it would take a long time for the dust to settle out of the air. In the morning the dust hung like fog, and the sun was as red as ripe new blood. All day the dust sifted down from the sky, and the next day it sifted down. An even blanket covered the earth. It settled on the corn, piled up on the tops of the fence posts, piled up on the wires; it settled on roofs, blanketed the weeds and wires.

from : John Steinbeck, *The Grapes of Wrath*

17 Equatorial rain

Borneo

'When we got there we really hit something' ... This, then, is the Rain Forest of Borneo, on the Southern slope of the Bawoei Mountains below the thunder factory that clings constantly to the bald dome of Batoetiban Peak. Above the solid blanket of foliage the supersaturated air can actually be seen carrying moisture higher and higher until it masses in solid white peaks of cumulo-nimbus clouds that suddenly blacken before your eyes and dump their reservoirs of water like burst balloons. Then it starts all over again. The whole process, from steam to cloud to cloudburst, might take place within an hour, the sun working furiously between showers to reclaim the moisture lost by precipitation. I don't recall seeing any birds in this locale, but if there were any they must have webbed feathers.

While the evolution of a raindrop is playing continuous performances above the Rain Forest, there is no change whatever in conditions underneath the tree crowns. Storms come and go above, but beneath the crown it rains all the time, and it is perpetually so dark on the jungle floor that it matters little if the sun outside is shining brightly ... Every leaf is a catch basin for the rain, and it drizzles its catch through with the annoying persistence of a leak in the roof. If the sun remains long enough to dry out the top leaves, there is still the moss, a vegetable reservoir capable of storing enough leakage to outlast a Texas drought. Moss grows and swells and soaks and reproduces on top of itself in a devouring cycle of destruction by suffocation. Trees are thickly coated with a decaying slime down which water constantly courses in greasy rivulets, and when you lean against the slime, your arm sinks in, while water spurts between your fingers. Trees and vines only a few inches in diameter look to be several feet thick because of this hoary shroud of death. Underfoot the boggy carpet slips and skids and tears just when you need your footing most. Fallen trees moulder overnight and form great mossy mounds over which you must claw and scramble while a rotting smell steams up your nostrils and your body is plastered with slime. Once on top of the mound you slip off on the other side and fall on your back with a spongy splash.

And the Rain Forest has another unpleasant side, too. Because of the tremendous heat and hundred per cent humidity, it has become the perfect incubator for poison in a thousand forms. Deadly snakes, spiders, insects and vitriolic vines breed there with a lavish contempt for the laws of survival ... We never felt safe. Always the way went up. Slipping in the moss, panting over fallen logs, struggling for air when there was only steam, worming among greasy tree trunks, we inched our way forward like a column of working ants. Each man carried his load on his back and a halo of gnats and flies around his head. His legs sank knee-deep in moss. There was no respite. A pause for rest meant nothing when you couldn't get a breath of air into your lungs. Once we crossed a small crystal brook in which the water ran ice cold. We all threw down our packs and rolled in the refreshing bath. Out of curiosity I tested the temperature with my dark-room thermometer. The stuff that struck us as ice-cold registered a neat 85°F. Still it did wonders to skins burned by poison vines and bites and chafed by sweat.

from : Charles C. Miller, *Black Borneo*

18 Total rain

Liberia

The problems of the country include a rainfall which, during the rainy season, can only be described as total rain—sometimes 200 inches in six months. It blankets the land and washes away the roads. It falls in a hot atmosphere and rises up again in steam. Everything grows at an almost dangerous rate. Not only jungle plants, crops and tropical fruits, but moulds and lichens as well. In unfortunate shades of grey and matt black, these crawl up the walls of newly built houses and establish themselves in the angles of stairways in office blocks and descend from below the eaves. New buildings, stopped midway in an austerity campaign dictated by an over-extended economy, can look like ruins thousands of years old within months.

from : Dennis Kiley, 'Liberia : swift change under policy of the open door', *The Times*, January 17, 1969

19 The excitement of rain

Northern Territory, Australia, 1964

If you have not felt or smelled the soothing deliverance of solid rain for four years and, on top of that, another three years previous to those four, two tremendous deluges inside a few hours and within your region are more than enough news to fill the radio waves to you and to every anxious settler for one hundred miles and more around.

So ran the tidings from Ayers Rock late in November 1964 : 'It's come !' Out of a cloudless sky, hundreds of miles over the limitless plain to the south, out of nowhere and almost in a flash, two whirling dust-storms-cum-rainstorms, several hours apart, gathered up the Rock in their midst and left it glistening and gurgling with the sound of falling waters.

Such an experience, unusual at any time, is even more strange for anyone who has seen the desert only under open skies in its accustomed mood of transcending silence. It left our small party, on whom the blessing descended, refreshed in body, elated in spirit and riding excitedly on the higher planes to which the experience of a traumatic natural event can rapidly lift the human mind.

First you are aware only that a vast, swirling, mauve-and-yellow cloud of dust is bowling across the desert in your direction. Then, from the lee of the Rock and lulled into a false sense of security by the shelter of a car, you are aware that the sky above and around has been completely blotted out. As the gloom gathers, its purples and mauves and orange-browns grow more intense, and the wind begins to shriek; there comes to everyone an eerie feeling, a sensation of being about to witness the end of the world.

Then are vouchsafed the deliverance, the soothing wetness, the huge drops streaming down—the rainstorm itself. The airstrip is quickly a murky no-man's-land.

The road is a ditch of puddles, a flowing drain, a Venetian canal (with our car a stationary, stalled gondola), and then a river fed by a delta of creeks surging out from the Rock. They in turn fed by a hundred waterfalls, cascading solid plumes of foam and spray thundering down several hundred feet from the lower bastions of this lonely fort. What a sight to gladden an explorer's heart!

An hour afterwards, with the car again able to move forward two miles or so out in the desert you still ask the question "Where's all this water coming from?" You cannot hear the waterfalls from this distance, but they continue to flow unabated. The wonder of it all is that the desert sands and the sunny skies would pretend no storm had passed this way at all.

From another angle—Ayers Rock, after the storm and bathed in sunlight, appears like a shimmering, silver-grey blanc-mange that could easily wobble over.

from : Richard Piesse, 'Storm over Ayers Rock',
Walkabout, March 1966

20 Escape in the wadi

Aden, South Arabia

Nearing our destination, we had to descend into a river bed cast between sheer rock faces about two hundred feet high either side of us—the whole being about seventy-five yards wide.

About a quarter of an hour into this impressive wadi the rain suddenly started to come down as I have never seen rain. The driver suddenly became very scared and parked the vehicle on a piece of higher ground on the left and I, not knowing much about these things, the driver had to do some smart talking to persuade me to get out of the car and climb the rock face. I reluctantly followed him and we found an overhanging rock. Under this we sat, soaking wet and shivering cold. Suddenly a great wall of water swept down the valley making what had been a dry river bed into a raging torrent.

It would have been dark by now but for the half hour long continuous flash of lightning. The noise of the thunder and the rushing water echoing between the cliff faces was something not easily forgotten.

from : Mora Dickson, *A World Elsewhere*

21 Monsoon: the farmer's point of view

India

After the Spring harvest is over, all the land rests. The farmers know that nothing will grow in the coming months because the time of great heat is coming. Day after day the earth dries a little more in the hot sunshine. It dries until it cracks. Over all the land there is a vast drought. Small rivers practically disappear. Gardens dry up. The people stay in their houses in the daytime. The village seems lifeless. No one works at anything except the things that must be done—feeding the animals, eating a little themselves, and watching the grain supplies get lower and lower in the bins and jars. . . .

At night the searing wind usually dies down, and the people come out of their houses for a breath of air even though it is hot. They look at the sky and shake their heads when they see stars instead of clouds. How much longer must they wait?

The rains normally break at the end of June. The first rain usually comes in the night. The people have seen clouds as they went to bed—those long awaited clouds—and they hope that before morning they will be wakened by thunder.

And then it comes. The skies seem literally to break open. The sound is like the crashing of cymbals in an orchestra, with an under note of drumbeats. The rain comes down in sheets and splashes back in fountains from the hard earth. When a little of the top is softened, the ground begins to soak up the water.

Along with that first rain comes a welcome coolness. People who have gasped for every heated breath they drew get up early to enjoy the difference.

In the morning everything looks fresh and washed. The dust is gone from the leaves. The land looks alive again. There is a peculiar smell about, a bitter odour of bruised plant stems and of clogged drains and of cattle and people. After a day or two of hard rain, the smell goes away, and there is left only the lovely freshness of wet fields and straw.

Even the smell of smoke from morning fires is different. The birds find their voices again and from somewhere deep in a thicket a wood dove sounds his plaintive thanksgiving for the new season.

The village children run outdoors and hold up their faces to the downpour to see if they can drink any of it. They hunt for pools and go wading. They get soaking wet and their mothers do not scold. They know that everyone's skin will be damp because of the hot steamy air for two and a half months to come. . . .

After the rains begin they last for almost three months, if the monsoon is strong and brings normal moisture. For some time it pours daily with no change. Then there may be a day or two of sunshine, or even a ten day period of no rain. Then the skies open and the rain pours down again. The parched earth soaks up all it can, like a giant sponge.

This is the time when the crops for the autumn harvest are planted. The rice farmers are busy at once. Out early with their bullocks, ploughing in the mud, after the first downpour. They churn the ground into a paste and then smooth it with boards on which they ride. Then the rice fields are ready for sowing. In three weeks the young plants will be large enough for thinning out and for transplanting to other fields that have been prepared for them. The rice will be ready to harvest in September . . .

If the sun comes out and shines for ten days at a time between showers, the man on the land begins to watch the sky anxiously. He wants to see clouds there. The new plants will dry up, or the un-sprouted seed will shrivel in the earth and never come up at all. The seed may be lost before there is a crop to worry about.

In such a season, with shining intervals that last too long all the talk of the men in the panchayat* at night time is gloomy. At the other extreme there can be too much rain and then there will be floods. Water courses over fields : animals are drowned; the walls of mud houses are undermined and cave in, and the roof falls down on top of the sorry heap.

After an experience like that the village slowly dries itself out and takes stock of the damage. The farmers clear up the wreckage and plant another crop. Meanwhile they draw on all the courage they have.

from : Jean Bothwell, *Men and Monsoons*

* Village council

22 Getting about a parish

Queensland, Australia, nineteen-fifties

In the dry months of the year, from April to the end of November, I can get about in this large parish fairly easily. The roads are not metalled, of course, and in England they would be described as cart tracks, but in a truck you can depend on averaging fifteen miles an hour, so that most of my parish lies within a couple of days' journey of the vicarage. In the wet season, however, travelling is very difficult. About fifty or sixty inches of rain falls in three months; the rivers, which are dry for the rest of the year, turn into swollen torrents, and much of the country is submerged in floods. In the wet no motor vehicle can move a hundred yards outside the town without getting bogged, so that there is little movement in the countryside; station managers get in the stores that they require for four months in November and seldom appear again in Landsborough before the beginning of April. A horse is the best way to get about the country then if one must travel, but the crocodiles are rather a nuisance in the floods and the incessant rain makes camping very unpleasant.

from : Nevil Shute, *In The Wet*

23 Following the lightning

South Africa, nineteen-sixties

'Is it really true', Charles Leonard was asking Ben, 'that these little fellows follow the lightning about?' ...

Yes, it was true, he told them now. Indeed they would be surprised if they only knew the immense role lightning played in the lives of all living things in the desert. It was in a sense *the* light of their lives. It was to them what a compass was to a sailor in a storm, or faith in us. In times like the present all living things in the desert waited with desperate anxiety for the lightning to come. When it did the transformation in them was unbelievable. It was as if suddenly they had rediscovered their lost purpose. No matter how famished and thirsty, they would be renewed at their first glimpse of it. Wildebeest, hartebeest, eland, zebra, gemsbuck, and, hard on their heels, wild dogs, leopard, lion and hyena would follow after it from one end of the vast wasteland to the other.

For instance, in one great drought, he had seen some thousands of springbuck nibbling, listless and gaunt, at the last stubble and

23

scrub around an immense pan. That very evening the lightning flared along the horizon in the west. The next morning all the buck had vanished, but the writing of their spoor in the sand was plain; they were making fast for the west. In the same drought he was helping to take supplies to some 'Khalagadi, dwellers at one of the few permanent wells in the desert, where they were said to be dying of hunger. On the way he ran into a group of Bushmen, no better off than those with us now. He gave them food and water and proposed giving them more next day. That night the first lightning appeared in the west. In the morning they were gone, and their neat little footprints too were directed to the west.

'But suppose the lightning fails them,' Charles Leonard asked.

'I don't think it fails them in the end,' said Ben.

from : Laurens Van Der Post, *The Heart of the Hunter*

24 Wind and waves over an atoll

South Pacific

My nerves were now keyed to a point beyond fear; nevertheless, I realised the perilousness of our situation. Matauea Point was not more than five feet above sea-level and the highest point on the Islet did not exceed fifteen feet. What should we do when the seas started breaking over the land itself?

We huddled together in the middle of the house, or rather in the framework of the house, with the sleeping mat to our backs. Rain came in torrents, soaking us with the first downpour. With chattering teeth I thought how nicely a pint of brandy would go down. Little Sea and Desire dozed in my arms, apparently quite comfortable.

By four in the morning the gale was at its height, blowing with such violence that we could no longer sit with our backs to it but must lie flat on the ground. Nuts, fronds and trees had ceased falling, for most of them had long since been blown into the lagoon, and weaker trees had gone down in the first gust. No gale can break down or uproot a sound, mature coconut palm—it will bend its sixty-foot bole to the ground without breaking; but one log which rolled toward us with grand velocity reminded me that the danger was not past. We could not see it but we heard the crash it made when it struck a coconut stump to windward. . . .

Little Sea was shaking my shoulder and screaming into my ear.

I was roused from my wide-awake nightmare and at length grasped the meaning of her words :

'The seas are coming! The seas are coming, Ropati!'

Dawn was breaking, a leaden, joyless dawn. I could dimly see the outlines of ragged palms with most of their fronds carried away, while the few remaining ones lay out horizontal and stiff in the mighty gale.

Then I heard a deafening roar as though the Islet were being wrenched loose from its foundations and whirled to oblivion in one annihilating avalanche of water. The next instant what remained of the house was flooded two feet deep in a foaming torrent that rushed pell-mell across the Point.

'The canoe! the canoe!' cried practical Little Sea.

Knowing that the mast stays were in the canoe, I ran out and in a moment had moored it to a coconut palm. It was no sooner done than a second wave foamed over the Point, three feet deep. I jumped into a tree and watched the Pacific Ocean washing beneath me. Little Sea and Desire were clinging to another tree nearby.

I had not noticed in the excitement that the wind had abated and was even then diminishing by perceptible degrees. Within the next five minutes it was dead calm again. It is at such times that the seas rise, for during the height of the gale they are flattened by the wind.

The next wave took the skeleton of the little house, flooding the Point a good six feet deep. Fortunately, instead of uprooting the trees we were roosting in, it banked about two foot of sand over the whole length of the Point. But waves are fickle things, and as the next one might sweep away all the sand that had been brought in, and a good deal more besides, we took advantage of the lull between the third and fourth waves to run inland to higher ground.

It was an eerie experience watching those great seas piling over the Islet, carrying débris, birds, fish and gigantic masses of coral which had been wrenched from the reef. The two girls took advantage of every lull to jump down and gather their dresses full of the fattest fish; but I remained where I was, not wishing to be put to the test of a quick scramble up the straight stem of a coconut palm.

By midday the seas had given up their attempt to wash Danger Island into the marine ooze, leaving a tattered and torn Ko Islet strewn with dead fish, mangled trees, coral boulders, and drowned sea-birds.

from : Robert Dean Frisbie, *The Book of Puka-Puka*

25 A tornado hits a farm

South Dakota, U.S.A., 1962

It was raining lightly on May 14th, 1962, and spring showers are always welcome on the Great Plains. Farmer Emil Ziebart of Ethan, a town in south-eastern South Dakota, glanced at the churning clouds massing in the south-west. He decided there was just time to plough another furrow before supper. Nearing the end of the round, he checked the sky again. A greyish-black cloud wall about half a mile wide loomed over his neighbour's tree grove. Below it hung a funnel-shaped mass, tapering towards the earth. Then suddenly, as he stared, horrified, the trees disappeared, flicked up as easily as a vacuum cleaner sucks up dust specks.

He jerked the plough from the earth and turned the tractor towards home. Behind him, advancing, the cavernous cloud mouth gaped hungrily.

He jumped from the tractor, raced towards the shelter belt of trees on the west side of his farmyard, dived headfirst through the wire fence and grabbed the nearest tree trunk. There was a strange, ominous silence. Emil Ziebart gasped for breath in the weighted, Stygian air. He could hear only the pounding of his heart. Then there was a stupendous Niagara of sound and he felt a heavy blow on his back. He dug his face into the ground as the tornado roared over him.

Soon the black, omnivorous wall, the pressure, the horrifying noise were gone. Ziebart raised his head slowly. The top of the tree he was clutching was not there. Uprooted trees lay grotesquely like piles of rotting weeds, their roots hanging limp. Twisted, spiky pieces of tin, shattered lumber, an overturned corn picker, huge drifts of last year's corn stalks, dead chickens—all lay in chaotic heaps as far as he could see. Beside him was a naked pheasant, only its remaining neck plumage identifying the lifeless form.

Dazed, Ziebart stood up. He shook his head. Something was wrong. He must be confused about directions, he decided. Where were the barn, the silo, the granary, the chicken houses—all his buildings? Gone. There was nothing standing, just mountains of débris.

Fearfully, he peered beyond for his house. He saw the remains of the front steps, leading up into empty space. Then he saw his home, completely lifted from the foundations, jammed against the tortured trees, roof fragments dangling pitifully like shattered human limbs. And his family?

He scrambled drunkenly over the littered mess. 'Oh God! They're dead! It's taken everything. They're gone!' It was the immemorial cry of man against nature's cruelty.

Emeline Ziebart had not turned on the radio or TV that May afternoon, and did not hear the tornado warnings. While her freshly-baked banana cake cooled on the kitchen table, she put several loaves of bread into the oven. She noticed it was raining outside. Suddenly, an explosive crash startled her. The house shuddered convulsively; windows popped out.

'Tornado!' she shouted. 'Joey! Diane! Run for the basement!'

The three dashed wildly into the basement and crouched beneath the stairs, seven year old Joey between his mother and his sister, Diane, 17. Instinctively Mrs. Ziebart pushed Joey down flat, she and Diane protecting his body with theirs. Superhuman powers pressed them viciously against the cement floor.

Then—was it one minute later, or five?—everything was quiet. The tornado had passed over them, its suction taking even their hiding place, the stairs. Above them was the open sky. Wreckage surrounded them—the washing machine, tubs, heavy pipes, severed electric cables, lumber—and mud everywhere. As they clambered out of the basement into the yard, fears flashed through Emeline Ziebart's mind. Where was Emil? Crushed beneath the tractor? Dashed to pieces in the field?

Suddenly she saw her husband—and he saw them at the same moment. He began to run, stumbling over the rubble. The four met and silently clung to one another. It was Diane who spoke first: 'Thank God! We're all alive!'

from: Helen Rezatto: 'Tornado Alley's week of terror', reprinted with permission from May 1963 British *Reader's Digest* © 1963
The Reader's Digest

26 Wind in the desert

Libya

In the big dune country south of Shebaba we were hit by a sand-storm. The Arabs drew their burnouses completely over their heads and huddled close to the recumbent camels. Through a slit in my burnous I saw loose sand rush along the ground like a fast flowing river. Sand bounded up the long slopes of the dunes and streamed off the precipitous edge in giant swirling plumes. Dunes actually melted, writhed, changed their shapes as I watched. One small dune marched up a great dune's back. Another dissolved and disappeared, and where there had been a hill there was only flat ground and driving sand. The air was thick and white as milk and crowded in

27

upon the lungs. The sun was an indistinct blob as if seen through frosted glass.

It was interesting for the first three hours. Then the stifling sensation increased, thirst began to assert itself, and the sand penetrated into the ears, nose and throat. There was no chance to get water or food. To rise would mean to be blown away bodily before the wind. The air was like the heat from a blast furnace. The best insulation was the sand that was piling up around and on top of us. There was a choice between sand outside the burnous and breathing carbon dioxide inside. We breathed carbon dioxide. It was easy to understand how desert travellers die of suffocation during such storms. It was twenty-eight hours before the screaming, grinding roar of the wind and sand abated and we could crawl out, weak and stiff, from our burial mounds.

from : William Price, *Incredible Africa*

27 Dust in the wind

Pakistan, 1963

Last night soon after I went out to dinner one of the dust storms, for which Pindi is famous, blew up so that within five minutes everything and every one in the room was coated in dust; you could see it on the food and feel it in your mouth and smell it horribly. Then all the lights went out and, what was far more disastrous, the fans stopped and we all sat in lamp-light, streaming sweat and grinding dust with our pilau.

You'd think the people here would take this heat in their stride but the papers go to town on it with banner headlines . . . Evidently being born to it doesn't make people immune. In summer factory-production goes down and the general efficiency level drops in the Civil Service, business, etc. Coming from sun-starved Ireland it takes time to adjust to the custom of avoiding the sun : it seems so *odd* to sit at lunch with curtains drawn and lights on.

from : Dervla Murphy, *Full Tilt*

28 Hot dry wind

Ukraine, U.S.S.R., nineteen-sixties

One wind kills with ice and snow; the other destroys with fire and dust. I never experienced the latter but I read with awe Paustovsky's description of one such wind which blew for a fortnight in his childhood near far-away Kiev.

'It came,' he writes, 'laden with sand, whirling and whistling and sending flurries of birds' feathers and chips of wood flying through the air. A heavy haze obscured everything. The sun had grown shaggy suddenly and as red as Mars. Broom-trees swayed and crackled. A heatwave scorched my back. My shirt seemed to be smouldering. Dust crunched between my teeth and pricked my eyes. By the first evening the sand-drifts were deep against the wattle fences; by morning green leaves were so dry that they turned to powder at the touch of a hand and trees stood as bare and black as in autumn. Women's wailing filled the cottages while men sat glumly in the shelter of walls prodding the soil with sticks saying : "It's turning as hard as rock. The grip of death is on the land, that's what it is, and we have nowhere else to go." . . .'

I mention these winds not only because they are so savage a feature of the Russian climate and must have some subtle influence on the character of the people—they blow, for instance, right through Russian music—but also because they are a natural challenge which brings out the best in Soviet Russia. In its mass attacks on 'natural problems' Soviet Russia is at its most impressive. The child Paustovsky had asked his parents why a Chinese wall could not be built to stop this devastating invasion of wind from the deserts of Central Asia, and was told it was impossible. Today the impossible is being performed.

I flew twice low over the plains between the Black Sea, the Caspian and the interior, and I was profoundly impressed by the vast belt of trees that the Russians have planted to break up the winds and shelter the cultivated earth.

from : Laurens Van Der Post, *Journey into Russia*

29 Effect of wind in winter

U.S.S.R.

White mist—a crystalline veil of air-suspended ice hangs in the near distance, and only a mile from the village you would be swallowed up in a swirling white world. There is not a stir in the silent air, but your eyes dazzle at the particles and they seem to swirl. The steel air gnaws and bites at your cheeks, a stiffening of frost arches at the corners of your eyes, and presently out of the padded silence the lightest of winds stirs the surface of the snow lifting spicules of ice into white wisps and trails, and suddenly it whips one of these across your face like a razor-slash. You turn your back only to meet a stinging slash from the other quarter, and if you must stay out in these conditions your earflaps, peak-flap, high fur collar, and a gloved hand together will seem a feeble shield. And this is but the lightest of winds. Every illusion you may have had about enduring Russian cold is undone by wind, and a five-mile-an-hour breeze has a grip like an iron mask. Twice that speed is already a blizzard. Windy weather is frostbite weather, and with ten degrees or more of frost, and a moving air, one must watch for the white, bloodless patches or, in the ghoulish phrase of the medical book, 'spontaneous amputation may supervene.'

This is the weather which ravages peasant faces, giving many of them an immobile, flattened appearance all the year, or leaving them with zigzag ears and nibbled noses which heal in clean new skin and come to look like deformities and not the wounds of winter.

from : Wright Miller, *Russians as People*

30 Roar of the Föhn

Switzerland

'At the end of every winter comes the Föhn with its deep-toned roar, a sound which the Alpine dweller hears with fear and trembling but for which he knows a terrible longing when he is far from home.

'Men and women, wild beasts and cattle sense the approach of the Föhn many hours in advance; even the mountains seem aware. Its advent, which is nearly always preceded by contrary winds, is announced by a warm deep-sounding rush of wind. Within a few seconds the blue-green of the lake becomes an inky black; the water is suddenly agitated and white crests of foam appear. Soon the lake, which but a few minutes before was utterly calm, begins to hurl its angry surf against the shore like a thundering sea. At the same time the countryside seems to close in nervously, to contract as if in fear. One can now pick out individual rocks and peaks which shortly before appeared to brood in the remote distance; and villages which previously looked like far-away specks, can now be seen so clearly that every roof, gable and window can be distinguished. Mountains, meadows and houses crowd in like a timorous flock, and then comes a rushing, rumbling sound as the earth begins to tremble. Waves whipped up from the lake are flung far through the air like wisps of smoke and one hears, especially at night, the incessant roar of the storm's desperate battle with the mountains. Later comes news of overflowing streams, battered houses, smashed lake-craft and men missing from their villages.

'When I was a child I dreaded the Föhn and even hated it. With the first stirrings of youth however, I grew to like this bold rebel, this ever young harbinger of spring. I loved the way it plunged into its wild battle, full of vigour, exuberance and hope, the way it laughed and stormed and groaned as it chased along the ravines, devouring the snow from the mountains, ruthlessly twisting the tough old firs and breaking them with a sigh.'

from : Hermann Hesse, as quoted in *Swiss Life and Landscape*
by E. Egli

31 Windlessness and English fog

England, 1960

Born and brought up in England, I find it hard to realise that there are people who have never seen a real fog. A sea fog—the scientifically-minded call them advection fogs—yes. They occur in many waters where warm, moisture-laden air passes over the colder water surface and is cooled to dew point. But there are not so many places in the world where the inland or radiation fog is common ...

Whether it is what the Londoner calls a 'peasouper' or the grey fog of the open country, it is still a strange, eerie, and somewhat frightening phenomenon, quite unpredictable. Seen from a car at night, it is a grey, impenetrable wall, each minute droplet of water reflecting the gleam of the fog lamps so that the straining eyes of the driver can see nothing, not even the edge of the road. Then the 'cat's eyes' are the only guide and I have driven sixty miles at a steady thirty miles an hour and never seen a thing except those cat's eyes coming up in a steady stream beyond the bonnet.

These fogs usually occur in the autumn, particularly November, for then the sun is still warm enough to draw moisture up into the atmosphere, and the nights are cold and clear, producing the necessary drop in temperature. One October, I remember taking five hours to drive the thirty miles to the coast. This was at night, on a road that had no cat's eyes, and I drove completely blind, my wife leaning out of the side window and reporting the distance from the edge of the road every few seconds for mile after weary mile. The strain of that drive was so great that I spent the remainder of the night fighting the wheel in my sleep as imaginary cars came at me out of the fog.

But it is not only at night; in broad daylight I have been forced to turn back, unable to penetrate for more than half a mile through the fog—and that was not in an industrial district, but trying to get out of my own village, where I knew every twist and turn of the road. Other times, I have progressed in jerks, the fog suddenly lifting and then as suddenly clamping down again.

But when the fog lies thin in layers, then it is at its weirdest. Then sometimes you drive just below it, as though a canopy had been stretched above the road.

Once, when I owned a little, low-slung sports car and was groping my way through thick fog, a coach went roaring past. The driver could see the hedges on either side, his head just above the fog-layer. It sounds absurd, but a little farther on, in a slight dip, I passed him, driving with my head just under the fog, whilst he in his turn was driving blind.

from : Hammond Innes, *Harvest of Journeys*

32 Just normal

Southern Chile

The squall line fled away to the north-east, the sea smoking dark below it. Soon water and sky, which had been one, separated. From the south-south-west the waves marched by, six to the mile, forty feet from trough to crest, capped by seven feet of breaking water, which the wind seized as it rose from the sheltered valleys and hurled ahead in glittering sheets. The smudge on the horizon took shape as a black, uncompromising island cliff : Cape Horn.

Rain, hail, fog, wind, snow these are the normal here, at the southernmost tip of South America. Here the Andes founder in a wreckage of islands, peninsulas, channels, bays and sounds. Clouds sit low on the mountains, and waterfalls pour out of them. The hardy trees grow close along the ground, where the wind thrusts them. It is a land where penguins hobnob with ostriches, glaciers run into the sea and raspberries grow in the turf; and all this no further south of the equator than Lincoln is to the north of it ...

'Here you have to grow a windbreak to protect the windbreak you have to grow to protect your flowers. Here you can wake up to a black frost any day of the year!'

Everywhere the houses are covered with painted sheet metal and roofed with corrugated iron. It looks dreadful, but nothing else will keep out the wind. The brilliant yellow of a barn, the scarlet of a roof, shout for warmth and recognition in this country of the huge dull skies. There is no time and no background for 'taste', even where there is money.

from : John Masters, 'Journey to the end of the Earth',
The Daily Telegraph Magazine, September 16, 1966

33 An ideal climate!

Queensland Coast, Australia, nineteen-fifties

Our climate, as any one in the neighbourhood will tell you, is ideal. There is the wet, of course, which makes life rather sodden for a while, and admittedly we get a cyclone now and then, but no one seriously disputes our claim that the weather is—normally—just about perfect ...

Of course there was the ten-months drought a few years ago; but that was quite abnormal. Our average annual rainfall is eighty inches, and we simply do not have droughts. Nor do we have bush-fires. The scrub just won't burn, and anyone who has tried to get rid of lantana by putting a match to it, has learned the meaning of frustration—so it was entirely owing to the abnormal conditions that we spent most of that December racing from one farm to another, brushing breaks, and burning back as the flames came romping up the gullies towards our pineapples.

As for frosts, it is only very rarely that we see a light, silvery powder on the ground in some low-lying spot, and the time when four farms lost about twelve acres of pines between them must be regarded as the exception that proves the rule. We do cop the winds a bit, particularly the westerlies, and the north-westerlies, and the

33

easterlies come in from the sea pretty fiercely, and the southerlies are sometimes bad, too. But it is well known—having been established as part of the district's folklore since old Mrs. Hawkins was a girl—that no wind lasts more than three days; even if one does go on for three weeks, you will notice that there is nearly always a sort of lull after the third day. Cyclones just have to be accepted; at least we never get them in the winter, though there was that July a few years ago when we had three—but that was quite abnormal, too.

Naturally one expects the wet to be wet, but when we have got it over, the rest of our eighty inches comes down as needed, at well-spaced intervals. So we were rather shocked one year when, instead of taking itself off at the appointed time, the wet settled down with us. Aunt Isabelle—blandly ignoring the reassuring noises made by politicians—always referred to it as *la pluie atomique*; but be that as it may, there was hardly a break in the rain from February to September. This was a grievous blow not only to our pockets but to our local patriotism, for we are proud of our climate.

from : Eleanor Dark, *Lantana Lane*

Notes to Section 1

The bold figures indicate extract numbers

1 An example of mid-continental winter cold which is also experienced in North America, where, however, greater affluence and higher expectations of comfort have so far led to more widespread efficient central heating, air-conditioning and car travel, insulating man from the outdoors.

2 Store cattle were being moved on the hoof from newly opened ranges halfway between Prince George and Bella Coola in British Columbia. This account shows the utter vulnerability of man and beast exposed to cold in a sudden bad spell. The latitude (52° 25′ N) approximates to that of Ipswich, England.

PRINCE GEORGE (53° 50′ N, 122° 50′ W) 2218 feet (676 m) above sea-level

| | Mean daily temperature | | | | Absolute daily temperature | | | |
| | maximum | | minimum | | maximum | | minimum | |
	°C	°F	°C	°F	°C	°F	°C	°F
January	5	23	−16	3	12	54	−49	−57
July	24	75	7	44	39	102	− 2	28

Contrary to popular view, British Columbia has a 'mild' climate only at a few spots along the coast, e.g. Prince Rupert:

PRINCE RUPERT (54° 20′ N, 130° 20′ W) 170 feet (52 m) above sea-level

| | Mean daily temperature | | | | | Absolute daily temperature | | | |
| | maximum | | minimum | | | maximum | | minimum | |
	°C	°F	°C	°F		°C	°F	°C	°F
January	4	39	− 1	30	January	17	62	−19	− 2
August	17	62	9	49	July	31	87	4	39

The above figures illustrate the effect of the warm drift of surface waters along the coast, which helps to warm onshore winds. The interior has both north winds bringing great cold, and föhns causing warm spells when the westerly air-streams hop over the coastal range. A large part of British Columbia is high and cold.

3 Great Falls, near Pine Falls (50° 51′ N, 96° 11′ W) is about the same latitude as Penzance, England. Like most of Canada it has long cold winters and very short springs. The nearest town for which figures are available is Winnipeg, 80 miles (129 km) away:

WINNIPEG (49° 50′ N, 97° 15′ W) 760 feet (232 m) above sea-level

| | Mean daily temperature | | | | Absolute daily temperature | | | |
| | maximum | | minimum | | maximum | | minimum | |
	°C	°F	°C	°F	°C	°F	°C	°F
January	− 8	17	−25	−13	8	46	−44	−47
February	−11	12	−23	− 9	8	47	−44	−47
March	− 3	27	−15	5	23	74	−39	−38
April	9	48	− 3	27	32	90	−28	−18
May	18	65	4	39	38	100	−12	11
June	23	74	10	50	38	100	− 6	21

4 The incident occurred between In Guezzam and Agadez (at approximately 17° 42′ N, 7° 0′ E) on the desert run of 2000 miles (about 3220 km) from Algiers to Kano. The track was lost while trying to make a detour round a stretch of road with a particularly bad surface. Apart from the hazard of sand, the rocky, rutted roads soon shake a car to pieces. The second driver had been left with nomads owing to fever. There is more traffic, especially lorries, across this area today between October and April, but the climatic conditions and road surfaces—apart from 200 miles (320 km) of tarmac outside Algiers—are not changed and travellers have to be wary. Summer travel is impossible by car owing to the furnace heat. The mean maximum daily temperatures for Agadez, which we can assume are for early afternoon, are as follows. They are shade figures. Night temperatures average 25 to 30 degrees Fahrenheit less.

AGADEZ (16° 58′ N, 7° 59′ E) 1706 feet (520 m) above sea-level

Mean maximum daily temperature

	°C	°F		°C	°F		°C	°F
January	30	86	May	42	108	September	39	103
February	33	91	June	42	107	October	38	101
March	37	99	July	40	104	November	35	95
April	41	105	August	37	98	December	31	87

Absolute shade maximum 46°C (115°F) and ground in the sun 78°C (172°F). Rainfall average 7 inches (178mm). The evaporation rate is very high.

5 ASUNCIÓN (25° 21′ S, 57° 30′ W) 456 feet (139 m) above sea-level
There is no winter as it is known in Britain.

	Mean daily temperature				Absolute daily temperature			
	maximum		minimum		maximum		minimum	
	°C	°F	°C	°F	°C	°F	°C	°F
January	35	95	22	71	43	109	12	54
June	22	72	12	53	37	98	− 2	29
August	26	78	14	57	38	101	− 1	30

6 The constant need to lose moisture in a humid climate which is inhibiting to evaporation induces lassitude. People from tropical countries feel more energetic in Western Europe, except during cold, sunless spells. Statistics reveal a very constant relative humidity throughout the year in both Singapore and Kuala Lumpur, and a constant range of temperature expressed by the monthly averages. A humidity of 75 per cent and over is uncomfortable. As it is a large town, Singapore tends to be a heat island and the warm seas keep night temperatures up. Kuala Lumpur's climate is affected by the presence of trees. Periods between rains are normally more sunny in the tropics than in the Western European zone.

SINGAPORE (1° 17′ N, 103° 51′ E) 33 feet (10 m) above sea-level
Mean annual relative humidity at 0900 hours = 79 per cent
at 1300 hours = 73 per cent
Mean annual rainfall = 95 inches (2413 mm)

Mean annual temperature				Absolute annual temperature			
maximum		minimum		maximum		minimum	
°C	°F	°C	°F	°C	°F	°C	°F
31	87	23	74	36	97	19	66
				(over 39 years)			

KUALA LUMPUR (3° 9′ N, 101° 41′ E) 127 feet (39 m) above sea-level
Mean annual relative humidity at 0700 hours = 96 per cent
at 1300 hours = 63 per cent
Mean annual rainfall = 96 inches (2438 mm)

Mean annual temperature				Absolute annual temperature			
maximum		minimum		maximum		minimum	
°C	°F	°C	°F	°C	°F	°C	°F
32	90	23	73	37	98	18	64

7 Windsor is fairly near Detroit (42° 25′ N, 83° 5′ W) where a mean temperature of 23°C (73°F) and an absolute maximum of 41°C (105°F) is experienced in July. Belleville (44° 15′ N, 77° 37′ W) may be compared with Toronto, where the mean temperature is 21°C (69°F) and the absolute maximum 41°C (105°F) in July. Winnipeg's mean temperature of 19°C (67°F) represents an average of the maximum 26°C (79°F) and the minimum 13°C (55°F). The absolute maximum is 42°C (108°F) in July. The nights in July average out at 4°F cooler in Winnipeg than in Toronto, thus bringing down the average.

8 Estancia Huanaluan is close to Maquinchao, Argentina (41° 15′ S, 68° 50′ W). It is about 2000 feet (610 m) up and has a severe winter. Cipolletti (38° 57′ S, 67° 59′ W), about 200 miles (322 km) farther north, is 889 feet (270 m) up and has mean day temperatures of 32°C (89°F) and night temperatures of 13°C (56°F) in January. The absolute maximum is 42°C (107°F), and the minimum 3°C (37°F) in January. Mean precipitation at Cipolletti is 6 inches (152 mm). On the ranch they rely on river water and bores.

9 Camdeboo (the thirst land) is an extension of the Great Karoo. The farm is 11 miles (18 km) from Pearston (32° 33′ S, 25° 7′ E) on the road between Somerset East and Graff Reinet. It was possible to establish it because there were bore holes and a dammed-up lake. Cradock, the nearest place whose statistics are available, is 50 miles (80 km) across country and between hills. Rainfall is light, 13 inches (330 mm) and on average falls on only 42 days of the year. In one year on the farm only 1 inch (25 mm) was experienced.

CRADOCK (32° 8' S, 25° 36' E) 2861 feet (872 m) above sea-level

| | Mean daily temperature | | | | Absolute daily temperature | | | |
| | maximum | | minimum | | maximum | | minimum | |
	°C	°F	°C	°F	°C	°F	°C	°F
January	31	87	14	58	42	107	4	40
February	29	85	14	58	41	105	4	40
March	28	82	13	55	39	103	3	38
April	25	77	9	49	37	98	— 1	30
May	21	70	5	41	33	91	— 4	25
June	16	60	2	35	27	81	— 7	19
July	18	64	1	34	28	83	— 7	20
August	21	69	3	38	32	89	— 5	23
September	23	73	6	43	37	98	— 4	24
October	26	78	9	48	39	103	— 1	31
November	27	81	12	53	41	106	1	34
December	29	85	13	55	42	107	4	39

10   Palermo (38° 0' N, 13° 19' E) 233 feet (71 m) above sea-level, is often quoted as having an ideal 'typical' Mediterranean climate. Its average temperatures suggest that it is favourable to man. 'Mediterranean' regions of the world lie between deserts and humid Western-type temperate areas. We sometimes forget that the summers should be thought of as being extensions of desert climates. This is particularly true in the south of the European Mediterranean area. Here there is a wide variety of conditions due not only to the latitude. True Mediterranean conditions can only be found on the coasts, the interiors of bordering countries being mountainous or sufficiently extensive to have greater extremes. The mean monthly temperatures for Palermo are:

	°C	°F		°C	°F		°C	°F
January	11	52	May	22	71	September	24	76
February	12	53	June	23	74	October	20	68
March	13	55	July	26	78	November	16	61
April	16	60	August	26	79	December	13	55

These are made up as follows:

| | Mean daily temperature | | | | Absolute daily temperature | | | |
| | maximum | | minimum | | maximum | | minimum | |
	°C	°F	°C	°F	°C	°F	°C	°F
January	14	58	8	47	22	71	2	35
February	16	60	8	47	26	78	0	32
March	17	62	9	49	33	91	— 1	31
April	19	67	12	53	30	86	6	42
May	28	83	15	59	35	95	9	48
June	28	82	19	66	39	103	11	52
July	30	86	22	71	41	105	15	59
August	31	87	22	72	45	113	17	63
September	28	83	21	69	41	106	11	51
October	24	75	17	62	32	90	9	48
November	19	67	13	55	29	84	5	41
December	16	61	10	50	26	79	3	37

Rainfall:

Mean monthly rainfall

	ins	mm		ins	mm		ins	mm
January	5	127	May	0·8	20	September	1·2	31
February	3·6	91	June	0·2	5	October	3·7	94
March	2·6	66	July	0·1	2·5	November	3·9	99
April	1·7	43	August	1·6	41	December	3·5	89

Heavy rain falls on 77 days in a year on average. It is very sunny and, with irrigation, there is a long growing-season.

11 Americans talk of the 'long hot summer'. Of recent years it has been associated with disquiet and political unrest. New York has a much more extreme climate than might be expected from its position (40° 45′ N, 74° 0′ W) and nearness to the Atlantic.

12 The evaporation rate by day may exceed 100 inches (2540 mm) and light rain evaporates as it touches ground. Cloudless skies increase heat loss at night. In the cool season, dew is sometimes formed on the dunes by morning.

13 It is possible to collect a small quantity of water at night by a simple apparatus consisting of a collecting vessel, a piece of plastic over a hole in the ground and a stone or other object to weight the centre of the plastic over the collector in the hole. Condensation in the night does the rest— water collects on the underside of the plastic and drops into the collector. Deserts cover about one-third of the world's surface, and are mainly in the warm areas. The Sahara, for example, is about twice the size of the U.S.A. Although fresh-water supplies from beneath the surface are exploited, and there is also oil, coal and iron ore, it will be a long time before such wide open spaces are conquered.

14 Chilas (32° 25′ N, 74° 5′ E) nearly 3000 feet (910 m) above sea-level. This extract comes from a writer travelling from Ireland to India with her cycle, 'Roz'. Some of the nullahs she describes originate in glacial melt-water and flow for a few hours in the heat of the day for much of the year. They are in full spate by 1800 hours and dry up during the cold of the mountain night. Some vegetation and shade result.

15 This is an area which has not only a light average rainfall, but in which the amount can vary enormously from year to year. Bore water is often both hot and saline.

16 The classic name 'Dust Bowl' was applied to Oklahoma in the nineteen-thirties. Similar conditions were experienced by other midwest states, including the Canadian state of Saskatchewan, where farmers had to give up in drought years. The term is now applied to other regions of the world where marginal land has been (or is being) overcropped or overgrazed in near-drought conditions, and the top soil has been (or is being) blown away. Large, hedgeless, treeless fields are particularly vulnerable, especially in monocultural farming. In North America public conscience led to government action and the bad areas were largely stabilised by strip-cropping, contour ploughing, rotation of crops and the use of bore water.

We are now aware of the danger of making fresh dust bowls, but large-scale mechanical farming, the natural enemy of soil conservation, is increasingly undertaken.

17 This description is applicable to other equatorial areas that experience a very high rainfall.

18 The effect of excessive humidity on material things is one of the trials of wet places. Monrovia (6° 18′ N, 10° 47′ W) has an average of 202 inches (5130 mm) of rain a year, of which on average 170 inches (4317 mm) fall in six months. The mean daily maxima range from 27°C (80°F) to 31°C (87°F), and the nights from 22°C (72°F) to 23°C (74°F). The absolute maximum temperature is 34°C (93°F) and the minimum 13°C (55°F). Relative humidity at 0730 hours ranges on average between 95 per cent and 87 per cent, and at 1130 hours from 86 per cent to 76 per cent—that is, at discomfort level.

19 Ayers Rock (25° 23′ S, 131° 5′ E) rises 1143 feet (348 m) out of the desert 250 miles (402 km) from Alice Springs in the centre of Australia. It is visited by 10,000 tourists a year who come to Alice usually by plane or train. The road is still very bad. From Alice to the Rock you come by coach or car across the red desert, preferably in the cooler season. Very few will have seen the rock wet.

20 The Aden area normally has a rainfall of less than 5 inches (127 mm). The presence of wadis probably indicates a wetter period in this area at some time in the past—perhaps an extension of the influence of the south-west monsoon. Now the occasional torrential rains cause a build-up of flood-waters which flush out the wadis.

21 Too often we think about the monsoon and its causes rather than about the farmer. The monsoon is in many places uncertain. Drainage, water conversion and irrigation are linked in a pattern of necessity.

22 Australians refer to the seasons as the 'Wet' or the 'Dry' over much of the continent, because rainfall is the key to climate. Seasonal variations of rainfall are greater than the seasonal variations in temperature except in the extreme south. Desert nights in the centre can be very cold at all seasons, especially in June and July. Immigrants sometimes underestimate the heat they are likely to meet in Australia. The north is approximately the latitude of Nigeria, the south that of Spain. The absolute maximum in Darwin is 41°C (105°F) and in Adelaide 48°C (118°F).

23 The 'little fellows' are the Bushmen of the Kalahari, the former inhabitants of much of South Africa and now pushed into the desert by the Hottentots, Bantus, and Dutch and English settlers who occupy the better lands. The Bushmen, like the animals, have an instinctive knowledge of many things, including the fact that lightning means rain and food.

24 Puka-Puka, Danger Islands (10° 53′ S, 165° 49′ W). Coral islands and atolls are always at risk, owing to their lack of altitude, from storm waves (surges) and from tsunamis (waves associated with earthquakes, sometimes thousands of miles away). The speed of travel of a tsunami can be from 100 to 700 miles per hour (160–1126 km).

25 North America is peculiarly susceptible to major tornadoes and her great plains are known as 'Tornado Alley'. This is due to the major topographical features which allow moist tropical air from the Gulf to come into violent conflict with cold north or north-westerly air-streams. Along this front from time to time secondary lows of exceptional depth form and move with the front at about 20–45 miles per hour (32–72 km). Once detected, their route can be approximately forecast and warnings sent out. The destruction they cause is due both to the winds within, whirling at 200–500 miles per hour (320–800 km), and to outward suction (due to the partial vacuum which lies in the centre of the tornado). A second tornado may follow on roughly the same track as the first.

26 Shebaba Sebha (27° 9' N, 14° 29' E). Names such as khamsim and sirocco are given to hot winds carrying desert sands. Even a slight wind causes distress, as can be noticed on a dry sandy beach. In Australia, east coast towns have been darkened by clouds of red dust. In south-eastern areas a wind of this kind is called a 'brickfielder', after the name given to a dust-laden wind from the former brickfields near Sydney.

27 Rawalpindi (33° 38' N, 73° 8' E), May 27, *before* the monsoon rains and during dry heat.

28 Outside Kiev, the black earth is under the plough and subject to gullying and erosion.

29 The plains of Russia and North America are especially susceptible to wind. Northers which blow for a day or two in winter can lower Gulf temperatures by 10°C (108°F). The Russian steppes are subject to winds from the region of extreme cold in Siberia. Russia in Europe is subject to blizzards originating along the cold front of Atlantic depressions.

30 The föhn blows for a few days at a time, in winter. It is caused by a deep depression north of the Alps attracting warm air from the Mediterranean. This air is further heated and dried by compression as it roars down the narrow valleys. The Chinook of the High Plains of North America is similar to the föhn. It occurs when warm, moist, unstable air, after rising over the Rockies and descending, arrives as a dry warm wind. Housewives in Calgary have been known to take advantage of the mild, dry conditions to hang washing out for a blow during the break in a long frozen-up winter. On an occasion such as this, Calgary has reached 16°C (61°F) in January, 19°C (66°F) in February and 24°C (75°F) in March. The mean temperatures for these months are January, −11°C (13°F), February, −8°C (17°F), and March, −3°C (26°F).

31 The worst effects of fog are felt on the motorways and at airports. Train services are also slowed down. The pea-souper is now rare owing to the clean-air policy in major cities where only smokeless fuels are permitted. England also experiences sea and hill fog or mist.

32 Southern Chile is lightly peopled. This area has been noted for storms from the time the first sailing ships battered their ways round. Punta Arenas has little rain but is cold for the latitude (Cape Horn 55° 50′ S; Lincoln, England, 53° 14′ N)..

33 A light-hearted piece with much truth in it and a warning, if ever there was one, to look behind the averages—useful as these are to give us a basis of comparison between the climate of one place and another.

2

Man's tenuous hold
on the Earth

'Even today, if only by its more dramatic interventions, a relentless nature makes us painfully aware of the uneasy terms on which human groups occupy and utilise the surface of the earth.'

W. G. East

This section attempts to make statements concerning some of the more difficult environments with which people have to contend. It is not intended to be read as descriptive physical geography but rather as an illustration of the quotation above.

Whilst there is a fair areal coverage, it is hoped that circumstances in one part of the globe and at one particular time will help us to understand those in other places and at other times.

1 What do we know of the Earth?

General

Roads avoid the barren lands, the rocks, the sands. They shape themselves to man's needs and run from stream to stream. They lead the
farmer from his barns to his wheatfields, receive at the thresholds of
stables the sleepy cattle and pour them forth at dawn into meadows
of alfalfa. They join village to village, for between villages marriages
are made.

And even when a road hazards its way over the desert, you will
see it make a thousand détours to take its pleasure at the oases. Thus,
led astray by the divagations of roads, as by other indulgent fictions,
having in the course of our travels skirted so many well-watered
lands, so many orchards, so many meadows, we have from the beginning of time embellished the picture of our prison. We have elected
to believe that our planet was merciful and fruitful.

But a cruel light has blazed, and our sight has been sharpened. The
plane has taught us to travel as the crow flies. Scarcely have we taken
off when we abandon these winding highways that slope down to
watering troughs and stables or run away to towns dreaming in the
shade of their trees. Freed henceforth from this happy servitude,
delivered from the need of fountains, we set our course for distant
destinations. And then, only, from the height of our rectilinear
trajectories, do we discover the essential foundation, the fundament
of rock and sand and salt in which here and there and from time to
time life like a little moss in the crevices of ruins has risked its precarious existence.

from : Antoine de Saint-Exupéry, *Wind, Sand and Stars*

2 Men and mountains

India, nineteen-thirties

Clusters of little mountain huts clung to the hill-sides, and round
about them were tiny fields made by prodigious labour on every possible bit of slope. They looked like terraces from a distance, huge
steps which sometimes went from the valley below right up almost to
the mountain top. What enormous labour had gone to make nature
yield a little food to the sparse population! How they toiled unceasingly only to get barely enough for their needs! Those ploughed
terraces gave a domesticated look to the hillsides and they contrasted
strangely with the bleaker or the more wooded slopes.

44

It was very pleasant in the daytime and, as the sun rose higher, the growing warmth brought life to the mountains and they seemed to lose their remoteness and become friendly and companionable. But how they change their aspect with the passing of day! How cold and grim they become when 'Night with giant strides stalks o'er the world' and life hides and protects itself and leaves wild nature to its own. In the semi-darkness of the moonlight or starlight the mountains loom up mysterious, threatening, overwhelming, and yet almost insubstantial, and through the valleys can be heard the moaning of the wind. The poor traveller shivers as he goes his lonely way and senses hostility everywhere. Even the voice of the wind seems to mock him and challenge him. And at other times there is no breath of wind or other sound, and there is an absolute silence that is oppressive in its intensity. Only the telegraph wires perhaps hum faintly, and the stars seem brighter and nearer than ever. The mountains look down grimly, and one seems to be face to face with a mystery that terrifies. With Pascal one thinks : 'La silence éternel de ces espaces infinis m'effraie.' In the plains the nights are never quite so soundless; life is still audible there, and the murmuring and humming of various animals and insects break the stillness of the night.

But the night with its chill and inhospitable message was yet distant as we motored along to Almora. As we neared the end of our journey, a turn in the road and a sudden lifting of the clouds brought a new sight which I saw with a gasp of surprised delight. The snowy peaks of the Himalayas stood glistening in the far distance, high above the wooded mountains that intervened. Calm and inscrutable they seemed, with all the wisdom of past ages, mighty sentinels over the vast Indian plain. The very sight of them cooled the fever in the brain, and the petty conflicts and intrigues, the lusts and falsehoods of the plains and the cities seemed trivial and far away before their eternal ways.

from : Jawaharlal Nehru, *An Autobiography*

3 Primitive fear of the mountains

Mt. Cameroon, Africa, nineteen-fifties

Mount Cameroon affected us personally during our five years at its foot, brooding, enormous, amorphous, it was often unseen but always felt.

For the students the knowledge that the climb of the mountain lay between them and their return home cast a shadow across the course.

They, too, on clear days would crowd to the windows to gaze on it, their expressive faces mirroring clearly their feelings; doubt and anxiety generally but sometimes determination ...

Course by course, however, the mountain expedition went well. A varying number of students reached the top and all got some way up. At this stage I had no real fears about Mount Cameroon ... But in one ascent, within an hour of one another, two separate students collapsed and died of fright. Quite what happened was never very clear, but a form of hysteria seized each young man, a combination of fatigue, cold and mental fear. For many this was the first time that they had experienced the sensation produced by cold, and the shivers down the spine, the discolouration of finger-tips, eyes watering, ears tingling, all seemed portents of approaching dissolution. Each lad, at a given moment, began to shout 'I want to die'—and did so ... The knowledge that psychology is giving us only today of how closely sickness and accident are associated with the will has always been apparent to Africans ... One of the two dead men had been a Cameroonian and local opinion was composed of a combination of genuine tragedy and a savage exaltation that their mountain had, after all, repelled strangers.

from : Mora Dickson, *New Nigerians*

4 Beware of the hills in winter

Lake District, England

It was very early in April, for the holidays allowed to a junior bank clerk gave me no later choice. The fells above Ullswater showed ink-black slopes beneath a scowl of wintry cloud when we set out from Glenridding on our first day to cross Helvellyn to Wythburn and thence to walk over into Langdale.

The rain ceased as we climbed the shoulder of Birkhouse Moor, and we entered a freezing mist, out of which grew at length a startling helmet-head of white—the rocky cone of Catseye Cam. We trod snow now, deep soft powder-snow, and with every 100 feet of ascent the wind smote us with increasing fury, flailing our bare knees with its lash of frozen particles. We had had the sense to avoid Striding Edge for the easier Swirrel Edge in such weather, but even on the narrow part of Swirrel we found ourselves in trouble. Path there was none, or the deep snow hid it. A blinding whirl of white swept up from the depths on our left where Red Tarn lay invisible in its wild hollow 500 feet below. Some rocks, looming blackly out of the blizzard above us, were the cause of an ill-advised divergence to the left which brought us on to the snowy steeps directly above Red Tarn and beneath the edge of the summit plateau. There was snow beneath the new-fallen powder, and when we started up the slope on hands and knees, myself leading, there was insufficient footing for our illshod toes. With gloveless fingers we clawed at the yielding surface, while the white blast drove at us and I felt for the first time that rapid double draining of warmth and strength which has been the last earthly sensation of many a mountaineer. I had just seen, fifty feet overhead and grinning spectrally through the flying powder-snow, the pale cornice tooth with icicles, when I heard an agonised shout from George. He was sliding helplessly backwards down the snowslope. The steely waters of Red Tarn, glimpsed through a gap in the flurry of white, framed his blue-mackintoshed figure like a medallion. There was nothing I could do.

On this occasion there was no startling transition on the part of the mountains from friendliness to enmity; possibly because we had already begun to think of our peak as an adversary strongly armed against us. But I remembered the shock of realisation that in all the white and whirling space around us there was no pity for our plight. We had trusted too carelessly in the benevolence of the inanimate hills; we had more to learn before we could call them friends.

A rock protruding from the snowslope halted George's slide. He started up again, this time to one side of the deep groove made by my own grovelling, and reached the level I had attained. Foot by foot we scrabbled desperately up to the cornice. Fortunately it was only a small one, with a break in the ice-toothed overhang just where it was needed. We clawed our way over the rim—and at once the gale seized on us and literally bowled us across the summit and down the easier slopes on the other side. Half an hour later we were thawing our frozen hands in the wet mosses of the little stream that tumbles down the fell sides above Wythburn.

from : Showell Styles, *Blue Remembered Hills*

5 Mountains as barriers

Ecuadorian Andes, nineteen-forties

At a quarter past five the next morning a jeep rolled up to the hotel entrance, and an Ecuadorian captain of engineers jumped out and reported himself at our service. His orders were to drive us to Quivedo, mud or no mud. The jeep was packed full of petrol cans, for there

47

were no petrol pumps or wheel-tracks along the route we were to take . . .

It was good going all along the range as far as the mountain village of Latakunga, where windowless Indian houses clustered blindly round a whitewashed country church with palms in a square. Here we turned off along a mule track which undulated and twisted westwards over hill and valley into the Andes. We came into a world we had never dreamt of. It was the mountain Indians' own world— east of the sun and west of the moon—outside time and beyond space. On the whole drive we saw not a carriage or a wheel. The traffic consisted of barelegged goat-herds in gaily-coloured ponchos driving forward disorderly herds of stiff-legged dignified llamas, and now and then whole families of Indians came along the road. The husband usually rode ahead on a mule, while his little wife trotted behind with her entire collection of hats on her head and the youngest child in a bag on her back. And all the time she ran she spun wool with her fingers. Donkeys and mules jogged behind at leisure, loaded with boughs and rushes and pottery,

The farther we went the fewer the Indians who spoke Spanish, and soon Agurto's* linguistic capacities were as useless as our own. A cluster of huts lay here and there up the mountains; fewer and fewer were built of clay, while more and more were made of twigs and dry grass. Both the huts and the sun-browned wrinkle faced people seemed to have grown up out of the earth itself, from the baking effect of the mountain sun on the Andes' rock walls . . .

We went on up over sun-smitten slopes without a bush or tree and down into valleys of desert sand and cactus, till we climbed right up and reached the topmost crest, with snowfields round the peak and wind so bitingly cold that we had to slacken speed in order not to freeze to bits as we sat in our shirts longing for jungle heat. For long stretches we had to drive across country between the mountains, over scree and grassy ridges, searching for the next bit of road. But when we reached the west wall, where the Andes range falls precipitiously to the lowlands, a mule track was cut along shelves in the loose rock, and the sheer cliffs and gorges were all about us. We put all our trust in friend Agurto as he sat crouched over the steering-wheel and always swung out when we came to a precipice. Suddenly a violent gust of wind met us; we had reached the outermost crest of the Andes chain where the mountain fell away sharply in a series of precipices to the jungle far down in a bottomless abyss 12,000 feet beneath us. But we were cheated of the dizzy view over the sea of jungle, for as soon as we reached the edge thick cloudbanks rolled about us like a witches' cauldron. But now our road ran down unhindered into the depths. Always down, in steep loops along gorges and bluffs and ridges,

* The driver

48

while the air grew damper and warmer and ever fuller of the heavy deadening hothouse air which rose from the jungle world below.

And then the rain began. First gently, then it began to pour and beat upon the jeep like drum sticks, and soon the chocolate coloured water was flowing down the rocks on every side of us. We almost flowed down too, away from the dry montain plateaux behind us and into another world, where stick and stone and clay slope were soft and lush with moss and turf. Leaves shot up; soon they became giant leaves hanging like green umbrellas and dripping over the hillside. Then came the first feeble advance posts of the jungle trees, with heavy fringes and beards of moss, and climbing plants, hanging from them. There was a gurgling and splashing everywhere. As the slopes grew gentler, the jungle rolled up swiftly like an army of green giant growth that swallowed up the little jeep as it splashed along the waterlogged clay road. We were in the jungle. The air was moist and warm and heavy with the smell of vegetation.

Darkness had fallen when we reached a cluster of palm-roofed huts on a ridge. Dripping with warm water we left the jeep for a night under a dry roof. The hoard of fleas that attacked us in the hut were drowned in next day's rain. With the jeep full of bananas and other southern fruit we went on downhill through the jungle, down and down, though we thought we had reached bottom long ago. The mud grew worse, but it did not stop us, and the robbers kept at an unknown distance.

Not till the road was barred by a broad river of muddy water rolling down through the jungle did the jeep give up. We stood stuck fast, unable to move either up or down along the river bank. In an open clearing stood a hut where a few half-breed Indians were stretching out a jaguar-skin on a sunny wall, while dogs and fowls were splashing about and enjoying themselves on top of some cocoa beans spread out to dry in the sun. When the jeep came bumping along the place came to life, and people who spoke Spanish declared that this was the river Palènque, and that Quivedo was just on the other side. There was no bridge there, and the river was swift and deep, but they were willing to float us and the jeep over by raft. This queer contraption lay down by the bank. Curved logs as thick as arms and legs were fastened together with vegetable fibres and bamboos to form a flimsy raft, twice the length and breadth of the jeep. With a plank under each wheel and our hearts in our mouths we drove the jeep out on to the logs, and if most of them were submerged under the muddy water, they did bear the jeep and us and four half-naked chocolate-coloured men who pushed us off with long poles.

'Balsa?' Herman and I asked in the same breath.

'Balsa.' One of the fellows nodded with a disrespectful kick at the logs.

The current seized us and we whirled down the river, while the men pushed in their poles at the right places and kept the raft on an even diagonal course across the current and into quieter water on the other side. This was our first meeting with the balsa tree and our first trip on a balsa raft. We brought the raft safely to land at the farther bank and motored triumphantly into Quivedo. Two rows of tarred wooden houses with motionless vultures on the palm roofs formed a kind of street, and this was the whole place. The inhabitants dropped whatever they might be carrying, and black and brown, young and old appeared to be swarming out of both doors and windows. They rushed to meet the jeep, a menacing, chattering tide of humanity. They scrambled on to it and under it and round it. We kept a tight hold on our worldly possessions while Agurto attempted desperate manoeuvres at the steering wheel. Then the jeep had a puncture and went down on one knee. We had arrived at Quivedo and had to endure the embrace of welcome.

from : Thor Heyerdahl, *The Kon-Tiki Expedition*
(translated by F. H. Lyon)

6 Avalanche

Switzerland

It is quite an experience to witness an avalanche from a safe distance. Suddenly one stops dead and pricks up one's ears. There is a low rumble like thunder as a mass of snow plunges down over a precipice like a cloud or a gigantic fall of fine white spray. It touches a broad ledge of rock, makes another leap into the open and plunges once more into the depths. Only then does the thunder of the first impact on the rock edge reach the onlooker. The avalanche, still seething and foaming rolls on down the hillside and the impressive spectacle comes to an end. In the spring the peasants have to remove the stones from the slopes over which the avalanche has passed, for the pastureland must be cleared. It is an endless task which goes on year after year.

For centuries the Alpine villages have sought to protect themselves by means of the ancient forests on the steep slopes above the villages. These *Bannwalder* are almost sacred and none of their trees may be felled. In many places there is a superstition that the hand which wields an axe against one of these precious trunks will begin to bleed. Artificial barriers are also erected; walls are built and ditches dug and these have become like the mighty avalanche obstructions high in the mountains above Davos, a characteristic feature of the Alpine countryside. Houses, stables and even churches are provided with avalanche wedges, against which the hurtling masses of snow break and scatter, while roads and mountain railways are taken through avalanche galleries.

Afforestation is encouraged by these defensive measures, for while an avalanche can tear an easy passage through sparse young woodland, a comparatively old wood can arrest its progress.

The avalanche rushes in among the trees with furious attack, but the wood holds and stands unyielding in the path of the aggressor, staying its onslaught and keeping the Alpine people secure.

It has been said of jungle people that an encounter with a tiger will leave its mark forever in their eyes. I have seen something of the sort in the face of the Alpine peasant who has known an avalanche disaster.

from : Emil Egli, *Swiss Life and Landscape* (translated by E. Brockett)

7 Mountain earthquake

Assam, India, 1950

My wife leapt out of bed shouting 'Earthquake!' I seized the lantern, and together we rushed outside, only to be thrown immediately to the ground. The lantern went out.

A dozen yards away our boys were crawling out of their tent. We yelled to them to join us, and although they had not heard our shouts, a minute later they crawled across to where we lay.

All four of us held hands and lay flat, waiting for the end.

My first feeling of bewilderment had given place to stark terror. These solid mountains were in the grip of a force that was shaking them as a terrier shakes a rat. Yet frightened as we were by the din and violent earth tremors, we spoke quite calmly to each other.

The earthquake roared on. Something was pounding the ground beneath us with the force of a giant sledgehammer. Our once-solid ground felt like no more than a thin covering, stretched across the valley floor, and attached by its edges to the mountains. It seemed that the very foundations of the world were breaking up under the violent blows, that the crust on which we lay would crumble like an ice flow in a rough sea and hurl us into a bottomless pit.

Besides the roaring of the earthquake itself, there was another more familiar sound—the crash of rock avalanches pouring into the valley on every side. The mountains themselves seemed to be falling into

51

the gorge as cliffs broke in half and boulders poured down into a hundred scuppers with a clatter and a rumble.

Not far from our camp the mountain rose steeply for hundreds of feet to a higher terrace. Surely the slope would give way and we should be crushed to death or buried alive.

But presently the battering ceased, and the noise died away except for an occasional rock avalanche. Then without warning came four or five explosions in quick succession, seemingly high up in the dark sky. They sounded like ack-ack shells bursting. It was the cease-fire; everything became quiet, and the madness was over for a while . . . Not until weeks later did we learn the magnitude of the earthquake. Over thousands of square miles it created havoc. All communications were disrupted. Avalanches buried whole villages and flung rock dams across rivers. When the dams burst, devastating floods raced down valleys, sweeping everything in their path.

Fortunately in this sparsely settled region the loss of human life, though in the hundreds, was surprisingly small for such an upheaval.

from : F. Kingdon-Ward, 'Caught in the Assam-Tibet Earthquake',
National Geographic Magazine, March 1952

8 No place for a plane

Kashmir, nineteen-sixties

We took off punctually at 2.30 p.m., when the heat was rising up so frenziedly from the plain that we fell, rather than bumped, in and out of air-pockets . . . Soon the plain was left behind and we passed over the terrain that I had cycled through on the Ashad Kashmir detour. Then this region of brown, rounded foothills and deep green valleys was replaced by a landscape of naked rock peaks, giant glaciers and vast sweeps of loose shale. We were flying so low that it was, in a sense, the next best thing to trekking through this area, which even the hardiest tribes have never attempted to inhabit and which has been trodden by no more than a few of the bravest traders and mountaineers. Yet only in one sense was it the next best thing; when we passed the 26,000 foot Nanga Parbat whose triple peak dominated the thousands of snow mountains which stretched to the horizon in every direction, I suddenly became acutely aware that this was the wrong approach to a noble range. One should *win* the privilege of looking down on such a scene, and because I had done nothing to earn a glimpse of these beauties I felt that I was cheating and that this nasty, noisy little impertinence, mechanically transporting me, was an insult to the mountains. You will probably accuse me of a tiresome outburst of romanticism—but I'm not sure you'll be right. The more I see of unmechanised places and people the more convinced I become that machines have done incalculable damage by unbalancing the relationship between Man and Nature. The very fact that we think and talk as we do about Nature is symptomatic. For us to refer to Nature as a separate entity—something we admire or avoid or study or paint—shows how far it is we've removed ourselves from it.

During the last fifteen minutes of the flight, however, I had no time for such quasi-philosophical speculations, for by then we had left behind the prosaic world of passenger transport and entered the sphere of aerial acrobatics. Here the mountains are too high for a Dakota to fly over them, so we were confined to a rock-strewn gorge which in my opinion is far too narrow for a Dakota to fly *through*. It is said that at this point even hardened air-travellers begin to think of alternative routes back to Pindi. The sensation of looking out to see rough rock-walls apparently within one and a quarter inches of the wing-tips is not a pleasant one. I am assured that there are twenty yards to spare on either side, but I stick to it that from the passenger's point of view this is, morally speaking, one and a quarter inches! When we came out of the valley we descended so abruptly that I got an excruciating pain in my right ear—it was so severe that I could think of nothing else and forgot to be afraid of the landing.

from : Dervla Murphy, *Full Tilt*

9 The spate of Tweed

River Tweed, Scotland, 1683

'There's been an awfu storm up i' the muirs.' Now Tweed, unlike all rivers of my knowledge, rises terribly at the first rain and travels slowly, so that Tweedsmuir may be under five feet of water and Peebles high and dry. This makes the whole valley a place of exceeding danger in sultry weather, for no man knows when a thunder storm may break in the hills and send the stream down a raging torrent. This, too, makes it possible to hear word of the flood before it comes, and by God's grace to provide against it.

The green was soon deserted. I rushed down to the water side houses, which were in the nearest peril, and in shorter time than it takes to tell we had the people out and as much of their belongings as were worth the saving; then we hastened to the low lying cottages on Tweed green and did likewise. Some of the folk seemed willing to

53

resist, because as they said, 'Whae kenned but that the body micht be a leear and they werena to hae a' this wark for naething?' For the great floods were but a tradition, and only the old men had seen the ruin which the spate could work. Nevertheless, even these were convinced by a threatening sky and a few words from the newsbearer's trenchant tongue. Soon the High Street and the wynds* were thick with household belongings, and the Castle hill was crowded with folk to see the coming of the flood.

By this time the grim line of black had grown over half the sky and down fell great drops of rain into the white sun-baked channel. It was strange to watch these mighty splashes falling into the little stagnant pools and the runlets of flowing water. And still the close thick heat hung over all, and men looked at the dawnings of the storm with sweat running over their brows. With the rain came a mist—a white ghastly haze which obliterated the hills and came down nigh to the stream. A sound, too, grew upon their ears, at first far away and dim, but increasing till it became a dull hollow thunder, varied with a strange crackling, swishing noise which made a man eerie to listen to. Then all of a sudden the full blast of the thing came upon us. Men held their breaths as the wind and rain choked them and drove them back. It was scarcely possible to see far before, but the outlines of the gorge of Neidpath fleeted through the drift, whence the river issued. Every man turned his eyes thither and strained them to pierce the gloom.

Suddenly round the corner of the hill appeared a great yellow wave crested with white foam and filling the whole space. Down it came roaring and hissing, mowing the pines by the waterside as a reaper mows down hay with a scythe. Then with a mighty bound it broke from the hill-barrier and spread over the haugh.† Now, the sound was like the bubbling of a pot ere it boils. We watched it in terror and admiration, as it swept on its awful course. In a trice it was at the cauld,‡ and the cauld disappeared under a whirl of foam; now it was on the houses, and the walls went in like nutshells and the rubble was borne onward. A cry got up of 'the bridge,' and all hung in wonder as it neared the old stonework, the first barrier to the torrent's course, the brave bridge of Peebles. It flung itself on it with fiendish violence, but the stout masonwork stood firm, and the boiling tide went on through the narrow arches, leaving the bridge standing unshaken, as it has stood against many a flood. As we looked, we one and all broke into a cheer in honour of the old masons who had made so trusty a piece of stone.

from : John Buchan, *John Burnet of Barnes*

*Narrow lanes
†Low-lying meadow
‡A dam composed of loose stones

10 Flooding of a city: Florence

Italy, 1966

The following is a letter written to her family in England by a student working in a jeweller's shop on the Ponte Vecchio.

It rained and it rained and it rained. I am very, very tired. For the past two days I have been up to my knees, at least, in slime, mud and water, in the icy wind looking for the jewels that were in the shop that was.

You could not possibly imagine the havoc and destruction that have been wrought here. The city seems to be in ruins; it is only a miracle that more people were not killed but it happened that Friday was a national holiday so everybody was at home. If the shops had been open, goodness only knows how many would have died.

The Arno broke its banks—or walls should I say?—at about five on Friday morning and within a few hours practically the whole of the city was under water. Not only this, but half the streets had turned into raging torrents twelve feet deep. The street where we live was at least six feet deep in water on which floated masses of filth, oil, petrol and a motley of chairs, tables and cars. The street that runs at right angles to ours was a torrent, as if it were the river itself; cars came tossing down as if they were feathers and moving so fast it was hard to believe.

Next morning Franco went out and bought a little food, very little because none of us had any money and it was very cold. Our street was then free of water but about two feet deep in mud and filth. We walked to the Lungarno and looked. I have never been so shocked in the whole of my life. The bridges were still standing, but with whole trees and steel girders wrapped round the supports. The stretch of the Lungarno between the Ponte Vecchio and Ponte Santa Trinita wasn't any more. That between Ponte Santa Trinita and our bridge was devastated. The river wall had been torn away and whole sections of the road had been ripped up and hurled into the shops, all of which were quite ruined. Cars were piled one on top of another as if the victims of some ghostly crash.

We picked our way through to Piazza del Duomo; everything was gone. Piazza della Stazione was a lake, all the shops had been reduced to pulp. Outside what had been one of the most beautiful shoe shops in Florence, the owner and wife were crying (that sounds melodramatic, but it was not).

Piazza del Duomo was the worst. The baptistery rose out of the mud with the water and oil mark on its sides at least twelve feet up; the bronze doors are ruined* and Ghiberti's Gates of Paradise have

* Since repaired

panels missing; the inside of the baptistery was deep in filth. I don't know, but I hope that they managed to salvage Donatello's St. Mary Magdalene which was inside. It appears that the force of the water opened and shut the gates of the baptistery so much that the pediments fell with the side supports. Somehow seeing the baptistery was too much and I burst into tears. It just seemed that no one had done anything to avert this disaster.

We next ventured to the Ponte Vecchio, which was one of the cruellest sights of all. The shop where I had worked was really indescribable. Those shops on the left side of the Ponte Vecchio had taken the brunt of the water's force. There is hardly anything left. Even the floors have been ripped up, there is nothing there. The three shops that belong to the family for whom I was working are practically finished; it seems that they have lost everything. There are no windows left on the river side, so that everything that the river carried with it came in. Whole trees, sticks, twigs, everything you can imagine, was piled nearly as high as the shops themselves and under it all about two feet of thick mud.

First, therefore, we have to lift all the top layers, for if anything is there it is underneath the mud. Yesterday I didn't move from the bridge for seven and a half hours, trying to find anything that was left. Today the same; as it is, we have only succeeded in moving about a tenth of the filth. Everything has to be checked by hand before it is thrown away, in case there is anything in it; I found about thirty pieces of jewellery yesterday, ironically enough, mostly charms. Apart from that which I found there was very little else.

Since we have no electricity we have no heating and it is cold here, we do not eat anything hot. Using gas is dangerous—not that we have gas, but other people in our house have so we all club together. Bread costs five shillings [25p] a pound (about) and the opportunists are abroad in many fields.

Today they began to do something with the roads. Since I do not possess a pair of boots I hit on the idea of wrapping my feet in plastic bags tied up with old stockings, but unfortunately due to density of the mud they break. So, if bootless, one goes around with mud-caked feet. Luckily when it dries it rubs off (the only trouble is shoes take at least four days to dry, if not more). It is dreadful in many respects too. I am filthy dirty, and all lavatories are foul due to lack of water; soon I will have nothing dry or clean to wear. We try to go to the station every day to get water, but it is very heavy stuff to carry . . .

Your ever loving, but rather cold, wet and hungry daughter.

from : Vivien Flaxman, 'After the flood', *The Guardian*,
November 12, 1966

11 Avoiding flood: Rhine rift valley

Germany

For nearly two hundred miles it passes no town except Breisach, perched on an outlying hump of the Kaiserstuhl hills. Strasbourg and Karlsruhe are large inland ports, but the cities and even the docks are set away from the Rhine for a very good reason. For centuries the great river, carrying the water of the melting snows from Switzerland, Austria and Liechtenstein, has twisted and turned, sweeping first one way and then the other under its own momentum to change its course to such an extent that over the ages it has worn for itself a bed of shingle buried in silt, a plain which is in places nearly twenty miles from side to side. It is upon this plain that the farmers of Alsace grow their maize and tobacco, and those of Baden on the opposite shore cultivate the best asparagus in Germany yet the actual course of the river will be a single channel perhaps a couple of hundred yards across, flanked by the swamps which show where not so long ago the river lay.

Crossing such a plain, the turbulent Rhine has always been unpredictable. A violent flood was no uncommon event in former centuries and overnight the river might desert its course for a new one— as in 1296, when the town of Breisach itself, perched on its private hill on the left bank was transferred to the right bank by a sudden shift of the flooded river. So capricious was the behaviour of the Rhine, that settlements built upon its banks were liable to be swept away in the torrent from the melting snows of the Alps, and natural prudence led the people of the plain to build their towns well to the side of the course. Except for Mannheim—an artificial and relatively modern creation—there is no single town actually set upon the river, all the way from Breisach to the point where the Rhine strikes against the hills of the Taunus near Mainz and has to behave itself in a more orderly fashion.

And so for miles the Rhine flows, but through nowhere at all. The modern bed is an improved and corrected one with floodbanks set well back, but apart from an occasional inn where a ferry crosses from shore to shore the river is flanked only by its fringe of deserted swamps and thickets, with a line of poplars standing upright along the top of each bank, a row of sentries standing to attention, lining for mile upon mile the route of the royal Rhine. The poplar guardsmen are mute and unbending and it is the ships themselves which give life to the scene between their ranks.

from : Roger Pilkington, *Small Boat to Bavaria*

12 A new 'cut-off'

U.S.A., eighteen-fifties

The water cuts the alluvial banks of the 'lower' river into deep horse-shoe curves; so deep, indeed, that in some places if you were to get ashore at one extremity of the horseshoe and walk across the neck, half or three-quarters of a mile, you could sit down and rest a couple of hours while your steamer was coming around the long elbow at a speed of ten miles an hour to take you on board again. When the river is rising fast, some scoundrel whose plantation is back in the country, and therefore of inferior value, has only to watch his chance, cut a little gutter across the narrow neck of land some dark night, and turn the water into it, and in a wonderfully short time a miracle has happened; to wit, the whole Mississippi has taken possession of that little ditch, and placed the countryman's plantation on its bank (quadrupling its value), and that other party's valuable plantation finds itself away out yonder on a big island; the old watercourse around it will soon shoal up, boats cannot approach within ten miles of it, and down goes its value to a fourth of its former worth. Watches are kept on those narrow necks at needful times, and if a man happens to be caught cutting a ditch across them the chances are all against his ever having another opportunity to cut a ditch . . .

When the water begins to flow through one of those ditches I have been speaking of, it is time for the people thereabouts to move. The water cleaves the bank away like a knife. By the time the ditch has become twelve or fifteen feet wide, the calamity is as good as accomplished, for no power on earth can stop it now. When the width has reached a hundred yards, the banks begin to peel off in slices half an acre wide. The current flowing round the bend travelled formerly only five miles an hour; now it is tremendously increased by the shortening of the distance. I was on board the first boat that tried to go through a cut-off at American Bend, but we did not get through. It was toward midnight, and a wild night it was—thunder, lightning, and torrents of rain. It was estimated that the current in the cut-off was making about fifteen or twenty miles an hour; twelve or thirteen was the best our boat could do, even in tolerably slack water, therefore perhaps we were foolish to try the cut-off.

At the end of our fourth effort we brought up in the woods two miles below the cut-off; all the country there was overflowed, of course. A day or two later the cut-off was three-quarters of a mile wide, and boats passed up through it without much difficulty, and so saved ten miles.

from : Mark Twain, *Life on the Mississippi*

13 Flood plain

China, nineteen-twenties

The river burst yet another dyke and another before it was content with the space it had for itself, and then it wore away these walls of earth until none could tell where a dyke had been in that whole country, and the river swelled and rolled like a sea over all the good farming land, and the wheat and the young rice were at the bottom of the sea.

One by one the villages were made into islands, and men watched the water rising and when it came within two feet of their doorways they bound their tables and beds together and put the doors of their houses upon them for rafts, and they piled what they could of their bedding and their clothes and their women and children on these rafts. And the water rose into the earthen houses and softened the walls and burst them apart and they melted down into the water and were as if they had never been. And then as the water on earth drew water from heaven it rained as though the earth were in drought. Day after day it rained.

Wang Lung sat in his doorway and looked out over the waters that were yet far enough from his house that was built on a high wide hill. But he saw the waters covering his land and he watched lest it covered the new-made graves, but it did not, although the waves of the yellow clay-laden water lapped about the dead hungrily.

There were no harvests of any kind that year and everywhere people starved and were hungry and were angry at what had befallen them yet again. Some went south, and some who were bold and angry and cared nothing for what they did joined the robber bands that flourished everywhere in the countryside. These even tried to beleaguer the town so that the townspeople locked the gates of the wall continually except for one small gate called the western water gate, and this was watched by soldiers and locked at night also. And besides those who robbed and those who went south to beg, even as Wang had once gone with his old father and his wife and children, there were others who were old and tired and timid, and who had no sons like Ching, and these stayed and starved and ate grass and what leaves they could find on high places and many died upon the land and water.

from : Pearl Buck, *The Good Earth*

59

14 Victory over a river: Yangtze-Kiang

China, 1954

Walk along the high dyke that is wide enough for a cart and an ox-cart to pass. Like a rampart of earth and stone it stands on the edge of a vast lake. Here it was that two years ago my companions helped in the fight against the raging waters that threatened to overwhelm their homes . . .

'They were both team-leaders and organised groups of women to carry soil as well as carrying it themselves,' Miss Chen says . . . 'It was at the beginning of July, and July is the month of typhoons. Rain fell continuously for over a week and the flood-level rose alarmingly. In addition a gale was blowing and whipped that great expanse of water into huge waves that battered the dyke and threatened to destroy all of our work. Teams of men were working frantically to lay down matting rafts to break the force of the waves while others brought earth and stones to raise the level of the dyke. But it was clear that unless something more was done to protect it, it would give way under the battering.

'So in order to protect it, six hundred youths and girls linked arms to form a human chain. For a week they stood in shifts with their backs pressed against the wall of the dyke and took the force of the waves on their own bodies. For a week they never left the dyke. When the waves receded they came out and lay on the bank. When the waves rose they went back again. On 7th July, when the wind was at its strongest and the waves highest, Ji-ying stayed in the water all through the night and into the day.

'Once she was so exhausted that she slipped down the bank, but the wave caught her and threw her back and her companions pulled her out again. That time they were sixteen hours without a break. Food was taken to them and they ate where they stood. When the waves were high they could not eat.

'When at last they came out they could not raise their arms, they could not use them. They had to be put to bed and fed like babies. It was for this she was made a veteran flood-fighter.'

from : Dymphna Cusack, *Chinese Women Speak*

15 Windmills behind the dykes

Holland, nineteen-sixties

It wasn't until I had made several visits to Holland that I realised the Dutch used them mainly to solve their water problems. At one time they had over seven thousand of them, the wind in their swirling sails providing the power to lift the water, step by step, a metre at a time, from the polders to the canals.

At Kinderdijk, some ten miles east of Rotterdam, you can find the biggest cluster of the remaining twelve hundred; mill after mill, one behind the other, standing down there in the sunken polder lands with their big sails spread like dumb giants in perpetual conclave. They are still working, these mills, still lifting the water above the roofs of the little thatched houses snugged against the dyke. I introduced myself to one that was painted green with carved front board decorated red and white. It was pretty as a picture, standing, archaic and wonderful, in a field full of buttercups and Frisian cattle. Faded canvas sails were stretched across two of its four arms and it was turning to a moderate breeze with a zing, zing, zing of power.

'In winter I haf four sails up,' the mill-keeper told me.

'Four sails?' I said. 'But in winter the wind is stronger.'

'*Ja*. But in winter more water, eh?'

Water, always water. Every single drop of rain to be laboriously lifted ten, fifteen, twenty feet. 'Come. I show you inside.' He was more like a seaman than a windmill-keeper with his black clothes and sailor's cap. We went through the wind-blown spray of the big iron wheel that was scooping the water up one step farther on its way to the sea. Clogs lay in a neat yellow row outside the door, the way you see them throughout all the country areas of Holland, and inside was a small cosy room full of women and children. The women were still and silent, only their fingers moving as they sewed, and the only sound was the rumble of the mill's great cog-wheels beyond the curve of the centre wall. The clogs, the crowded room, the straining, grinding noise of the mill's efforts—so it had been since the Dutch created the first polder.

There is a scheme now to preserve these old windmills by converting them to the production of electricity and so giving them the chance to earn their keep, for as water-lifters their days are numbered; in the new polder of the Zuider Zee two or three big diesel pumping stations suffice to keep the water level down in a hundred thousand acres.

from : Hammond Innes, *Harvest of Journeys*

16 The redoubt had fallen

East coast, England, 1953

'Get up! Come quick! The sea's come over! The sea's come over!'

The redoubt had fallen. The enormous sea that all day had pounded the east coast from the Humber to the North Foreland had come over at last.

One huge wave looking like all those that had gone before it came in foaming and tumbling upon itself, moving with the speed of a racehorse towards the high-tide line, where instead of retreating it careered on. Careered, foaming and frothing, through and over the myriad pebbles of the wave-shaped barrier of stones, drawing behind it curiously smooth, the huge black membrane of the sea. Another wave followed, and then another and another, a whole succession of them, until the stone barrier was engulfed totally, and only a reef of angry white water marked where it had once been.

The waves now coalesced and drove on. In seconds they had filled and overflowed the shallow bowl of the marsh; had swept up the heavy high-prowed fishing boats that the men had drawn up high for safety and tossed them splintering and bruising into the dripping branches of the fir woods on the lower hill slopes. Spray flew up into the dense canopy of fir needles, encrusting them with salt, while at ground level the water swirled round the resin-dripping trunks, sucking out the light earth from between the shallow roots until the trees tilted sideways with groans of protesting wood, and then crashed into the seething water and were carried out into the flood.

Further up the coast the sea had already crashed the iron-bolted breakwaters; had piled up over the concrete front and then, thunderously joining with a local river that had burst its banks, had erupted into the small seaside town with such a violent rush of waters that in a few seconds it had been turned into an inland sea . . .

In one man's home the water was three-quarters of the way up the kitchen window. For a second or two he clung to the submerged sink taps, breathing in the freezing air and looking out through the smashed glass at the drowned world outside. It was a scene of utter desolation. The wind had got up again in flurries of sleet, whipping the waves white, blowing the ragged black clouds in mad tatters over the slate-coloured sky. From what he could see the sea was littered with flotsam; with shapes that could have been boats or beach huts or the swollen carcasses of drowned animals. For a moment he thought with terror how easy it would be to be sucked out through the window and into that terrible world outside to join those tossing shapes which rolled and eddied with such appalling lack of purpose. To prevent such a thing he guided himself carefully along by the sink edge, holding on for dear life against the current which seemed to be flowing more strongly here than it had done anywhere else ... He began to swim, but in the darkness had the terrible sensation that he was making no headway, that the mask of water that kept rolling up over his face was not caused by any forward movement but by the natural resistance to the current of a stationary object. He swept his arms wide, touching the moving walls of the passage, and then he swept them down, and there was nothing. He was being swept backwards.

He now ceased to think at all, but became a machine thrashing against the current. He worked, kicking, shouting, grimacing, thrusting away the wall of swift oncoming water, battling for the light which was fast receding inside his head like a diminishing spark.

It was his body that reached the submerged doorway into the hall. It was his clever, water-wrinkled hands, the muscles inside them taut and twitching with painful eagerness, that stretched down and then braced him against the jambs and, not caring whether he took breath or not, drew him screaming down, under and through.

He emerged into light, vomiting water and moaning, drawing the marvellous light back into his lungs. But his arms wouldn't let him rest. They drove him protesting nearer and ever nearer to the light, drove him frenziedly through stiller and yet stiller water until, with a curious half turn, he found himself lying like a stranded fish in the shallow water which covered the upper stairs.

from : Elizabeth Mavor, *The Redoubt*

17 Water everywhere

England, July 1968

Wednesday's foul weather brought for most of us no more than vexation, disappointment or wet feet—another day's cricket washed away. From others it snatched their homes, even their lives ...

One fact must always be relevant when floods are discussed. It is the changing texture of our wet islands. Primaeval England was like sponge; it sucked up much of the rain which fell on it and released it only gradually. Civilisation has since covered large areas with impermeable tarmac, concrete and buildings; the landscape in between is also balder, progressively denuded of moisture-conserving forests, undergrowth and hedgerows; fields are in general better drained. The resultant England has been compared to a vast roof, off which the water pours dangerously fast. The risks are two. One is that of flooding where the lower reaches of the rivers are not properly adapted to

63

the increased flow; perhaps some of the water which poured through people's houses on Wednesday night would in earlier days have been held in the soil. The other risk, graver and less obviously remediable, is a growing shortage of underground water, for which civilisation has an ever more insatiable appetite. Floods and dessication often go together and are nature's punishment for those who heedlessly upset her balance.

from : The Daily Telegraph, July 12, 1968

18 Spring-thaw floods

U.S.S.R.

In March the sun becomes warm enough to melt a little snow each day on sheltered roofs and sills and pavements facing south. Soon the streets begin to run with streams of thaw, though at night these turn again to treacherous sheets of ice. Almost every ceiling drips with water, and the porters climb on to the roofs with their aluminium shovels, hurling down masses of snow to compete with the natural avalanches which slide off with a noise like trains approaching. The nights are white with the mist of meeting thaw and frost, the incautious foreigner leaves off his heavier clothing and gets bronchitis, and in the misty dark one trips and falls full length over a new kind of obstacle—great cylinders of ice six inches in diameter, which have at last dropped out of the battered downpipes where they have been collecting all the winter. In April peasants bring pussy willow into town, and in a few more days the *rasputitsa* will begin—the appalling state of 'roadlessness' when all outside the towns is mud and icy slush and flood, when villages for a short period are completely isolated and neither sleigh nor cart, lorry nor tractor can stir . . .

In the countryside every stream must be bridged afresh, each year, as soon as the spring floods subside. For in this land of a million waters there are few metalled roads and only they, as a rule, are carried on permanent bridges. Elsewhere the dirt roads are roughly patched in May to make approaches to the crossings, fresh piles are driven into the river bottoms, and rough-hewn bridges with rattling floors are built on top. Sometimes a convenient unit of the army does the job engineer fashion, but otherwise the peasants must improvise in the ancient way, unless they prefer—with or without the approval of the local Soviet—to continue splashing through a ford of perhaps a hundred yards in width, until in five months time the ice returns.

from : Wright Miller, *Russians as People*

19 Desert travellers

Gobi Desert

An aerial view of the Desert of Gobi on a midsummer day would show a burning arid waste of dunes interspersed with monotonous rolling expanses of gravel and crossed by occasional ridges of high mountains whose foothills dwindle to low rocky mounds. The whole plain is shadeless and exposed to scorching heat under a pitiless sun. All living creatures seek shelter from its fierce rays and the roads are deserted, for the reverberation of heat makes travel almost impossible.

By night it is quite otherwise, and as darkness falls the desert quickens into life. Scorching heat gives way to a sudden chill which rises from the ground and strikes the traveller with a cold impact which makes him lift his head to catch the warmer upper stratum of the air as a relief from that too palpable cold. Soon that layer too will be permeated by the chill, and he will wrap a sheepskin coat around him in an endeavour to keep warm.

At this hour the observer would see caravans emerge from all the oasis inns and move slowly in various directions. Long trains of two hundred camels roped together in strings of twelve, stretch out in thin lines over the narrow tracks; caravans of large carts, each laden with a thousand pounds of merchandise, follow one another across the plain; these join up for safety and keep within hailing distance of each other. Pedestrians carrying their own baggage balanced over the shoulder from the two ends of a pole come from many places and look like swinging dots as they move briskly at first, but later settle down to the inevitable pace of Gobi travel.

Half-way through the night all these travellers are seen to halt. This is the moment when caravans moving in opposite directions meet and greet each other. Carters recognise friends from other towns, but there is no more talk between them than is necessary from the passing of needed warnings. Camel-drivers on their immensely long journeys are alert for all unusual sights or sounds, and often carry letters to be handed to those whom they may meet at some halting-place. Pedestrians lay down their loads, rest aching shoulders and drink from their water bottles, squatting lightly on their heels for a while before they make the second half of the stage. All these men speak but little and there is no easy chat on a desert night journey, nor is loud conversation ever heard; desert talk is always spare, subdued and unhurried for the spaces teach men to be sharers of their dignity, and to scorn noise and tattle as only suited to the vulgarity of towns. Moreover, in the still air voices carry dangerously well, and silence becomes a cautionary instinct.

The sand deadens the sound of wheels, and camels' soft padded feet move quietly between the dunes. The camp watch-dogs might give a sharp sound by day, but at night they follow at the camels' heels or leap on to the back of one beast and lie there until the halt is called, when they jump down to take on duty. The sonorous monotonous camel-bell has no sharp clang, but only a deep dull boom, and the rythmic dip of the camel's neck keeps it in perfect measure. This bell is such a part of desert quiet that it breaks silence without disturbing it. When the great carts draw up for the mid-stage halt, a heavy smell of opium often comes from the pipe of some smoker hidden behind the curtains who lies there listless while the drivers exchange their greetings and then move on again.

Not only humans but innumerable small animals and insects come from their hiding places as soon as darkness falls. All through the hours of heat they have slept in the tunnelled world which they have burrowed for themselves a few feet underground, and of which the openings are on the sheltered side of many a tiny sand-mound, blown up round the foot of a tuft of camel-thorn or of a low bush of scrub. All through the night the little live things move ceaselessly, silently and invisibly over the sand, and only by chance does a traveller become aware of their presence; after sunrise however he sees the sand patterned with all kind of beautiful markings left by small rodents, beetles, centipedes and other insects which scuttle back to their sleeping quarters with the first ray of sunshine . . .

With the rising sun, the aerial observer could watch all the caravans reaching their respective destinations at the end of their night's journey. The camels kneel among the sands to have their loads removed, and wide-open doors of oasis inns wait to receive the tired wayfarers who, throughout the night, have covered another thirty-mile stage of the desert road. By divergent ways they come, meeting at the welcome *serai*, and disappear into the darkness and quiet of inn cells to pass the day in sleep.

from : Mildred Cable with Francesca French, *The Gobi Desert*

20 Inhospitable land of the permafrost

Polar fringe, nineteen-fifties

Gradually as we flew north, the trees thinned out and we came to the edge of the permafrost, or tundra. This is land which is permanently frozen hundreds of feet down. Only a thin top layer has a chance to thaw during the brief summer, so only small, creeping, shallow-rooted plants can grow there, and mosses and lichens. There was not much of it and it showed as patches of brownish, dead-looking areas between the trees, as if the land had leprosy. We began to see drumlins—elongated hills and lakes pointing north and south, straight as rulers, where the slow-moving glacier had grooved the land—and strangmoors—wavering string-like peat ridges, formed by a slow, mysterious action of frost on earth . . .

It was dead and horrible country, ancient sea bottom, wet, forbidding, full of mosquitoes and quaking bogs. Nobody could live there, our pilot told us, and it was no good for anything. Its stunted spruces were too thin for logging, its soil too soggy for farming, there were no minerals to speak of and trapping was almost impossible due to the difficulty of getting around. Besides hardly any animals lived there . . .

The barren permafrost areas gradually ate up the landscape as we moved north. The tundra was full of stagnant puddles with tawny-coloured bogs along their shores : the country was soggy and arid at the same time. Since there is little air circulation over the vast, flat inland stretches of Canada's tundra the rainfall is slight—less than that of the Sahara desert. But the land is always wet. With a bed of impermeable frozen soil the water cannot sink into the earth, nor can it run off the flat surface. The weather is so cold that there is little evaporation, so all the moisture in the earth is used, and the low plant cover is comparatively lush. But if the climate should become warmer and the permafrost melt, as they say it had been doing lately, the Canadian tundra might become a vast desert, the biggest on earth.

Then there was a new sight in the misty distance—the old shore line of Hudson Bay. The water of this inland sea has receded during many centuries, and the ancient beaches rise in a series of rippled, terraced ridges. Beyond the ridges we could see a thin white line, the bay itself, still frozen. Shortly after that we circled low over Churchill . . . The ice was an enormous, cracked expanse, gleaming like polished steel hurting the eyes, and the whole horizon was white from reflected ice. Here and there we saw drifted snow in geometric wind patterns, looking like huge triangular footprints. Sometimes there were patches of fog below us, more brilliant and blinding white than the ice, and occasionally we passed over open water. In the sun it was of deepest, purest blue, flecked with tiny pieces of ice that looked like whitecaps.

The plane stopped briefly at Coral Harbor on Southampton Island . . . It was a great stretch of flat brown-grey tundra with snow peeling off in dirty strips. It contained a Canadian air forces base and communications post with a little recreation hut labelled 'Southampton Inn : Guests Welcome'. Around the hut drifted snow was piled to the roof.

'When will summer come here ?' we asked.

'This is summer,' they said.

The tundra was lifeless and terrible. Where the snow had melted off there was a thin slippery layer of mud with absolute iron hardness underneath. In a few places the sun had dried the land and there one walked in a halo of stifling dust. The twelve men who were posted there for six months to two years felt imprisoned by the dead, unmoving land. But there was a saving grace—the bay. It gave them a feeling that they could get away, or that anyway they could rest their eyes on something that could get away, something that could move.

from : Katherine Scherman, *Spring on an Arctic Island*

21 Tundra: breeding place for mosquitoes

Alaska, U.S.A.

When the surface of the ground thaws out in the north it is pitted with pockets of water which have never drained in a million years. It is all one great big soured swamp—mosquito country. The circling midnight sun incubates the mosquitoes relentlessly twenty-four hours out of the day, as it increases and forces all life at this season. The water pockets, lying beneath a covering of spongy moss sometimes two feet thick, are every place you step. They are even on the sides of the hills, where hummocks of earth have frequently been distorted and thrown up by the frost of winter and carved into queer shapes. There is not a human being, not even a native, to be found inland during the summer for trackless hundreds of miles of mountains and swamp. Only on the arteries of the big rivers can you find a human being.

It does not take a wise person to keep out of these trackless muskeg swamps. Cross country hiking over the terrain is just unknown; nobody does it ... Bud tore his mosquito net ever so slightly as he wandered among the scattered spruce trees of the darkening swamp. This set us to wondering just what would happen to an unclothed man turned loose to the mosquitoes here.

It was our belief that such a man would become blind within three hours from their bites and would be a dead man possibly within the next thirty-six hours. 'In fact,' said Bud, 'that's just what the Indians did at one time. They took the clothes off their prisoners, tied them to trees, and turned them loose to the mosquitoes.' Since the mosquitoes of the north carry no fevers or diseases and there is but relatively little poison in each insect, others of greater experience have told us that the cause of death, aside from exposure, would be from loss of blood.

It was midnight when we arrived back at our boat, dripping with perspiration and followed by such swarms of insects that they looked like clouds about our heads. Clapping Bud on the back of his once-white ski jacket between the shoulder blades, my gloved hand covered as many as a hundred or more mosquitoes in that small area, black, crawling, bobbing, probing with their beaks. We were alive with them ...

They thudded against our jackets audibly, pierced through woollen shirts and pants alike with their long-probing beaks, crawled up underneath mosquito head nets and down necks and up under the hair line into the scalp.

from : Constance Helmericks, *We live in Alaska*

22 The frozen continent

Halley Bay, Antarctica, nineteen-fifties

At first we could only plot the coastal cliffs by radar, for they could not be seen through the snow and bad visibility, but soon the ice still fast to the coast forced us farther and farther from the cliffs until we were steaming down a twenty-mile-wide ice-free channel some fifteen miles off-shore. Everywhere huge stranded or floating tabular icebergs were scattered along our course ...

By the evening of 27th January the *Theron* was some forty miles north of Halley Bay. That night, in perfect weather, we sailed along a magnificent ice cliff coastline with a broad belt of unbroken sea ice still lying before it. In our imagination it seemed like the white cliffs of Dover, the sandy beach bleached by a perpetual sun, the holidaymakers represented by basking seal.

The ice cliffs were in fact the front of an ice shelf, a mass of floating ice attached to the land and varying in thickness from a few hundred to perhaps fifteen hundred feet. The surface of an ice shelf is normally level or gently undulating and at times large or small masses break away from its edge and move out to sea as tabular bergs.

As we approached Halley Bay, a series of small embayments or clefts began to appear in the regular front of the ice shelf. Each of these had preserved its own small area of sea ice from which drifts of snow extended almost to the top of the ice cliffs behind, but it was not until we reached Halley Bay itself that a way could be seen leading to the very top. At last, beyond a headland of ninety-foot ice cliffs, we saw two small black figures waving from the sea ice edge. David Dalgliesh, and one of his party, George Lush, had come to guide us to the base site some two miles inland and invisible from the sea. Soon a boat was lowered to put out ice anchors and to bring them both aboard. While we were exchanging greetings the Auster was being lowered over the side, a second party was preparing to go sealing, while yet another set about the usual collection of ice for our water supply.

On 20th January it was possible to make our first inland reconnaissance flight . . .

Now we were flying low through the mountains on an easterly course, but climbing steadily as we followed the most likely looking glacier past the grey-black ridges and peaks. Here and there red and yellow rocks varied the scene, while below the wind-swept surface of the glacier showed blue where the snow had been stripped from the ice beneath. We imagined the tracked vehicles with their heavily-loaded sledges, attempting to climb these steep and slippery slopes. True, the crevasses lay revealed and might therefore be avoided, but this also reminded us that where the snow still lay it must hide many treacherous pitfalls.

At 6,000 feet we found ourselves about 1,500 feet above a wide snowfield which fed the glacier we had been following and which also declined southward. Turning on to a southerly course we flew out over a huge east–west glacier which we were later to know as the 'Recovery Glacier'. This was forty miles wide and at least as long as the Slessor Glacier, although the upper reaches have not been seen. While the north side is flanked by the length of the Shackleton Range, the south side is marked by a line of rocky peaks which we called the 'Whichaway Nunataks',* and a precipitous tumbling slope of ice which continues the line of the nunataks for many miles to east and west. Beyond the main line of the Whichaways a few rocky outcrops thrust through an undulating and somewhat crevassed expanse of snow and ice. Circling the most southerly of these, which stood at about 5,000 feet, we scanned the southern horizon with binoculars and saw nothing but rising, and undulating snowfields. Here and there a white gleam seemed to indicate a crevassed area, but no further mountains could be seen and we felt certain that we were looking over the high Polar Plateau itself. Satisfied, too, that in this area a suitable site for South Ice could be found and that the proximity of the nunataks would aid the location of the station from the air, we turned back to land at Shackleton after five hours and twenty minutes.

from : Vivian Fuchs and Edmund Hillary, *The Crossing of Antarctica*

* Peaks appearing through an ice sheet

23 The southern tip

South Patagonia, 1958-62

I celebrated my fiftieth birthday in the Karakoram. It was doubtless this melancholy event that impressed me with the urgency of making definite plans for an expedition to Patagonia before I became too senile for such an undertaking. Even so I might have done nothing about it if it had not been for young Geoff Bratt ... On the subject of Patagonia it was not difficult to arouse his enthusiasm; its warmth brought mine to the boil and we agreed to go there together the following year.

Patagonia is not a country. The name refers to the whole of the mainland of South America south of the Rio Negro in Latitude 40°S. The bulk of this vast territory, lying in Argentina to the east of the Andes, consists of prairie, some of it flat, much of it hilly, nearly all of it dry, treeless and covered with coarse and open scrub. It is a stark, inhospitable land which, until late in the nineteenth century, was inhabited only by a few scattered Indian tribes. It was only then, towards the end of the century, that white men came, mostly direct from Europe or from the Falkland Islands, to settle there as sheep farmers, first along the Atlantic coast, then gradually further inland. Indeed the settlement of Patagonia is so recent that even today many of the estancieros are the sons and daughters of those original pioneers.

The Chilean part of Patagonia, except for a small area in the extreme south is utterly different. Most of it is wild, rugged and uninhabited, a region of tempest and torrential rain, of fantastic geographical form and strange natural phenomena. The Pacific coast immediately west of the Andes, is split by a perfect labyrinth of fjords which bite deep into the mainland and form an archipelago, a giant jigsaw of islands 1,000 miles long. The climate is sub-arctic, and the glaciation so extensive that, although the mountains are not particularly high, they are as spectacular as any in the entire range. There are two great ice-caps, which are the only examples of their kind outside Polar regions. Many of the innumerable glaciers which radiate from these, flow down through dense 'tropical forest' (as Darwin described it) and thrust their massive fronts into the intricate system of waterways surrounding them. Parrots and humming birds inhabit these forests ...

Most parts of the main range, even many on the eastern side, can only be approached by water, and because of the weather, the use of small craft on the lakes and fjords is liable to be a hazardous business. The glaciers in their lower reaches are often so broken and crevassed that it is virtually impossible to travel on them, and lateral moraines rarely provide an easy line of approach, as they usually do on the

Himalaya. In the foothills the forest often presents an impassable barrier, particularly on the western side of the range, where the wind has twisted the stunted trees into a low-lying mass of tangled trunks and branches. It is these obstacles which have prevented most expeditions to the area from achieving more than a limited objective or covering a very small proportion of the region.

from : Eric Shipton, *Land of the Tempest*

24 Men against the Chaco

Paraguay

As to whether life in the Chaco, even in its lyrical moments, is of Arcadian type, each must judge for himself.

Certainly there is little sense of the pressure of human affairs or time, let alone the more important matters of the world today ... The clock's attempts to hammer our lives into some temporal shape are bound to fail : in the Chaco, the hour, like every newcomer has made no real conquests. The day's life is 'antès' or 'depuès de mediodía' (before or after midday); and men's daily activities plotted from some unknown departure point at dead of night, long before the sun lifts over the forest; a fix is taken at noon, and the day's final position checked against the sun's swift declension, which distributes over the western horizon only the most impecunious legacy of hovering light.

One man alone in this immense calorific pulsing Chaco, catching with difficulty his breath in the furnace winds, stepping carefully against serpents and other untrustworthy creatures—what is he but live roasting flesh? Country life is held to be 'free' (especially by successful businessmen); but this freedom examined, is generally found to mean freedom from the inconvenience, imagined as well as real, of town life. And with this, all that has been proved is a preference in inconveniences.

But here too, life is largely built on a causeway of avoidance : of the hottest part of the day, the haunts of poisonous snakes, piraña-populated water, deep swamps, being caught alone far from the house without a horse, darkness, being lost. This Arcadian profile conceals a bone-structure of constant seige : by drought, cattle sickness, insects, pests, floods, cattle thieves. Arcadia then, perhaps only in the vision of those unoccupied with such hostilities, and of course by its contrast with the mechanical and social exigencies of a provincial metropolitan life.

This equation of beauty and violence called Chaco is a vast animal republic, whose horizons are galaxies of palms; rivers of birds irrigate its skies; and on its dusty grassy folios countless creatures, some of the earth's strangest, daily print the designs of their beautifully evolved bodies. It has conceded to man a few enclaves and corridors, in which he finally becomes like the inhabitants in at least one aspect : a discovery that it is unnecessary to sustain himself by belief in his future and evocation of his past . . . If Arcadia, then, an existentialist Arcadia.

from : Gordon Meyer, *The River and the People*

25 Tropical forest: a close possessive world

Zaire

Anyone who has stood in the silent emptiness of a tropical rain forest must know how Stanley and his followers felt, coming as they did from an open country of rolling plains, of sunlight and warmth. Many people who have visited the Ituri since, and many who have lived there, feel just the same—overpowered by the heaviness of everything; the damp air, the gigantic, water-laden trees that are constantly dripping, never quite drying out between the violent storms that come with monotonous regularity, the very earth itself becoming heavy and cloying after the slightest shower. And above all such people feel overpowered by the seeming silence and the age-old remoteness and loneliness of it all.

. . . The World of the forest is a closed, possessive world, hostile to all those who do not understand it. At first sight you might think it was hostile to all human beings, because in every village you find the same suspicion and fear of the forest, that blank impenetrable wall. The villagers are friendly and hospitable to strangers, offering them the best of whatever food and drink they have, and always clearing out a house where the traveller can rest in comfort and safety. But these villages are set among plantations in great clearings cut from the heart of the world around them. It is from the plantations that the food comes, not from the forest, and for the villagers life is a constant battle to prevent their plantations from being overgrown.

They speak of the world beyond the plantations as being a fearful place, full of malevolent spirits and not fit for anyone to live in except animals and Bambuti, which is what they call the pygmies. The villagers, some Bantu and some Sudanic, keep to their plantations and seldom go into the forest unless it is absolutely necessary. For them it is a place of evil. They are outsiders.

from : Colin M. Turnbull, *The Forest People*

73

26 Advice to an airman bailing out over jungle

Rain forests

If you have bailed out over a rain forest, the chances are about 100 to 1 that your fall will not carry you through the double forest roof or canopy. You will be suspended by chute and shroud lines well above the forest floor. The distance above ground will depend upon the height of the trees and the density of the overhead forest canopy. You will have to free yourself from the chute and improvise some means of getting down. You might descend hand-over-hand on a large liana, or pull yourself to the trunk of a tree and slide down. The large rain forest trees have few or no branches except at the crowns.

... The first few hours are hours of decision. Should you improvise a camp and stay put until a rescue party finds you? Should you go in search of the others who bailed out? Are you physically able to endure travel? You are a prisoner of the rain forest; above you is a solid roof of vegetation and 20 to 50 feet on all sides are trees that blend into a solid wall. You cannot be seen from a rescue aircraft even if the pilot is flying at tree-top level. And the pilot cannot read you on the radio, for your small set is not effective when used under the thick canopy roof.

If you want your survival experience to be of short duration you must start walking. The chances of finding or encountering one of your fellow survivors is slim indeed unless on the way down you saw him land close by. Your radio will not reach him nor will shouts and gunshots be of much aid to establishing contact; sound has very limited range in the rain forest.

... Start early in the morning and put in a long marching day, broken by frequent 10- to 15-minute rest periods. Drink plenty of water to make up for heavy sweating. It is important to keep alert, to study your surroundings, and to select your route with care. It's not easy when you are tired—you must force yourself to do it.

If you reach a high point in the jungle, look for rivers, lakes or clearings in the distance. If you see something you want to head for, such as a large clearing, use your compass to get its direction. Distances in the jungle are very deceiving—a clearing may appear close at hand but may take a day or two to reach. Ordinarily, a compass route to your destination will not be a straight line. Dense secondary vegetation, swamps, fallen trees, rivers, and other natural obstacles will require that you make frequent detours. All changes from the direction in which you are marching should be noted, preferably on a sketch of your route, so that you can correct for them later. Use your compass frequently, once every hundred yards or so, to maintain a straight course. This will keep you from circling, and will help to make you more alert to your surroundings.

... The highways of the jungle are the trails and the streams; use them.

from : Nesbitt, Pond and Allen, *The Survival Book*

27 Overwhelming nature of Amazon forests

Brazil, circa 1912

It is a rare traveller who goes through those forests, guided only by a compass and his lore of the wilderness. That for months I had never been out of sight of the jungle, and yet had rarely ventured to turn aside from a path more than a few paces is some indication of its character. At the camp where we were staying I was told that once a man had gone merely within the screen of leaves and then no doubt had lost for a few moments, his sense of direction of the camp, for he was never seen again.

... This forest since we entered the Pará river, now a thousand miles away, has not ceased. There have been clearings of the settlements from Pará inwards; but as Spruce says in his journal, those clearings and campos alter the forest of the Amazon no more than would the culling of a few weeds alter the aspect of an English cornfield. The few openings I have seen in the forest do not change my clear impression of a limitless ocean of leaves, its deep billows of foliage rolling down the only paths there are in this country, the rivers, and there overhanging, arrested in collapse. There is no land. One must travel by boat from one settlement to another. The settlements are but islands, narrow footholds, widely surrounded by vast gulfs of jungle.

Sometimes we pass single habitations on the water-side. Ephemeral huts of palm-leaves are forced down by the forest, which overhangs them, to wade on frail stilts. A canoe is tied to a toy jetty, a sad woman and several naked children stand, with no show of emotion, to watch us go by. Behind them is impenetrable foliage. I cannot help remembering the precarious tenure on earth of these brown folk. The easy dominance of the wilderness, and man's intelligent morsel of life feebly resisting it, is made plain when we suddenly come upon one of his little shacks secreted among the aqueous roots of a great tree; cowering as it were between two of the giant's toes.

from : H. M. Tomlinson, *The Sea and the Jungle*

28 Coniferous forest

Central British Columbia, Canada, 1953

When we landed at the North-East tip of the lake after our 50-mile journey by boat, we came face to face with the reality of the forest. It swept down from the hills to the water's edge, making it difficult for us to land stores or walk along the strand; a month later the water level had fallen by some six feet exposing a narrow beach as the swollen lake had gradually cleared the last winter's snow and ice. Before we could pitch camp however, we had to fell trees and clear away undergrowth, hacking out a place for each tent. At night, as we tried to sleep, the loneliness of this desolate place, the cries and scufflings of strange creatures and the general eeriness were hard to take. With dawn, the night's mist and cold gradually gave way to sunshine and warmth which brought out clouds of blood-sucking insects. There were mosquitoes and blackflies but most effective of all were the 'noseeums' which lived up to their name.

We set out to explore the forest. It was quite unlike anything we had been led to expect from our previous limited excursions into Western European woodlands that had been tended for centuries—culled, replanted and spaced out in tidy rows. This looked like virgin forest—nature in the raw. Myriads of trees were struggling for life, pines, firs, birches, poplars, crowding in closely—fully-grown trees, saplings and half-grown specimens fighting for room. There were dead branches suspended, rotting as they fell. Here and there were whole dead trees that crumbled shockingly beneath our feet, dropping us in a cloud of dust and scuttling insects. It was an awesome dark cavern, the sun shut out by a close canopy of interlacing evergreens, cool and heavily scented! The difficulty we had in penetrating can well be imagined. Branches swept the ground, scratching our faces and clinging to our clothing as we pushed a way through. We stumbled on rough stones and through wet places, keeping close together for comfort, chopping a way through here and there and blazing the trees to make sure of the way back. Besides streams in many places we encountered the dreaded 'Devil's Club', a plant like giant rhubarb but covered with minute spines which caused septic sores to break out wherever they scratched our skin. At times we found ourselves crossing, and sometimes following, beaten tracks through the tangle of trees. These tracks were clearly not man-made; in fact fresh droppings suggested that they were moose tracks. Knowing the beast to be both large, and fierce when met face to face, we kept a careful watch and were prepared for swift upward flight into the branches above us should one appear. We followed a track leading uphill and presently came to a break in the forest cover. The sudden sunshine brought a sense of respite, and relief from the weight of the melancholy conifers. We looked down on to a sea of greens of infinite variety, and saw at last, a finger of the lake far below. This gave us for the first time, a visual bearing on our position. Lower down the hillside we had been completely dependent on our compass for the direction in which we were travelling.

Out in the sun for a moment, we found, amongst the tufted grasses, a tangle of thorny twining growth that had sprung up where the trees had gone. We helped ourselves to wild raspberries and strawberries from plants heavy with fruit, before plunging back into the dark forest. In other clearings, on lower ground, we broke out into what looked like bright green mossy grass, but proved to be trembling, sucking bog—the muskeg. As we tried to cross it, the ground quivered with every step—a little further and the skin might break, we felt, and we should disappear without trace, so we hastily retreated and took a longer safer route.

What remote, deserted difficult country this was! There were minerals waiting to be taken from the hills, but transport costs would have been too great to make it worth while. Winter is fierce here for all the warmth of the summer we were experiencing. But it was the overwhelming nature of the forest that seemed to be the major factor in life. It was even rumoured that light planes routed over the area had been known to disappear without trace.

When, on one occasion, we travelled to the far end of the lake, to our amazement we came across a cord road. It led to a wooden shack, where we discovered a young couple trying to make a home and farm a few acres. What courage! This was still pioneer country.

A special contribution by R. L. King

29 Fire in the bush

South Australia, 1962

I was one of the lucky ones who escaped death with barely a minute to spare. The air smelt of danger—the above-century heat drew out a strong odour of eucalyptus, and the wind was scorching : radio, press and television announced a day of acute fire danger.

At mid-morning a curl of grey smoke rose from the valley below . . . we learnt later that a youth lit the fire deliberately to demonstrate his fire-fighting prowess.

We watched that smoke and the direction of the wind anxiously, and gathered our most important documents into a satchel. The car stood on the road, ready for flight. Midday, but we couldn't eat. We cleared fallen leaves from the guttering round the roof, filled the water pump (which we carried on our backs for three days and nights without rest), shut all doors and windows, and packed our suit case—the car was small and we wanted room for a pensioner couple.

There was still nothing to see, but suddenly I heard an ominous roaring and crackling. In less time than it takes to tell, the fire roared one thousand six hundred feet up the mountain and cut off the only road out. Burning leaves were falling faster than we could put them out. Grass and shrubs burst into flame like a giant cracker on either side of the road a few feet from the car.

And that rushing wall of flame, reaching high above the tops of the trees, was tearing uphill at about 40 miles an hour.

We struck downhill on a mud track potholed and long disused. For fully two weeks I was struck numb of feeling by the absolute horror of that moment. The car jolted and the roof rack fell in our path. The precious seconds we lost then almost spelt our death. The fire front had reached the bottom of our garden, only 215 feet away. We abandoned the case on the bare earth. But when we returned only the handles were left.

The fire swept on to new victims, and we circled back on the main road, expecting to view the ashes of the house. We had our lives, and the loss of all but the clothes we wore seemed unimportant.

A miracle had happened. As well as our lives, we had the bonus of a house unscathed. But the last of the 80 trees there had been in the garden was still burning and brushing against the wall. The neighbouring house was filled with flame and crumbled in a heap of molten glass and twisted iron. The sweating soot-blackened men of one of Australia's network of volunteer fire brigades arrived just in time to save our house.

That was only the start. The fire had burnt the undergrowth and left the crowns brittle and brown. With a change of wind the fire could double back again, and a crown fire is worst of all, as it can drop to the ground at any point enclosing the firefighters in a death trap.

For three days and nights we patrolled our lonely spur, putting out smouldering logs, watching whole hillsides blaze from valley to peak in a few seconds. We breathed smoke, our eyes smarted with smoke, we smelt of smoke and sweat, and we scanned the encircling hills for signs of smoke rising from fresh outbreaks.

We sweltered in woollen clothing, as fire kills by direct radiation of heat before the flames arrive. Food ran out, and I drove two miles to the store, never sure whether the next bend would bring me into the fire. Telephone calls were banned, except for emergencies, and strictly timed. Hundreds left their offices to join our battle against the fires; hundreds more were turned away, as the army cordoned off all roads to the hills. Thirty miles away the air was filled with smoke and blackened leaves fell into the sea.

The last night was the most harrowing. While the fire was in our hills, there was some comfort in knowing that down there, through the haze, was a city of 1,500,000 where life was going on normally. When the fire reached the outer suburbs and the hills all around us were aflame, so that the slightest wind could bring any one of a dozen fires down on us again, I wanted to run away and just let the house burn.

It didn't, though. In the early hours of the morning rain came. The hundreds of weary, ragged fire fighters went home for their first sleep in days—those who still had homes. Instead of the steady roar of fire trucks there was silence. Mounds of orange peel lay where the men had stopped for but a few minutes to rest; chimney stacks were gaunt where once there had been a house. The ground was black and bare, the trees were black, and the roads were deserted.

from : 'Fire in the Bush—Melbourne, 1962', *The Times,*
February 13, 1967

30 Shock in the night

Mexico City

It was the morning of 28th July and still very dark when I woke with the strange sensation that my bed was moving about. It took a few seconds before the truth dawned on me : I was in an earthquake; and a few more while I wondered what to do.

I was on the fourth floor of a six-storey building which was rocking like a big ship in a heavy sea, only faster. The lights had failed and the thought that there was a distinct possibility that the building might collapse made me instinctively want to get under something. There was a table, I knew, at the far end of the room, so supporting myself against the wall I groped my way unsteadily towards it. I soon found I could no longer stand up, so continued on all fours until at last I reached the table and crawled underneath it.

There I sat feeling very frightened, and very foolish, while the shock waves heaved the building back and forth and the floor-boards creaked ominously in time with the violent undulations of the earth and the eerie swish-swish, swish-swish of displaced air. Beyond, through the windows of my room, I was more vaguely aware of the more persistent roll of thunder and a livid sky rent by lightning. Sitting ignominiously under my table there was nothing I could do save wait—until either the building collapsed or the tremors ceased. It was not the first time I had experienced the presence of death and I felt perfectly philosophical about the outcome; I should either survive or I shouldn't.

The earthquake lasted over ninety seconds; in my own mind it was like a whole life-time which might well have continued into eternity. But instead it stopped short; the swaying and the swishing died down and as the earth became steady once more, the vague experience of eternity vanished back into the temporal. For a minute or so there was a deathly silence and all was still. Then out of the far distance came the wailing of a siren, then another and another; the ambulances were out in search of the dead and injured.

My own reactions were now quite unexpected. I suddenly felt an overwhelming surge of emotion; my heart was beating fast and I found that tears were coming into my eyes. The full impact of the extraordinary experience now struck me—the utter impotence I had felt while caught in that violent spasm of the earth and the humbling thought that I had been spared a lonely death beneath tons of falling masonry while others, in those long seconds of waiting, must certainly so have perished.

from : Peter Townsend, *Earth, My Friend*

31 Waving spires: the Lisbon earthquake

Lisbon, Portugal, 1755

There were three major shocks that day in Lisbon and hundreds of shocks as the lurching earth settled to take up new pressures ... The second shock lasted about three minutes. From the river Tagus, where sailors on the anchored ships had watched with horror the first collapse, a fantastic sight was presented. The master of one English ship saw the whole city waving backwards and forwards like the sea when the wind first begins to rise. Lisbon is built on many sharp hills which at the time projected a great number of convent and church spires into the sky. The master of another ship compared their movements to the waving of a field of corn in the wind ...

The Tagus at that point was four miles wide, an estuary still normally well enough protected by a river bar. As Braddock [an English merchant] looked at it he could see it heaving and swelling in a most unaccountable manner, since the weather was still dead calm, as it had been all morning. Then, out in the estuary, he saw a high wall of water rising as if the sea were forming into a mountain. Foaming and roaring, the wave swept towards the shore at high speed. As the crowd on the waterside understood what was happening they broke and ran, anywhere away from the water, back into the devastated city. But the hissing waters caught them. [After the third shock] the great fire had started. It was to burn out all the centre of Lisbon. It was to continue for nine days.

from : Allen Andrews, *Earthquake*

32 The eruption of Vesuvius AD 79

Italy

Being got at a convenient distance from the houses, we stood still in the midst of a most dangerous and dreadful scene. The chariots which we had ordered to be drawn out were so agitated backwards and for-wards, though upon the most level ground, that we could not keep them steady, even by supporting them with large stones. The sea seemed to roll back upon itself, and to be driven from its banks by the convulsive motion of the earth. It is certain at least that the shore was enlarged, and many sea animals were left upon it. On the other side a black and dreadful cloud bursting with an igneous serpentine vapour darted out a long train of fire, resembling flashes of lightning but much larger... The ashes now began to fall upon us, though in no great quantity. I turned my head, and observed behind us a thick smoke, which came rolling after us like a torrent.

I proposed, while we had any light, to turn out of the high-road, lest we should be pressed to death in the dark by the crowd that followed us. We had scarce stepped out of the path when darkness overspread us, not like that of a cloudy night, or when there is no moon, but of a room when it is shut up and all the lights extinct. Nothing then was to be heard but the shrieks of women, the screams of children, and the cries of men; some were calling for their children, others for their parents, others for their husbands, and only distinguishing each other by their voices; one lamenting his own fate, another that of his family; some wishing to die from the very fear of dying; some lifting their hands to the gods, but the greater part imagining that the last and eternal light was come to destroy the gods and the world together. Among them were some who augmented the real terrors by imaginary ones, and made the frightened multitude falsely believe that Misenum was actually in flames.

At length a glimmering light appeared, which we imagined to be rather the forerunner of an approaching burst of flame (as in truth it was) rather than the return of day. However, the fire fell at a distance from us, then again we were immersed in a thick darkness, and a heavy shower of ashes rained upon us, which we were obliged to shake off, otherwise we should have been crushed and buried in the heap.

from : Pliny the Younger, *Letters*

33 Lava swallows a village

Italy, nineteen-forties

Away to the right I caught a glimpse of the front of the lava choking a narrow street and spilling steadily forward. It was black like clinker and as it spilled down along the street, little rivulets of molten rock flowed red.

The air was full of the dust of broken buildings now. My mouth and throat were dry and gritty with it and the air shimmered with intense heat. I could no longer hear the roar of gases escaping from Vesuvius. Instead my world was full of a hissing and sifting—it was a steady, unrelenting background of sound to the intermittent crash of stone and the crumbling roar of falling plaster and masonry.

Then the next building began to go. I watched, fascinated, as a crack opened across the roof. There was a tumbling roar of sound, the crack widened, splitting the very stone itself, and then the farther end of the building vanished in a cloud of dust. There was a ghastly pause as the lava consolidated, eating up the pile of rubble below. Then cracks ran splitting all across the remains of the roof not five yards away from me. The cracks widened, spreading like little fast-moving rivers, and then suddenly the whole roof seemed to sink, vanishing away below me in a great rumble of sound and disappearing into the dust of its own fall.

And as the dust settled I found myself staring at the lava face itself. It was a sight that took my breath away. I wanted to cry out, to run from it—but instead I remained on my hands and one knee staring at it, unable to move, speechless, held in the shock of seeing the pitiless force of Nature angered.

I have seen villages and towns bombed and smashed to rubble by shell-fire. But Cassino, Berlin—they were nothing to this. Bombing or shelling at least leaves the torn shells and smashed rubble of buildings to indicate what was once there. The lava left nothing. Of the half of Santo Francisco that it had overrun there was no trace. Before me stretched a black cinder embankment, quite flat and smoking with heat. It was impossible to think of a village ever having existed there.

It had left no trace and I could scarcely believe that only a few minutes before there had been buildings between me and the lava and that I'd seen them toppling, buildings that had been occupied for hundreds of years. Only away to the left the dome of a church stood up out of the black plain. And even as I noticed it the beautifully symmetrical dome cracked open like a flower, fell in a cloud of dust and was swallowed completely.

from : Hammond Innes, *The Angry Mountain*

34 Eye-witness account of the Mt. Peleé eruption

Martinique, West Indies, 1902

I saw St. Pierre destroyed. It was blotted out by one great flash of fire. Nearly 40,000 people were killed at once. Of 18 vessels lying in the roads, only one, the British steamship *Roddam*, escaped and she, I hear, lost more than half on board. It was a dying crew that took her out. Our boat arrived at St. Pierre early Thursday morning. For hours before we entered the roadstead, we could see flames and smoke rising from Mount Peleé. No one on board had any idea of danger. Capt. G. T. Muggah was on the bridge and all hands got on deck to see the show. The spectacle was magnificent. As we approached St. Pierre, we could distinguish the rolling and leaping red flames that belched from the mountain in huge volume and gushed high in the sky. Enormous clouds of black smoke hung over the volcano. The flames were then spurting straight up in the air, now and then waving to one side or the other a moment, and again leaping suddenly higher up. There was a constant muffled roar. It was like the biggest oil refinery in the world burning up on the mountain top. There was a tremendous explosion about 7.45 soon after we got in. The mountain was blown to pieces. There was no warning. The side of the volcano was ripped out, and there hurled straight towards us a solid wall of flame. It sounded like a thousand cannon. The wave of fire was on us and over us like a lightning flash. It was like a hurricane of fire, which rolled in mass straight down on St. Pierre and the shipping. The town vanished before our eyes, and then the air grew stifling hot and we were in the thick of it. Wherever the mass of fire struck the sea, the water boiled and sent up great clouds of steam. I saved my life by running to my stateroom and burying myself in the bedding. The blast of fire from the volcano lasted only for a few minutes.

It shrivelled and set fire to everything it touched. Burning rum ran in streams down every street and out into the sea. Before the volcano burst, the landings at St. Pierre were crowded with people. After the explosion, not one living being was seen on land. Only 25 of those on the *Roraima*, out of 68, were left after the first flash. The fire swept off the ship's masts and smoke stack as if they had been cut by a knife.

from : Fred M. Bullard, *Volcanoes*

Notes on Section 2

The bold figures indicate extract numbers

2 Mountains for most men are barriers, sources of flood waters, of avalanches and rock falls, the home of spirits, and so hostile to settlement for both physical and spiritual reasons. People who climb mountains for pleasure and to enjoy the scenery are few; they have only done so for a little over a hundred years. The similarities between mountain peoples, and the fact that they enjoy living in the mountains, is discussed in other sections, as is the poverty and backwardness of some mountain communities. Jawaharlal Nehru enjoyed the mountains, but realised that for people who had to live in the Himalayan foothills, life could be far from easy. Almora, India, 29° 38′ N, 79° 42′ E.

3 Mount Cameroon (4° 45′ N, 8 55′ E) is 13,350 feet (4069 m) high. Mora Dickson and her husband were responsible for a training centre at Man O'War Bay where the purpose was to give young men, from all parts and of all races of Nigeria, training in personal resource, endurance and initiative, which would encourage them to help their country in its new state of independence. It was rewarding work but had its sorrows. Strangely enough a similar case has been reported on an endurance course, on cold moorland in England, during military training.

4 Helvellyn (54° 31′ N, 3° 1′ W) in the English Lake District, is a small mountain by world standards, only 3118 feet (950 m). The summit can be attained by an easy scramble in summer, though even then mist and rain can come up suddenly. Many school parties visit the Lakes in April when conditions can be as 'Alpine' as this author experienced them. It is then that leadership is fully tested, and careful kitting out and training of the party pay dividends. Adequate footwear, windproof clothing, the odd bar of chocolate and the exposure blanket that fits into a matchbox, often repay forethought. The author was a hill-walker who became an experienced mountaineer. Similar conditions can prevail in all high spots of the British Isles in midwinter and early spring, and can catch the unwary.

5 Latakunga (Latacunga), 0° 50′ S, 78° 35′ W. Climatic changes with altitude and aspect are illustrated, and also the condition of unsophisticated people in isolated areas. Quivedo is on the river Palènque; it joins the river Guayas on which Guayaquil stands. The author was seeking balsa wood in order to make a raft for a cross-Pacific voyage from South America to the Polynesian Islands. He wished to test the feasibility of his theory that primitive navigators, who depended on ocean currents and winds, could have reached Polynesia by following this route.

In order to reach the jungle-covered coastal plain, the author had to travel by a roundabout route, first by air to Quito, then by track through intermontane plateaux, over the Andes, and down to the undeveloped coastal plain. A friend of the compiler who visited this area many years later reported little change in road conditions. The poverty of the inhabitants can be illustrated by quoting a bus fare—1 $ U.S. per 200 miles (320 km approx.).

6 Sites for mountain homes must be chosen with great care, to avoid not only rock falls and avalanche tracks, but also the cold site where the sun strikes late, or the wind whips up, or frost creeps down, or floods tear down narrow stream tracks and wash away homes and arable land.

7 The mountain chains of most recent origin are particularly liable to disturbance. The author was seeking botanical specimens when he experienced this Assam-Tibet earthquake which changed the course of rivers and caused whole mountain ranges to disappear.

9 'Throughout the world floods cause greater loss of life than any other natural disaster', F. W. Lane, *The Elements Rage.* In Peebles (55° 40′ N, 3° 12′ W) this flood followed a long drought when the Tweed had dried up to a series of pools and shallows on this reach. A century is not long in the life of a river and men can build on the flood plain without being aware of the danger. Great boulders seen in the narrow valleys of trickling streams are sometimes puzzling phenomena, until one realises how much the flood waters can rise as the stream and its tributaries come down in an exceptional spate.

10 Florence (Firenze), 43° 47′ N, 11° 15′ E. The mean rainfall is 5.1 inches (130 mm) in October and 4.6 inches (117 mm) in November; the year's total is 36 inches (914 mm). The higher ground from which the Arno flows would have more. Florence lies low in old marshland and has had floods before, but nothing to equal that of 1966, which caused distress to art lovers all over the world. The river banks have been strengthened and raised, and the city has made a remarkable recovery. Flood marks well over one's head show on walls a long way from the river.

11 Like the towns, the autobahn is also well back from the river. Both sides of this road are strip-farmed for a variety of crops, including maize, tobacco, vines, sugar beet, poppies, wheat, sunflowers, potatoes, hops, and apples, pears and cherries on the lower slopes. Small church spires locate villages situated on terrace sites and approached by side roads. Above are the forested hillsides. Breisach, 48° 2′ N, 7° 37′ E.

12 This extract vividly describes the formation of a new cut-off. Note the period, the eighteen-fifties. Since then the levées have been raised time and again and are reinforced with concrete. The Mississippi runs at a high level above the flood plain. Despite vast overflow lakes for the storage of storm waters, it is said that over ten million people in U.S.A. are still subject to flood hazards. Elsewhere in the world there are millions more who live and work on flood plains. Many of these areas are fertile, and it is likely that about one-third of the world's present food supplies come from them.

13 Enormous areas of China are subject to floods. They are due to melt-waters from the mountains, monsoon rains, and the deposit of silt in the rivers which has raised the water to above the level of the plains. The rivers are confined by dykes, most of them of earth. Concerted efforts of recent years have strengthened the dykes and diverted flood waters to storage lakes, but flooding remains a problem as in many other river basins in other parts of the world.

14 The young people were fighting the river, and fighting for their new way of life after the poverty and distress of their forefathers. Organisation kept them together as a larger-than-family unit.

15 Half the Dutch people live behind dykes on polders below sea-level and are not aware of it in the ordinary way. In Amsterdam all large old buildings are built on wooden piles. Under the royal palace there are 14,000; the main railway station is on 'made' land.

16 Low land on both sides of the North Sea has from time to time suffered extensive flooding. It occurs when gales have coincided with spring high tides, causing the sea to be pounded up against the shore and up the rivers, and to breach the coasts. In England on this occasion in 1953 many were killed, and in Holland 1800 died in the polder floods. Since then, coastal defences have been reinforced and redesigned on both sides of the North Sea. It is said that given the right combination of rain, wind and tide much of London is still vulnerable to severe flooding. A flood barrier to control the tidal surge is to be built across the Thames in the Woolwich area. Many new housing estates above London are built astride tributaries of the Thames, on land formerly avoided, and in recent years have been badly flooded in consequence. Flood-water channels are to be cut to reduce this flooding.

17 'Water everywhere' is written about England, but it applies to all those places where we are covering the absorbent surface of the land. The same effect can be observed on a small scale in the patio-type garden.

18 Spring-thaw floods are acute in Siberia where there are enormous north-flowing rivers. They are so wide that there are few crossings, and the ferries have particular difficulties both in spring and in autumn. In winter the river is used as a road, and sledges and horses are still commonly seen in use for short journeys.

19 This picture of the unwelcoming Gobi (Shamo) desert is still true of life in most of desert Asia. An exception is Ulan Bator, the capital of Mongolia and a modern town, connected with towns in the U.S.S.R. and China by air and railways. The roads after a few miles are little more than well-marked tracks. Lorries are still infrequent in the Gobi; you might meet one in a hundred miles or you might not. You will certainly meet nomads from time to time, though many of the people have now settled down.

20 Southampton Island (64° 30′ N, 80° 0′ W) is Canadian. Conditions are of course applicable to tundra elsewhere. According to a Russian scientist a quarter of the earth's surface is permafrost, and certainly half the U.S.S.R. is permafrost. Winter is the best time to get about by land despite the cold, because the ground is frozen solid.

21 The Tanana River, Alaska, in spring. Mosquitoes are a menace from the equator to the subarctic. Attempts are made to keep down their number by spraying the breeding grounds in some areas. They are not much trouble in the British Isles except for a short time in the year, but in much of Canada and the U.S.A. for example, as soon as the central heating is turned off and the double-glazing comes down, up go the mosquito screens.

22 Halley Bay, approximately 76° S, 30° W. The vast frozen continent under the ice cap may one day yield minerals. International interest centres

87

on scientific research, including the study of earthquakes, weather patterns, and human endurance and life patterns. One station (American), established at the South Pole and fitted and refuelled by air, reports a movement of the geographic South Pole in twelve years of half a mile (0·8 km). Winter work proceeds underground or outside in a temperature of −49°C (−56°F) and blizzards in which the winds can reach 150 miles per hour (240 km).

23 Southern Patagonia is still practically uninhabited except by a handful of nomadic Indians who live on the sea and forest foods which are enough for their simple needs. They are practically untouched by the twentieth century.

24 An unusual view of 'Arcadia'. The Chaco, with a population of some 94,000 and covering about 270,000 square miles (nearly 700,000 km²)—three times the size of the United Kingdom—is situated mainly in Paraguay, but it also extends into Brazil and Argentina.

5 This is a description of the Ituri forest (1° 20′ N, 27° 30′ E) but it could be applied to other forest areas. There is a feeling of oppressiveness, hostility, and of being watched by unseen eyes.

27 Belém (Pará), 1° 27′ S, 48° 29′ W. There is no real change in the forest since the time when this extract was written. River and hydrofoil transport is probably no greater, as the extract was written at the time of a rubber-boom on the Amazon. Belém has an airport, and flights across to Rio and other coastal towns are now commonplace. There is a road from Belém to Brasilia and the coast; otherwise the rivers are still the roads.

28 This was a schoolboy expedition from England whose purpose was to study, map and experience a tough area, in this case the interior plateau of British Columbia (at approximately 54° 30′ N, 124° 30′ W). Note the dissected nature of the plateau.

29 Fire is a hazard in all forest regions, especially in Australia during the dry, hot summer. In Europe, the Mediterranean forests are also at risk, and constant watch must be kept and fire breaks maintained.

30–34 The world's earthquake belt is so extensive that probably 200 million people live within range of severe quakes. The fold mountains that cross the world from east to west, ring the Pacific, and form the submarine ridges in the oceans, are the main areas of instability. Most earthquakes have little effect on people's homes, but on average three times a year a large town, or group of towns, suffers a major disaster from a shock or series of shocks of intensity 8–12 on the Mercalli scale (which runs from 1 to 12).

The Tokyo earthquake of 1923 was responsible for the death of 100,000 people; 170 shocks were experienced in six hours and a great fire was fanned by high winds. Lisbon in 1755, and San Francisco in 1906 were also raked with fire. Agadir (Morocco) 1960, Dan-Isfahan (Iran) 1962, and Skopje (Yugoslavia) 1963, suffered almost complete collapse owing to the severity of the shocks and the nature of the buildings. In 1970 Peru suffered a major shock in which 50,000 people were killed and one million made homeless in the total destruction of Chimbote and the surrounding towns.

Chilean earthquakes are frequent; Concepcion had two major shocks in 1939 when Valdivia lost its harbour and islands, and fishing villages along the coast disappeared, and another in 1960 when a quarter of the people of Chile were in danger and the coast had to be remapped. Killer sea waves (tsunami) caused by earthquake shocks can affect coasts thousands of miles away. The Pacific Islands and Japan both suffered from the Chilean shocks.

Japan is a particularly vulnerable area; there are minor tremors almost every day and periodic major quakes. The Japanese have put up earthquake-proof buildings of flexible steel-and-concrete construction, 512 feet (156 m) high, which they hope will swing like a willow and withstand typhoon winds of 175 miles (280 km) an hour. They have also suggested the possibility of exploding atom bombs below the surface to release earth tension. New Zealanders—in another vulnerable area—keep their towns well spread out and live low, in bungalows in the suburbs. They, too, have almost daily tremors, and a major earthquake on average every eight years. Naturally their scientists research into the instability of the earth's crust and the use of resources such as natural steam for generating thermal electricity.

Many earthquakes precede or accompany volcanic activity. 530 active volcanoes exist, mostly around the Pacific, with a maximum concentration of seventy-seven in Indonesia. The fertility of weathered volcanic soil encourages close settlement around many volcanoes. Towns destroyed by earthquakes or volcanoes are nearly always rebuilt—such is the tenacity of man.

3

Coming to terms with environment

This section takes up the theme of the first two. The opening passages illustrate how some people have managed, through trial and error, to exist with limited resources and to establish a reasonable way of life under conditions that would be difficult if not intolerable to those raised in softer climes. Later extracts show how some simple people have been affected by contacts with men and ideas from areas of the world with more advanced technology. Finally, there are a few passages about people who, with the aid of modern skills, can—for greater convenience or from necessity—create a micro-climate and social build-up of their own, and, by means of improved transport, penetrate fast and far into the wilds. Change is accelerating and we must look to an exciting future as men carry their essential environment into space and under the seas.

1 Aboriginal hunter's skill

Western Australia

He knows the secrets of bird and animal life. The goanna* runs along the ground and soon outstrips the speeding native, and cannot be caught, but hold! the native whistles and the speeding goanna hears this sound. In a flash it freezes, erect and immobile, thinking its arch enemy the hawk is swooping down to kill. The bandicoot† runs into a hollow log and cannot be dug out with a primitive stone axe. The black man hisses down the log like a snake and out comes the bandicoot to escape its mortal enemy and so is killed and eaten. For that is the lore of the aboriginal, who survives by learning the secrets of the animals and birds around him.

Camouflage, mimicry and the keen insight of the trained naturalist—all this learning is brought to play in his struggle to live. A hollow log thrown into a water-hole with one end closed up becomes an ideal fish-trap. At early morn or during the night when evaporation is least, the muddy water of a pool becomes clear on the surface. When the pelicans come along to feed on the little fish of the Marlingi water-hole, the latter hide away from their enemy by going into these log traps. Then comes the native, who, diving down, picks up these log-traps; putting his hand over the open end, he carries it out to the bank and empties the fish on the ground for his family. Here is a good morning meal for his family.

The emu speeds along the ground and quickly outstrips the fastest hunter. The black man knows this and does not hunt them that way, for he has an easy method. He simply lies on the ground then whistles aloud and waves his legs about, for he knows the emu's weakness is inquisitiveness. It becomes attracted by the sounds and the waving of legs, so up it comes to see what is wrong. The result is a good meal for the black man. Crocodiles, kangaroos, hawks, ducks, fish all are caught this way. I write of these few things to show that the native lying under a tree is simply obeying the great primal law that the 'maximum food must be taken with the least energy'. The lazy black man and the rich white man are obeying the same law.

from : W. E. Harney, *North of 23*

* Iguana, large lizard
† Australian insect-eating marsupial (pouched)

2 Dependence on game

Kalahari, South Africa, nineteen-fifties

They [the Bushmen] started at once unloading the game, and went straight on to the skinning and cutting up the animals with skill and dispatch. I watched them absorbed in the grace of their movements. They worked with extraordinary reverence for the carcasses at their feet. There was no waste to mock the dead or start a conscience over the kill. The meat was neatly sorted out for specific uses and placed in separate piles on the skin of each animal. All the time the women stood around and watched. They greeted the unloading of each arrival with an outburst of praise, the ostrich receiving the greatest of all, and kept up a wonderful murmur of thanksgiving which swelled at moments in their emotion to break on a firm phrase of a song of sheer deliverance. How cold, inhuman and barbarous a civilized butcher's shop appeared in comparison.

from : Laurens Van Der Post, *The Heart of the Hunter*

3 Camels and their uses

Australia

In a dust storm camels can close their nostrils, or almost close them, and still get enough air for breathing. The nostrils meet, forming a long straight slit, lined on each side with short, soft hair which filters the air. Another clever arrangement for travelling in dust storms is that the camel's eyelids are only about fifty per cent opaque, and through them the camel can see more or less where it is going. Often through thunderstorms at night I have distinctly seen a flash of lightning with eyes shut, so if our own eyelids were less opaque we'd be able to see through them enough to keep walking on flat desert country.

I was told that camels cannot swim, and was inclined to believe it as they seem to have lived in desert country always. However the day came when I was riding a camel and came to a river in flood and went in. The camel swam well while I hung on to the saddle expecting to have difficulty in keeping it headed for the opposite bank; but that was not necessary—he swam straight across about thirty yards. Climbing up the muddy bank on the other side was even less difficult. A camel goes down on its knees and thus is in a more serviceable position; the back legs hold its rear end high and its knees get a better grip than its feet would. It does that whenever a steep grade is encountered, especially a sandhill . . .

A camel goes up hindquarters first, like cattle, and just the opposite to a horse. While sitting with a load on and its brisket on the ground taking most of the weight, it seems to know what weight it has on, and what special effort it must make. The brisket is a round, protruding mass of gristle about ten inches across. It raises its hindquarters until its hind legs are as straight as they can be, which is far from as straight as the hind legs of a horse. Both legs go up evenly. That amounts to lifting only half the total weight. With hindquarters and and load propped up at the back, this makes the front legs open up at the knees, the forequarters rising a bit as they are pushed forward till the knees take the weight and the brisket is off the ground. The camel is then kneeling on the ground with hind legs right up and it has only to rise enough to be able to straighten its front legs to be fully up on all fours. This means that the job is more than half done. It sways its body a little, forwards and backwards, and on a back sway lifts one knee up till the foot of that leg is straightened out on the ground. It uses the momentum of a sway to assist in this, but it cannot do this when rising from the second knee, so it does the rest a bit quicker. Its body is propped up by three legs and the fourth, one front leg, is propping the fourth quarter from the knee up. It has little more to do and does it quickly, the straight front leg taking the weight while it smartly lifts the other and straightens it with the foot on the ground.

It is a clever arrangement, as the load goes up in stages, a proportion at a time. The biggest strain is on the two hind legs giving the first lift. If the load is too great the camel gets it nearly up then flops back on the ground again. This is painful and makes him yell. Once the hind quarters are up, no matter how heavy the load is, they always succeed in getting up on to their front legs.

When sitting down again, they go down on their knees first and the back legs fold up as their hindquarters go down steadily and avoid the final bump on the ground. That must be painful, but the brisket takes most of the bump. It was always a wise thing to choose soft or sandy ground for pack camels to sit on . . . Once on its four legs, any camel will carry more than it can lift or get up with. A horse's back is concave, but a camel's is convex, built on the arch principle, and that makes it better for carrying a heavy load, so much so that it seems as if nature designed their arched backbones for load carrying. The distance that camels could carry heavy loads was surprising to those that had been accustomed to other pack animals. When they come to an uphill grade they go into low gear by making shorter steps.

Camels have broad feet, about nine or ten inches across, the most useful of any draught animals. The soles are black and not unlike motor tyres. They wear wonderfully and have two short, broad claws at the front end where the soles are thickest.

They don't sound or look right for getting a grip of the ground in a heavy pull, but they used to do so very well and in heavy sand they stood alone.

[*About camels as draught animals.*] In a heavy pull the camels were 'stood up' first, each camel pressing forward into the collar until his chains were tight but not making any special effort to pull. Each driver had his own way of getting them 'stood up', calling out the names of this and that camel that was lazy or inattentive. They knew, and he knew, when the time was about right for the special effort, and this was usually signified with a whistle. Then they lowered the whole body by a few inches and the wagon was pulled forward slowly, taking minutes to cover its own length. In the heaviest pulls they did well to move the wagon only three feet at a time. If they were allowed to choose their own time to stop, then the choice would be made by the laziest; he would stop and they'd all stop. The driver had to discourage that in every way he could think of, swinging the whip in a threatening circle and keeping within reach of the ones that he expected would be the first to stop pulling. Once they were well trained to heavy pulling they would take it very calmly and not get excited or upset with fright... In heavy pulling no animal could beat the camel. If he could not move a wagon he would try again and again, being unique in that respect among draught animals...

The number of camels to a wagon varied. On the road from Nannine to Wiluna... the right proportion was fourteen camels to fourteen tons. This was a very good road and they would have pulled twenty tons except for a long sandy plain they had to cross. In the more rugged country in the north-west half a ton a camel was about right for three shafters and five sets of three in front of them, eighteen in all. A larger team would reduce the capacity of each camel because the leaders would be too far from the wagon. The closer they were to the wagon the more they could pull, but bush roads allowed no more than three camels abreast and so limited the effective size of the team...

The camels were superior to any other draught animal in a drought. If they had to go two days and a night without water it was not serious. Like donkeys they did not need shoeing. They could be worked for years without a spill.

from : H. M. Barker, *Camels and the Outback*

4 Usefulness of the desert grass

Gobi, Mongolia

The sturdy desert grass called by the Chinese *gi-gi-stao* counts as one of his most valuable harvests and is of use to him in endless ways. When still young and tender, if chopped with a big fodder-knife, its green shoots are suitable for horse fodder, but the plant grows quickly and before long its stalks are so hard that even camels pass it by. When it reaches its full height of seven or eight feet it is cut, garnered, and serves many purposes.

In farms which have to maintain the strongest resistance against natural encroachment, the ridge of the dune is cleverly supported by loosely knotted desert grass, and this net-like barrier is most effective in holding back the wind-lashed sand-waves. During the winter months the grass is woven into mats which cover the mud bed, and are also used to line the mud roof of the oasis shack. The same mat, woven in another shape, forms the chassis of the village cart, and also makes its awning. A very long mat forms a circular bin which holds the winter store of grain and fodder. The winnowing-fan used on the threshing-floor for tossing the grain is also made from it, and in the kitchen it is used as a sieve for sifting particles of mud from the wheat. Small children, collecting every scrap of animal manure in and around the oasis for fuel, use a basket plaited from this *gi-gi-tsao*, and the broom with which the innkeeper stirs the dust in his guest-rooms consists of a bunch of grass, tied round a stick. The carter, on desert stages, fashions from it a makeshift curry-comb to groom his mules, and the only rope or string which the desert provides is grass twisted either coarsely or finely. The planks of the bridge which the farmer and his sons throw across the irrigation canal are held in place by strands of the same grass, and the bridles and halters of horses and bullocks are made from it.

Inside the home the woman at her hand-loom uses a weaver's comb and reed made from the grass, and she also plaits from it a ladle with which to lift dough-strings from the boiling water. The iron cooking-pot is scrubbed clean with a scouring brush of the stiffest stalks firmly tied together, and carefully selected stems, cut to exact length, are used as chopsticks. Over the kitchen stove hangs a grass hold-all in which the woman keeps her primitive cooking accessories, and by stripping off the outer sheath and boiling the pith, a wick for the vegetable-oil lamp is supplied.

During the summer heat a curtain made of desert grass, held in place by twisted thread, hangs in the door-frame and keeps out the flies but lets in the air, and the desert nomads make a most charming dado for their tents from the stalks decorated in intricate geometrical patterns with home-dyed and hand-twisted wool. It is also used to weave the hurdles which enclose the lamb, kid and baby-camel nurseries, and serve as camouflage for the encampments.

This same grass is used by the desert child to make his playthings; from it he learns to plait the most entrancing little toys, necklets and bracelets. When the cicada begins to sound its queer tearing call in the great heat, every child cuts the grass to make a tiny cage to hold one of the fascinating tree-hoppers, for in the Gobi the caged cicada is comparable to the caged canary of a Western nursery. The Gobi baby's rattle, too, is a hollow ball of twisted grass enclosing a large bead.

In cases where the dwarf iris is pulped and made into paper the sieve on which the pulp is drained is made of desert grass, and it is from this sieve that each sheet of paper is lifted to the whitewashed walls on which it is sun-dried. Were it not for the abundant growth of *gi-gi-tsao,* on desert steppe-lands the standard of comfort in an oasis home would be much lower than it is now.

from : Mildred Cable with Francesca French, *The Gobi Desert*

5 Value of the oil palm

Guinea Coast, West Africa

The people in tropical lands have arranged their diet almost exclusively of vegetables. In this it is possible to see the influence of the physical environment, but the influence of the hard facts of civilization cannot be neglected. As a whole, in making use of nature people in the hot, wet belt turn almost exclusively to the vegetable kingdom for their tools, clothes, and dwellings. Like the people in the Far East, they belong to a 'vegetable civilization'. They have evinced the highest degree of ingenuity in getting the best out of certain plants. The innumerable possibilities afforded by the bamboo are well known; and in Northern Ceylon the palmyra tree (*Borassus flabellifer*) has no fewer than 801 uses, whilst the oil palm (*Eloeis guineenis*) is quite as valuable to the people of the Guinea Coast and is really the basis of daily life.

The fibrous husk of the nut yields oil which is used in the preparation of all kinds of food. The nut is eaten raw. Its oil, though less esteemed, is chiefly used for making cosmetics. After the extraction of the oil, the fibres are carefully kept, dried, and used for kindling fires. The ashes of the male flowers take the place of table salt. When the stalk which bears the bunch is teased out, it makes a good brush for whitewashing walls with lime or kaolin. A fibre used for mending broken calabashes is taken from the spathe covering the bunches. The leaves are made into roofing screens to protect young plants from the sun, fish-fences, and baskets for carrying on the back or in the hand. The veins of the leaflets are used for making little fly-whisks which the chiefs carry in their hands. The spines of the fronds serve as rafters. When cut into thin laths, they make rat-traps or snares for birds, and when flattened, they give rough paddles. The juice from the spine is used for healing cuts. The fluff taken off the bases of the leaves catches fire easily and is used as tinder. The central leaf-buds are eaten raw or cooked as palm cabbage. Among the Fangs it is boiled with red pepper to form a remedy for bronchitis. The sap which flows from a hole cut in the central leaf buds is made into palm wine. The roots are chewed as an aphrodisiac. As soon as the tree is felled, the trunk is attacked by the larvae of a big beetle (*Rhynchophorus ferrugineus*), and these 'palm worms' are a popular dainty.

Most investigators into the diet of peoples in the hot, wet belt have found that the diet does not contain the quantity of calories needed by a manual worker.

from : Pierre Gourou, *The Tropical World*

6 Subsistence farming in the tropics

Mexico

In the Tropics many families depend upon perennial garden plots managed by the husband and wife with the help of their children. The traditions they follow probably represent a type of tillage older than grain-raising or the domestication of animals. We have encountered remnants of this subsistence agriculture wherever we have explored off the beaten track in the mountains of tropical America and Mexico, regions in which the year falls naturally into two seasons. One is Dry Season, when evaporation exceeds rainfall. The other is Wet Season, when the converse is true.

After a few weeks of Dry Season, dead wood exposed to air burns easily. It is then that we have watched the strange birth of subsistence-gardens, each rising like the legendary phoenix from the ashes of a jungle fire. The peasant farmer prepares for this event by deliberately girdling or cutting the forest trees. As soon as the brush is dry, he ignites it, and ashes fall to the soil as a quick fertiliser. Promptly the cleared space is stocked by hand with a wide variety of useful plants, often in tiers of vegetation. Vines soon creep over the ground. Beans climb the dead trees or even the cornstalks. The profusion of leaves suggests chaos, for a few of the plants are in rows. Yet the soil is covered with valuable plants and may remain so for several years.

Agriculture by these primitive methods fits well into the life of the family. Some products are ready almost every day, and no sudden need for extra help arises. Whenever a bit of soil is exposed by removal of a plant, it is used immediately as space in which to start another. Often the same plant yields a variety of different products as it ages : pot herbs from your foliage; decorative flowers; fruits; starch-filled rootstocks; perhaps fibres from the mature stem, or a fermentable juice. Other plants from this culture show outstanding productivity and a long succession of products : bananas, yams, and cassava (manioc-source of tapioca starch). In consequence the idea of a harvest time is foreign to this style of agriculture . . .

We were aghast to see fires lit so widely, to find valuable timber going up in smoke. Agriculturalists experienced in these lands assured us that a new network of roots would form within weeks and keep the steep soils from eroding. They insisted that methods suited to temperate zones did not work as well as the burn-and-plant system traditional in tropical America.

At the time we did not realise that on a great many subsistence farmlets, man really lives at peace with his land. He asks little from it, and does almost nothing to encourage higher yields. When the forest re-invades, he lets it come as part of a casual rotation of crops. Instead of weeding out saplings to protect his garden, he allows them to grow. Then, towards the end of Wet Season, he girdles trees in a fresh area and starts a new garden patch. By the time his surviving children have grown and some of them inherit the land, the earlier areas will be jungle again and ready for another round of use.

A majority of these patchy gardens, whether viewed from a plane or from the ground, seem glued to mountain slopes as though applied by a paper-hanger. On the farmlet the peasant follows parental precept. He may be illiterate, and completely unaware that his system achieves a good rotational cropping of the land. Only where greater productivity is required of the land has it been necessary to codify farming procedure, to argue the relative merits of a two-field alternation between row crops and hay, as against a three field system demanding less of the soil.

In Latin America the burn-and-plant method has been successful for centuries in all areas so remote from a centre of civilisation that no pressure for greater productivity is felt. Only when the peasant raises more food than is needed for his own family's subsistence is he likely to harm the land.

from : Lorus J. and Margery Milne, *The Balance of Nature*

99

7 Masai home life

Kenya, nineteen-fifties

One of the scrawny mothers of the tribe, clad in skins, took me into her hut. It was made of withies twisted together between upright sticks like a basket, with plenty of daylight showing through. The roof was of mud plastered over a cap of withies and it had an air of marked impermanence, for the Suk are nomads.

Possessions were down to the bone. A few hollow gourds stoppered with cows' tails in a woven bag hanging on a wall; a clay pot, upside-down on a stick, for milking into; a spear tucked into the side of the hut; a few hides in a corner. Nothing else. Two low platforms, perhaps a foot high, made of sticks bound with thongs, provided elementary beds. Sunlight dappled the floor as it probed chinks in the walls. A smell of wood-smoke, rancid fat and cow dung—rather pleasant. The old girl hawked and spat as she talked and her neck coils twinkled in the sun and shadow . . .

No cooking stones in this hut, such as you find in all the huts of cultivating people. There is no need to cook. Curdled milk and blood is the staple, and meat roasted on the ends of skewers. Sometimes nowadays they trade hides for grain, and then the women pound and cook it like their harder-working sisters of the uplands. But only now and then : for them no delving, no hoes, no *pangas*.* The pastoral life they know to be best because it does not turn women into slaves of the hoe. They have no envy for their sisters who bend their backs in the hot sun to dig, weed and harvest.

from : Elspeth Huxley, *A New Earth*

8 Life in the village

Guinea, nineteen-forties

The tops of the thatched huts glistening as the first bright rays of morning light disperse the mists of the night. Birds singing for the new day. Clatter from kitchens built out behind the main houses and attached to the dwellings with palm-covered passages. Smoke from these kitchens curling lazily into the clean bright air like little lost clouds as breakfasts are cooked. The odours of steamed corn meal mixed with black-eyed peas, palm oil, crawfish, and hot pepper. Girls going to the well outside the village with great calabashes balanced on their

* Heavy knives

heads. Children running to the stream to bathe with home-made soap boiled up from palm oil and the leachings of ashes. Vigorous brushing of the teeth by twirling a fuzzed-out fibrous root against each tooth. Men singing as they go to the *efe* to work the farm. A busy new day beginning in the village.

This was just any day, but there were special ones so full of delight for a small boy that the excitement was almost more than one small body could contain. Feast days when the trained horses danced to the drums! House-building days when every able-bodied man in the town lent a hand to help raise a new dwelling! All of them were careful to protect the illusion of us small boys who were under the delightful impression that we were being helpful. We must have been in the way, darting in with thatch and tie-ropes proffered before they were needed, but that was all part of the gaiety of house-raising. Women cooked and served great quantities of food, and the men sang heady songs of brave deeds, of valour in war and the hunt.

The actual materials of the houses were simple earth-things—a framework of stout poles laced together with saplings. The walls were plastered with clay mixed with cow-dung; the roof was thatched with thick bundles of palm leaves tied to the roof poles. Laughter and song and goodwill were necessary materials, too, and seemed like integral parts of the whole. My grandfather's royal palace was built of these same materials and was different from the rest of the structures only in arrangement and size. It consisted of many large and small rooms built around an immense central council chamber where the sub-chiefs and elders met in conference.

Our houses were good houses, not grand but good. They kept out the scorching heat of the sun and the downpour of tropical storms. At night they were lighted by little clay lamps containing palm oil which were suspended from the ceiling by raffia cords. Our parents had beds made of mahogany wood with sinews laced across them to keep the country cloth pads off the earth floor. Children bedded down on thick raffia mats called *canda* which could be rolled up during the day. With the door of the house closed against the weather and the night-prowling creatures, the small yellow light flickering down on a family sleep-time scene, a village house seemed, and still seems to me, a secure and happy kind of home. Some of the laughter that goes into the building of the house seems to stay in it.

If housing is measured by the quality of the living done within its walls rather than by the amount of plumbing installed, there is nothing very much wrong with an earthen house.

from : Prince Modupe, *I was a Savage*

9 East African childhood

Kenya

I was not yet four years old when my sister was born. I had got used to sleeping away from my mother's care, having been so long with my uncle. On my return, together with other male youngsters of very nearly the same age, I began to sleep in my grandfather's hut. (The girls of this age also would sleep away from their parents' homes and at some grandmother's house.) Because there was no older sister in the family, and my mother had to go off to work in the *shamba** every day, it wasn't long before I was obliged, though still a very young child myself, to become the day-to-day 'nurse' for my baby sister. For my mother to make me succeed in this function, she had to train me—to give me instructions and see how well I carried them out. I had at first to do some of the things while she watched—feed the child on porridge, for example. Such training took us into the planting season of the following year. As her *shamba* work increased, so did my nursing duties.

In our home the day would start with early morning duties for all the members of our household except the baby, Mang'ong'o Alusa. My father would put out our animals, which included cows, goats and sheep. He would then sharpen the farm tools and go to the farm, very often without breakfast. My mother would fetch water from the river, clean *shiko*, that area of the house occupied by our domestic animals at night, and breast-feed Alusa. On my arrival from Grandfather's hut, which used to be at sunrise, I would be sent to look for fire from other homes; if, that is, my mother had been careless about keeping hers burning through the night. I would build or stir up the fire in the fire-place, and leave it for my mother to make breakfast. This breakfast was of maize meal, which was meant for my father. I would be asked to eat *bujeni*, the remains of the previous day's supper. My mother would check Alusa's porridge, which had been made out of millet flour and stored in a gourd for ready use. Sometimes the porridge turned out to be sour, but it would still serve the purpose, my mother believed. She would then wake up the baby to give her the last feed for the morning. And lastly, before moving off to the *shamba*, she would give me instructions : Do not leave the home unguarded, she would tell me, for fear that thieves would steal our property. Do not leave Alusa crying for long periods of time, for that would be dangerous to her health. Feed her when she cries. Guard the chickens from wild cats and the chicks from wild birds. Be helpful to visitors and strangers who ask you for information. Finally, she would promise to bring me a present—a piece of fruit, a potato—

* Farm plot

when she returned from work. Then she would leave, not to return until very late in the evening.

As soon as my mother left, loneliness would set in. I was in charge of a huge house and, judged by present day standards, it was a very dark, extremely untidy and even filthy house. The outside was frightful, too. There were known to be wild cats which would come to catch our chickens. Thieves might come at any moment, too. All of these thoughts would frighten me constantly in my early days of home-guarding and baby-nursing.

As Alusa slept for long hours, I would decide to do some of the things I had seen my mother do, but which she had not particularly asked me to do. I had seen her grind millet and prepare and cook bananas; so I would keep busy with one or two of these jobs until Alusa would wake up. Then I would feed her according to instructions : shake the gourd that contained the porridge, lay Alusa on my lap with the head resting on my stomach, fold my left palm and fingers so as to make a curved cup to be placed below her mouth. Into this curve I would pour porridge until her mouth was submerged. As soon as the porridge touched her mouth, Alusa would suck it in. If she refused to suck it, I had been told to stop feeding her. But, of course, I had noticed my mother force the baby to suck by closing her nostrils with a finger, thereby forcing her to breathe through the mouth. As the mouth was submerged in porridge, the breathing would inevitably force the porridge down the gullet. At first I feared trying this trick; I would simply hold her until my mother returned from work.

Sooner or later, I discovered that in the meantime I could go away and—when Alusa was sleeping—play with other 'nurses' from the neighbouring homes. At first we were afraid to go because our parents had given us strict orders to remain at home. But having established among us the place where we would play whenever a chance came we would gather there as soon as possible after the parents had gone to the *shambas*.

Here we would come with our siblings. We would sit them or lay them on the ground and the five of us would go on playing. We would attend to our babies only when they cried excessively. Then we would sing lullabies to make them go to sleep quickly, hurriedly feed them, or perhaps tie them, still crying on our backs and continue playing. Neither our babies nor we ourselves had any clothes to put on, so there was no problem of washing napkins! Neither were children and babies supposed to be bathed lest they catch disease. Yet when we did try to bathe ourselves as well as the babies, the only objection our parents would raise was that the process involved our leaving the homes unguarded. This was true, since we had to do the bathing at a river, where we energetically engaged ourselves in play activity.

As the four of my playmates were girls, they would have with them containers in which to draw water, thereby helping the mothers in other home duties as well as nursing.

Another activity of ours was that of collecting and carrying firewood. At first I was reluctant to take part in this because it was felt essentially to be girls' work. But my mother encouraged me to do it—in fact at one stage she threatened to refuse me food if I did not bring firewood during the day! Games such as hide-and-seek, and 'make-believe' play—imitating mother at cooking, death ceremonies, riddles, house-building (using maize-cobs), harvesting, beer-party scenes, circumcision ceremonies—all of these would engage our energies and vigour as we guarded the homes and cared for the babies.

It was my duty as Alusa's nurse to offer her toilet 'training'. For toilet paper, I was instructed to use *mavuya*, a special type of leaf, soft enough to resemble the feel of our present-day toilet paper. Nurses were all instructed to use *mavuya* whenever babies defecated. As Alusa grew older she was usually told, either by my mother or by myself, to excrete on the grass. But many children in our location, fearing the cool dew in the early morning, would go alongside the house, or even in the house itself. There were no latrines as such; grown-ups went into the bush. Hence there was always an uncultivated piece of land near the home for this purpose.

When my mother returned from work, she would look round the house and at the baby to see if I had done my duty well. If Alusa's eyes were red, she would know Alusa had cried a lot during the day. If the gourd was still full of porridge, she would know Alusa had not been fed. She would then deduce that I had left her uncared for and had gone off to play. I would be reported to my father who would decide the punishment for the offence and who would inflict that punishment, usually a beating. If all was well, on the other hand, my mother would breast-feed Alusa, lay her down to rest, and begin to prepare our evening meal. I would be released to go out and play with the other children ...

Before Alusa was a year old, her breast-feeding was supplemented with solid foods, just as mine had been a few years before. The first of these foods was banana. My mother would chew the banana until it was ready for swallowing, remove it from her own mouth, and give it to Alusa in small bits. This practice would be highly unwelcome today; but it was the way the parents in Idakho society imagined babies without teeth and without strong chewing muscles should be fed on solids. Later black *bushuma*, made out of millet flour, was introduced and this when given to the baby would not have been chewed by a grown up. Instead, it would be given along with some slippery type of vegetable called *lihu* which made swallowing without chewing easy.

As I had to use these solids as well as the porridge for feeding Alusa, I found that my responsibilities as a nurse increased. During the day I would prepare and cook bananas in order to provide a meal not only for Alusa but for myself and my playmates as well. This was a risky business. Many a time in those days nurses had been known to set houses on fire while cooking in the absence of grown ups. If I was going to cook bananas, say, for Alusa and me, I would have to find firewood, to fetch water from the river, to wash the cutlery after using it, to feed Alusa, to use a knife without harming myself, to place dangerous materials out of Alusa's reach, and to allow myself time for play. How well I remember one particular time when I had prepared porridge for our lunch. As I was dishing it out on the plates, the container slipped and both my hands were covered with hot porridge! By the time a neighbour arrived to cool my hands with wet soil, I had had enough pain to teach me always to fear touching anything hot.

from : Joseph A. Lijembe, 'The Valley Between', in *East African Childhood—Three Versions*, edited by Lorene K. Fox

10 Building a log cabin

Pennsylvania, American Colony, mid eighteenth century

I will proceed to state the usual manner of settling a young couple in the world.

A spot was selected on a piece of land of one of their parents, for their habitation. A day appointed shortly after their marriage for commencing the work of building their cabin. The fatigue party consisted of choppers, whose business it was to fell the trees and cut them off at proper lengths. A man with a team for hauling them to the place, and arranging them, properly assorted, at the sides and ends of the building, a carpenter, if such he might be called, whose business it was to search the woods for a proper tree for making clap-boards for the roof. The tree for the purpose must be straight grained and from three to four feet in diameter. The boards were split four feet long, with a large frow, and as wide as the timber would allow. They were used without planing or shaving. Another division were employed in getting puncheons for the floor of the cabin; this was done by splitting trees, about eighteen inches in diameter, and hewing the faces of them with a broad axe. They were half the length of the floor they were intended to make.

The materials for the cabin were mostly prepared on the first day and sometimes the foundation laid in the evening. The second day was allotted for the raising.

In the morning of the next day the neighbours collected for the raising. The first thing to be done was the election of four corner men, whose business it was to notch and place the logs. The rest of the company furnished them with the timbers. In the meantime the boards and puncheons were collecting for the floor and roof, so that by the time the cabin was a few rounds high the sleepers and floor began to be laid. The door was made by sawing or cutting the logs in one side so as to make an opening about three feet wide. The opening was secured by upright pieces of timber about three inches thick through which holes were bored into the ends of the logs for the purpose of pinning them fast. A similar opening, but wider, was made at the end for the chimney. This was built of logs and made large enough to admit of a back and jambs of stone. At the square, two end logs projected a foot or eighteen inches beyond the wall to receive the butting poles, as they were called, against which the ends of the first row of clap boards was supported. The roof was formed by making the end logs shorter until a single log formed the comb of the roof, on these logs the clap boards were placed, the ranges of them lapping some distance over those next below them and kept in their places by logs, raised at proper distances upon them.

The roof and, sometimes, the floor were finished on the same day of the raising. A third day was commonly spent by a few carpenters in levelling off the floor, making a clap board door and a table. This last was made of a split slab and supported by four round legs set in auger holes. Some three-legged stools were made in the same manner. Some pins stuck in the logs at the back of the house supported some clap boards which served for shelves for the table furniture. A single fork, placed with its lower end in a hole in the floor and the upper end fastened to a joist served for a bed stead, by placing a pole in the fork with one end through a crack between the logs of the wall. This front pole was crossed by a shorter one within the fork, with its outer end through another crack. From the front pole, through a crack between the logs at the end of the house, the boards were put on which formed the bottom of the bed. Some times other poles were pinned to the fork a little distance above these, for the purpose of supporting the front and foot of the bed, while the walls were the supports of its back and head. A few pegs round the wall for a display of the coats of the women, and the hunting shirts of the men, and two small forks or bucks horns to a joist for the rifle and shot pouch, completed the carpenter work.

In the meantime masons were at work. With the heart pieces of the timber of which the clap boards were made, they made billets for chunking up the cracks between the logs of the cabin and chimney, a large bed of mortar was made for daubing up those cracks; a few stones formed the back and jambs of the chimney.

The cabin being finished, the ceremony of house warming took place, before the young couple were permitted to move into it.

The house warming was a dance of a whole night's continuance, made up of the relations of the bride and groom, and their neighbours. On the day following the young couple took possession of their new mansion.

from: Joseph Doddridge, *Notes on the Settlement and Indian wars, of the Western Parts of Virginia and Pennsylvania*

11 Modern cave houses

Shensi, China, 1963

People in our part of the country prefer living in caves. This is largely because our loess soil makes cave-building easy and the result is a nicer and better insulated dwelling than an ordinary house. I must have built a good forty caves in my day. My father taught me how to build them, but I'm no specialist. Anybody can build a cave.

There are two kinds of cave : earth ones and stone ones. The earth caves are dug into the hillside. The first thing to do is to find a place with the right kind of soil, hard yellow loess soil. You cannot build a cave where the soil is sandy ... An ordinary cave of normal size, 18-19 chi* long, 9-10 chi high and 8-9 chi wide, including making the kang and cooking stove and chimney, takes about forty work-days. A house of the same size takes the same or a little less, but it isn't so practical and costs more to heat.

Having selected a place where the earth seems to be of the right kind, you smooth the hillside so that you have a vertical face. In doing this you will see what the soil is like to work with. Next, you make a first hole of two by seven chi and dig in for roughly three chi before you start enlarging. As you dig, the kind of soil will show you how large you can make the cave. The harder and closer the soil is, the larger you can make your cave, and vice versa. Having dug out your cave, you polish the earth walls to make them smooth, then you plaster them with mud made of loess earth. All this time you leave the outer wall untouched, using just the little opening that you made at the beginning, but once the cave is finished you open up this wall so that you have a door and a window. The window is a lattice frame with paper stretched over it. This makes a good window that

* One chi is 13¼ inches (about 33 cm)

lets in the light but keeps out the wind. Nowadays we also use glass a bit; but glass is expensive and it is seldom one sees a piece more than two by three chi. Besides, glass is not always practical, and it calls for considerably more complicated structure for the lattice.

At first, caves are slightly damp, but they dry out after three or five months. If the soil is of good quality and hard and firm, you can then build additional caves and store-rooms leading off from the first cave. But if you do that, you make the passages between them rather narrow, roughly two by seven chi.

You cannot build this sort of cave by yourself. It needs several of you. We usually exchange work and help each other. Up here in northern Shensi people prefer, as I said, to live in caves, because they are warmer in winter and cooler in summer; but down in central Shensi people prefer to live in houses.

But earth caves don't last well, and they can also be dangerous. Even if the soil is of good quality, an earth cave seldom lasts more than two or three generations. Often only thirty years . . .

A stone cave calls for more careful planning and considerably more work. You can take it that each stone cave takes roughly 400 work-days. The three caves in this row took the work of seventy men for a whole month. They are thus considerably more expensive to build than both earth caves and ordinary houses; but, while an ordinary house won't go more than thirty years without major repairs, a stone cave will stand for four or five hundred years and not need a thing doing to it. In theory stone caves are indestructible. The only thing requiring maintenance is the paper and woodwork of the windows, for wood will rot in time. But in an ordinary house there is a lot that can rot and fall and need replacing.

In principle it is best for a cave to face south, because then it will be warmed by the winter sun, which hangs low, and the summer sun, which stands high in the sky, won't reach in; but you cannot pay much attention to that, where earth or stone caves are concerned, for they have to be sited according to the condition of the ground. I have built caves facing all quarters of the compass, but wherever I could, I have avoided making them face east or west.

Caves, of course, are built with cooking stoves and chimneys, but with both earth and stone caves we usually make an additional out-side kitchen for use in summer. That helps to keep the cave cool in summer and the women consider it an advantage to be able to work outdoors. When we do this, we site the outside kitchen in a shady place.

In many places you have to be careful about drainage, when build-ing stone caves, but here with us the subsoil water is fairly far down and we have good stone. We have not needed any special drainage either at the school or for this row. We begin by digging the foundations. We excavate ten chi down. The hole corresponds to the outside measurements of the cave-to-be. Then we make a foundation of tamped loess. If this is done carefully, it becomes almost as hard as concrete. On this foundation we build two stone walls, which are the inner long walls of the cave. We make a stone floor. When these inner walls reach a height of six chi above the stone floors we build the inner short walls. Then we reckon out the vault. This has to be a semicircle and rest on the two inner long walls. We don't calculate with paper and brush. We are farmers and we cannot write or calculate on paper; but we know how it has to be. The inner short wall is a measure for the vault. We put up a frame in the cave and build the vault with stones. This calls for a lot of work, for each stone has to be cut so that it fits exactly. But you soon learn to tell from looking at a stone how it has to be done.

Once the vaulting is finished the cave will stand for hundreds of years. After that we build the outside walls. The smallest distance between the inside of the outer wall and the outside of the inner wall is five chi. The same goes for the distance between the outsides of the inner walls if one is building several caves one beside the other as in this row. This intervening space is filled with tamped loess. The outside walls of the cave are built up six chi, plus the height of the vault, plus five chi, because the vault has also to be covered with trodden loess. Here too, five chi is the smallest permissible distance between the highest point of the vault and the top of the layer of beaten loess.

Built in this way, the roof needs no maintenance; and although grass grows on it, and we let our goats graze there, no damp can get into the cave. For the sake of drainage we make the roof slope inwards and a gutter of baked clay there to take the water away. Neither rain nor frost nor weeds can crack the roof. Up in the north, however, where they build similar caves, but of sun-dried bricks, which aren't strong enough to bear the load, the clay roof has to be trodden every year.

from : Jan Myrdal, *Report from a Chinese Village*

12 Isolated croft life: Sutherland

Scotland, nineteen-fifties

Really there are very few adults these days who possess the mental and emotional self-sufficiency necessary for leading satisfactory existences in these remote parts. When the daylight lasts for only five or six hours, when the Never Silent—as the Norsemen called the wind—howls down the corries and the snow is lying so deep that even the deer are unable to reach the croft in search of food, then one learns what it means to be cut off from the outside world, and either one grows to accept and appreciate spells of complete isolation, or else the isolation begins to sap one's confidence and to terrify.

From mid-September to April or May we were alone in the croft, and for weeks, sometimes months, we saw nobody except each other. Even the postman was rarely able to call in during winter for a chat. The croft was at a fairly high altitude and we had snow every year. Yet on a sunny day with the snow lying on the hills and round the croft we would take a walk to a lower altitude and picnic on the grass. Some days in winter could be extraordinarily mild and pleasant.

As the hours of darkness lengthened our days became relatively shorter. We seldom rose before nine and were in bed by nine-thirty. Reading in bed was strictly forbidden because of using up too much paraffin ... We never wasted a scrap of candle grease or a drop of paraffin. When there was a heavy deluge of rain during winter only a thin light was able to penetrate the leaden sky and the day was spent in semi-darkness. We cooked and ate by lamplight, religiously turned out the flame when the meal was finished, and allowed ourselves a brief two hours of light again after supper before turning into bed. The animals' propensity for sleep through a spell of bad weather was remarkable. Except for the briefest exits to answer the calls of nature they would lie comatose for hours on couch, carpet or in box, and were very little trouble. We cut their food down when they took next to no exercise.

Keeping goats and a pony meant that however treacherous the weather there was always the necessity to cross over to the byre twice a day in order to milk, feed and water them. Even this short journey of ten strides could be arduous. Several times, to my delight, I watched Aunt from a window going along the path on hands and knees because the force of the gale prevented her from standing upright. I too had to take my turn at milking when one of these fierce gales was blowing and make my way across in this ignominious position, but it was never so funny then. When a gale was blowing hard from the east it was often impossible to open the back door and we were compelled to use the front one only. A strong westerly gale meant using the back door only. In this kind of blustery weather we never opened a window; we got all the fresh air we wanted on the brief crossings to and from the byre. After a heavy fall of snow during the night it would take us a hard morning's work to free the doors and to dig a path to the byre from the croft. Our preliminary exit on these occasions had to be through a window because the weight of snow jammed the doors tight. Sometimes when it had been snowing for

several days on end and the snow reached eight or nine feet—up to
the roof of the croft—we would dig in shifts from morning till late at
night, working by lamplight, in order to keep the path clear and the
windows free from the pressure of snow. Surrounding our domain
would be an impenetrable white wall. I would stand on a box in the
high narrow path way we had cleared and stare over the snow wall
across the white countryside, enjoying the sensation of being completely marooned and cut off from the rest of the world.

One of the most difficult lessons we had to learn was to be content
to do very little, during winter especially, for quite long periods. From
the merest toddlers it has been so dinned into us that we should be
continuously busy throughout the day—Satan finds work for idle
hands, and so on—that when one first attempts to discard these
teachings and sit contentedly doing absolutely nothing it is by no
means easy. The mind is both guilty and bored. But all tendencies
to try filling in the idle minute must be rigorously suppressed. It is
fatal, living in these parts, if the mind and hands are continually
seeking for something to occupy them. When the stockings have been
darned, the animals fed, the hour not yet come to light the lamp and
read, then surely one should be able to sit for a while without feeling
restless or guilty. Yet modern conditioning and upbringing have made
the art of relaxing and emptying the mind of petty concerns and
worries a feat difficult of attainment by most. Nevertheless we eventually learnt to accomplish it to the dismay of energetic friends when
they came to stay.

from : Rowena Farre, *Seal Morning*

13 Happy and creative life on a prosperous farm

Tibet, nineteen-fifties

When it grew dark our lamps would be lit. They consisted of shallow
saucers filled with oil of mustard with one or more wicks of cotton
in them and half over the edges, and they stood on slate shelves which
jutted out from the walls. There was one of these lamps in the byre
too. This was the only form of domestic artificial light we ever knew.

When she had finished the milking mother would bring the milk
into the kitchen in wooden pails. These pails were made of juniper
wood brought by my father from the mountains. At regular intervals
a handicraftsman would come in from Balangtsa to make it into tubs

and bowls. He was also a general handyman who could do any necessary repairs. The best bowls were reserved for the curdled milk. These were particularly strong and they were decorated with carvings on the outside. But the greater part of the fresh milk would be poured into a large copper container and then boiled. A small amount was put to one side to be used with the tea. Always, before the milk had boiled, mother would put a large scoopful to one side to thicken. The next day the cream would be taken off and put into a special wooden tub. After a few days this tub would be filled to the brim, and then its contents went into the butter churn—though we could sometimes wheedle mother into letting us have a spoonful of it with our tea. Before it had completely mixed with the tea we would take a delight in pushing it below the surface with our hard rusklike pieces of bread. Fresh cream was a treat, but we were allowed to drink as much as we liked of the buttermilk, which always had fascinating little globules floating round in it. If mother wanted to make cheese she would boil up the sour milk once more, after which she would pour the white mass into a sieve and keep it in a cool dark room for a while, where it slowly dried into the crumbly cheese we ate for break- fast with our tsampa. The greenish whey that dripped through the sieve was given to the animals.

My mother, who was an excellent cook and knew how to prepare the most tasty dishes, did almost all the work in the kitchen herself. There was a small table against one wall and on this she used to make the pastry and the delicious rolls which are amongst my favourite food today. She was renowned for her pastry throughout the village. She also used to make the best yeast, so much so that the other peasant women would come round and beg for some of it—always to the accompaniment of great praise. We used to have rolls both with and without yeast, but the ones we liked best were those that were baked in oil, or even butter. As a baking oven my mother used an iron tin in which she scattered glowing coals.

We had to have our grain ground in the mill by the village stream in Balangtsa. At exactly fixed times my father would turn up there pulling the mule behind him with the grain sacks on its back. In payment, one-tenth of the flour ground from the grain was left with the miller.

We ate potatoes at nearly every meal, and meat when it was available, but we didn't care much for pork, preferring beef; best of all we liked mutton. Fresh meat was really more or less confined to the autumn when the sheep were fattest and we had slaughtered. If fresh meat came on the table in summer it was because an emer- gency slaughtering had been carried out for some reason or other. Sometimes, too, wolves would pull down one of our animals, and we would eat the rest, if any. The favourite cut from the sheep was the ribs where the layer of fat was as thick as your finger. It was eaten boiled or roasted, but also raw and as dried meat.

When a sheep was slaughtered every single part of it was used, from the skull to the trotters. The intestines were drawn, carefully washed and then used as casing for blood, sausage, tsampa flour and pieces of fat. The lungs were regarded as a special delicacy. And the trotters, once the outer horny substance was peeled off, tasted excellent. We children used to love to look on when the intestines were filled and turned into sausages which, boiled or roasted, made excellent eating. We liked to roast them ourselves. The kidneys, embedded in sheaths of fat, also went into the glowing embers. Tripe was another highly prized delicacy, and it was carefully washed and prepared with herbs and spices like salad. Some tripes which were left over from the autumn slaughtering were used for storing butter in. Otherwise for the rest of the year there was only dried meat. It was easy to dry in the open because our village was so high that there were only a few weeks in the summer when there was any danger of things going bad. In summer we lived chiefly on vegetables and salads. A favourite salad delicacy was a kind of radish which mother pickled in a wooden tub with sour gherkins. We usually used wooden spoons to eat with, but sometimes chopsticks. After use all these table utensils would be tucked into the interstices between the wall panelling.

But our staple food was tsampa flour. All flour obtained from roast grain or roast leguminous fruits was called tsampa. There are wheat tsampas, pea tsampas and maize tsampas, but the usual variety is barley tsampa. The barley is roasted in the kitchen. Sand is put into an iron frying-pan and heated over a fierce fire, and the grains are then poured on to it. As soon as they touch the hot sand they split open and a wonderful smell pervades the room. The contents of the frying pan are then poured into a sieve through which the sand runs away. The first crisp, golden brown grains are always eaten by the family straight away. The barley roasting is carried out only at long intervals, but then usually a whole day is devoted to it. The roasted grains are then shovelled into sacks and taken to the miller to be ground into tsampa flour, which is then eaten with tea, milk or beer, or just on its own.

The preparation of the dough demands a certain skill. For example, you sprinkle tea into a wooden dish and then pour tsampa flour on top of it, then turn the dish with the left hand in a clockwise direction whilst at the same time you stir the mixture in the opposite direction with the middle finger until it has reached the desired consistency. As children we were not adroit enough for this performance, so in order that none of this precious mixture should be lost, mother taught us to prepare the dough in a leather bag held closed with one hand whilst its contents were thoroughly kneaded with the free hand. For

113

the big ones at table there was a dish with three compartments containing butter, tsampa flour and pieces of dried cheese respectively. This dish was then passed round in a circle. When each of us had sufficiently kneaded the dough in his own wooden bowl, he would make little balls of it and put them in his lap or line them up on the table in front of him. Tea or soup was then poured into the empty bowl, and the meal could begin. Our eating-bowls for daily use were made of birch wood, and of such a size that they could easily be held in one hand. For the children, of course, there were smaller bowls. Each bowl differed a little from its neighbour, and the most sought after were made from gnarled roots. When the wood was being turned the most astonishing patterns would come to light, and it was the beauty and clarity of the graining which made a bowl highly prized. ... Woollen cloth was woven by craftsmen who went from farm to farm, and set up their looms in the yards. They would weave pieces about eight inches wide and many feet in length; these pieces were then sewn together edgewise. The thread used to sew them was spun by my father during the long winter evenings. Wherever he was, standing or sitting, his hands were always occupied making something or other. The Tibetan peasant is never idle, and if just for the moment his hands do not happen to be making anything, the rosary is slipping bead by bead through his fingers. My mother made all the clothes for the children, and a proper tailor was called into the house only to make the gala clothes of my mother and father. I can remember watching him with wide-open eyes and marvelling at his skill with the needle. In cutting out shirts he would always fold the stuff and then press the fold by sticking forward his dirty neck and pulling the fold across it. I always used to laugh when after that a dirty mark appeared on the light material.

Along the edges of our fields my father used to grow enough jute to supply thread for our boots. When the jute had been dried out on the roof of our house my father would dampen it again, beat it with a stick, then remove the outer husk and spin the fibres into thread or yarn. The cow leather for the soles of our boots was bought in Balangtsa. We had no leather of our own because we never slaughtered cattle in our own yard, but always sold them. In summer we went round bare-footed, but in winter we used to wear out so many boots that the cobbler had to come to our house several times during the winter and attach new leather soles to the stuff tops of our boots. My father always had the leather ready soaked so that all the cobbler had to do when he arrived was to cut out the soles and sew them on to the old ones.

In addition to the cobbler, the tailor and the weaver, other tradesmen also came into the house to work; for instance, the carpenter and the carpet maker. These artisans, and also passing caravan drivers, would live in the guest room next to the cow byre, sleeping on a broad bench which took up the whole of one wall. And if they had animals with them then these were provided for too. In the yard there was a round base made of cemented stones to take our big prayer-mast, which was over thirty feet high. Round this base were large irregular stone slabs which served as feeding troughs. There were also holes worked in these stones to which halters could be fastened.

The prayer flag itself was a long white piece of cotton material about a foot wide, covered over and over with prayers. It reached from the top of the mast right down to the stone base below, and occasionally it had to be renewed. Before certain feast days we would take a suitable piece of cotton material to a neighbour who possessed the wooden blocks for printing prayers on the flag, and have it covered with prayers like the old one. We brought our own printer's ink along —father had previously scraped soot from the kitchen ceiling, and from the bottom of the cooking pots, and mixed it with size.

We bought the glue from the itinerant vendors who made it themselves from cow hooves, bones and skins. There were many itinerant pedlars of this kind who went from village to village and from house to house offering all sorts of goods for sale. I think the jolliest visitor for us children was the potter, whose donkey was almost hidden by the many pots some of them many feet high, hanging round him. In our house we had three of these great green-glazed pots, and as a rule they didn't have a very long life. During the winter one or other of them would probably burst from the cold, despite the fact that it was carefully swathed in sheep skins. In summer when we needed more water, two other containers stood outside the kitchen.

... In early summer the sheep were shorn, and we children had to help in earnest, holding the feet of the sheep, which kicked out wildly in a panic when they were being shorn. But we liked shearing time, when the wool piled up in the yard into white mountains waiting to be packed into jute sacks, work which was invariably accompanied by a good deal of shouting and jollity.

It was not until there was no longer so much work to be done in the fields that the sacks were again brought out, emptied, and the wool soaked in great wooden tubs before being washed, teased and hung up to dry. When a large quantity of wool had been spun my mother would colour the thick ropes with dyes made from the bark of trees, earth and plants.

... In autumn the grain harvest would be brought in. The sheaves were spread out in front of the house, and moving around in circles the horses pulled a six or eight-sided stone roller over it. The barley obtained in this way was shovelled into baskets which were then held high and gradually emptied in order to let the wind do the work of winnowing, and carry away the chaff. The straw would then be piled up in the nearest fields often higher than the house; and these heaps were wonderful places for us to play in during the winter months. For example we would scoop ourselves out comfortable holes in them, and then pay each other visits.

...During the winter when there was snow on the ground for five months we would build huge snowmen, making their eyes with pieces of burnt wood. And we slid down the slopes so often that in the end we had slides as highly polished as mirrors. But our greatest fun was to shoot down steep inclines on a short plank shouting at the tops of our voices.

At the age of six I discovered another place to play : on our flat roof, to which we would climb by means of a ladder. It wasn't easy for me to clamber up the rungs because they were very wide apart, being, of course, intended for adults. On the outside the roof had a protective wall, and I could just about look over it. Herbs for incense, yak dung and wood were piled up there to dry. But on the courtyard side there was no such protective wall, and, in addition, the roof sloped slightly inwards towards the yard. Now I was very fond of flowers and I discovered to my delight that all sorts of lovely flowers were growing in the protection of the warm chimneys, and with the help of my sister I now planted many others. My parents didn't much care for these roof expeditions of mine. My mother was afraid I might roll down, and my father was afraid that many flowers might make the roof leak.

...From up there you could see Kyeri. Kyeri means something like "Mountains of Happiness", and for me it has certainly become the embodiment of a happy childhood. It was under Kyeri that I experienced the love of my parents and my brother and sister, that I rode on our horses over the flower dotted pastures, and accompanied the herdsman and his beasts. It was towards Kyeri that our prayers were directed, because Kyeri was the throne of our protective deity and bore his name. Throughout life the idea of terrestrial and heavenly happiness will always be connected with Kyeri. For me Kyeri has become the symbol of full life.

from : Thubten Norbu (as told to H. Harrer), *Tibet is my Country*

14 Transhumance and a problem people

Pakistan, nineteen-sixties

We left Kagan at 6.30 a.m. and found the road so blocked by migrant traffic, moving up the valley to summer pastures, that it took us three hours to cover six miles. The road was all downhill, but cycling remained out of the question—one simply pushed and edged one's way through dense masses of buffaloes, cows, camels, horses, mules, donkeys, jennets, goats, sheep, kids, lambs, men and women and children.

... Recently, the government, who want to plant the high pastures with young trees, proposed to the Kochis that they should settle permanently on land in the Punjab, given to them by the State: but the tribes were so devastated by the idea that President Ayub ordered it to be dropped. For at least 3,000 years, and probably longer, these people's ancestors have been on this trek—up every June, down every October—and any other way of life would be as inhuman as caging a tiger. Actually they are quite well off by Pakistani standards, with their own meat, eggs, milk and butter, and clothing from their sheep and goats. To acquire supplies of flour, tea, sugar and salt they barter their superfluous animals. An incredible amount of silver jewellery is worn by the girls, from two years old and upwards, and by the women; some of it is very ancient and all of it is beautiful. On these long treks tiny babies are carried concealed in cloths on their mothers' backs, toddlers ride on their fathers' shoulders or on one of the animals and everything above the age of four walks sturdily, like a good Kochi. Often little girls carry top-heavy loads of pots, pans and miscellaneous household goods on their heads and sometimes little boys are in sole charge of a flock of thirty or forty animals. New born or delicate foals or calves (except camel calves who can apparently cope with life right from scratch) are tied to some animal, other than their mother, or are carried on the men's shoulders. Puppies, hens and chickens go on the buffaloes' backs; when there's a halt one sees the fowls flying down and scratching and pecking while the humans make tea and the animals eat their fodder, and then when the signal is given to start again they fly back to their moving roosts. Each kind of animal wears a different-sounding bell and the result is quite symphonic.

from : Dervla Murphy, *Full Tilt*

15 On the Roof of the World

Pamirs, U.S.S.R.

There are great glaciers to be traversed, some of them as long as from London to Brighton,* which lead to passes never before used by white men. The ascent is coated with ice and the whole surface like a sheet of glass. The way leads down and up among the Pamirs, the Roof of the World. One might imagine that this is a tableland, that

* Fifty miles (80 km)

movement is unrestricted, with plains stretching away to the horizon. The reverse is the case; the 'roof' is no tableland, but rather a mighty mass of lofty, high-pitched ridges and gables, with narrow valleys, hollows, or leads between them. Such soil as there is has been formed by the detritus of avalanche-swept shale and gravel, and it is among these interminable and formidable leads that the inhabitants gain a scanty subsistence by herding a few flocks.

... They are a sociable and hospitable people, but they decline to live in houses. Instead they have the *khirga*, or felt tent, a circular construction on a lattice framework, from twelve to twenty-five feet in diameter. The lattice-work walls are about four feet high and from them wooden rods are stretched to a hoop forming the crown of the tent. The framework is covered with felt made from goat and camel's hair and an opening left at the top to let out the smoke. The tent is bedroom, sitting room, dining room, and kitchen, all in one. The Kirghiz tell you that it has no equal; you can set it up or take it down in twenty minutes. Could I do that with my house, a Kirghiz chief asked!

... The wants and ambitions of these simple, carefree folk are few. The yak provides several of them, a queer creature that revels in the cold and seems to fade away in the slightest heat. Its nearest ally is the bison of North America and in colour it is generally black. Found at a greater altitude than any other animal, except perhaps the burhel or mountain sheep, it thrives on the coarse grass growing there. The yak is an accommodating creature and, apart from being used for riding and the transport of goods, provides milk and cream, from which a cheese is made, whilst the flesh is not unlike beef to eat. Yak dung is the principal fuel; it gives out great heat and is a precious asset, being collected and then dried in the sun for storage and use during the winter months, for the cold weather lasts from September until the following June.

from : P. T. Etherton, 'The Lure of Solitude', in *Traveller's Quest*,
edited by M. A. Michael

16 Attempt to collectivize the Kirghiz

U.S.S.R., nineteen-sixties

The Russians have given them industries too, taught them to grow sugar beet, cotton and other crops on irrigation along the edges of the desert. But all of them in heart, and many of them in practice, are nomads still. Deep in their mountains, they move with their flocks in winter from one rich sheltered meadow to another, in summer high up on the mountain slopes dressed in their quilted gowns, leather boots with skin overshoes and white felt hats with black brims. Their *yurtas*, felt tents spread on lattice frames, are easily transported on horses or camels. Where they are pitched for days at a time in some rich valley they achieve an ancient splendour with carpets spread on the grass inside, blankets and colourful cushions piled against the sides, guns, knives, scabbards, bridles and skin bags full of *koumiss*, the mares' milk they love, suspended from the walls. This nomadic way of life too the Russians say is now collectivized. When I asked how, they said that mobile radios, creameries, schools, dispensaries, co-operative shops, film projectors, our old friends the 'zoo-technicians' are allocated to every nomad group and accompany them everywhere on their seasonal round among those profound mountains. But there is nothing tame or collectivized about the look they bring to bear on Tashkent.

from : Laurens Van Der Post, *Journey into Russia*

17 Film truck in modern Mongolia

Mongolia, 1966

Apart from a lama temple or two, Ulan Bator today is a completely modern town ... and ... boasts a well-stocked department store, an opera house, a university, an Academy of Science, a Grand Hotel (reputedly the best in the Communist world), a stadium and a large new hospital. A number of up-to-date factories, mostly geared to Mongolia's pastoral economy, include a meat-canning factory, a tannery, a boot-and-shoe factory, and a wool mill equipped with the latest British textile machinery.

In such an immense country a population of less than a million is thinly spread. On all sides a vast expanse of green rolling steppe stretches away to a distant horizon of hills. In a hundred miles you may encounter another truck. Or you may not. Probably you will just meet a shepherd with his sheep or a herd or two of horses or cattle. Or a little group of exotic-looking, high-cheekboned nomads on the march, with all their worldly belongings loaded on to a string of camels ...

Here and there we came, as we drove, on a little cluster of *gers*, the traditional Mongolian round white tents of felt stretched over a collapsible wooden framework, in which the bulk of the population still live and which they carry with them on their camels when they move. It was in these that we paused on our way, to get out of the cold and into a warm Mongol family atmosphere and eat strange meals of tea and cheese and great bowls of *airag*—fermented mare's milk—in the centre of a circle of friendly, grinning, curious faces. Fermented mare's milk is delicious, effervescent and more than slightly intoxicating.

Strictly speaking, there are no proper roads in Mongolia—just a whole series of widely divergent tracks across the plain from which you select the most promising. Further south, the steppe turns gradually into desert or *gobi*, a mixture, like most deserts, of patches of scrub, salt flats and sand dunes and great stretches of nothing in particular, turned into a wilderness 700 years ago, or so they say, by the trampling of Genghis Kahn's myriad cavalry.

After stopping repeatedly on the way, to film the great herds of wild horses that drift about the steppe, and then getting hopelessly lost in the darkness amongst the innumerable divergent tracks, we did not complete the first stage of our journey until five the following morning—only to find, to our amazement, that, after crossing 200 miles of steppe, we were staying in yet another luxury suite with sitting-room and bathroom attached and a Chinese toothbrush and tube of toothpaste laid out for each of us in case we had left ours at home. After a few hours' sleep, we set off again for Karakorum.

On the way we stopped off at a *negdel* or collective farm, where we saw more horses than ever and witnessed a fantastic display of rough-riding. The Mongols have remained a nation of horsemen. It was they, they claim, who invented the saddle, who practically invented riding. In fact, it was in Mongolia that the first horse made its appearance. To this day, each Mongolian man, woman and child is ready to jump on to a horse and gallop off, and they expect visitors to be able to do the same.

... Communism and collectivisation have altered the life of the average Mongolian *arat* or herdsman less than one might think. Stock-breeding and livestock rearing remain the basis of the national economy. The Mongol is still basically a nomad. His home remains his circular *ger*. It is here that he and his family are born, live and die. It is here, too, that the traveller, wherever he comes from, will find a friendly welcome and lavish hospitality.

What may in the long run have more effect on Mongolian life is the introduction of arable farming. For centuries the Mongols refrained on religious ground from disturbing the soil and its spirits, and as recently as 1929 only 8,000 acres were under cultivation in the whole country. Now a vast ploughing-up programme has enabled Mongolia to supply her own requirements of wheat and to export some as well.

Mongolia strikes one today as a prosperous-enough country. People on the whole are well-fed and well-dressed, cars are still scarce but bicycles and motorcycles are beginning to make their appearance, and there is always a horse for everyone. In the shops in Ulan Bator there are plenty of consumer goods imported from Russia or China or from the other Communist countries.

Politically, Mongolia has much in common with any other Communist state. 'What', the Mongols asked me after a tour of elaborately-insulated polling-booths on election day, 'do you think of our elections?' 'Admirable,' I replied, 'except that you have only one party.'

And yet it would be a mistake to assume that Mongolia is no more than an outlying province of the Soviet Empire. The Mongolian People's Republic, strategically poised between Russia and China, gives in many ways a greater impression of independence than do some Communist countries in Eastern Europe.

One reason for this, I suspect, is that the Mongols are so intensely proud of everything Mongolian.

from : F. Fitzroy Maclean, 'Into Mongolia', *The Daily Telegraph Magazine*, September 30, 1966

18 Transistors in the desert

Egypt, 1966

We had taken the route from Gaza and just south of Naklin, completely desolate with nothing but sand and more sand, we met an Arab camel driver ambling along with his herd. By dress and general appearance there was nothing to distinguish him from his forebears of 1,500 years ago. Except for one difference. Round his neck hung a transistor radio and he was listening to the news from Cairo.

I have always considered that because of its equal effect on the illiterate as on the literate, radio in the developing countries will, in the foreseeable future, provide the most effective means of mass communication, and here was the perfect demonstration that this could be so.

Radio is extremely flexible in presentation and immediate in transmission, and without doubt provides the principal means for the greater proportion of the population in the Middle East to obtain information and entertainment.

Its influence is immeasurable. The coffee shop, the traditional meeting place of the Arab, has its static set, which is seldom silent.

There are very few of the Arab states that have not established broadcasting services. Powerful transmitters are used to obtain the maximum coverage and broadcasting is carried on both medium and short wave frequencies. The programme schedule transmitted is in the main well balanced and full use is made of the effectiveness of the propaganda value of the medium.

from : The Times, December 30, 1966

19 Rapid change in a primitive community

Manus Island, New Guinea, 1928 and 1953

I saw in 1928 nearly naked savages living in pile dwellings in the sea, their earlobes weighed down by shells, their hands still ready to use spears, their anger implemented with magical curses ... With training as an anthropologist, I was equipped to understand their tight limited little world, their language spoken by only two thousand people, their complex system of kinship relationships and exchanges of shell money and dogs' teeth by which they maintained their precarious hold on the fringes of their island world. I learned to talk with them, to observe their taboos, to ask the right questions when an adult was ill : 'Which ghost is striking him down?' 'Why?' 'Has he confessed yet? Has he paid expiation yet?' I learned to interpret sudden periods of silence or angry outbursts of outraged virtue. As long as I spoke their language and used their ways of thought, they understood me. But they had no way of understanding my ideas and values, even of making the simplest assumption about why I would tie up their wounds and still less of why I should have left some far away country and come to live in their village, except for simple crude gain. When I left, every house in the village sounded the death beat on the house drum, quite appropriately, for I was dying to them. No one could write me a letter, and no letter that I could write, if it could have been read would have had any meaning beyond the mere statement that I was alive somewhere in a world stranger than the abode of their dead.

In 1953 I stepped ashore on the new site of Peri village now built on land with 'American-style' houses ... A few minutes after I arrived a letter was handed to me. Translated it read :

'Dear Missus Markrit : This letter is to ask you whether you will help me teach the children.' An elected official brought in an exercise book in which he had written down a long set of rules for modern child care, feeding, discipline etc.

The experience of opening this letter, of reading the 'notes' written by people whom one had never visualised as becoming part of the modern world, with whom, in truth there had been no hope of real two-way communication, had a quality that I had never imagined. I felt almost as if someone—and I was not quite sure who it was, they or I—had been raised from the dead. Someone who, not knowing it, had been dead and had lived again.

I realised for the first time the relative emptiness of my earlier years among the people of Peri, among all the non-literate peoples of New Guinea, who had been so deeply comprehensible to me while I remained incomprehensible to them. I had known of course that this lack of understanding existed, that, while I could count on affection, on loyalty and even on some intellectual enjoyment when we discussed some intricate point of kinsmanship terminology or dogs' teeth exchange, I could never hope to be 'real' to them in the way they were 'real' to one another... Quite suddenly that June evening in 1953, I knew that today all of us, the people of Peri and of the other Manus village, the boys who had run my house for me twenty-five years ago, now tall mature men with households of their own, and the weight of office on their shoulders, lived in the same world.

from : Margaret Mead, *New Lives for Old*

20 Aboriginal woman in the technical age

Western Australia, 1948

I first saw her on the seat of a rotary hoe, driving it round a forty-acre field, and got a glimpse of her flashing teeth and pleasant smile as she went by in a cloud of dust, the engine humming away, while round and round sped the hoe digging up the soil of a peanut farm so that the crop could be planted before Christmas. At dinner I ate the bread she baked, saw her dishing out food to the natives, and heard the orders she gave them for the evening's work on the farm ... I have seen her driving a Chev truck through the bush with a load of logs aboard, pausing to let the engine cool down, she would lift up the hood and peer beneath at the engine to try to rectify some fault within.

from : W. E. Harney, *North of 23*

21 New skills for the Eskimos

Arctic

The mechanical aptitudes of the Eskimo are certainly remarkable. I heard at first hand the story of an Eskimo boy whom I met at a missionary school at Aklavik, on the Mackenzie Delta, 120 miles north of the Arctic Circle. He was given a present of a watch and he did what every boy wants to do, but what only an Eskimo boy would dare to do. He immediately took the watch to pieces. The chapel bell rang. He put the pieces in his cap and stuffed it in his pocket, and, after chapel, went to bed. The next day he put that watch together again. Which is one reason why the Canadian Government are now training Eskimos as highly proficient watchmakers, radio engineers etc.

The explanation of the mechanical aptitudes of the Eskimos is fairly obvious when you come to think of it. It is a high degree of Natural Selection. For 4,000 years the Eskimo has survived in the snow deserts, the Barrens. Only those with acute eyesight and a photographic memory could thus survive because, travelling over wide expanses of snow-covered landscape which drifts and changes, pin-pointing permanent landmarks becomes a natural and instinctive subconscious faculty. They develop a blueprint mind. Combine that with fingers which have to be nimble and with the fact that, through all these thousands of years, they have had to improvise. They had no wood because they lived beyond the tree line. They had no metal, except some native copper around Coppermine River, in the Central Arctic. They had the pelts and bones of the sea and land creatures which they hunted. They had slate and soapstone.

I have met Eskimos who, until thirty years ago, had never seen a white man and who had lived in the Stone Age. They made their bows—remarkable weapons—by laminating articulated caribou bone, and springy whalebone, bound with caribou sinew . . .

Yet those same Eskimos would step unconcernedly into an aircraft, handle a radio set or take a geiger counter with them to find uranium, on the way to their trap lines. But still, in the Long Night, they carve their traditional soapstone and ivory figurines.

from : Ritchie Calder, *The Inheritors*

22 Huskies versus the skidoo

Hudson Bay, Canada, 1966

This spring at dusk, I flew into Rankin Inlet on the west coast of Hudson Bay. Through the cloud of white powder snow churned up by the aircraft, I saw a dozen yellow autoboggans dart across the drifts and line the runway. Their Eskimo owners were obviously enjoying the easy speed of the vehicles. I stood at the door of the plane and like a die-hard at the end of the horse and buggy era, felt like yelling, 'Get a dog team'.

I am not a sentimentalist. I don't feel nostalgic about the vanishing igloo with its snow platform and seal oil lamp. The temperature inside those picturesque mounds of snow seldom rose above 32°F [0°C]. When it did, the walls began to melt and drip. And when you woke up in the morning a shower of hoar frost from the fur blankets fell down your neck.

But the Eskimo sled dogs—the Qimminik as they are called by the Eskimos—are another thing again. They have been a living vital part of Eskimo life for unrecorded generations—probably since the day an early hunter trained a young wolf cub to harness thousands of years ago. Their record of achievement and endurance is as old as the unfolding story of the North.

... Food for the ravenous huskies has always been a problem in the barren lands. The dogs will literally eat anything they can get their teeth into. Skin lines, harness, skin clothing, kayaks. In earlier days all these had to be piled out of reach on top of the igloo; today they are taken into the house. The huskies will also eat other dogs, foxes— even people who have the misfortune to fall and flounder (like a seal) in the snow in front of them. The two exceptions to the wholesale rule are wolf flesh, which a husky scorns even on the verge of starvation, and the liver of the polar bear, toxic because of its high concentration of vitamin A. (The dogs would probably eat the liver too, if their owners didn't make a point of throwing it beyond their reach into the ocean.)

In the summer months the voracious dogs are often turned out of camp to forage for themselves. They survive on lemmings and on shrimps, mussels, and animal life cast up on the stony shore line at low tide. But with the coming of the first snow, they are back in the settlement, ready to work, knowing they can expect a ration of fish, vitamin-rich seal, or walrus meat during the months when the Eskimo hunter depends on them for vital transportation.

The North is a harsh land; the sturdy sled dog is equipped to meet its challenge. In dark winter storms, he curls in a ball outside the hunter's igloo. His outer coat of dense coarse hair is four to six inches long; beneath it he has a thick inner coat of warm oily wool. Some hunters admit that their dogs may move into the lee of an igloo or discarded snow blocks at the height of a blizzard; others swear that their dogs always sleep with their noses into the wind—sensitive alert systems that pick up a scent miles away on the clear arctic air.

I have seen an Eskimo settlement brought to life two hours in advance by dogs who announce the impending arrival of visitors in long-drawn howls. By the time the distant figures appear on the snow-bound horizon, kettles are boiling for tea, and the whole settlement is ready to welcome the guests.

The same keen sense of smell has often made the difference between food and hunger in a settlement. A hunter exploring off the frozen shoreline for seal at their breathing holes may suddenly find his team veering inland toward a herd of caribou a dozen miles away, or a polar bear loping between the hummocks.

The search for game, however, has lost some of the urgency that it had in the borderline existence of the early years. Today more Eskimos have regular 9 to 5 jobs, or earn an income from char fishing or an arts and crafts program. A nomadic people are settling down around the community school that their children attend, the nursing station, store, craft centre, and airport. They are buying permanent houses, lighted by power from the community power plant and serviced with water by a community water truck. A trapper with a fast skidoo is able to cover his lines in a third of the time that it took him to do it by dog-team. He is inclined to leave his family in the settlement instead of packing them around to temporary camps in search of game.

At Rankin Inlet, where community life and regular wage employment became established during the operation of the Rankin Inlet Nickel Mine, skidoos are the popular way to travel. In mid-February, this year, there were forty-one skidoos in the settlement and forty-one dogs including house pets. The next week the Hudson's Bay store sold another two skidoos. At Baker Lake where the people still move out onto the land to hunt and trap, skidoos are not as popular.

'A skidoo burns gas, right?' one Baker Lake trapper said in explanation. 'The fox smells it. You lose him. You wouldn't see me using a skidoo round a trap line '

Trapper Paul Kablalik of Rankin disagrees. 'I trap all the time with a skidoo and I get plenty of white fox. But I'm careful. I use two pairs of mitts. One just for baiting and handling the traps.'

Over two thousand miles from Montreal at Grise Fiord on Ellesmere island, Appaliapik implies that he wouldn't use a skidoo if you gave him one as a gift. 'Two or three men are buying them, but I'm staying with dogs. I can depend on them.'

'Dependable?' comments a Rankin Inlet skidoo-owner, 'Last year I was twenty miles up the coast and my dogs, the whole team of them, lit out for home and left me to walk. A blizzard came up and I nearly froze. How do you like that?'

Memorana of Holman on Victoria Island says that he wouldn't take the chance of hunting without dogs. 'Many times they've saved my life. Once I shot my last bullet into the thigh of a huge polar bear. My dogs ringed him, held him back until I tied a knife to my tent pole and finished him off.'

There are pros and cons from every corner of the Arctic with those in favour of dogs coming from most outlying and northern camps ...

The immediate future of the husky is in the hands of his individual owner. At least one cautious Eskimo is playing the changing situation from all the angles. He traps in the Inuvik area with a new yellow skidoo. But riding behind the skidoo on a toboggan is his entire dog-team, heads erect, deep-chested, noses pointed into the wind.

from : Alex Stevenson, 'Qimminik—the Huskies', *The Beaver*,
Winter 1966

23 Houses for Inuvik

Arctic Canada, 1963

With the town's completion, the Eskimo moves ... into wooden houses with baths, toilets, electricity, constant hot water, radio and television ... The engineers relied mainly on pilings for the larger buildings and the use of gravel pacs—thick layers insulating the building from the ground for the smaller ones. The piles also allow ventilation between buildings and ground. Without this, heat from the building would melt the permafrost and eventually collapse the foundations.

The town had to have well-designed water and sewerage systems. The normal method outside the Arctic is to install both below the frost line. But at Inuvik this meant a depth of 1,000 feet.

Yet at any lesser depth pipes would freeze solid. Even if these could be well insulated and the fluid on the pipes kept warm, the problems of underground maintenance would be impossible. Inuvik's solution : box-like containers running above ground with the pipes inside them.

Even so, a hot water pipe had to be run alongside to keep them from freezing. These warm pipes also heat the houses.

With the town's completion, cabins used by the construction crews have been converted into small houses that are being sold cheaply to the Eskimos.

from : Francis Dickie, 'Arctic town that beats the frost',
The Daily Telegraph, June 6, 1963

24 Significance of the jeep

Africa and general

Whoever invented the Land-Rover, or perhaps its father the jeep, did more than anyone since the inventor of the high-velocity rifle to change the face of Africa. The high-velocity rifle enabled men to wipe out the wild animals, the Land-Rover enables them to destroy the last of the wilderness, to bring the last captive back in chains. That stocky, snub-nosed, undefeated little olive-green object, the mechanised pack-mule has carried administrators, policemen, soldiers, doctors and technicians into the heart of darkness to obliterate the most secret haunts of civilisation-shunners, human and animal. It has brought blackboards to nomads, vaccines to mountain-tops, law courts to fishermen, police posts to the depth of the desert. With the Land-Rover there is nowhere that white men cannot go and nowhere they have not been, and are not penetrating like a stain of oil, wiping out for ever the majesty, the antiquity, the mystery of Africa. The death of the elephant and the coming of the pylon; the end of the warrior and the beginning of the clerk.

from : Elspeth Huxley, *A New Earth*

25 Coming to terms with the North

Canada, 1969

The Canadian north offers much to those who wish to find themselves.

It is massive, with swaggering pioneers to match Panavision scenery. There are acres and acres of elbow room for the restless. The villages are often isolated but the bush plane links them to the outside. Nevertheless, they retain a dogmatic separateness as though the other world out there was none of their business ... Although the small bush plane has changed much, and it is possible to get anywhere in a few hours, to come down in the bush or be lost in the bush is like being plunged back into another age. Survival in those conditions is almost solely dependent on the ability of the victim to resist panic and to use the bush to ensure survival. Rivers can be used as highways, if you know how to make a raft. Food can be found but it has to be stalked. There are many small animals that can be caught with a knife or string and patience.

The hard life is there, just outside the back door. It can be wooed or you can play at pioneering by proxy, as many of the new settlers prefer to do. Furs no longer fetch a good price, and the gold can be scooped up by huge floating factories operated by a handful of men. Asbestos, oil, silver and many other minerals are now the big industries in the north.

Service towns and villages spring up where a new strike is made. Air-conditioned, centrally heated luxury cabins are the rule not the exception. Few new settlers would come to an isolated township without the assurance of such comfort.

But even with these aids life is still tough. No matter how many mosquito screens on the cabins or how well the area has been sprayed, it is normal to accept daily bites. The town itself might be safe from wild life but no one goes into the bush without a rifle.

Day to day life revolves around and overlaps the pressures brought about by a hostile environment. Although it is foolish to try to beat it, it is possible to use these natural forces and learn to take steps to avoid disasters. This is a basic requirement for all those who wish to make the north their home.

Many new settlers never get beyond learning to make the elemental adjustments. One needs to become accustomed to the smell of rancid insect repellent, to going without frequent baths, to the dust and lack of a balanced diet. But it takes time also to realize that the generosity and friendliness shown you is real. The northerners want you to stay. They want you to believe in them and their hopes. They love people who want to live, and they love their country. They recognize the enormous potential of the country and want to share it.

from : Barrie Biven, 'In the steps of pioneers',
The Times, February 26, 1969

26 Learning to live with air-conditioning in the tropics

Rangoon, Burma, 1959

I reside in a flat at the top of the office building. It is a strange place —hot, dusty, noisy and very large, with four complete bathrooms with hot and cold running water; yet there are only two bedrooms. Fortunately one of them is air-conditioned, and in fact I find myself living in two little air-conditioned boxes : in the manager's office downstairs and in the back bedroom upstairs, where I can shut out the noise and dirt of the city—as long as there is electricity to keep the air-conditioner running.

As there often isn't, it's important not to become too dependent upon air-conditioning to beat the heat. In the old days, the preferred method was heavy drinking, which certainly enabled some to forget how hot it was, but, even before the days of electricity, the limitations of this method were recognized and the punkah was invented. This was a heavy cloth which was hung from the ceiling and pulled to and fro by a man at the other end of a connecting rope, usually passed through a hole in the wall to the other world.

Electricity brought the fan, ceiling and table, but chairborne empire builders still had to suffer papers being blown away, or employ a peon to hold them down, and the fan didn't stop sweating. Air-conditioning actually changes climate by reducing temperature and humidity to create an artificial hill station. Papers don't blow about, and one doesn't stick to them because one doesn't sweat. However, shutting oneself off is bad (and wholesale air-conditioning isn't practicable); one ought not to create exclusiveness. I claim that air-conditioning increases my efficiency in an office in the middle of an oriental bazaar, but it must be admitted that it emphasises the gulf which separates the sort of people who can have it from those who can't, and those who would be unhappy with it. For one thing some don't like the noise of it night and day.

Of course, there's another way to beat the heat if there's no humidity to beat as well, by the use of kuss-kuss. During a hot dry season, relief is obtained by erecting bamboo frames over the windows, to hold dried grass in position, and the former punkah-wallah is employed to throw buckets of water at it (from the outside, of course). This makes the room comfortable inside as long as the grass is kept wet, and the water kept outside. The coming of electricity brought a refinement called a desert cooler, which consists of a big fan fitted into the window frame, under a pipe with holes in it, arranged so that the water drips in front of the fan and causes a draft of moist air to surge through the room. This has an advantage over air-conditioning in that the room need not, indeed must not be sealed, but kept open to create a draught, but it's no good when the air is already over-humid. It's all a question of where one is, and my two little air-conditioned boxes suit me just fine.

from : A letter from Ralph Wyeth

27 Living under cover: Churchill

Manitoba, Canada, 1960

There is also a modern 'fort' at Churchill, part of the defence system of the north, and I saw it that night, driving to it in the Hudson Bay factor's car down a dirt road with the glint of water, frosty and pale in the starlight. A military checkpoint, and then buildings looming up, black shapes above the scoured and bulldozed silt of the old river bed, and as we penetrated deeper, the place became a blaze of lights, and the buildings, illuminated, looked raw and insubstantial. Impermanent, unwilling tenants of this hostile country, they were strangely deserted; not a soul about. It was science fiction come to life—an earth-born settlement on the moon, with all human life extinguished.

We parked by a bulldozer that was scraping out the foundations for yet another barrack block, and after some searching in the dark, found a door. The buildings were strangely short of doors. An interminable corridor, suddenly and miraculously full of people, and then we were in the foyer of a cinema. It was a big theatre and there must have been a thousand people there, many of them children, some in thick Norwegian-patterned sweaters, others in singlets or sports shirts, for the central heating had the temperature up in the eighties.*

And after the cinema, half a mile of crowded corridors, electrically lit and centrally heated, brought us to the Officers' Mess. Everywhere you went in this extraordinary camp it was the same—corridors leading to married quarters, to canteen, to offices, to barrack blocks, garages and airfield. The place was built to hold several thousand, and no person need ever go out in the teeth of the elements.

from : Hammond Innes, *Harvest of Journeys*

28 Winter life of the Finns

Finland, 1967

Finland has about the worst winters in the world. Other inhabited areas in Russia, Sweden, Norway and Canada have similary low temperatures, but Finland occupies higher latitudes (60 and 70 degrees North), so the winter is darker. And no other country is so extensively encased by sea ice.

The climate has coloured every aspect of Finnish life. One example of this is the considerable winter vocabulary which has evolved to

* Fahrenheit

express the nuances of snow and ice conditions. On the practical level, Finland produces the most advanced ice-crushers and the most expert heating engineers.

There is no doubt that the predictability of the Finnish winter's intensity and duration has been an advantage. Finns plan for it. Central heating is regarded as a necessity and not, as still in Britain, as a luxury. Finns keep their houses round the 75 degree Fahrenheit mark—considerably hotter than the average British centrally heated house.

In Finland, insulation is tackled at source by the building-component factories. All components available on the market meet specifications necessary to keep warmth in. Double-glazing is normal, triple-glazing is also familiar, and some windows are metal coated to reflect indoor heat.

The 77 per cent roof heat-loss which British heating pundits complain of is quite unheard of in Finland. Mr. Unto Kilpinen, Helsinki's chief engineer of the District Heating Department Of Electricity Works, made a startling comment pointing out that at the coldest peak in Finland, *less* heat is consumed than in Britain's coldest spell, simply because Finnish houses are properly insulated. The 'do-it-yourself' double-glazing, 'background' heat and 'occupancy patterns' of British sales talk just do not enter the Finnish vocabulary. Finns turn on full heating systems in September, and run them through to March or even May. The 'occupancy' pattern is irrelevant.

Central heating has for a long time been tackled on a community basis in Finland, which makes it infinitely cheaper and more reliable. District heating, as it is called, was introduced first in Copenhagen, Hamburg and New York, but in recent years the system has made most marked progress in Finland, and in the per capita use of communal heat, Helsinki leads the world.

District heating links piped radiator systems in subscribers' houses to communal power plants . . .

Helsinki is one of the most consistently gaily electrified capitals in Europe. Many pavements are heated. The doors of department stores are open to the street, insulated by a sheet of rising hot air. The new main bus station, with a shopping arcade, is being built completely underground.

Their technological control over winter suggests that all that modern Finns have left to combat is winter blues. "There comes a time," explained one Finnish business woman, "when you can't fight them any more, and then you sink. We almost enjoy melancholy, like Chekhov's characters."

The combination of cold grey mist and only five hours of daylight which is Helsinki's in mid-winter, acts like some mild, wearying depressant. The snow blanket is sometimes crisp, sometimes slushy, sometimes greying, but it never, apparently, diminishes. The sky reflects the off-white monotony. Birch trees make the only definite incision into the gauze-textured air, giving new suburbs like Tapiola and Otanemi, the faded unreality of a Japanese print from a distance.

Nearly every hall has a tiled floor to cope with drips from icicled outdoor clothes. Invariably the tiles are white, and a row of brightly coloured felt slippers is offered to visitors in place of their boots.

The weekly sauna is a recuperative necessity, as well as a treat. Finns are said to build their saunas first and live there while building the house. Nearly every family who do not own their own have access to a shared sauna in the basement of their block. Every lakeside sauna has its ice-hole, and even in the suburbs Finns will leap, hot and steaming, to the end of their gardens to immerse themselves in mounds of snow.

Forced to spend so great a percentage of their time indoors, few peoples have focused so much attention on their houses. Architects and designers in Finland are national heroes whose own houses are much-photographed, emulated prototypes.

The consistently high quality in building is inevitable. Poor workmanship would come apart under winter pressures.

from : The Daily Telegraph, November 10, 1967

29 English family from the tropics fits into urban life

U.S.A., 1964

This time we're writing from a rut (but we're not all the way in yet), and suffering from the snags of over-development (but enjoying it all the same). We live in a dormitory area across the Potomac River from Washington, in a small two-bedroom unit in a very large block of flats. It is air-conditioned and centrally heated, and completely equipped—that means a garbage disposal unit instead of a dustbin, a letter box in the corridor outside the door and a swimming pool squeezed into something called landscaping. It's not quite 100 per cent suburbia because the nearest drugstore, super market, gas station and hamburger stand are over a mile away, and that's because we live in the shadow of the Pentagon, which takes up a lot of space. It's the home of the U.S. Army and is the largest office building in the world in terms of ground covered, and is protected from the encroachment of other buildings by the world's biggest car parks. We're on the edge of one of them, the one which has a heliport on one side and Washington's busiest airport on the other. All these bits of civilization need a great network of roads and we are surrounded by super-highways with three and four lanes in both directions on which cars either flash by at sixty plus miles per hour, or are completely immobilized in a traffic jam, because these super-highways aren't wide enough. There remains only one 'ordinary' road in our vicinity and that will have to be replaced very soon because the traffic will be much worse after completion of new blocks of flats which are being built on three sides of us. One of these is going up immediately outside our windows and is going to be the biggest in the Washington area by some standard or other.

And so we have aeroplanes overhead, helicopters lower down and motor cars and concrete mixers down below, but it's not as noisy as you'd expect because we keep all the windows shut. The rent includes the cost of a steady flow of homogenized, vitaminized, mechanised air.

The climate no longer justifies a hardship allowance because air-conditioning has solved the problem of the long humid summers. Although we knew about the delights of spring and cherry blossoms we have been surprised at the beauty and length of autumn.

One standard by which we judge the livability of a place is the potential for getting away from it, and we have found so many places to visit at week-ends that we've been away camping right up to mid-November.

from : A letter from Annette and Ralph Wyeth

30 Life in a spacecraft

Outer space, 1965

'It's easier to fly in space than to pilot an aircraft, once you've mastered the controls,' says Frank Borman . . .

'One of our biggest problems,' says Jim Lovell, 'was the same thing that everybody faces here on earth—eating, sleeping, and housekeeping. We were worried that we'd sort of get pushed out of the spacecraft with all the debris that would accumulate. So we spent many hours prior to the flight finding little spots and crevices in the spacecraft where we could pack things. We would eat three meals a day, and Frank would very nicely pack the containers in a small bag, and at the end of the day he would throw it behind the seat. We managed to get nine days' debris behind those seats.'

The spacecraft returned surprisingly clean.

'Other Gemini crews,' says Lovell, 'have reported that they became increasingly tired due to the fact that one person would be on watch and the other sleeping, and communication between the ground and the spacecraft would wake the sleeping person. So we decided to sleep simultaneously.

'We worked on a Houston day. Our watches were set on Houston time. We had a regular work day, had three meals a day, and then at night we went to bed. We put up light filters in the windows and didn't look out, and to us it was nighttime.

'We had absolutely no sensation of movement. Our world was inside the spacecraft. We even had some books along. Frank had one which was quite apropos : It was called *Roughing It*, by Mark Twain !'

from : Kenneth F. Weaver, 'Space rendezvous', *National Geographic Magazine*, April 1966

31 Learning to travel in space

Outer space, 1962

The doctor also asked me what physical reactions, if any, I had experienced so far from weightlessness. I was able to tell him that there had been none at all; I assured him that I felt fine. I had had no trouble reaching accurately for the controls and switches—there had been no tendency to get awkward and over-reach them, as some people had thought there might be. I could hit directly any spot that I wanted to hit. I had an eye-chart on board, a small version of the kind you find in doctors' offices, and I had no trouble reading the same line of type each time. After making a few slow movements with my head to see if this brought on a feeling of disorientation, I even tried to induce a little dizziness by nodding my head up and down and moving it from side to side. I experienced no disturbance, however. I felt no sense of vertigo, astigmatism or nausea whatever.

In fact, I found weightlessness to be extremely pleasant—and very convenient for a space pilot. I was busy at one moment, for example, taking photographs, and suddenly I had to free my hands to attend to something else. Without even thinking about it, I simply left the camera in mid-air, and it stayed there until I was ready to pick it up again. That this strange phenomenon seemed so natural at the time indicates how rapidly man can adapt to a new environment. I am sure that I could have gone for a much longer period in a weightless condition without being bothered by it at all. Being suspended in a state of Zero G is much more comfortable than lying down under the pressure of 1 G on the ground, for you are not subject to any pressure points. You feel absolutely free. The state is so pleasant that we joked that a person could probably become addicted to it without any trouble. I know that I could. The only catch that I can think of on a space flight is that you would have to be careful about the kind of food you carried along. Anything crumbly like biscuits could be a nuisance, for the pieces would float around and get in your way. But I think that an Astronaut could easily take a plain old ham sandwich up with him—complete with mustard.

from : (John Glenn) The Seven Astronauts
of Project Mercury, *Into Orbit*

Notes on Section 3

The bold figures indicate extract numbers

1-2 Both peoples are primitive. They have been dispossessed of good lands and driven by force of circumstance into the desert or semi-desert. Both must be admired for their skills and knowledge of animals. The Australian aborigines seem to be more affected by contact with the white man. Once hunted by them, the aborigines are now protected and often work as cattle-men. See also Section 4, extract No. 32, which gives the other side of the coin.

3 A fascinating study of a usually disliked animal, by a man who loved the beasts he worked with for over twenty years. Camels are still used over vast areas of the arid and semi-arid Old World countries. They had their day in Australia as beasts of burden and team animals, being used in thousands in every state but Victoria, carrying ore, wool, stores and bore casings, and pulling ploughs and the scoops used when building dams. They naturally drink as other animals do, and have to be trained to go without water. This is possible because they can tolerate a rise in body temperature to 40·6°C (105°F) before they need to lose heat by water loss from the blood stream.

4-5 These are examples of the many gifts of nature used by inventive people with limited resources. The oil palm, a native of the West African forests, has become a plantation crop in other tropical areas. It has two fruiting seasons a year, and provides a useful cash crop. The forest people of West Africa are only short of food when cut off from supplies, as in refugee camps. See also Section 7, extract No. 35.

6 This suggests the suitability of subsistence farming in an area of periodic leaching of the soil and great heat; also that a wide variety of crops grown to cover the ground holds the land in better heart than European methods which expose the soil. Subsistence farming is found all over the tropical world. In some areas, including Malaya, however, large patches of forest are being cleared so that a single crop can be grown, and we shall have to see what effect this has on the land.

7 Life reduced to its simplest. These are movable homes. See also Section 7, extract No. 11. Some of the men have taken jobs.

8 Here the quality of life is stressed and a sense of happiness is evident. Many homes of this kind are still to be found in West Africa.

9 The young boy had enormous responsibilities, but was supported by living in a clan community. It is to such a community that his responsibility as an adult will be pledged, and to this community he must contribute wherever he is working. The boy's intelligence is clear; this is a picture seen through his eyes.

11 China is notoriously short of timber (even for coffins), but there is mud for bricks and in Shensi the wonderful loess and rock. An earth cave may only last thirty years, but a stone cave lasting several hundred years gives a sense of timelessness. Again in this extract we see the value of team-work, and man's pride in his work and in the finished job.

12 This is a lesson in enforced idleness and contentment with a simple life. The Scottish crofts are isolated—rather a contrast to the Irish. Today many of them are holiday homes, or deserted in favour of flats in the towns. Of those that remain, electricity has reached some, but isolation by snow has to be faced in winter, and crofters must be self-sufficient people.

13 The working day only began after the religious ceremonies had been performed in the altar room. This farm, over 10,000 feet (3000 m) above sea-level, was the home of the Dalai Lama as a child. The description of what life was like was given by his brother. Tibet has been 'liberated' by the Chinese from its traditional religious authorities; the Dalai Lama who left the country in 1959 was declared a traitor in 1964. In 1965 Tibet became an Autonomous Region of China. It is difficult to believe that life on farms such as this can have changed fundamentally. In this account, security, creativity, and a warmth of family life are very apparent. A contented and independent-minded people with a reasonable standard of living are not good subjects for change, as were the poverty-stricken masses of Chinese. No doubt some of the younger people will have left for education in China, acquired new skills and brought back some consumer goods and new ideas. It is unusual to find a description giving such a complete 'feel' of a mountain farm, many of whose features are to be found also in European farms in high mountainous places. The impact of electricity, ski-lifts and panoramic roads, however, is changing the picture faster in Europe's remote places. It is probably the plane that is most likely to affect Tibet.

14 The Kochis are a nomadic people practising transhumance from the plains to the high foothills of the Himalayas. So far they have been un-restricted by the government.

15–16 The Kirghiz are a people suited to the high mountains and inter-montane plateaux of Kirgizia and the eastern Pamirs, taking in their stride the collectivizing agents of the government. The felt tents are usually referred to as *yurtas*, but sometimes the term *khirgas* is used.

17 Mongolians are basically a nomadic people in high desert and poor steppe-land, prosperous in cattle-rearing and stock-raising, and still very independent and horse-orientated like their forebears. Mongolia as a whole enjoys the highest standard of living in Asia, apart from Japan. The Peoples' Republic of Mongolia became communist in 1921. The unenviable position of being a buffer state between two idealogies has its advantages too, in foreign aid. It would appear that the Russians have contributed most largely.

18 The transistor radio is found in peasant homes all over the world. It is an enormous influence for good or ill—probably the greatest of the age for the largest number of people. The size of the market is ever increasing. A large proportion of the sets are Japanese.

19 This shows the extraordinarily fast development of an intelligent but formerly ignorant people—ignorant, that is, by Western standards. Events have been accelerated by a world war, and by the interest of young Australian pioneers in New Guinea.

138

20 This was unusual in 1948.

21 The Eskimos have great mechanical aptitude and are able to live in areas and under circumstances that others would find intolerable unless supported by modern technology.

22 This kind of conflict between old and new methods is inevitable as the Arctic is gradually developed and exploited. In order to buy a skidoo the Eskimo works for money, and naturally his whole outlook on life changes.

23 Contrary to general belief, the Eskimo only built an igloo occasionally when on hunting expeditions; wherever possible he built a turf-house or used a tent as a base. The houses described in the extract are an improvement. It suits the government and the oil firms to gather the Eskimos together and employ them as part of the labour force for strategic and commercial developments. Unfortunately the Eskimos have inherited the role of second-class citizens. They were not considered when their ancient hunting grounds were parcelled out for sale. If they had been, they would now be one of the wealthiest races in the world.

24-25 The importance of transport for penetrating difficult areas and bringing new ideas to backward places, and the advantage of fast transport in enabling a man to make a return trip quickly, can be universally applied. The question of breakdown is always implicit.

26 The author is an expatriate who spent over twenty years in the tropics. Rangoon has a mean rainfall of 103 inches (2600 mm) and high temperatures all the year, with an absolute maximum of 41 °C (106 °F) and an absolute minimum of 13 °C (55 °F). Relative humidity is high, especially between June and September when both morning and evening figures range only between 85 per cent and 89 per cent (the monsoon is from May to September).

27-28 Churchill, 58° 45′ N. Helsinki, 60° 15′ N. Northern Finland is nearly 70°N. See also Section 1, extracts No. 1 (Russian winter). Enclosed, indoor living creates tensions and can have a serious effect on people.

29 This extract is concerned with adaptation to town life. The city is the place of culture and opportunity, and the trend towards urbanisation is likely to accelerate.

30-31 These extracts highlight men coming to terms with a new environment—space. Housekeeping problems have been simplified since Jim Lovell's flight.

4

The less fortunate ones

The emphasis in this section is on people in different parts of the world who have found conditions too difficult for them to attain a satisfactory standard of living acceptable today. Naturally a good many of them live in backward or in developing countries, but the sophisticated societies have their black spots. A glance at some of the historical extracts will establish that some of the problems are not new in a world context. Whilst social conscience is more alive to the well-being and sensitivity of others that ever before, thanks to the communications industry, the small men of this world are still overridden in the name of expediency; there is still lack of understanding.

THE LESS FORTUNATE ONES

1 Underdevelopment and people

General

The roads and railroads are insufficient, the communication system is erratic, the factories and the tools for agriculture are mostly lacking. Few people have enough education and training to take part usefully in the development process ...

Whatever wealth underdeveloped countries have is often concentrated in the hands of a few people who live in comparative opulence surrounded by overwhelming poverty. An underdeveloped country's banking system is embryonic; small loans have to be obtained through money lenders who are often little better than extortionists ...

Exports typically consist almost entirely of raw materials.

from : Paul G. Hoffman, *World without Want*

2 Muscle power: avoiding the sentimental

General

Elephants pulling logs, the flat-hatted Indonesians pounding their earth with wooden blocks, the Sudanese heaving water from the Nile in petrol-tins, look to us disenchanted town-dwellers like timeless tokens of nature's wisdom which we in the West are perverting with our restless ingenuity. We must not seek our lost romanticism in the miserable lives of millions whose modes of living few of us would wish to adopt for more than a day. The disparity in mechanical power between us and the 'powerless' areas of the world is in itself serious enough : mechanical power is the fuel for any wealth-producing community. But worse still, existing mechanical energy in these power-starved nations is most unequally distributed. It is wholly concentrated in ports and cities. In the vast hinterlands 1,000 million people—one in every three people on earth—labour in the manner of ancient Babylon. The women are packhorses, the waterwheels are turned by men or oxen, human muscles are harnessed to a yoke of unchanging hopelessness. This is one aspect of underdevelopment where statistics based on averages can look very misleading.

It is bad (and impressive enough) to be told that the mechanical energy supply of a vast subcontinent like India would be insufficient for New York City. But nine-tenths of even that pittance of power derives from Bombay, Calcutta, Madras, Delhi, the power stations, and giant dams; go beyond these and you find where the city and the concrete end, there end the pylons, the roads, the mechanical aids to free men from perpetual slavery to their environment. The transition to 'nothing' is dramatically evident. A perfectly good road ends as if cut by some invisible wall. A hideous concrete street lamp similar to those gracing our own suburbs lights up a corner of a West African roadway; and ten yards farther on—the wilderness. The drift to the city is quickened by this internal disparity of energy. Within the city or the port the contrast between the possession of mechanical power and reliance on human muscle has reached ludicrous dimensions. A photo-electric cell opens the doors of a bank, whereas, barely a mile away in the harbour crates full of fragile, high-precision instruments are lifted from the hold on the backs of men.

from : Stephen Hearst, *2,000 Million Poor*

3 Sampans on the Yangtze-Kiang

China, nineteen-fifties

I watch the innumerable junks and sampans fighting the same battle their predecessors have fought for thousands of years.

Beside us a sampan, piled with rice-bags, edges its way inch by inch across the river. They use the wind to help them and the sail swells in a sudden gust. The sampan surges forward and one wonders at its progress under a sail that is as much hole as cotton.

They lose the wind. The boat is tossed like a chip on the water. The man bends to the oar, chin dug in, lips pulled back in a snarl, his body glistening with sweat, the muscles of his arms like cords. The woman clings to the stern oar that serves as rudder, pressing all her frail weight against it, her head thrown back and her eyes closed in an agony of useless effort. The racing current takes them and while we watch they are carried a half a mile downstream.

All around the same drama is being played out on a larger or smaller scale.

We pass a big trading boat, high of prow and stern rowed by eight men on a long swing oar who walk backwards and forwards across the deck without cease, propelling the vessel across to the shore we have left. What a few hundred tugs could do here in the saving of human energy in the daily-struggle against the big river that must wear out body and heart!

from : Dymphna Cusack, *Chinese Women Speak*

4 Toil and its reward in fishing: Penang

Malaya

On the beach the Tamil fishermen are hauling in their net. They haul on their ropes in two long files stretching from the edge of the sea. Their net, attached at either of its ends to each of these ropes, is almost half a mile out to sea. We can see where the net is, for a boat bobs above it and follows it in.

As the fishermen haul, they chant. I do not know what it is that they chant, but it rises as though from the dust of India. One man leads and calls in a high and rythmical intonation; promptly the others give the reply. At the same time they haul on the ropes. And slowly the net moves shorewards. As each man reaches the point where the rope piles into huge coils he goes to the front again and attaches himself to the rope with a line that is passed round his waist. Most of the purchase, therefore, comes from his waist.

They are thin and wiry little men, these Tamils, with skins so dark that they are almost black. The cloths that they wear at their waists are drawn tightly into their loins so that their buttocks are exposed; thin emaciated, hollow buttocks. It is extraordinary, this steady application of energy. The sweat gleams on their black skins and little balls of muscle stand out on their thin limbs, and for well over an hour they work without pause, straining at the dripping rope. Their splaying toes rip up the sand. The sun pours down and dances viciously off the water so that a man can see only if his eyes are almost closed. And over it all the monotonous, repetitious chant and counter-chant.

The net approaches to within a hundred yards of the beach and suddenly the rhythm of the chant changes—faster, more insistent. The caller cries out in a louder voice and the answer comes more urgently. The black bodies lean more heavily against the rope, and feet in unison hit the sand and the fight for a grip in the holes that other feet have made. The sun falls towards the western hills and becomes hotter, and the little black boat bobbing on the silvering sea comes slowly towards us. We can see the rope running along the surface of the sea all the way now to the net and the black boat moving in the sun's reflected fire.

A tall grey-beard, dressed, it seems, in nothing but a western-style shirt and a white turban, goes to the water's edge and turns and faces the men. He stands in the blinding heat like an ancient prophet, raises a hand to heaven and calls with all the power of his lungs, and then throws himself at the rope and hauls so that his body is almost parallel to the ground. At once the timeless answer is given, yet faster, and with a more pronounced and furious rhythm. One, two, three, four; one, two, three, four; and the sand flies as the feet stamp into its softness. I had never seen this operation before and I think it is one of the most exciting things I have ever seen. I stood there transfixed, among an ecstasy of sound and movement and colour, and I think that if a man lived who combined the genius of a Beethoven, a Pavlova and Leonardo, he could produce nothing so beautiful as this nor anything so vital and stirring.

The net is only a few yards from the beach now. For the last time the rhythm changes and the call and the answer becomes a one-two rhythm; one-two; one-two. In their stamping, dancing gait the men run away with the rope and the net lies black and heavy on the wet sand.

Quite suddenly there is quiet and the sound of the sea is heard again, and the men come down to see what the reward for their hours of toil is to be. Under three obscene jelly-fish, each eighteen inches across, squirms the thin, grey body of a flat-headed sea snake. Besides these things there is enough fish to fill a small basket.

from : Donald Moore, *We live in Singapore*

5 Porterage: mid twentieth century

Nyasaland (now Malawi), 1949

We climbed for an hour. I remember I had just taken off a sweater and looked at my watch, when I heard the first yodel. It sounded for all the world as if it might have been in the Austrian Tyrol or any of the mountain slopes of Switzerland, and I asked Quillan if there was another party of Europeans ahead of us.

'Oh! No,' he said, with a laugh. 'Europeans don't come here if they can help it. These are departmental native bearers coming down with sawn cedar from above. They always call like that to one another particularly when it is misty. You will soon see them. But it is a funny thing about mountains, they always make everyone want to yodel. We didn't teach these blokes. It is their own idea, it just came to them; a gift from the mountain.'

He explained that they were so short of good wood in Nyasaland that they were cutting cedar at Chambe, sawing it up by hand and carrying it down the mountain, each length separately on the head of black porters.

'It is hell for them,' said Quillan, 'but they don't mind and we have got to do it. We make it up to them by feeding them and paying them as well as we can, but we don't like it. We intend changing it as soon as Vance finishes his road on top. At the moment we get more carriers than we can use, because there's a semi-famine on and they want the food.' Just then another yodel soared up like a bird close by. I became aware of a strange, thick, resinous, spiced, oily scent, and Quillan said 'Do you mind getting off the track, please.'

There seemed to be a deep sheer drop on our right, so using saplings we pulled ourselves up on to a steep slope to the left of the track. I heard the pad-pad of heavily burdened feet coming out of the mist above, then someone breathing and puffing with every cell of his lungs, followed by a smell of human sweat mingling with the scent of resin, and a native balancing a heavy, thirty-foot beam of cedar on his head, came out of the mist towards us.

I thought it wrong, somehow, that laden and breathing as he was, he should feel compelled to raise his hand and say 'Morning, Bwana!' Besides, he was just on the edge of a precipice.

'He gets ninepence [4p] a day and some food, for doing that,' said Quillan. 'I'd be damned if I'd do it.'

From now on we passed dozens of carriers coming down the mountain at regular intervals. Quillan always took the same punctilious care to make way for them. We began to talk less. The track became steeper and we had to use our hands as well as our feet in places.

from : Laurens Van Der Post, *Venture to the Interior*

6 Porterage remembered by a young African

Nyasaland (now Malawi), nineteen-forties

There were no roads in our area at that time, and whenever a white man happened to be passing by, there would be scores of Africans carrying his luggage, and sometimes carrying him. Our chief had received word that a white Government official would be visiting our area and the other parts of the district, and he picked out several men from the village to carry his loads. My father was among them.

The journey was long and tedious, and it took them a long time before they finally got to our village, as the white man and his carriers were going from village to village spending a night in each. I had never seen a white person before, and when the day arrived when he was due in our village, hundreds of us stood beside the path, awaiting his arrival. I saw a line of tired men, my father included, all carrying on their shoulders or on their heads chairs, tables, a tent, boxes, and many other things. It looked as though the white man was moving to some other place. Slowly they passed us with no words and no smile on their faces. Behind these men was a sun-tanned white couple. The man was walking elegantly, not seeming to care about his heavily burdened carriers. His wife was lying luxuriously on a stretcher held by four of the strongest men of the group. They passed us, and we followed them until we came to a river where I saw the white man, who did not like to wade across the river, jump up on the back of an African. I watched the bearer as he staggered across the river, and wondered what would happen if that man slipped and fell, dropping his burden. But he did not.

We followed them still farther to the place where the carriers had set up the tent. I saw the chief bringing a fat bull as a gift to the white man, and other people bringing eggs, chickens, onions and other gifts. I wondered how really important he was that people would so willingly give him bulls and chickens and other precious things. My mother and others in the village had told us children that he owned the country.

from : Legson Kayira, *I will Try*

7 Power and poverty: a paradox

General

Only those who have seen the nature of poverty in these countries can possibly measure the consequences. A typical scene in a tropical country is that of a bullock-team raising water from a well. To the chanting of the drivers, the bullocks trudge backwards and forwards under the relentless sun, lowering buckets into the well, hoisting the water and tipping it into the water courses to irrigate the thirsty soil from which both men and beasts get their food.

These peasants are poor, desperately poor, yet they use the most expensive power in the world—muscle power. Bullocks have to be bought, tended and fed, yet even with the meagre food and pitiful earnings of the men who drive them, the energy-equivalent which they produce costs twenty times as much per unit as the energy output of Britain's Calder Hall atomic energy station.

A great many people in the world are poor because they, of necessity, use calories in their most expensive form as food, and energy in the most uneconomical way as muscle-power. Although we may glorify muscle-effort—and indeed laud it in the performance of athletes—it is deplorably inefficient. The advance from the steam-engine to atomic power, from the pulley-belt to automation, has represented the emancipation of Man from muscle-slavery.

Fully to grasp the difference between muscle power and mechanical power one has to think of a transatlantic liner. If that liner were a trireme, with slaves pulling on the galley oars, it would need 3,500,000 slaves to row it in five days from Southampton to New York.

The paradox of power is that those who are power-deficient are power extravagant. When we go round the house switching off lights to keep the electricity bill down, we might think of the Indian villager burning cow-dung to cook his food for his muscle power. Because he burns that dung, instead of using it as manure, his soil is undernourished, his crops are undernourished, and he is undernourished.

from : Ritchie Calder, *The Inheritors*

8 Poverty and porterage on the road

Kashmir, 1965

We met one other traveller today—a frail and half-starved young man who was carrying a huge wooden crate on his back and could barely stagger along the rough track under its weight. I gave him my lunch of four hard-boiled eggs and he ate them so fast I was quite alarmed, fearing he'd die of indigestion and that I'd have done more harm than good. Now I basely and bitterly regret my generosity, as I myself am almost dying of starvation, and this village can't even produce an egg. At the moment I'm waiting while clover is being cut in a near-by field to be stewed for my supper . . .

The filth in these villages is beyond all, the poverty is the most extreme I've met since leaving home and the skin-diseases are too dreadful to be described. Everyone stinks to high heaven—even in the open air it's overpowering and inside the little stone huts it's almost lethal. Now two grinning boys of about twelve have just appeared beside me, carrying a hideous-looking cloth full of mulberries. The method is to lay a cloth under a tree, climb into the lower branches and shake the fruit down. I'm too hungry to resist their juicy sweetness so, in spite of the cloth, will devour them. They are, of course, the chief source of sugar for the Gilgitis.

from : Dervla Murphy, *Full Tilt*

9 Impact of Bombay

Bombay, India

India is the poorest country in the world. Therefore, to see its poverty is to make an observation of no value; a thousand newcomers to the country before you have seen and said as you. And not only new-comers. Our own sons and daughters, when they return from Europe and America, have spoken in your very words. Do not think that your anger and contempt are marks of your sensitivity. You might have seen more : the smiles on the faces of the begging children, that domestic group among the pavement sleepers waking in the cool Bombay morning, father, mother and baby in a trinity of love, so self-contained that they are as private as if walls had separated them from you : it is your gaze that violates them, your sense of outrage that outrages them. You might have seen the boy sweeping his area of pavement, spreading his mat, lying down; exhaustion and under-nourishment are in his tiny body and shrunken face, but lying flat on his back, oblivious of you and the thousands who walk past in the lane between sleepers' mats and house walls bright with advertise-ment and election slogans, oblivious of the warm, over-breathed air, he plays with fatigued concentration with a tiny pistol in blue plastic. It is your surprise, your anger that denies him humanity. But wait. Stay six months. The winter will bring fresh visitors. Their talk will also be of poverty; they will show their anger. You will agree; but deep down there will be annoyance; it will seem to you then, too, that they are seeing only the obvious; and it will not please you to find your sensibility so accurately parodied.

Ten months later I was to revisit Bombay and to wonder at my hysteria. It was cooler, and in the crowded courtyards of Colaba there were Christmas decorations, illuminated stars hanging out of windows against the black sky. It was my eye that had changed. I had seen Indian villages : the narrow, broken lanes with green slime in the gutters, the choked back-to-back mud houses, the jumble of filth and food and animals and people, the baby in the dust, swollen-bellied, black with flies, but wearing its good-luck amulet. I had seen the starved child defecating at the roadside while the mangy dog waited to eat the excrement. I had seen the physique of the people of Andhra, which had suggested the possibility of an evolution down-wards, wasted body to wasted body, Nature mocking herself, incap-able of remission. Compassion and pity did not answer; they were refinements of hope. Fear was what I felt. Contempt was what I had to fight against; to give way to that was to abandon the self I had known. Perhaps in the end it was fatigue that overcame me. For abruptly, in the midst of hysteria, there occurred periods of calm, in

149

which I found that I had grown to separate myself from what I saw, to separate the pleasant from the unpleasant, the whole circular sky ablaze at sunset from the peasants diminished by its glory, the beauty of brassware and silk from the thin wrists that held them up for display, the ruins from the child defecating among them, to separate things from men. I had learned too that escape was always possible, that in every Indian town there was a corner of comparative order and cleanliness in which one could recover and cherish one's self-respect. In India the easiest and most necessary thing to ignore was the most obvious. Which no doubt was why, in spite of all that I had read about the country, nothing had prepared me for it.

But, in the beginning the obvious was overwhelming, and there was the knowledge that there was no ship to run back to, as there had been in Alexandria, Port Sudan, Djibouti, Karachi. It was new to me then that the obvious could be separated from the pleasant, from the area of self-respect and self-love. Marine Drive, Malabar Hill, the lights of the city at night from Kamala Nehru Park, the Parsi Towers of Silence. These are what the tourist brochures put forward as Bombay, and these were the things we were taken to see on three successive days by three kind persons. They build up a dread of what was not shown, that other city where lived the hundreds of thousands who poured in a white stream in and out of Churchgate Station as though hurrying to and from an endless football match. This was the city that presently revealed itself, in the broad, choked and endless main roads of suburbs, a chaos of shops, tall tenements, decaying balconies, electric wires and advertisements, the film posters that seemed to derive from a cooler and more luscious world ... And the courtyards behind the main streets: the heat heightened, at night the sense of outdoors destroyed the air holding on its stillness the odours of mingled filth, the windows not showing as oblongs of light but revealing lines, clothes, furniture, boxes and suggesting an occupation of more floor space. On the roads northwards, the cool redbrick factories set in gardens; Middlesex it might have been, but not attached to these factories any semi-detached or terrace houses, but that shanty town, that rubbish dump.

from : V. S. Naipaul, *An Area of Darkness*

10 Inca descendants on the Alto Plano

Peru, nineteen-fifties

They eked out a miserable existence at bare subsistence level. They lived in filthy vermin-ridden huts and had not water or sanitation. They were nearly always hungry and numb with cold. They lacked the will, the ability, or the means to improve their lot and seemed, instead, to have slipped back each generation. Until the United Nations' officials came,* they had no idea how to go about increasing the yield of the few crops they grew, crops which, so officials told me, had been better cultivated by the far-off Incas. They had no idea how to build a path, let alone a road, and would splash knee-deep through boggy land for years without attempting to drain it. They countered epidemics, which took heavy toll of young and old, by fantastic remedies suggested to them by their own witch doctors. They had a superstitious explanation for all that happened. They knew of nothing outside their own limited experience. Since no one ventured out of the valleys no one brought back new ideas. Some isolated groups admitted they did not know there had been a world war. They had never heard of television, telephones or the cinema though they had seen and heard machines which flew overhead. The United Nations' officials worked patiently with little reward. The Indians seemed to be sunk in a stupor into which their ancestors had descended when the Inca ruling class had been dispersed. They had lost everything in a national tragedy that had no equal. They lost their emperor and god, their faith, their homes and their farms. They were driven from big communal centres which were highly organized and had to take refuge in the most inaccessible and in-hospitable parts of the Cordillera and the High Plateau to prevent their womenfolk being violated, to save themselves being sent into slavery in the mines, or on the great estates which had been stolen by the *conquistadores*. They also wanted to escape the awful atrocities...

United Nations medical teams told me how they found the Indians suffering from economic and social degradation as well as from malnutrition and diseases of many kinds. The wives worked with the men in the fields and then slaved until it was too dark to see in the dingy mud huts they called home. The breadwinner sometimes mortgaged his entire working life to some Spanish profiteer for small sums needed to buy seeds. Families lived together with their animals in one crowded room and the air reeked with the smell of stale urine and excreta, animal and human. The whole family huddled together for warmth on animal skins on the hearth in the winter irrespective

* In 1954 the United Nations began their International Labour Organisation in Peru, by 1964 reaching 400,000 out of 7 million Indians.

of sex. In high summer the harvest was reaped in a new crop of babies who died unless they were hardy . . . many of the children died from smallpox, which was endemic, or from whooping cough, tuberculosis or half a dozen dread parasitic diseases. Their diet was deficient in protein and fats. Even if they had a few domestic animals and birds, wild turkeys from the jungle they had tethered and tamed, or little black pigs or poultry, the meat, milk and eggs these produced were for sale, not for family consumption. The money obtained from them was badly needed to pay for seeds.

from : W. Byford Jones, *Four Faces of Peru*

11 Poverty's millionaires

India, 1961

It is a natural assumption, made mainly by those who have never known real poverty, that a poor man can never be in doubt about his problems. He does not have enough for what economists would define as his 'absolute' needs, such as food, clothing, and housing, and therefore he must want more. Depending on one's philosophy of life, it is said, one may or may not be inclined to exert oneself for luxuries. Beyond a certain state of affluence one may not even be clear as to precisely what one needs. But it should not be necessary to tell a hungry man that he requires food and that he must work to obtain it.

Yet Balappa, a landless agricultural labourer in Gangawati *taluk* of the State of Mysore, has returned from work though the time is only noon. He was fortunate to get work today. But now he is reclining against the wall of his hut smoking a *bidi*.

'How is it you are back so early? Are you not going to work for the rest of the day?'

'No,' is the brief reply.

'Why?'

'I am tired.'

He is a young man; has a wife and a child and one cow.

'How much have you been paid for half a day's work?'

'One and a half *seers* of *jowar*.'

'But are you able to get work all the year round that you can afford to take it so easy?' I persist.

'No.'

'Then what do you do when you have no work?'

'Sit at home and borrow and eat. What else can I do?'

'Why don't you work for the whole day when work is available and save for lean times?' I ask again, unable to restrain myself from offering gratuitous advice.

'Oh, I have to get grass for my cow. If I work in the afternoon as well, when will I get the grass for the cow?', he says, throwing away the still smoking stump of the *bidi* with a gesture of dismissing the debate.

It is not food alone that Balappa lacks for many days in the year. His clothes are torn and dirty, and his house is a small one-room mud hut with a thatch which his family shares with the cow. But he relaxes by the time it is noon and, of his own choice, does not go back to work even when it is available. He possesses nothing but poverty; yet a millionaire could not care less.

from : Kusum Nair, *Blossoms in the Dust*

12 The poor have too much to lose

General

The poorest people sometimes seem like good candidates for change. They have so little to lose, economically and socially, it is argued, that they are taking no great risk in adopting the new. Many developmental programs in such fields as agriculture and health have been directed toward this target group, both because of the philosophy of dire need and because of the belief that they will be receptive. But experience again shows that the lower socio-economic groups are usually the poorest candidates for change . . .

Fear renders the poorest people incapable of trying new things. They know that their productive capacities, with traditional means, will provide a bare subsistence, but their margin of survival is so slim that they feel they cannot risk even a tiny amount to experiment with something that is new and untested . . . the most receptive people are those who are neither at the top nor the bottom of the local socio-economic scale. They have enough so that they can gamble with limited experiments without unduly threatening their well-being, but their position is not so secure that the attraction of greater income, as well as the possibility of satisfying other felt needs, is a strong motivation to action . . .

The attitude to fatalism is closely allied to the forces of tradition and constitutes a barrier of equal strength. In industrial societies people have proved to their satisfaction that a high degree of mastery over nature and social conditions is possible. An undesirable situation is not a hopeless block, but rather a challenge to man's ingenuity. In industrial societies people have come to believe that almost anything can be achieved; at least, any reasonable plan is worth a serious try.

But in non-industrial societies a very low degree of mastery over nature and social conditions has been achieved. Drought or flood is looked upon as a visitation from gods or evil spirits whom man can propitiate but not control. Feudal forms of land-tenure and non-productive technologies may condemn a farmer to a bare subsistence living. Medical and social services are lacking, and people die young. Under such circumstances it is not surprising that people have few illusions about the possibility of improving their lot. A fatalistic outlook, the assumption that whatever happens is the will of God or Allah, is the best adjustment the individual can make to an apparently hopeless situation.

from : George M. Foster, *Traditional Cultures and the Impact of Technological Change*

13 What form should aid take?

Liberia, nineteen-sixties

'How was the trip?' I asked.

'Fine, fine.' His enthusiasm seemed somehow watered down. 'How was yours?' I gave him a quick run-down of some of my impressions. 'I moved round quite a bit up-country,' he told me, 'but I can't say that I liked a great deal of what I saw. Things are happening of course but there was not enough involvement of the people at the lower levels. At least that's the opinion I got while up there. You see, they're building roads. O.K. But it's always with a few bulldozers, a couple of white technicians and a handful of African labourers. At the same time hundreds of men are sitting around idle in the villages. I figure they could do the job just as well without the bulldozers and lots more local labour. It would give the people a stake in what's going on. I figure it this way. Back home everybody wants to help Africa and they're pouring money over here. That's fine, but the money should be for the things the Africans cannot do for themselves.

from : E. R. Braithwaite, *A Kind of Homecoming*

14 Wasted potential

India, 1969

We must identify ourselves with the villagers who toil under hot sun beating on their bent backs and see how we would like to drink water from the pool in which the villagers bathe.

Mahatma Gandhi

Gandhi, with his unshakable faith in the people, told us to adjust the pace of our progress to the capacity of the common man; not to allow machines to replace man and animal power but to use them only to supplement it so as to realize the full potential of our- human and cattle population.

... India, as Gandhi saw it, was divided into two parts—the urban sector, comprising about twenty per cent of the population, and the rural sector, including more than 500,000 villages, containing about eighty per cent. Given a proper land system, he said, conservative subsistence farming coupled with handicrafts could enable all our population, even with the present rate of increase, to be maintained out of our own resources for a long time provided we were prepared to forego temporarily some of the trimmings of progress and to put first things first.

Take, for instance, our needs in fabric. There is no part of India where with proper training and organization every man, woman and child cannot provide him or herself with these from locally available resources with the help of indigenous tools that cost next to nothing, within a period of six months...

The salient features of his system of economy were : (1) Intensive small-scale diversified farming, as opposed to mechanized, large-scale monoculture, or collective farming, the total yield, as against yield per agricultural worker, being the highest under this system; (2) development of cottage crafts as ancillary to agriculture; (3) a cattle-based economy, with strict enforcement of the law of return, viz. to return to the soil in organic form what is taken out of the soil, without which the health and fertility of the soil and the population living on it cannot be fully maintained; (4) maintenance of a proper balance and relationship between human and animal and plant life—social health and stability being essentially the product of such a symbiosis; and (5) adoption of what Dr. Schumacher has called intermediate technology, and voluntary protection for both human and animal power against the competition of machinery as the price of social insurance.

There are unutilized natural resources in our villages lying at the very doorsteps of the people who need them, not enough for commercial exploitation but sufficient for their basic needs. The same applies to wee bits of time and labour of millions of hands. Proper utilization of these tiny bits, Gandhi affirmed, could provide our needy masses in the immediate present [with] what no central planning, helped even by foreign aid on a colossal scale, could do.

from : Pyarelal Nayar, 'Sufficiency from small resources', *The Times,* October 13, 1969

15 Pressure on the land: the Nile Delta

Egypt, 1966

One is never out of sight of human figures and seldom out of sound of the human voice. Every square inch of cultivated land, every drop of irrigation water, is meticulously utilised. Liberal doses of artificial fertilizer supplement the bounty of nature and the labour of man to produce three crops a year on the same plot of irrigated land. There is no shortage of labour. Willing hands are available in abundance for any work for which wages will be paid, whether it be the excavation of some ancient burial-ground, the repair of a road or a bridge, the digging or dredging of a canal, the repair of a boat, the building of a house or unloading of a truck. There is, in the Delta, and to a lesser extent in Upper Egypt, an overwhelming impression of that land-hunger, that over-population which is Egypt's perennial social and economic problem . . . It is this increasing population enfeebled by endemic diseases but no longer decimated by epidemic plagues and periodical foreign or civil war, which fills up the villages, depressing the price of labour, and overflows into the towns, creating slums, beggary and destitution.

from : John Marlowe, *Four Aspects of Egypt*

16 Malaria, germs and worms—endemic

Tropics and general

I have seen at first hand what malaria means in most parts of the world. It is definitely one of the principal causes of the shortages of food in tropical countries. The malarial season often coincides with the transplanting of rice or its harvesting, or both. Two out of every three of the peasants who might have been working on the land at those critical periods have been sick of the fever. The result has been poor crops through inadequate husbandry. In other parts, as in the north of Thailand, the malarial season has coincided with what might have been a second growing season. The peasants without undue food shortages to themselves, have settled for a single crop, although they might have produced two, and might have provided a surplus for export to other hungry peoples . . .

It is also reckoned that millions of tons of foodstuffs are wasted in feeding the disease germs and parasites in the human body. A gross example is, of course, the intestinal worms which are universally prevalent among the people of the tropics. A peasant may work a third of his life just to feed his tape-worm. But it applies also to the innumerable germs which batten on the human victim and make it impossible for him to absorb the food which he eats or prevent him from producing food which he might eat.

from : Ritchie Calder, *The Inheritors*

17 Syphilis brought to primitive people

Sandwich Islands, (Hawaii), eighteen-thirties

I spent one evening, as had been my custom, at the oven with the Sandwich-Islanders; but it was far from being the usual noisy, laughing, time. It has been said that the greatest curse to each of the South Sea Islands was the first man who discovered it; and every one who knows anything of the history of our commerce in those parts knows how much truth there is in this; and that the white men, with their vices, have brought diseases before unknown to the islanders, which are now sweeping off the native population of the Sandwich Islands at the rate of one-fortieth of the entire population annually. They seem to be a doomed people. The curse of a people calling themselves Christian seems to follow them everywhere; and even here, in this obscure place, lay two young islanders, whom I had left strong, active young men, in the vigour of health, wasting away under a disease which they would never have known but for their intercourse with people from Christian America and Europe. One of them was not so ill, and was moving about, smoking his pipe, and talking, and trying to keep up his spirits; but the other, who was my friend and *aikane,* Hope, was the most dreadful object I had ever seen in my life—his eyes sunken and dead, his cheeks fallen in against his teeth, his hands looking like claws; a dreadful cough, which seemed to rack his whole shattered system; a hollow, whispering voice, and an entire inability to move himself. There he lay, upon a mat on the ground, which was the only floor of the oven, with no medicine, no comforts, and no one to care for or help him but a few Kanakas, who were willing enough, but could do nothing. The sight of him made me sick and faint . . .

The next day I told Captain Thompson of Hope's state, and asked him if he would be so kind as to go and see him.

'What! a damned Kanaka?'

'Yes, sir,' I said; 'but he has worked four years for our vessels, and has been in the employ of our owners, both on shore and aboard.'

'Oh! he be damned!' said the captain, and walked off.

from : R. H. Dana, *Two Years before the Mast*

18 Scurvy: curse to sailors and emigrants

At sea, eighteen-thirties

The scurvy had begun to show itself on board. One man had it so badly as to be disabled and off duty, and the English lad, Ben, was in a dreadful state, and was daily growing worse. His legs swelled and pained him so that he could not walk : his flesh lost its elasticity, so that if he pressed in it would not return to its shape; and his gums swelled until he could not open his mouth. His breath, too, became very offensive; he lost all strength and spirit; could eat nothing; grew worse every day; and, in fact, unless something was done for him, he would be a dead man in a week, at the rate at which he was sinking. The medicines were all, or nearly all, gone, and if we had had a chest-full they would have been of no use, for nothing but fresh provisions and *terra firma* has any effect upon the scurvy. This disease is not so common now as formerly, and is attributed generally to salt provisions, want of cleanliness, the free use of grease and fat (which is the reason of its prevalence among whalemen), and, last of all, to laziness. It never could have been from the last cause on board our ship; nor from the second, for we were a very cleanly crew, kept our forecastle in neat order, and were more particular about washing and changing clothes than many better-dressed people on shore. It was probably from having none but salt provisions, and possibly from our having run very rapidly into hot weather, after having been so long in the extremest cold . . .

The next morning about ten o'clock, 'Sail ho!' was cried on deck;

158

and all hands turned up to see the stranger. As she drew nearer, she proved to be an ordinary-looking hermaphrodite brig, standing south-south-east, and probably bound out from the Northern States to the West Indies, and was just the thing we wished to see. She hove-to for us, seeing that we wished to speak to her, and we ran down to her, boom-ended our studding sails, backed our maintopsail, and hailed her : 'Brig ahoy!' 'Hallo!' 'Where are you from, pray?' 'From New York, bound to Curaçao'. 'Have you any fresh provisions to spare?' 'Aye, aye! Plenty of them!' We lowered away the quarter-boat instantly, and the captain and four hands sprang in, and were soon dancing over the water and alongside the brig. In about half an hour they returned with half a boat-load of potatoes and onions, and each vessel filled away and kept on her course . . .

It was just dinner-time when we filled away, and the steward, taking a few bunches of onions for the cabin, gave the rest to us, with a bottle of vinegar. We carried them forward, stowed them away in the forecastle, refusing to have them cooked, and ate them raw, with our beef and bread. And a glorious treat they were. The freshness and crispness of the raw onion, with the earthy taste, gave it a great relish to one who has been a long time on salt provisions. We were ravenous after them. It was like a scent of blood to a hound. We ate them at every meal, by the dozen, and filled our pockets with them, to eat in our watch on deck; and the bunches, rising in the form of a cone, from the largest at the bottom, to the smallest, no larger than a strawberry, at the top, soon disappeared. The chief use, however, for the fresh provisions, was for the men with scurvy. One of them was able to eat, and soon brought himself to, by gnawing upon raw potatoes and onions; but the other, by this time, was hardly able to open his mouth, and the cook took the potatoes raw, pounded them in a mortar, and gave him the juice to drink. This he swallowed, by the teaspoonful at a time, and rinsed it about his gums and throat. The strong earthy taste of this extract of raw potato at first produced a shuddering through his whole frame, and, after drinking it, an acute pain, which ran through all parts of his body; but knowing by this that it was taking strong hold, he persevered, drinking a spoonful every hour or so, and holding it a long time in his mouth, until, by the effect of this drink, and of his own restored hope (for he had nearly given up in despair) he became so well as to be able to move about, and open his mouth enough to eat the raw potatoes and onions pounded into a soft pulp. This course soon restored his appetite and strength, and in ten days after we spoke the *Solon*, so rapid was his recovery that, from lying helpless and almost hopeless in his berth, he was at the masthead furling a royal.

from : R. H. Dana, *Two Years before the Mast*

19 Lack of understanding in hospital

South Africa, nineteen-sixties

I recall a visit I once made to the hospital of one of the Johannesburg gold mines. The English matron was justifiably proud of the
shining cleanliness, but she complained that the Bantu patients were
always trying to untuck their blankets and to wrap them round themselves, but, I asked, wasn't that the way they had always treated
blankets? Of course it was, she agreed, but you couldn't possibly
have that sort of thing in hospital. It would make the wards look
so untidy.

Yes, I suppose it would. And yet, looking down the ward at all
those black men with fear in their eyes, I wished that tidiness and
cleanliness were not so important, and that they could lessen their
fear and their pain by wrapping themselves in their blankets as they
would have done in the remote and dirty kraal that to them was
home.

from : Vernon Bartlett, *Tuscan Retreat*

20 Rural need

Tanzania, nineteen-sixties

I flew early one morning in a very small aeroplane to Dodoma, 300
miles inland and West of Dar-es-Salaam. At mid-day the sun, beating vertically on this landscape, flattens it distortedly. But fly over it
early when the shadows are as vivid as the light and you see the
variety in the topography, a huge and engrossing complex of slopes
and pinnacles and turrets coloured in subtle mergings of blues and
greys and greens. But it is not easy country for men to manage.
The sun glints on so few spurts of water that when you spot one
you are likely to feel pleased with yourself, like a hill-hiker spotting
deer.

Staring down at this land held in such relief, sometimes skimming
close to a purple ridge of rock, I could pick out clusters of houses
bunched at the ends of thin tracks in the bush. There were seldom
more than half a dozen dwellings in one spot. Their neighbours
would be on the other side of the next hill.

These were the people I had been discussing the day before with
a young community development worker ... The poor families, the
ones living on the bare subsistence crops they scrape together with
untutored method, were well known to Basila. They are the bulk

of her country's population. She had been telling me of the dragging weight of hardship which accompanies the lack of readily available water, which is one of Tanzania's main problems. Passing slowly over the land I understood her point more clearly.

Living hand to mouth in this territory, without road or water pipe, people followed a daily routine of grim essentiality. A mother would begin her day at 5 a.m. or earlier, setting off on a walk of perhaps five miles to the nearest water hole. She would probably have a baby wrapped into her clothing on her back and possibly another in her arms. At the water hole she would find a queue of other women and children who had made the walk from their own little settlements just as she had. The water she collected in a gourd or an old dried milk tin would at best be less than clear; at worst it would be contaminated.

Basila had emphasised the physical obstacles in the way of progress to a better life. How could she teach hygiene to people who had no water to wash with? She thought that one of the first requirements in Tanzanian rural life was for a major programme of well digging. 'Let's say,' she said, with an impressive practicality, 'that two miles is a reasonable distance for a family to walk for water.'

That was the voice of reality, one which was not looking for an urban transformation of rural backwardness. Tremendous improvements are possible in the quality of rural life in the most forbidding areas of the poor world, and they can be effected by the kind of measures which may sound depressingly modest in meetings of impatient planners in air-conditioned offices. Method has to be relevant to resources.

At Dodoma I saw an example of this pragmatic approach. The region is plainland which bakes dry for six months of the year. Its prevailing characteristic is gauntness; the people are gaunt, so are their cattle and so is the bush. The Gogo tribe live here in a brutish parody of the pastoral ideal, insulated by their privation. The struggle for survival is the constant in their lives and it gives them a weary resilience of the kind the rich world likes to romanticize with a label like 'primitive pride'.

There is certainly a stubborn toughness here, a fortitude that keeps them wandering with their starved herds looking for grazing when the land is brown and brittle in drought. There is also suffering ...

What sort of life presents itself to most of the children who grow up? Home is a succession of temporary mud-and-pole shelters, often no taller than big dog kennels. For the lucky there will be school, of a rudimentary sort under a teacher with an educational standard equivalent to that of an American or European bright twelve year old. They will suffer recurrent malaria and intestinal diseases and be old by the time they are forty-five.

But there is a glimmer of hope for a much brighter prospect for the generation which will follow the one growing up now in this area. Some very practical help has arrived at Hombolo, and the children of the late seventies may well enter a different world because of it. Hombolo is being taught to use the land, instead of being ruled by it.

I found the kind of farmers' training centre which works at Hombolo repeated in many of the places I visited in other countries; but I do not think I found one which had a harder job. The stubbornness developed by people who have to live in such harshness is naturally applied to all external influences, not just to adverse climate. Peter Marks and his wife, Ann, the young English couple who started the centre (the money being provided by the Somerset FFHC* committee), had to win over the people as well as tame the land.

The setting was chosen deliberately for its intractability, on the grounds that if it could be made to bloom, so could anywhere else in Tanzania. When Marks arrived in 1963 he was driven by Land-Rover up to a little rise in the bush and told he could begin as soon as he liked. Standing beside one of the cattle pens, where some of his healthy African animals grazed and snuffled, I looked beyond the farm fences at the kind of stuff he had to clear: a stubby, prickly vegetation broken up by enormous grey trees. I do not think that after Dodoma I shall ever use the word 'wild' about any European landscape again.

The place looked as if it belonged far more to animals than to people: burningly hot, stinging with flying bugs and, when we stopped talking, imbued with a silence which felt to me to be watchful. Marks soon let me know that I was not being fanciful about the place. It is jungle. Leopards had prowled about the fences. ('The barbed wire just gives them pause for thought. It wouldn't keep them out if they were desperate for food. They'd clear it like a little gate.') Vipers and adders were commonly seen in the compound. A python, fourteen feet long, had been killed in the grounds of the leprosy hospital near by. One of Marks' staff had brought home an eight-feet-long spitting cobra.

These alarming exotica, of course, did not form the main obstacles to Marks' work. The huge variety of insects which attacked his crops, the shortage of water, the suspicion and deeply buried customs of the people; these were what he fought.

There are thought to be a million cattle in the Dodoma region. They are the people's capital, their declaration of status as well as their savings account. For much of the year they are as fleshless and knobbly as hat stands. The people trade with them, use them for daughters' dowries, squeeze miserably little milk out of them, bleed them now and again and mix the blood with maize to make

* Freedom from Hunger Campaign

something resembling a northern Englishman's black pudding. But they seldom slaughter.

When Marks began his operations there were about 20,000 of these bleak animals grazing like a packed flock of buzzards in the area. As he cleared the bush the pack came crowding in. Grazing land is common land here, and under these circumstances no training in the control of pasture is possible. Marks began to fence. The Gogo people, outraged, set fire to corners of his station.

It was an unpromising beginning, but as the centre got under way it taught the one clinching lesson to the local people that if they followed its methods they could make money.

Farmers spent a week at the centre, living in cement-and-asbestos dormitories which represented a far higher standard of housing than they were used to. They also ate better, their usual diet of maize and beans supplemented by onions and tomatoes introduced from the school farm. Marks kept the teaching simple in order to maximize the effect, and he cautiously estimated that seventy per cent of farmers who had taken courses were now doing the basic, but quite novel, things they had been taught.

Now they were planting seed in rows, spacing it adequately, using the abundant cattle manure on the land, conserving fodder. Only when you realize that these matters were revolutionary to them do you understand what is contained in the word 'ignorance' as applied to rural life in the poor world ...

The people here were still assimilating the first influences of the modern world: methodical farming, balanced feeding—and an assured water supply from a reservoir newly built about a mile from the training centre. Stand taps have eased some of the women's domestic labour, but have not helped to cut down the heavy incidence of intestinal diseases ... It is a social custom again. As soon as you mention latrines the barrier goes up immediately. There is a strict privacy about this subject. The people use the bush, and a man will never go to the same place as his sons; young men will not go to the same place as their mothers and so on. We haven't been able to get across the idea of a single latrine for the family.

The effects of such a situation grow worse, of course, if people are encouraged by facilities such as water taps and permanently available farming advice to gather closely in one area. The totally primitive life, a semi-nomadic wandering and brief settling while the water and the grazing lasted, dispersed the people. Now the combination of bare feet and littered filth was undoing a great deal of the health work in the area. Here again it seemed that it would take a generation of exposure to modern ways to clear the obstacle of custom.

from : Arthur Hopcraft, *Born to Hunger*

163

21 This is a hungry year: Matabeleland

First the chickens die; there is no chaff from the pounding of the grain.
Then the dogs die; there are no scraps from the cooking pot.
Then the goats die; there are no leaves which they can reach.
The cattle die; there is no grass on the land.
This is a hungry year!

Gordon Ash

22 Waiting for the harvest

World-wide

As Old Man Peasant swung along, his eyes roamed the green fields
on either side. The wheat was waist-high, and the tips showed a
glimpse of the gold of the harvest, but the fields were sparse and the
ripening grain scanty. No better than his own fields. 'In two weeks,'
he calculated, 'it will be ready for the sickle.' His eyes narrowed and
the furrow in his forehead deepened. 'Two weeks!' a thought like a
tall wave broke over him, leaving him taut. 'Can we last that long?'
His wife had been very clever the way she had husbanded their
small store of food all through the cold season; and pride sat in his
eyes at the thought. What grain they had been able to save after the
flood last autumn she had divided at once into twenty portions—one
for each week before the harvest could be expected. Every week—
and every day—all six of them had been hungry . . .
   This morning the woman his wife had confided to him alone her
fears. There was food in the house for only three more days—one
scanty meal a day. The boy his second son and the girl his daughter
were both ill with starvation sickness; the small dreary faces of
Younger Son and Merry Mischief, the toddler, looked out of listless
eyes. Yes, said the woman his wife, they must sell something and
buy food. One of their two cooking pots must go, and after all what
was the use of hoarding two if you had not food to fill one? Thirty
cents was much less than the pot was worth, but it might buy rice
to keep them alive for a week. So Old Man Peasant had gone to
the grain shop in the village and turned away because the price had
been raised twice over; he had then walked the four hot miles to the
market town and was now wearily returning empty-handed, for it
was the time just before the harvest when only the rich could buy.
   Despair contorted the face of Old Man Peasant. He glanced at

the heavens and saw a meeting of the clouds in the western sky. Rain, so welcome when the crop is growing, would be no boon at this season. Rain would beat down and shatter the grain almost ready for the reaping. A sudden terror blinded Old Man Peasant; stalks lying flat and broken; grain unripened, rotting. Strength drained from his legs and he stumbled towards home, clawing the heavens, crying out to the god of the clouds, the god of the harvest . . .

Visualise a line starting from your front door, made up of the hungry of the world—many ragged and disease ravaged, with pinched faces. The line goes on out of sight over continent and ocean, around the world—twenty-five thousand miles—and returns to your front door. On and on it stretches, circling the globe, not twice nor five times, but twenty-five, and there is no one in the line but hungry, suffering humanity.

from : Donald K. Faris, *To Plough with Hope*

23 Ireland and the potato

Ireland, eighteen-forties

The whole of this structure, the minute subdivisions, the closely-packed population existing at the lowest level, the high rents, the frantic competition for land, had been produced by the potato. The conditions of life in Ireland and the existence of the Irish people depended on the potato entirely and exclusively.

The potato, provided it did not fail, enabled great quantities of food to be produced at a trifling cost from a small plot of ground. Subdivision could never have taken place without the potato; an acre and a half would provide a family of five or six with food for twelve months, while to grow the equivalent grain required an acreage four to six times as large and some knowledge of tillage as well. Only a spade was needed for the primitive method of potato culture usually practised in Ireland. Trenches were dug and beds—called 'lazy beds'—made; the potato sets were laid on the ground and earthed up from the trenches; when the shoots appeared, they were earthed up again. This method, regarded by the English with contempt, was in fact admirably suited to the moist soil of Ireland. The trenches provided drainage, and crops could be grown in wet ground, while cultivation by the spade enabled potatoes to be grown on mountain sides, where no plough could be used. As the population expanded, potatoes in lazy beds were pushed out into the bog and up the mountain, where no other cultivation would have been possible.

The potato was, moreover, the most universally useful of foods. Pigs, cattle and fowls could be reared on it, using the tubers which were too small for everyday use; it was simple to cook; it produced fine children; as a diet, it did not pall.

Yet it was the most dangerous of crops. It did not keep, nor could it be stored from one season to another. Thus every year the nearly two and a half million labourers who had no regular employment more or less starved in the summer, when the old potatoes were finished and the new had not come in. It was for this reason that June, July and August were called the 'meal months': there was always the danger that potatoes would run out and meal would have to be eaten instead, the labourers would then have to buy it on credit, at exorbitant prices, from the petty dealer and usurer who was the scourge of the Irish village—the dreaded 'Gombeen man'.

More serious still, if the potato did fail, neither meal nor anything else could replace it. There could be no question of resorting to an equally cheap food, no such food existed, nor could potato cultivation be replaced, except after a long period, by the cultivation of anything else. 'What hope is there for a nation that lives on potatoes!' wrote an English official.

from : Cecil Woodham-Smith, *The Great Hunger*

24 Locusts and the menace of hunger

Ethiopia, nineteen-sixties

'Locusts. A swarm so big we cannot measure it. It came this morning about seventy miles away at the town of JiJiga. Just after sunrise the locusts woke up and they have been eating ever since. The corn will be all gone soon.'

'Right, I'll go over straight away.'

I was joined by two assistants and we set out to drive the seventy miles to JiJiga to the swarm. Even before we got to the last reported position of the locusts we found them. They were hanging in clouds over the valleys like brown smoke. They were all over the road too and we could hear them squash and crunch under the tyres as we drove over them. In some places there were so many that the windscreen wipers had great difficulty in clearing the crushed locusts from the screen. At last we reached JiJiga and made our way through a crowd to the government offices. Even inside I could hear the farmers in the crowd, some were shouting and asking when the government were going to do something, some were just muttering to themselves and others were weeping.

I began to make arrangements for the poison teams to get to work on the swarm. We needed aeroplanes with poison sprays, cars with sprays, and poisoned bait to spread on the ground but by the time they could get to JiJiga it would probably be too late. We had not been warned in time. Then the first of the farmers came in. He was tired and dirty. He had been fighting the locusts since dawn.

'Sir, when will the poison people get here? Most of my corn has already been eaten. We have killed and burned many locusts but we cannot kill them all. We are ruined. My children have been beating drums all day and still the locusts come. We have dug deep ditches round our fields and have driven the locusts into them; we have burnt some of them but it's no use. My family will starve and it was going to be the best harvest we have had for years.'

And so it went on all day, with the reports getting worse and worse. In this swarm we calculated that there were over forty thousand million locusts. In one day this swarm could eat about eighty thousand tons of food. That's enough for about one million people, about the population of Birmingham, for six months. I can never forget what I saw on that day. The crops stripped bare of grain, the locusts glistening in the sky and the poor farmers wondering how they would feed their families in the coming months. That night I could not sleep even though I was dead tired.

The poisons kill the locusts if they touch them or if they eat them. The poisons are so strong that for each teacupful sprayed from an aeroplane enough locusts will be killed so as to fill your bath. Over twenty thousand of them. However, as each aeroplane carries one hundred gallons of insecticide many millions of locusts are killed each time the aeroplanes fly off.

Killing locusts is not the only problem of course. Before you can kill them you have to find them ... Locusts breed in warm damp sand and a steady wind will often make them swarm, and so weather forecasts and locust forecasts are closely linked together. As soon as a swarm is reported and the wind direction checked the control teams get busy.

from : Geoffrey Sherlock, 'Exploration Earth, Unit 2', BBC radio script

25 Dinner with the Chinese

China, 1966

Nowhere I have been in the world can people eat better than in China, or worse. Perhaps on second thoughts it is possible to eat worse in the Balkans, but that is an accepted nadir of nastiness; the penance of Chinese diplomats in Albania is one of the lesser-known hells of the Cold War.

There are therefore two ways of considering Chinese feeding. One is from the point of view of, say, the Small Peasant of Szechuan. The other is that of the gastronome, which all Chinese would like to be and which not a few are. The difference has existed since Confucius and before. Today it diminishes fast. Twenty years ago more than 30,000 Chinese died from starvation in the streets of Shanghai alone. They do so no longer.

Some 600 million Chinese live on what they can get and are grateful. What they get varies according to the caprices of nature and the dispensations of the Central Government, both of which are inscrutable. Hunger is not something you eliminate by legislation. The *average* Chinese today probably eats as much food in a year as the *average* American consumes (or throws away) in a month. In protein-content it is perhaps one two-hundredth.

But whatever it may be, it is considered and presented with decorum. The Chinese in their own midst are an extremely civil people; no one could exist in the dense congestion of a Chinese home without almost superhuman good manners.

from : James Cameron, 'Dinner with the Chinese', *The Daily Telegraph Magazine*, September 30, 1966

26 Prejudice overcome

China, nineteen-thirties

Yuan grew restless in the mild spring winds and these winds made him remember the little hamlet where the earthen house stood, and he had a craving in his feet to stand on earth somewhere instead of on these city pavements. So he entered his name in the new spring term into a certain class where teachers taught of cultivation of the land and Yuan, among others, was apportioned a little piece of earth outside the city, for practice at the land to test what they had learned in books, and in this bit of land it was part of Yuan's task that he must plant seeds and keep the weeds out and do labour of this sort.

It so happened that the piece Yuan had was at the end of all the others, and next to a farmer's field, and the first time Yuan came out to see his plot of land he went alone, and the farmer stood there staring, his face alight with grinning, and he shouted, 'What do you students here? I thought students only learned in books!'

Then Yuan answered, 'In these days we learn in books of sowing and reaping too, and we learn how to make the land ready for sowing, and that is what I do today.'

At this the farmer laughed loudly and said with a mighty scorn, 'I never did hear of such a learning! Why, farmer tells his son and his son tells his son—one looks only at his neighbour and does what his neighbour does!'

'And if the neighbour is wrong?' said Yuan, smiling. 'Then look at the next neighbour and a better one,' said the farmer and he laughed over again and fell to hoeing in his own field and he muttered to himself and stopped to scratch his head and shake himself and laugh again and cry out, 'No, I never did hear such a thing in all my days! Well, I'm glad I sent no son of mine to any school, to waste my silver to have him learn of farming! I'll teach him more than he can learn, I'll swear!' ... and Yuan looked and saw the farmer, a man strong and brown, stripped to the waist, his legs bare to his knees, his feet in sandals, his face brown and red with winds and weather, his whole look good and free. Then Yuan said nothing, but he smiled and without a single word he took off his outer heavy coat and then his inner coat, and rolled his sleeves up to his elbow and stood ready. This the farmer watched, and suddenly he cried again, 'What woman's skin you have! Look at this arm of mine!' And he put his arm by Yuan's and outstretched his hand. 'Put out your hand! Look at your palm all blisters! But you hold your hoe so loosely it would have rubbed a blister even on my hand.' Then he picked up the hoe and showed Yuan how to hold it in his two hands, the one firm and close to keep the handle sure and the other farther on, to guide the swing of it. And Yuan was not ashamed to learn, and he tried many times until at last the iron point fell true and hard and clipped away a piece of earth each time it fell, and then the farmer praised him and Yuan felt as glad as he did if he had a verse praised by his teacher, although he wondered that he did, seeing that the farmer was but a common man ...

Day after day Yuan came to work upon his plot of land and he liked best to come when all his fellows were not there, for when they came the farmer would not draw near at all, but worked in some more distant field of his. But if Yuan were alone he came and talked and showed Yuan how to plant his seed and how to thin the seedlings when they sprang up, and how to watch for the worms and insects that were eager and ready always to devour each seedling as it came.

And Yuan had his turn in teaching, too, for when such pests came he read and learned of foreign poisons that would kill them and he used these poisons. The first time he did this the farmer laughed at him and cried out, 'Remember how you watched me, after all, and how your books have not come true nor showed you how deep to lay your beans or when to hoe them free of weeds!'

But when he saw worms shrivel up and die upon the bean plants under the poison then he grew grave and wondering and said in a somewhat lower tone, 'I swear I would not have believed it. So it is not a thing willed by gods, these pests. It is something man can do away with. Something there is in books, after all—yes, more than a little even, I can say, because planting and sowing are of no use if worms devour the plants.'

Then he begged some poison for his own land, and Yuan gave it gladly, and in such giving these two became friends after a fashion, and Yuan's plot was best of all, and for this he thanked the farmer, and the farmer thanked Yuan that his beans throve and were not eaten as his neighbour's fields were.

It was well for Yuan to have this friend and to have this bit of land to work upon, for often in the spring-time as he bent himself upon the earth, some content rose up in him which he had never known.

from : Pearl Buck, *A House Divided*

27 The illiterate

West Africa

He arrived at seven-thirty, bright-eyed and cheerful and genuinely surprised at my cold greeting. I told him he was one and a half hours late and asked if he did not realise it. Didn't he notice the time? His reply was simple and completely disarming; he could not read, nor write, nor tell time.

So simple a thing, but it shocked me. I have encountered illiteracy in many ways and thought that none of its forms would surprise me. But I have never linked it with so everyday a thing as reading the face of a clock. It really shook me. Then when we were rolling smoothly along the highway out of Monrovia, I had a sudden thought, and asked him how fast we were travelling. The speedometer showed sixty miles per hour. He looked at it and merely said, 'Not fast'.

The sweep of the needle across the dial told him whether his speed was fast or slow; the numbers were meaningless.

from : E. R. Braithwaite, A Kind of Homecoming

28 Literacy brings new hope to peasants

Asia, nineteen-fifties

The surprising thing that happened was that two strangers had come from the city to drink tea with the farmers and road makers; they were squatting with the workers and talking surprising talk. They must be village men although they came from the city, for they talked farmers' talk and knew the ways of the land. But they talked other talk as well.

They said there was no reason why every man and woman in the countryside should not read and write. After loud laughter had greeted them they said it again. Reading and writing was no such trick as the scholars made out, they said. Ha! when one saw what fools could learn to read, why should it be thought such an impossible achievement? Indeed, it was really quite easy. An hour or two in the evenings of the winter season—and then a man could teach someone else. In fact they promised that in one week a man could learn to sign his name instead of his thumbmark, and in a few weeks he could pick up his newspaper and read what people outside the village were doing and saying.

But more—and by that time there was not a sound among the listeners—they said that a man who learned the twenty pages of the Primer could also read another little book which told new secrets of better ways to farm; of making old land take on the strength of its youth. Moreover, another twenty pages and he could learn how to keep himself well and how to keep his family from sickness. Here they showed two thin books, bright with pictures, and the pages covered with plain, big words. One page taught how dirt and manure getting into an open wound—say, into the bleeding chilblains of winter—could make a child sick, and perhaps lame, and even cause him to die. This they said about chilblains! Then they said that anyone who could read could also learn to figure. And right here Old Man Peasant pressed closer. He sucked in his breath when they told him of an old man who had learned enough to read to examine the money-lender's account against him and see just how much more he must pay to be free from his debt. Old Man Peasant had often felt a suspicion that for all his desperate trying, his debt was not getting smaller as fast as it should.

And, to crown all, the two men—one short and thin, one tall and booming—said they intended to teach the very farmers sitting there in the bazaar. That was their business, they said, to teach ordinary people to read and write. And one week hence they would return to begin.

No one believed them of course. It was some kind of trick, some kind of play. They were madmen who liked to put their dreams into words. Nevertheless, for the next six nights Old Man Peasant and his friends talked only of this thing which they had heard. If a man *could* learn to read what was good for the land, and how to keep his children well, and know what the moneylender wrote against him in the book! For these six days Old Man Peasant had no trouble to rise up of a morning. On the seventh night he was there at the bazaar shop when the two men—the tall booming one and the short thin one with the slow way of speaking—came striding in, one carrying a blackboard and the other a bundle of reed pens, inkpots, papers, and Primers.

from : Donald K. Faris, *To Plough with Hope*

29 You'll have to get off the land

South Dakota, U.S.A., nineteen-thirties

The owner men sat in the cars and explained. You know the land is poor. You've scrabbled at it long enough, God knows.

The squatting tenant men nodded and wondered and drew figures in the dust, and yes, they knew, God knows. If the dust only wouldn't fly. If the top would only stay on the soil, it might not be so bad. The owner men went on leading to their point : you know the land's getting poorer. You know what cotton does to the land : robs it, sucks all the blood out of it.

The squatters nodded—they knew, God knew. If they could only rotate the crops they might pump blood back into the land. Well it's too late. And the owner men explained the workings and the thinkings of the monster that was stronger than they were. A man can hold land if he can just eat and pay taxes; he can do that. Yes he can do that until his crops fail one day and he has to borrow money from the bank.

But—you see, a bank or company can't do that, because those

creatures don't breathe air, don't eat side-meat. They breathe profits; they eat the interest on money. If they don't get it, they die the way you die without air, without side-meat. It is a sad thing, but it is so. It is just so.

The squatting men raised their eyes to understand. Can't we just hang on? Maybe the next year will be a good year. God knows how much cotton next year. And with all the wars—God knows what price cotton will bring. Don't they make explosives out of cotton and uniforms? Get enough wars and cotton'll hit the ceiling. Next year, maybe. They looked up questioningly.

We can't depend on it. The bank—the monster has to have profits all the time. It can't wait. It'll die. No, taxes go on. When the monster stops growing, it dies. It can't stay one size.

Soft fingers began to tap the sill of the car window, and hard fingers tightened on the restless drawing sticks. In the doorways of the sun-beaten tenant houses women sighed and then shifted feet so that the one that had been down was now on top, and the toes working . . .

The squatting men looked down again. What do you want us to do? We can't take less of the crop—we're half starved now. The kids are hungry all the time. We got no clothes, torn an' ragged. If all the neighbours weren't the same we'd be ashamed to go to meeting.

And at last the owner men came to the point. The tenant system won't work any more. One man on a tractor can take the place of twelve or fourteen families. Pay him a wage and take all the crop. We have to do it. We don't like to do it. But the monster's sick. Something's happened to the monster.

But you'll kill the land with cotton.

We know. We've got to take cotton quick before the land dies. Then we'll sell the land. Lots of families in the East would like to own a piece of land.

The tenant men looked up alarmed. But what'll happen to us? How'll we eat?

You'll have to get off the land. The ploughs'll go through the door yard.

And now the squatting men stood up angrily. Grampa took up the land, and he had to kill the Indians and drive them away. And Pa was born here, and he killed weeds and snakes. Then a bad year came and he had to borrow a little money. An' we was born here. There in the door—our children born here. And Pa had to borrow money. The bank owned the land then, but we stayed and we got a little bit of what we raised.

We know that—all that. It's not us, it's the bank. A bank isn't

173

like a man. Or an owner with fifty thousand acres, he isn't like a man either. That's the monster.

Sure, cried the tenant men, but it's our land. We measured it and broke it up. We were born on it, and we got killed on it, died on it. Even if it's no good it's still ours. That's what makes it ours—being born on it, working on it, dying on it. That makes ownership, not a paper with numbers on it.

We're sorry. It's not us. It's the monster. The bank isn't like a man.

Yes, but the bank is only made of men.

No you're wrong there—quite wrong there. The bank is something more than men. I tell you. It's the monster. Men made it but they can't control it.

The tenant's cried : Grampa killed Indians. Pa killed snakes for the land. Maybe we can kill banks—they're worse than Indians and snakes. Maybe we got to fight to keep our land, like Pa and Grampa did.

And now the owner men grew angry. You'll have to go.

But it's ours, the tenant men cried. We—

No. The bank, the monster owns it. You'll have to go.

We'll get our guns, like Grampa when the Indians came. What then?

Well—first the sheriff, and then the troops. You'll be stealing if you try to stay, you'll be murderers if you kill to stay. The monster isn't men, but it can make men do what it wants.

But if we go, where'll we go? How'll we go? We got no money.

We're sorry, said the owner men. The bank, the fifty-thousand acre owner can't be responsible. You're on land that isn't yours . . .

Where'll we go? the women asked.

We don't know. We don't know.

And the women went quickly, quietly back into the houses and herded the children ahead of them. They knew that a man so hurt and perplexed may turn in anger, even on people he loves. They left the men alone to figure and to wonder in the dust.

from : John Steinbeck, *The Grapes of Wrath*

30 The Aswan High Dam and enforced migration

Egypt, 1964

Sometimes we made the effort to go down to the river in the late afternoons, when the worst of the heat was over, to try and breathe, which always seemed easier away from the heat-reflecting wall of rock behind the village. We would meet the women coming up from the river with the cans of water on their heads, and they would stop and talk. One old woman liked to sing a little song about Kom Ombo, how they were all going to Kom Ombo, where everything was green and the water coming out of taps—I remembered this later, when I saw Kom Ombo. The women were more reconciled to the move than the men; some seemed even to look forward to it. They felt, perhaps, that they had nothing to lose. Every evening the government broadcast to them telling them about the advantages of life in the new Nubia, urging them not to worry or be afraid, telling them evacuation dates and plans, and about the compensation that would be made, and there would always be a rather 'jolly' song about Nubia, calculated to hearten . . .

From a distance Nubian villages look like mediaeval fortresses— like the villages of the North West Frontier—with their long lines of high walls and projecting rafters.

This village [Wadi-es-Sebua] is like a place in a volcano crater, the sand strewn with black stones, and with strange rocks like lumps of lava. Tracks worn by human feet go off in all directions through the dust and sand and rocks and boulders and excrement.

Many of the houses look like the houses young children fashion out of plasticine, with uneven castellations, and at the top of the wall at each side of the gate a kind of chimney pot, all very cockeyed and childish, like the very primitive drawings in white and blue wash which decorate the houses. Behind the walls all is squalor—donkeys chewing dried stalks in a corner, a few turkeys and very small scrawny chickens with rumps bare of feathers chasing about in the dust, and in one corner, perhaps, a water-jar, and the shallow pan of a bath, and opening off, dark high rooms with bedsteads piled with rugs . . .

The first village to be evacuated would be Daboud, the nearest village to Aswan, and its equivalent of that name had already been completed here and we could visit it . . . Pumping stations were being installed to raise the Nile fourteen to fifteen metres. Ten thousand acres of land had been reclaimed and were ready for cultivation. Families would be allotted an acre each to begin with and given more later. Factories were being built, to be ready in two or three years; they would process milk, sugar and vegetables. By offering opportunities for employment in this way it was hoped that the boys would remain in the villages when their education was finished and not leave home for Aswan and Cairo; it was also hoped to attract the husbands back to their villages, so that a proper home life would be maintained, not as at present with the villages populated only by the women and old men and young boys . . .

Six months later I was to see the heartening beginnings of adaptation to the new surroundings, when I visited the village of Maharraka, where the people were busily whitewashing and decorating their new houses in the old Nubian manner, and women were gossiping together as they drew their clear piped water from the village taps. The children were all in school—I visited some of the classes—and there were a few animals about, donkeys and goats. At present the people must buy forage for their animals, which is a source of grievance to them. The information official from Aswan who showed me round was himself Nubian, and his mother and married brother were living there. He said, 'When the land is allotted they will be content'. In the meantime the women and girls work at the arts and crafts centres and produce some very attractive necklaces and other kinds of beadwork.

For the older people the emigration has undoubtedly been tragedy; some of them wept and begged to be allowed to die where they and generations of their families had been born, and where the family graves are, 'and the river we swam in as children,' said my Nubian guide, adding, 'all our memories are there.' But the emigration was inevitable; people cannot be left to drown, and for the younger generation the new Nubia of Kom Ombo does represent new life and hope—a better life, in line with modern ideas of education, hygiene, and good living. There could be nothing for the boys in the old Nubia but to grow up as their fathers and grandfathers had, to go eventually to Aswan, Alexandria, Cairo, to become hotel waiters, or doormen at apartment houses and for the girls nothing but a repetition of the hard life of their mothers and grandmothers, tending the beasts and cultivating the land for the one crop a year before the Nile flood rose and all was inundated, and to have husbands who would be with them for only a few weeks in the year, so that there could be no real family life any more than any real village community life.

from : Ethel Mannin, *Aspects of Egypt*

31 Flooding of the Gwembe Valley: they don't understand

Northern Rhodesia (now Zambia), nineteen-fifties

The news was received with the deepest gloom and anger. Nobody even suggested that the disaster might be prevented. Although it was a human decision to build the dam, it seemed more like a cataclysm of nature, an Act of God. At first, like [District Commissioner] d'Avray, the chiefs saw so many difficulties that they could not concentrate their minds on any of them, and the discussion drifted aimlessly. They asked the same practical questions that he had asked himself : where could the people go, and who would move them, and how could they live without their winter gardens? But intangible problems weighed more with them than any European, however sympathetic, could have expected to foresee. Would the souls of the dead allow the tribe to move? And what would happen to the shrines and holy places? These questions were to assume more and more importance as time went on, because the practical problems could be solved, more or less, by the District Commissioner, but the spiritual problems could only be solved, if at all, by the Tonga.

The argument went on and on all day. Beneath it there was fear at that meeting of an unknown future in an unknown place, and there was a feeling of deep unhappiness which could hardly be expressed in words at all. Whatever happened, it was clear even then that the tribe would be split in two. To the people in cities who had decreed the dam, the Zambesi was a frontier. The people on one side belonged to Southern Rhodesia [Rhodesia] and those on the other side to Northern Rhodesia [Zambia]. But to the Tonga, it had never been a frontier at all. They often crossed it, to borrow food or cut poles to build their huts, or to court new brides, or just to go to parties or call on relations. Many families lived half on one side and half on the other. But now it seemed that each government intended to drag its people back from the river, away into the hills, so that friends on the opposite bank would disappear and never be seen again.

And another source of unhappiness, equally deep but more difficult to define, was the thought that the river would be destroyed . . . All the Tonga villages were ramshackle places. The huts were easily built, and soon fell down again. For most of the year it was more comfortable to cook and eat and even sleep in the open air, and huts were only a necessity in the heavy rains and the comparatively chilly nights of winter. So it was quite a common event, when the land in the neighbourhood of a village was worked out, or the village became too dirty and insanitary, for bits of it to be abandoned and rebuilt somewhere else to form several little villages. But Chisamu like other villages on the river bank, was a more permanent habitation because its people owned some of the valuable permanent gardens on the flood plain which never lost fertility . . .

Home life in the village was extremely simple. Life is always simple for people who have no kind of artificial light, so that there is nothing they can do when the sun has set, except dance by the light of fires, or go to bed, or simply sit and gossip. Among the Tonga there was not even much of the ceremonial which diversifies the life of tribes who are more advanced . . .

The people of Chisamu, like all the Tonga, had always existed on the edge of disaster: the disaster of a failure of the rains. They lived entirely on corn porridge, flavoured by vegetables and fruit, and sometimes by meat or fish which they boiled till it was reduced to a kind of paste; and in any year when the rain was sparse and the river failed to overflow its banks, they starved. They had plenty of sheep and goats and some cattle, but they did not eat them; the sheep and goats were a kind of currency, used in paying for brides and settling other bargains, and the cattle were used for ploughing. There was a case of a woman who successfully sued for divorce on the ground that her husband was insane, because in time of famine he had killed his ox and begun to eat it. During the last few decades the government had never wittingly allowed any Tonga to starve to death . . .

The Tonga believed that when a person died, his soul should be inherited by somebody living. The inheritor of the soul was chosen by a family council during the funeral, and he also inherited some of the dead person's rights. If it was a man's soul, he might inherit the man's wives, and become responsible for his children; and if the man had daughters, the inheritor might claim a share of the price which was paid for them by their husbands when they married . . . This firm belief in souls, like other religions in other forms of society, tended to preserve and stabilise the Tonga community; and it had a specially conservative influence, because souls were usually found to want things done in the way they were done in their own lifetime, one or two generations back, and to resent any new ideas.

Behind this belief, the Tonga had a vague conception of a supreme God. But this God had little influence on their daily lives . . . The government census of Chisamu village showed 233 people; but hundreds of other souls lived in the village, and any Tonga would have known that their wishes and opinions were important. The souls of dead Tonga, no less than the living Tonga had to be persuaded to accept the Kariba Dam . . .

Everyone felt he might lose his own possessions and his own authority. The headman could not be certain whether he would still be headman, or whether the village, in some foreign land, would be split in pieces or merged with other villages; he foresaw that if he helped the government in the move and something went wrong, the people might turn against him. Men who had sweated to clear a patch of forest, and so been able to claim it for their own, saw all their labour wasted. Others who had inherited a winter garden by the river and hoed it and planted it every year since they were children could hardly bear to think of leaving it. Men who had built up a herd of goats by breeding and careful bargaining imagined them straying and dying on unfamiliar pastures. The Tonga had few possessions, but they valued them as high as rich men value fortunes; a score of goats, an acre of land, could represent the fulfilment of a life's ambitions.

Nobody in the government wanted to make the move more difficult or upsetting than it had to be, and so the search for new lands had been concentrated on distant, unexplored and uninhabited corners of the valley which would always remain above the flood line ...

The refusal to face the problem at all was part of the Tonga's easy-going lassitude. Everyone who had worked with them in the past had noticed how little physical energy they possessed. Now, for almost the first time they were being asked to make a mental effort, and it seemed to be beyond them. Alex [the district-officer for Chisamu] began to suspect that the climate was not the only reason for their laziness. It seemed to him that every single one of them was ill.

In this, he was not far wrong. he medical treatment the Tonga had received in the past from Europeans was negligible, and they were still living in the state of chronic illness which was general in Africa before Europeans came. But the impending move was bringing them one benefit. The government saw a risk that an epidemic of smallpox might follow the move, and so doctors were being sent through the valley, with portable aluminium dispensaries, to examine and treat and vaccinate every human being in it.

These doctors were already at work in some parts of the valley, and were shocked at what they found. The Tonga had a naturally good physique, but lack of treatment, and the climate, and their own insanitary habits, had made their health appalling. Almost all of them, it was found, had malaria and enteritis. The latter disease was spread by their custom of relieving themselves by the side of streams from which they drank. Like most other people, they disliked being watched while they did it, and in winter when the grass had died down, there was nowhere else but the beds of streams where they could hide. Most of them also had bilharzia—an internal parasite carried by water snails—leprosy, hookworm, yaws or goitre, or a combination of those diseases. Eye diseases and blindness were common. Nobody ever collected exact statistics of infant mortality, but it was certainly dreadfully high. One of the doctors who worked among them confirmed Alex's own impression when he said that a Tonga who actually had a day's good health would wonder what was wrong; and he was speaking half in jest when he said it. The Tonga, in fact, were living in a vicious circle. Malaria and mal-nutrition sapped their energy, and with less energy they grew less food, went hungry, and became even more susceptible to diseases. The most surprising thing was that they seemed so cheerful, and the only explanation of their cheerfulness was that such terrible condi-tions seemed to them the normal lot of man.

During 1957 and 1958, a scientific attack was begun on the Tonga's diseases . . .

The government had decided to invest two million pounds in removing the trees of two million acres of the Gwembe valley, before the flood began. The work was put out to contract and the con-tractors devised the quickest and most efficient methods of doing it.

The speed they achieved in sheer ruin and devastation shocked even the Europeans who happened to see it. The largest caterpillar tractors ever made were shackled together in pairs with lengths of battleship anchor chain, and driven roaring through the forest on parallel course, towing the chain in a loop behind them. The trees which were caught in the bight of the chain were dragged out of the ground, and anything else in the way was destroyed. The width of the swathe they cut, and the speed at which they drove depended on the density of the forest. In an average area, one pair of tractors could wreck thirty acres of forest in an hour. Groves of trees which had been landmarks to people who lived near by for as long as the oldest could remember disappeared in a matter of seconds. Behind the tractors, bulldozers pushed the wreckage into rows, and it was burned. The columns of smoke drifted over the valley, and ashes settled quickly, and at night the melancholy bonfires could be seen . . .

The payment of compensation, small though it was, has pitched the Tonga headlong into the use of money for buying and selling, instead of the use of goats. Several hundred thousand pounds were shared among them. They had to save most of it to buy grain until the new land was bearing, but some was left over. Where there is money, traders follow, and shops have sprung up to tempt them. The young women have met Europeans and people of other tribes, and realised that their nakedness was unusual, and bought them-selves cotton frocks and head squares and sandals; and look charming in them. And having discovered the delights of shopping, they have thought of new ways of making pocket money . . . The change to money will certainly upset the whole of the Tonga's social system. It may slowly put an end to polygamy. In the old days, the more wives a man could acquire, by making the customary payments to their fathers, the richer he eventually became, because his wives worked for him and their needs were humble. But when a man's wives need frocks and shoes, and other things which they see in shop windows, they become a financial liability instead of an investment...

from : David Howarth, *The Shadow of the Dam*

32 They just don't fit into the twentieth century

Australia

The aborigines don't live in caves, but in junked cars on the desert. Some work with crowbars, noodling for opal in the rubble the white miners have rejected. Most don't work. They sit or lie under the cars or in the narrow shade of the two stores. Most of the women are available to the miners on reasonable terms. The relationship is often semi-permanent, but only a few whites allow themselves to be seen with their aboriginal women by day. Most of the aborigines are drunk some of the time and some are drunk all the time.

Barney Lennon had an aboriginal mother and an Irish father. His face is strikingly handsome, his bearing dignified and sad. He is a gentleman and a gentle man. He sat on the ground among the women and children and grandchildren and babies and dogs of his family, in the burning shade of late afternoon, outside his battered caravan—the only aborigine in Cooper Pedy with even that much of a home. On the wall of the caravan hung a reproduction of a landscape by the aboriginal artist, Albert Namatjira.

'I don't know what's happened,' Barney said. 'There used to be a barrier between the whites and us. Now we're supposed to be equal, but it hasn't made anything any better... This was our land. The white man took it. No, he didn't give us anything for it. It was hard in the desert in the old days, but now they don't want us to live there. They say we'll die in the droughts. Is this any better?'

He looked past me at the wheelless Ford a quarter of a mile away, its seats on the ground, all the stuffing gone from them, and five aborigines sprawled there in the long shadows. Other cars dotted the waste. On an impulse I asked Barney Lennon if he, too, painted. He did. He showed me his water colours. They were obviously imitations of Namatjira's oils, without the power. But Namatjira had escaped—first, to fame; then, through alcohol, all the way. He is dead. Barney Lennon would never get away by either of these routes. Dust trails raced across the waste as the white miners drove out of town to their mines, each to his own, to work.

from : John Masters, 'Gold, camels and wise men, frankincense and myrrh', *The Daily Telegraph Magazine*, September 29, 1967

33 Migrant workers

U.S.A., nineteen-sixties

Daybreak in Cottonwood Row (Dingetown, you're likelier to hear it called), the Negro ghetto of Bakersfield, California, and the clumpy shadows of hundreds of waiting men—Negroes, Mexican, a few white—dissolve as they hasten to the farmers' buses pulling up : pay rates stated, no argument, and they bear off their day-haul gangs for picking the plums, nectarines and peaches, for cutting cotton field weeds, thinning grapes and topping sugar beets. But many are left behind, no work that day, so most probably no food.

... In almost every state in the Union except perhaps Nevada and Montana in these late summer weeks the migrant pickers are out, working usually from 'can't to can't'—from when you can't see the sun in the morning until you can't see it any more at night, getting money that forbids an adequate existence, living in shelters that stink and crawl.

At any given daylight moment in the fruitful seasons there are perhaps two million bent backs in the fields of the Great Society, an African servitude in the meadows of plenty.

Statistics differ uncertainly in these shifting sands for the population of this America is never permanently still enough for a head count—between crops, shaking along the roads in those rattletrap trucks—but there appears to be no official disagreement about that two million. They are a petrol-driven peasantry living in a sort of revolving slum which never more than brushes the suburbs and towns of affluent America. They are destitute and sunk in a way that the old harvest force of ornery individuals never was, in a way that the surviving hobo with his prickly, even pathological, pride in his own volition is not. The hobo has always hung on to the conviction that the next train ride may have a special significance; even the Okies had an objective, that dream California. These migrants cannot raise their eyes above the next row of beans.

There are in present-day America six major streams of seasonal migrants in constant monkey-on-a-stick movement. All have Southern sources and they flow Northward and ebb back when the crops are in.

There is the one originating in Florida, mostly Negroes, which climbs the Atlantic Seaboard, through the Old South into Delaware, New Jersey, New York and Pennsylvania, engaging in a great variety of harvests. There is one of Mexican-Americans which goes from Texas up into the North Central and Mountain States, most of the way on sugar beet but also picking vegetables and fruits. There is another wholly Mexican-American stream which leaves Texas and passes through Montana and North Dakota on wheat and small-grain harvests. There is a third from Texas, Spanish-American and Negroes, which splits—one working the cotton crops Westward to New Mexico, Arizona and Southern California, the other making for the Mississippi Delta. There is one, mainly whites of early American stock, which goes from Oklahoma, Arkansas and Western Tennessee, and fans North and West on fruit and tomatoes. There is the sixth, composed of migrants of mixed races, which shuttles up and down the Pacific Coast, harvesting and processing fruits and vegetables.

They go in families, even in communities, in single cars in motor-cades, in buses and trucks led by middlemen crew organizers who contract with farmers to deliver the manpower, and the woman and child power, and collect the better part of the financial reward. The migrants move because they have no other way of earning any money.

Since 1940 two and a half million farms have gone, simply wiped off the agricultural map of America by being either wrung dry and returning to scrub or being cannibalised by agribusiness units. The expropriated tenants, sharecroppers and small owners have been sucked into the migrant streams.

... It is a beastly, disproportionate way of staying alive, for there are seldom the means, once in the migrant stream, of avoiding fourteen-hour days when employed and desperate scourings of the country when not employed, of seeing your children inexorably drawn into the same bondage of poverty, of having no comforts or background or local attachment, of having no future expectations, of being shackled to an inhuman level of labor whose wage status is actually declining. In the 1910-14 period the farm laborer's average hourly wage was sixty-seven per cent of the average factory hand's; by 1945 it had dropped to forty-seven per cent; by 1963 it was down to thirty-six per cent.

'A hundred years ago we owned slaves,' a Congressman from a South-Western state said of the contract labor system. 'Today we just rent them.'

... 'If you ask the children what they want to be when they grow

183

up they say they want to be bean pickers. Why? They just don't know. That's all they know, picking beans and chopping cotton.

'They're not dumb. They're just behind, because their parents aren't interested in them having an education. They need to take them travelling, to earn money in the fields. If you take the kids to see the rodeo they crawl around on the floor looking for money people have dropped.

'They're loud and noisy, but they don't know how to play organized games. Most of them never did finish high school and never knew anything about sport. The teenagers go out in the fields and just hang around ... but these kids won't go out and mix with the town children. Probably it's because they feel odd man out.'

from : Kenneth Allsop, *Hard Travellin'* — *The Hobo and his History*

34 The refugees: a world-wide problem

China, nineteen-twenties

There were already other huts clinging to the wall behind them, but what was inside the wall none knew and there was no way of knowing. It stretched out long and grey and very high, and against the base the small mat sheds clung like fleas to a dog's back. Wang Lung observed the huts and he began to shape his own mats this way and that, but they were stiff and clumsy things at best, being made of split reeds, and he despaired, when suddenly O-lan said :

'That I can do. I remember it in my childhood.'

And she placed the girl upon the ground and pulled the mats thus and thus, and shaped a rounded roof reaching to the ground and high enough for a man to sit under and not strike the top, and upon the edges of the mats that were upon the ground she placed bricks that were lying about and she set the boys to picking up more bricks. When it was finished they went within and with one mat she had contrived not to use they made a floor and sat down and were sheltered.

Sitting thus and looking at each other, it seemed less than possible that the day before they had left their own house and their land and that these were now a hundred miles away. It was a distance vast enough to have taken them weeks of walking and at which they must have died, some of them, before it was done.

Then the general feeling of plenty in this rich land, where no one seemed even hungered, filled them, and when Wang Lung said, 'Let us go and seek the public kitchens,' they rose up almost cheerfully and went out once more, and this time the small boys clattered their chopsticks against their bowls as they walked, for there would soon be something to put into them. And they found soon why the huts were built to that long wall, for a short distance beyond the northern end of it was a street and along the street many people walked carrying bowls and buckets and vessels of tin, all empty, and these persons were going to the kitchens for the poor, which were at the end of the street and not far away. And so Wang Lung and his family mingled with these others and with them they came at last to two great buildings made of mats, and every one crowded into the open end of these buildings.

Now in the rear of each building were earthen stoves, but larger than Wang Lung had ever seen, and on them iron cauldrons as big as small ponds; and when the great wooden lids were prised up, there was the good white rice bubbling and boiling, and clouds of fragrant steam rose up. Now when the people smelled this fragrance of rice it was the sweetest in the world to their nostrils, and they all pressed forward in a great mass and people called out and mothers shouted in anger and fear lest their children be trodden upon and little babies cried, and the men who opened the cauldron roared forth :

'Now there is enough for every man and each in his turn !'

But nothing could stop the mass of hungry men and women and they fought like beasts until all were fed. Wang Lung, caught in their midst, could do nothing but cling to his father and his two sons and when he was swept to the great cauldron he held out his bowl and when it was filled threw down his pence, and it was all he could do to stand sturdily and not be swept before the thing was done.

Then when they had come to the street again and stood eating their rice, he ate and was filled and there was a little left in his bowl and he said :

'I will take this home to eat in the evening'.

But a man stood near who was some sort of a guard of the place for he wore a special garment of blue and red, and he said sharply :

'No, and you can take nothing away except what is in your belly' and Wang Lung marvelled and said :

'Well, if I have paid my penny what business is it of yours if I carry it within or without me?'

The man said then :

'We must have this rule, for there are those whose hearts are so hard that they would come and buy this rice that is given for the poor—for a penny will not feed any man like this—and they will carry the rice home to feed their pigs for slops. And the rice is for the men and not for pigs.'

185

Wang Lung listened to this in astonishment and he cried :
'Are there men as hard as this!' and then he said, 'But why should
any give like this to the poor and who is it that gives?'
The man answered then :
'It is the rich and the gentry of the town who do it, and some do
it for a good deed for the future, that by saving lives they may get
merit in heaven, and some do it for righteousness that men may
speak well of them.'
'Nevertheless it is a good deed for whatever reason,' said Wang
Lung, 'and some must do it out of a good heart,' and then seeing
that the man did not answer him, he added in his own defence, 'at
least there are a few of these?'
But the man was weary of speaking with him and he turned his
back, and he hummed an idle tune. The children tugged at Wang
Lung then and Wang Lung led them all back to the hut they had
made and there they laid themselves down and they slept till the
next morning, for it was the first time since summer they had been
filled with food, and sleep overcame them with fullness.

from : Pearl Buck, *The Good Earth*

35 Under stress in the cities: Pakistani immigrants

England, 1964

Most come by air in rather sad, depressed, bewildered huddles of
males, understanding not a word of the language, totally ignorant of
what this sunless, noisy, crowded world will offer them, heavily in
debt for their passages and passports, which are sometimes forged
and nearly always bribed for, and terribly homesick for the families
they've left behind.
A roof, a job. The first is not too difficult because plenty of Pakistanis are here already—the High Commissioner's estimate is one
lakh, or 100,000. Newcomers go straight to a kinsman or a fellow-
villager ...
No unskilled Pakistani worker—and nine out of ten are said to be
unskilled—can bring his wife. For one thing he can't possibly afford
it; he's sold and pledged and mortgaged everything he's got to come
himself; the whole object of the exercise is to make enough to pay
back expenses, send money to his family and buy a plot of land at
home and build a house. Since Muslim customs rigidly preclude his

wife's going out to work, she's bound to be an economic liability, not an asset as Jamaican wives are. Added to that, any Pakistani who does import his family must provide a much higher standard of accommodation than a West Indian needs to. He must have a separate kitchen and lavatory and at least two bedrooms, one for the couple, one for the children, and a third when the sexes separate at six or so. So wives and families are strictly for the rich—a status symbol. A few make do with English wives, not nearly so expensive, as they are prepared to work and, not being Muslims, permitted to do so; but, while often personally respected, as a class they are looked upon by the community, according to the sociologist Mr. Hamza Alavi, as 'a betrayal of the family in Pakistan'.

... Often a 'boss-man' or 'big uncle' collects everyone's rents, conducts any dealings that may be needed with authority, and exercises a rather nebulous control over his fellow-lodgers. He may be the senior elder of a family, or a man of some position in a distant village. As he is often elderly and non-English speaking, from an English point of view he is seldom the best intermediary, but that can't be helped.

How to fill their leisure time is the lodgers' major problem. There's nowhere to go and nothing to do. At weekends, those who are literate write long letters home for their illiterate fellows, as well as for themselves. They play cards. Now and again there's an Indian or Pakistani film. A few of the younger men play football and that's about all. They don't dance. The pub is out—not only for religious reasons, but because the driving force behind these uprooted men is all to save, save, save. A few fall from grace; there's even a Pakistani in Leeds who keeps a pub; but most of these are men who came before the rush, as seamen, and settled here.

Internally, the Pakistani community is deeply riven, both geographically, between east and west, and socially, between a thin top crust of highly educated, and the peasant mass. No one could be more sophisticated, intelligent, articulate and civilised than the educated Pakistani diplomats and doctors, professors and barristers— a small world but a choice one, adorned by graceful, charming wives.

from : Elspeth Huxley, *Back Street, New Worlds*

36 People under social stress

Jamaica, 1969

There are two Jamaicas. The only thing they share is a cost of living twenty per cent higher than Britain's. There is surface Jamaica : the tourists, the expatriates and a multi-racial ruling class which demonstrates the national motto 'out of many, one people . . .'

The other Jamaica is black, ill-educated and poor . . . Adult illiteracy is forty per cent, and education a disaster. Between 60,000 and 100,000 children are not enrolled in schools . . . Of those who enrol, a third are absent daily; of those who attend, half are in classes of 50 plus, one in five of 90 plus. Almost half of the primary teachers are untrained . . .

Jamaica's tragedy is less its poverty than the stereotype that denies and wastes its agricultural and human wealth : 'Jamaica can't make it' seems to be a national slogan. With land that can grow almost anything, it imports £20 million of food a year, including jam made from its own sugar in Britain; with a tradition of craftsmen joiners, many now working in High Wycombe, it lets hotels import furniture tax free . . . And the children drift from the land that can't support them to the towns, to become waiters or beachboys—ill paid and self-hating servants of a tourist industry that is mainly foreign owned and seems determined to turn a tourist paradise into a parody of Miami Beach.

from : Colin McGlashan, 'The two Jamaicas', *The Observer*, November 23, 1969

37 Economic pressure: the rat race

El Salvador, 1968

Because of the intense pressure of population on the land, more and more Salvadoreños have turned to manufacturing and commerce, and in this trend they have been actively encouraged by a government which gives special tax concessions to small businesses. As a matter of fact, this encouragement is scarcely necessary, for the Salvadoreños are among the hardest-working, shrewdest, and most financially adventurous people in the world. A Salvadorean entrepreneur thinks nothing of launching himself into business on a capital of one hundred pounds, and very often he has at least one other business on the side and his wife working too. Small wonder that San Salvador is one of the few cities in the world where you can buy an air ticket from an agency for less than the airline will sell it to you. The ticket agent is splitting his commission with the customer in order to get the business.

The storm centre of this frenetic buying and selling is the capital, San Salvador, which contains almost a fifth of the country's population. It is a roaring city with an acute case of schizophrenia. At one end is a run-down, rather squalid, area overgrown with garish neon signs and sprinkled with pavement hucksters selling every imaginable gew-gaw and knick-knack from round wicker trays perched on what look to be bar stools. At the other end it is all concrete and wide avenues, luxurious homes and the latest in daring architecture. The former zone is the old commercial centre of the town, now rather decrepit, where stand the curlicued monuments to the country's first stirrings of independence : the modern end of the town by contrast, has the monuments to the new prosperity—the crisp drive-in banks, the expensive restaurants, and the smart boutiques. The very, very rich have fled even farther, up the sides of the nearby volcanoes where they sit in homes that would grace a viceroy, and look through their picture windows at the superb spectacle of lightning playing over the peaks.

But life for the *campesinos*, the 'country ones', is something very different. Here is an existence far closer to the clichés of Central America. El Salvador's countryside is so thickly settled that almost every bush seems to surround the straw cone of a *campesino* hut. And when the evening comes, the roads swarm with files of white-clad peasants, plodding home from the fields, tyre-soled sandals on their feet, empty water gourds slung over their shoulders, and their machetes hanging in betasselled leather scabbards. The *campesino* is the backbone of the country, the solid basis of its life. He lives in comparative poverty (the per capita income for the entire country is less than £100 per annum) and he is utterly dependent upon the big landowners. Yet here too there is change, for a *campesino* who may never have tasted anything better than tortillas and beans now has the chance to break out of the endless grind of peasant life. Many a *campesino* now rides to and from his work on a Japanese bicycle, and in the fields it is not uncommon to see him behind the yoked oxen with a transistor radio so that he can listen to the government programme for literacy. The *campesinos* are vitally interested. They too want to learn how to read and write, and then join in the mad scramble for prosperity characterizing so much of the pace of life and work in their country.

But of course there is a long way to go. And here again the government blue books tell the tale. Adult literacy is probably less than fifty per cent, and the standard of schooling is appallingly low.

Prices are spiralling upward—rice is two shillings and twopence a pound, cheese five shillings, and lard more than three shillings and sixpence.* El Salvador must run faster to keep in the same place.

from : Timothy Severin, 'Pressure in El Salvador,'
The Geographical Magazine, January 1969

* 11p, 25p and 17½p

Notes on Section 4

The bold figures indicate extract numbers

1–8 These extracts are concerned with the heavy unprofitable use of man-power common to the vast majority of people on the earth even now. The porterage system in Africa and other tropical places inevitably drains away essential manpower from the villages, and involves heavy load carrying by people whose state of nutrition and general health may be far from adequate for such work. Some details of the building of the Tanganyikan Railway (Tanzania) provide an example of what porterage actually involved—6000 tons of materials were head-carried by porters in loads of 90 pounds (41 kg) over a distance of 90 miles (145 km) in three days in tropical heat. This heavy work (see extract No. 8) is forced on backward people by economic need. Extract No. 5: Mlanje in Malawi, 16° 2′ S, 35° 38′ E. The author of extract No. 6, Legson Kayira, walked 2500 miles (4000 km) from Malawi to Khartoum where he took a plane to the U..S.A. There he achieved an advanced education before returning to help his people.

9 V. S. Naipaul, an indefatigable and very observant traveller, was born in Trinidad of Indian descent. When visiting India he was able to wander, more or less unnoticed, in places where the white tourist could not have gone without attracting undue attention.

12 A timely reminder of some of the reasons for the apparent lack of self-help among the poor.

13 This extract questions the value of initiating vast schemes to help developing peoples without using available local resources as far as possible. What form should aid take? What are the economic and political reasons behind widespread aid and borrowing?

14 Quotes the words of Mahatma Ghandi who, aware of the special problems of the Indian sub-continent with a vast labour force and explosive population growth, advised the organisation of many hands and the retention of the craftsman, educated and motivated to use his full potential. Ghandi was of course an idealist, and called for self-denial, discipline and goodwill which are difficult to attain. He deplored the caste system which though officially banned does still exist. Some vast building and engineering projects are carried out by long lines of men and women using their bare hands, but many factories and works have been developed to employ some of the cheap labour available and, although 90 per cent of the people still get their living from the land, many of the young men seek work in the towns. Of those who do not make good, some join the pavement sleepers in painful anonymity, others return disillusioned to their villages and a status in society, however humble.

15 In this fertile area approximately 9 million people live on reclaimed, desalinated, dyked land. The government are fighting to maintain and extend the area to provide more land (see Section 8, extract No. 11). One endemic disease, bilharzia, has increased as a result of perennial irrigation.

17 Syphilis is one of the many diseases first carried to primitive peoples by Europeans. Captain Thompson's attitude towards the Kanakas was common at this period.

18 No one fully understood the reason for scurvy at this time (the 1830's). It is now known to be caused by a deficiency of vitamin C and a large intake of salt.

19 Many African hospitals are run on community lines with family cooking and nursing.

20 Miss Basila Renju, the daughter of a cash-crop farmer, was educated in Africa and England. This long extract stresses the value of small, individual improvement schemes and poses several problems common to other parts of the tropical world.

21–22 The meaning of hunger to man and beast is only too familiar in the world today. Millions of peasants suffer from the 'wait-for-the-harvest' hunger. It was one of the problems of emigrants from Europe and a common one in Britain until, as a wealthy country, she was able to buy goods from all over the world.

23 Monoculture and famine were common in Europe at one time, and famines still tend to occur wherever too much dependence is placed on one basic crop.

24 Locust swarms may fly for thousands of miles. In Africa international organisations have been established to provide a constant watch on likely 'outbreak areas' where newly formed swarms can be destroyed before they migrate.

25 The Chinese rarely eat meat protein which they consider wasteful; cereals, sprouted vegetables in great variety, and rape which bears oil, cotton seed, and sunflower seed are more profitable on the land available. The Chinese are obsessed with 'character', according to Lin Yutang, valuing best a mature man who retains an equanimity of mind under all circumstances —the training school for his patience being the large, cramped family and its demands.

26–28 These are illustrations of tradition, prejudice, illiteracy and poverty. The value of example rather than precept is brought out. It has been the custom nearly everywhere for those who escape the dreary round and achieve an education, to gather its fruits for the family in some white- or blue-collared job, rather than to sink back to the level of village teacher or soil their hands by farm work. This attitude is gradually being broken down; the example of the Israelis and others is helping to undermine age-old prejudice and teach self-help. See also Indian farmers, Section 8, extract No. 16.

29 This is fiction, but about a true situation. The tenant farmers on small farms ran into debt owing to the drought and the failure of the cotton crop, on which they depended exclusively to pay mortgages. The owners of big farms bought them out and sought to get a quick crop by large-scale ploughing before the land became completely useless. Thousands of people left for other parts of North America, where in years of depression they competed for jobs at low rates. In less wealthy countries, getting off the land in drought years still swells the refugee problem.

30 The Aswan High Dam benefits millions of people in Egypt, but the Nubians were forced to move as their land was flooded. Kom Ombo is a town on the east bank of the Nile, 40 miles (64 km) below the dam. There are rows of new houses, back to back, built to a design approved by the Nubians. The way of life of these people is changing. In Kom Ombo they have schools and other advantages, but boatmen have had to become farmers. The farmers have more land than before and are being taught more modern methods. The young learn new trades in factories for textiles, sugar and its residues, and dairying. The author saw both the old and the beginning of the new Nubia.

31 Although this is another extract about a people being moved to make way for a dam (the Kariba this time), the problem was quite different. The Tonga were a very primitive people who had to be persuaded to leave because their homes were to be drowned under a lake. They could not understand or visualise how this could come about. The story throughout shows the devotion of the District Officers and District Commissioners, of what was then Northern Rhodesia, to the cause of justice and to the good of a simple people, who had to be moved for the sake of others. After three years of patient negotiation, a pitiful revolt had to be put down and the people were eventually moved.

The move has revolutionised Tongan life. The women, seeing clothes and consumer goods and *money* for the first time, have stimulated the men's move to paid work. Compensation worked out at £10 per head in 1958—a large amount for a people who had never really used money before in their daily lives. At that time the labourers on the dam earned $1\frac{1}{2}$p per hour. The Tonga have been resettled on the valley sides; some of them fish, and others farm. They learn modern agricultural methods, practice co-operative marketing, and have schools and facilities for hospital treatment. Some really bad diseases are being cured, but bilharzia is increasing and two-thirds of the children have it. They are said to have lost their faith and replaced it with no other.

Lower down the Zambesi at Cabora Bassa a still bigger dam and hydro-electric power stations are being built.

32 There are few aborigines left in Australia; many were liquidated in the nineteenth century. They are an unwanted, dispossessed people.

33 The 'Okies' referred to were a preceding generation turned off the land in the 1930's when the Dust Bowl was formed.

35 More people under stress—in England this time. The English do not really fully understand them, nor they the English; they are the enterprising of their race.

36 This shows the waste of human lives in squalor and distress. It explains the large number of Jamaicans trying to find a way out of the impasse by coming to Britain.

37 El Salvador is another schizophrenic area, but with a difference. The fact that the country's only coastline is on the Pacific makes her particularly susceptible to the economic influence of Japan, the chief buyer of her cotton. Population pressure is considerable, with an average density of 165 people per square kilometre.

5

Pioneers and adventurers

This section traces some of the hardy, tenacious ordinary people who travelled into the unknown in the nineteenth and twentieth centuries. Most of them, whether settlers, explorers or exploiters, were poorly equipped by modern standards and their suffering and hardship show a direct relationship to their environmental difficulties. The successful ones poured their vitality into new lands. Often through ignorance or greed they exploited the land and its indigenous peoples. Although most of the extracts deal with people of European stock, it must be remembered that pioneers are thrown up by all people and in all periods of history. Today's pioneers are pressing into the still untamed parts of the earth, cushioned no doubt by technology, better equipped and more knowledgeable. They seek to tame the wilds, to release the earth's potentials. A few taking off into space or under the oceans take the essentials of their earth's environment with them.

The question of ethics is more urgent now than ever before. When, for instance, does pioneering become exploitation—of man, beast, plants, the air, the sea? Some of these questions come up in more detail in Section 6. Other forms of pioneer activities are dealt with according to context in other Sections.

1 On the California trail

U.S.A., 1846

My Dear Cousin,   May the 16, 1847.
   I take this oppertunity to write to you to let you now that we are
all Well at present and hope this letter may find you all well to/My
Dear Cousin I am going to write to you about our trubels geting to
Callifornia . . .
   we come to the big mountain of the Callifornia Mountain/the
snow then was about 3 feet deep/thare was some wagons thare thay
said that had atempted to croos and could not. Well we thought we
would try it/so we started and they started again with those wagons/
the snow was then up to the mules side/the farther we went up the
deeper the snow got/so the wagons could not go/so thay pack thare
oxens and started with us carring a child a piece and driving the
oxens in snow up to thare wast/the mule Martha and the Indian was
on was the best one/so thay went and broak the road and that indian
was the Pilet/so we wint on that way 2 miles and the mules kept
faling down in the snow head formost and the Indian said he could
not find the road/we stoped and let the indian and man go on to
hunt the road/thay went on and found the road to the top of the
mountain and come back and said they thought we could git over if
it did not snow any more/well the Weman were all so tirder caring
there Children that thay could not go over that night/so we made a
fire and got something to eat & ma spred down a bufalo robe & we all
laid down on it & spred somthing over us & ma sit up by the fire &
it snowed one foot on top of the bed/so we got up in the morning
& the snow was so deep we could not go over & we had to go back to
the cabin & build more cabins & stay thar all winter without Pa/we
had not the first thing to eat/Ma maid arrangements for some cattel
giving 2 for 1 in callifornia/we seldom thot of bread for we had not
any since I [remember] & the cattel was so poor thay could not git up
when thay laid down/we stoped thare the 4th of November & staid till
March and what we had to eat i cant hardley tell you & we had that
man & Indians to feed to/well thay started over a foot and had to
come back/so thay made snowshoes and started again & it come on a
storm & thay had to come back/it would snow 10 days before it would
stop/thay wated till it stoped & started again/I was a going with them
& I took sick & could not go/thare was 15 started & thare was 7 got
throw/5 weman & 2 men/it come a storme and that lost the road &
got out of provisions & the ones that got throwe had to eat them that
Died/not long after thay started we got out of provisions & had to
put matha at one cabin James at another Thomas at another & Ma
and Elizia & Milt Eliot & I dried up what little meat we had and

started to see if we could get across & had to leve the childrin/o
Mary you may think that hard to leve theme with strangers & did not
now wether we would see them again or not/we couldn't hardle get
away from them but we told theme we would bring them Bread & then
thay was willing to stay/we went & was out 5 days in the mountains/
Eliza give out & had to go back/we went on a day longer/we had to
lay by a day & make snowshows & we went on a while and coud not
find the road so we had to turn back/I could go on verry well while
I thout we were giting along but as soone as we had to turn back i
coud hadley get along/but we got to the cabins that night & i froze
one of my feet verry bad/that same night thare was the worst storme
we had that winter & if we had not come back that night we would
never got back/we had nothing to eat but ox hides/o Mary I could
cry and wish I had what you all wasted/Eliza had to go to Mr Graves
cabin & we staid at Mr Breen/thay had meat all the time & we had
to kill littel cash the dog & eat him/we ate his entrails and feet &
hide & every thing about him/o my Dear Cousin you dont now what
trubel is yet . . . thare was but [2] familes that all of them [through]
we was one/O Mary I have not rote you half of the truble we have
had but I have rote you anuf to let you now that you dont now what
truble is/but thank god we have all got throw and the onely family
that did not eat human flesh/we have left everything but i dont cair
for that we have got throw with our lives/but Dont let this letter
dishaten anybody/never take no cutofs and hurry along as fast as you
can . . .

VIRGINIA ELIZABETH B. REED

2 Bantu migration over the Zambesi

Africa

The Zambesi River. I had not seen it flying down to South Africa.
I now saw it spanning the land from horizon to horizon and felt how
puny we humans were in our flight over Africa. The great river
seemed to belong, was of a piece in the palette Nature held out below :
the stupefying extent of land and bush, over it limitless skies. It looked
like a gigantic serpent, milk-chocolate in colour as though thickly sweet
if one tasted of it; slow, lazy, sprawling, stretching itself across the
bows of the visible earth. Away in the farthest distance it seemed to
splinter into huge fragments and become dotted with islands, like an
archipelago. I thought of how down home legend has it that this
river was the supreme obstacle in the path of our peoples as they had
migrated south. Those men, according to the praise-poem histories of

197

some clans, had to *Zambesa* themselves on reaching its banks. *Uku-zambesa* is to divest yourself of clothing. They had to doff their togas of ochre-smeared ox-skins, the women their swinging skirts. Looking down I wondered how many white Southern Africans were aware of the persisting significance to some of us even nowadays of the name of the mighty river. I for one was thinking, as fellow passengers on the aircraft read their Rhodesian *Herald,* of those of our forebears who had been unable to swim and did not attempt the crossing; of those who did, and some proving unequal to the task, some were swept away, 'went with the river' or of the strong who swam but some of their number were food for crocodiles; and what of their treasure, the cattle? Such chapters in people's histories were demonstrations of one of Nature's principles, the survival of the fittest. Dimly remembered sagas like these have, I thought, conditioned our belief that : of our migratory peoples who perpetually hived off from parent stocks in search of *lebensraum* for their cattle, only the fittest, most enterprising survived. They persuade us that our forefathers were 'truly men' in the spirit, as we say, and in the realms of imagination. And we say the reason was because their motive was centred on some thing they prized above their own selves, cattle, round which they spun what they knew of poetry and artistic feeling. Had they been lesser men, we say, they would only have pitched up, at some sheltered spot, taken root, settled down and become mere cultivators.

from : Noni Jabavu, *Drawn in Colour—African Contrasts*

3 Pioneer family, 1922

British Columbia, Canada

Cyrus Lord Bryant is one of that visionary, doggedly independent breed of men who have opened up our tougher frontiers. Twelve years earlier, with his wife and four children, he had driven a wagon and six horses nearly a thousand miles from southern Washington into the interior of British Columbia.

They were on the trail for months. It was a tough trip. Winter cracked down on them suddenly and without warning. A harsh blizzard swished down out of the north-east before the little family had reached Alexis Creek. Cyrus' driving hand, his left one, froze almost solid inside of his inadequate leather glove.

It was growing dark when he swung his leaders around a narrow bend high up on the edge of a deep ravine east of Alexis Creek. The rear wheels of the wagon slipped on the icy road. The outfit slewed out so close to the edge of the precipice that one hind wheel dipped for an instant over space.

A gnawing wind stabbed the forty-below-zero* weather into the huddled bodies of Mrs. Bryant and the children. They bunched together around a coal-oil lantern beneath the waggon tarp.

At last, when their limbs were almost past the hurting stage and a sleepy numb feeling was creeping in on them, Bryant hauled the horses to a stop near the log cabins of Alexis Creek. Mrs. Bryant and the children were rushed into a rancher's house for frost treatment, and Cyrus took care of the ice-caked, frost-covered horses. Bryant left the coal-oil lantern burning beneath the waggon to keep their food from freezing.

Inside that oversized waggon box were the family's precious and most priceless possessions : family portraits, oil paintings handed down through the family for generations, Mrs. Bryant's jewelry and music— she was a gifted pianist and singer—Cyrus' pocketbook with a considerable sum of money. Their life savings to be invested in their future ranch and stock were carefully wrapped in oil paper and locked in a little fishing box. There were rare old books, the family's winter clothes, their winter's provisions, tools, saddles and extra harness. All these things added together were to be the start, the foundation of their new home and new way of life.

In the dark fifty-below-zero* dawn of the following day, Cyrus Lord kicked the black hissing ashes of what had once been that waggon box. He rooted out a fifty cent iron wrecking bar, an axe head and a few well-tempered horse-shoes. That was all. The coal-oil lantern had touched off the load.

The Bryant family was in a position that was more than critical. Here—without money—in a strange country, with winter upon them, Cyrus, his wife and his four children pitched blindly into the toughest proposition of their lives. A rancher advanced them grub and what clothing they could get by on. Cyrus cut and hauled logs out of the bush, and in a month's time had built a two-room cabin for the family. Later they moved on to Tatla Lake.

For years every member of the family worked from dawn to dark. In the Chilcotin, Cyrus hired out with his well-broke teams for cash, cows, sheep or vegetables. Mrs. Bryant helped shear the sheep, cleaned, carded and spun wool garments for the family and the neighbors. Thirteen-year old Alfred worked with an axe, a saddle horse and a rifle. The girls became as good as men at riding jobs and axe work.

After nearly four years of ceaseless privation and work, the family had once again outfitted themselves. With two waggons, a dozen cows and eighteen head of horses, they axed their way through the bush to a swamp meadow five miles from Anahim Lake.

* Centigrade

Here, on the banks of a twisting mud creek named Corkscrew, the family threw their combined strength into the building up of a new home and their future ranch. They worked steadily and unrelentingly for two more years. The girls axed down trees, bucked up wood, made new clothes out of moose hide, and patched old ones with gunny sacks and binder twine, moose hide and rabbit fur.

Mrs. Bryant put everything she had into making a home for the family. She had little to cook with—the vegetable garden wouldn't grow in the new and sour land. Alfred eked out their supplies of coffee, spuds and flour by contracting and driving pack trains for his neighbors a hundred miles down a narrow trail through the bush to the tiny fishing village of Bella Coola on the coast, where he picked up their supplies brought in from Vancouver by boat.

By the spring of 1934, the year of our arrival in the country, the Bryants had, through their courage, determination and terrific work, pulled themselves up and out of the almost bottomless hole into which the waggon fire had plunged them twelve years before.

... Cyrus Lord didn't seem to be particularly impressed by the fine job he and his family had made of house building, but as we sipped coffee from large white china mugs, around a big, broad-axed plank table near the stove, he carried on with his rapid-fire, short sentenced eulogy on draining and developing the vast marginal lands of the Anahim country.

I looked about at the structure... The walls of huge peeled jack-pine logs were thirty-eight feet long on one side and about twenty-eight feet wide on the other. Hand-hewn log partitions divided it into three rooms. The building was chinked with little peeled poles and moss. The floor had been made by splitting ten-inch logs through the middle, and hewing the split sides level with a broad-axe. They were laid flush with each other, the flat sides up, and to save nails, Cyrus Lord had pegged them to a row of log stringers, and then polished them with linseed oil. The floor was smooth enough to dance on.

The only evidence that this house was located more than 225 miles from shops and railroad was the complete lack of ornaments, up-holstered furniture, spring beds and heavy equipment. Freighting-in bulky or heavy paraphernalia by pack horse or waggon is a frustrating and discouraging business. It is impossible to average more than fifteen miles a day on a 450 mile round trip. A load of two tons, which is plenty for a four-horse team to lug over the hills, rocks and mud flats of the interior, becomes a mighty valuable poundage, when finally landed at Anahim more than a month after the freighter started out.

from : Richmond P. Hobson, Jnr., *Grass beyond the Mountains*

4 Grey nuns voyage to the Red River

Ontario, Canada, 1844

First let me tell you that the voyage is very laborious, and much more so than I expected. Nevertheless, God will do me the favour of letting me continue to the end. We have not had a good night's sleep, Mother Valade and I, since our departure, but our two younger Sisters are pulling through pretty well. Nearly all the time we have had bad weather, and when the rain stops we have contrary winds which hold us back greatly; when we have to camp, we are as a rule beset by rain and chilled with cold. There is a good fire, it is true, but while one side of us burns, the other freezes. The tent is pitched, an oilcloth spread beneath, and that is the bed. Believe me that is cool, especially when it has rained all day and it rains all night, which often happens. Our canvas house gives little protection and our clothes are wet through. I rarely undress. In spite of everything, I am filled with courage to carry out the sacred will of God, though it may well cost me something. On the rocks where we are camping today the snakes are numerous, the men have killed four of them. Yesterday we ran several quite dangerous rapids. The canoemen uttered cries of delight in clearing these rapids. I too enjoyed it but our sisters were pale with fright... When it comes to climbing rocks, pushing through thickets, crossing ravines on dry and rotten trees, I think twice about it—but there is no turning back.

from : Robert George Barclay, 'Grey nuns voyage to Red River', *The Beaver*, Winter, 1966

5 Prairie journeys

Nebraska, U.S.A.

We were at sea—there is no other adequate expression—on the plains of Nebraska. It was a world almost without a feature; an empty sky, an empty earth; front and back, the line of railway stretched from horizon to horizon, like a cue across a billiard board; on either hand the green plain ran till it touched the skirts of heaven... The train toiled over this infinity like a snail; and being the one thing moving, it was wonderful what huge proportions it began to assume in our regard. It seemed miles in length, and either end of it within but a step of the horizon. Even my own body or my own head seemed a great thing in that emptiness...

To one hurrying through by steam there was a certain exhilaration in this spacious vacancy, this greatness of the air, this discovery of the whole arch of heaven, this straight, unbroken prison line of the horizon. Yet one could not but reflect upon the weariness of those who passed by there in old days, at the foot's pace of oxen, painfully urging their teams, and with no landmark but that unattainable evening sun for which they steered, and which daily fled them by an equal stride. They had nothing, it would seem, to overtake; nothing by which to reckon their advance; no sight for repose or for encouragement; but stage after stage, only the dead green waste under foot, and the mocking fugitive horizon. But the eye, as I have been told, found differences even here; and at the worst the emigrant came, by perseverance to the end of his toil. It is the settlers, after all, at whom we have a right to marvel. Our consciousness, by which we live, is itself but the creature of variety. Upon what food does it subsist in such a land? What livelihood can repay a human creature for a life spent in this huge sameness? He is cut off from books, from news, from company, from all that can relieve existence but the prosecution of his affairs. A sky full of stars is the most varied spectacle that he can hope. He may walk five miles and see nothing, ten, and it is as though he has not moved; twenty, and still be in the midst of the same great level, and has approached no nearer to the object in view, the flat horizon which keeps pace with his advance.

from : R. L. Stevenson, *Across the Plains*

6 Hints to emigrants

England, 1886

The first few weeks on board a ship you hear nothing but lamentations, the passengers constantly discovering that they cannot get anything they want, or cannot use what they do get : they have not brought things with them which they ought to have or have encumbered themselves with much they had better have left behind, and making complaints of a like nature ... On board a ship very trifling things seem to acquire great importance; the general routine of life may be described as the pursuit of personal comfort under difficulties ...

It is better to have only such things as are intended to be worn on board and retain the means of purchasing, on arrival, the two or three necessary garments most suited for the season on arriving. Ready-made garments of all descriptions can be purchased within a few minute's walk of the landing-place of most Australian ports, and most of the articles are nearly or quite as cheap as at home. Shoes are the most expensive things, and it is worth while to bring a good stock ... Emigrants are usually furnished with lists of the most necessary articles, as hook pots, water cans, knives, forks, spoons, cups, basins, tin pails &c. Besides these, many little things are required to do things properly and with comfort, as a mop, a long birch broom, a short handled brush, a scrubbing brush and flannels, coarse cloths to wipe up slops in rough weather and a piece of bath brick ...

Procure before starting as many good sound onions as you can find room for. Raw onions are the thing often most readily eaten, and sometimes, indeed, the only things which can be relished after an attack of sea-sickness. With a piece of bread or biscuit they form a palatable refreshment, when the most savory dishes or richest confectionery would be refused ... almost as useful as onions are lemons ... It is a lamentable fact that so many ship doctors are intemperate and loose, and when sober so negligent and hardened to the sight of suffering that it is with difficulty the passengers can get proper attendance ...

There is a society in London (The Prayer Book and Homily Society) which provides emigrants gratis with little books and pamphlets suited for reading during the voyage, among which is a selection of psalms and prayers which are very appropriate to the vicissitudes of life at sea, and which all may read with benefit. At such a time all sectarian distinction should be as much as possible dispensed with, or merged within the higher truths of universal belief ... It is the best policy to be on terms with all that none would feel any malicious pleasure in seeing you brought down from the position you may start with ... The grade in society to which people belong is determined much more by the way in which they spend their money and leisure than by the way they make it.

from : Rosamund Smith, *Hints to Emigrants*

7 Starting a home in the bush

Australia

As the day increased, Stan Parker emerged and, after going here and there, simply looking at what was his, began to tear the bush apart. His first tree fell through the white silence with a volley of leaves. This was clean enough. But there was also the meaner warfare of the scrub, deadly in technique and omnipresence, that would come up from behind and leave warning on the flesh in messages of blood ...

203

There in the scarred bush, that had not yet accepted its changed face, the man soon began to build a house, or shack. He brought the slabs he had shaped for logs. Slowly. He piled his matchsticks. So the days were piled too. Seasons were closing and opening on the clearing in which the man was at work. If days fanned the fury in him, months soothed, so that time, as it passed, was both shaping and dissolving, in one.

But the house was being built among the stumps, that in time had ceased to bleed. It was more the symbol of a house. Its prim, slab walls fulfilled necessity. There were windows to let the light into the oblong room, there was a tin chimney, shaped like a matchbox, through which the smoke came at last. Finally he stuck on a veranda. It was too low, rather a frowning addition, but which did not forbid. Seen through the trees, it was a plain but honest house that the man had built.

If there had been neighbours, it would have been a comfort to see the smoke occur regularly in the matchbox-chimney. But there were no neighbours. Only sometimes, if you listened on the stiller days, you might hear the sound of an axe, like the throb of your own heart, in the blue distances. Only very distant. Or more distantly, a cock. Or imagination. It was too far.

Sometimes, the man would drive off into the distance in his high cart. Then the clearing was full of the whine and yelping of the red dog, left chained to a veranda post. Till in time the silence grew, and his yellow eyes watched it. Or a parrot flurried the blue air. Or a mouse glistened on the dirt floor of the house. The abandoned dog was at the service of silence at last. He was no longer attached, even by his chain, to the blunt house of the man's making.

The man always brought back things in his cart. He brought a scratched table and chairs, with mahogany lumps in the proper places. He brought an iron bed, big and noisy, of which the bars had been bent a bit by kids shoving their heads between. And he brought all those necessities, like flour, and a bottle of pain killer, and pickled meat, and kerosene, and seed potatoes, and a packet of needles, and oaten chaff for the shaggy horse, and the tea and sugar that trickled from their bags, so that you crunched on them, almost always, on the hardened floor.

The dog's collar almost carved off his neck when the man came, and there was always the joy and excitement and the smell of brought things.

Then, once, when the man had been gone some time, longer than normal perhaps, he brought with him a woman, who sat beside him in the cart, holding the board and her flat hat. When she had got down, the dog, loosed from his chain, craned forward, still uncertain of his freedom, on trembling toes, in silence, and smelled the hem of her skirt.

from : Patrick White, *The Tree of Man*

8 Englishwoman on the ranch

Patagonia, early twentieth century

Talcahuala was a flat sandy area of 225 square miles with a few water holes and was stocked with sheep. In places it was covered with a short prickly veldt-like grass but for the most part it consisted of dry undulating scrubland. One marvelled that any animals could be grazed here until one noticed the fern-leafed bushes whose fronds bore on the underside a mass of berries. These provided one of the most fattening foods for the sheep who sought it eagerly.

The only hills were those of the Sierra Colorada, a rowan-red ridge many leagues distant across the wastes of sand that stretched to the horizon, dotted with algarroba bushes. An almost constant wind blew over it which in summer seemed to come direct from a furnace. Temperatures of 99 degrees Fahrenheit were a commonplace, and many times during our stay at this ranch the thermometer rose to 100 degrees and over. At midday the heat smote one with an almost tangible force, so that if compelled to go out during these hours, one ran for the haven of shade just as in England we dash for shelter from the rain.

The ranch house, which was raised about six feet from the ground in order to allow a current of air to circulate beneath, was the usual clap-board structure, its paint scabby and weathered like the skin of a very old person. A corrugated tin roof caught and held every ray of the sun. In summer this tin roof attracted the heat so much that all who lived under it sweltered by day, while during the cooler night hours the tin continually contracted with a noise like gun shots. In the winter months the roof provided no warmth for the rooms underneath ...

Like an inquisitive stranger peering over someone's shoulder, the *molino* or windmill from which we obtained our well water loomed above the single story dwelling. The *molino* was situated at the back of the ranch, and its rotating metal sails made a pleasantly drowsy sound as they sang to themselves through the long hot forenoons. To the side of the compound were the stables, the out-buildings and a large empty quadrangle, dominated by a single tamarisk—almost a tree—the favourite roosting place for the entire hen population.

From 11 a.m. to 3.45 p.m. in summer the whole ranch became

inanimate. Not a figure would be stirring. The animals sprawled in the shade of the house, panting in unison, and only a lone dust devil, whirling madly, would spiral across an empty landscape which quivered with heat as far as the eye could see ... And the flies! Every drinking vessel had to be covered, and woe betide the unwitting person who omitted to place his saucer over his tea cup; otherwise a number of the creatures would commit suicide in it.

The kitchen just did not bear thinking about. One look at the odious haze flitting over everything caused my mother to feel ill ... Looking back, it is wonderful how my mother managed to remain sane and sweet-tempered and retain her sense of humour ... She could not engross herself in a good baking day, as it was considered undignified for the Señora to set foot in the kitchen. Not even a superman could have wrested a garden from our inhospitable ground, so she was denied that pleasure. All of us were heartily sick of the few cracked records which the wheezy gramophone could with difficulty be induced to play. My father's day was occupied entirely with the sheep, so that apart from mealtimes, he was visible only in the evening and was then too tired for much conversation ... And, as if this were not enough, the daily killing of sheep for meat and the inevitable cruelties connected with ranch work, caused her much distress. Dust, flies, heat, loneliness. The days must have seemed hideously empty to her.

Before our arrival there was not even any pretension to a garden, or even a shelter from the incessant wind, to break the harsh outlines of the ugly tin-roofed ranch house. However, my mother had come out here to make a home for her husband and child and a home she did make of it.

from : M. Robertson, *The Sand, the Wind and the Sierras*

9 Pioneering and creativity on the Kalahari fringe

South Africa

Africa is my mother's country. I do not know exactly how long my mother's family has lived in Africa; but I do know that Africa was about and within her from the beginning, as it was for me ...

Many years ago my father had bought a vast tract of land on the edge of the Kalahari desert. For fifty years no one had made any effort to develop it, and those broad acres were left there, lying parched and unwanted in the desert sun. There my mother went at the age of eighty. The only people who seemed willing to accompany her were displaced persons; there was a German geologist who had been interned during the war; a delicate Bavarian missionary, whom she made her secretary; and an Italian carpenter and mason, an ex-prisoner of war, who became her foreman.

A hundred miles from the nearest village, they pitched their tents and started looking for water, without which no permanent settlement was possible. At first they hired from private contractors the machines to drill for water. The German geologist's knowledge of his science and my mother's intuitive assessment between them determined where the drilling should take place. The first contractor drilled down to 150 feet, struck iron stone—or so he said—and refused to continue . . .

A second contractor drilling a few feet away from the first hole, after going down 147 feet, lost all his tackle in the shaft and moved away in disgust. A third contractor, drilling still in the same narrow area, found after 153 feet that he had sunk his shaft at an angle, and could not continue. He too went, bitter and deeply out-of-pocket. By this time no new contractor could be tempted to try his fortune at this notorious site. There was nothing for it but for my mother to buy her own drilling machine. The aged geologist was apprenticed for some months to one of the few remaining unestranged drilling contractors in the area, in order to acquire this new craft; then drilling was resumed in earnest.

Nearly three years had gone by out there in the Kalahari desert, with the burning suns of its summer, and the searing cold winds of its winter. One of the worst droughts in memory, bringing great storms of dust and sand, broke over them. But the party continued confidently.

Every morning at six my mother rang a hand-bell and handed her employees steaming bowls of coffee that she had made herself. 'Men are like that,' she says, 'they are like children who will get out of bed for food if nothing else.'

Having thus enticed them out of bed, she set them drilling. At 157 feet, only four feet deeper than the deepest shaft sunk by a contractor, they struck water.

'It was most dramatic,' my mother said. 'I was watching the machine at that moment quite by chance'—of course, her eyes never left it— 'when suddenly I saw it lurch slightly. All the slack in the rope of the drill disappeared. The bore was through the stone and in a deep vein of water. It came gushing up the shaft.'

So sure had she been all along that water would be found, that the pumps were there waiting; they had been waiting for three years ready to go up the moment that water was found.

There my mother is to this day, a slim, lovely, upright, gracious old lady, whose skin looks as if it has never known anything but a European sun. She is still active, vigorous, young in spirit, and convinced she will live to be a hundred and twenty. She builds, plants trees and orchards, and grows corn in a desert where neither corn nor grass grew before . . .

It has often occurred to me that the heavy burden of child-bearing —and my mother reared thirteen—has in a sense, been irrelevant to the deepest and most vital purpose of her life. I have never been able to believe that a woman's task in life is limited to her children. I can quite well conceive that in my mother, as with more and more women of our own day there is an urge to creativeness which lies underneath and deeper, above and beyond the begetting of children. These women have a contract with life itself, which is not discharged with the mere procreation of their species. Men recognise and try to honour this contract in themselves as a matter of course. Their contribution to life vibrates with their passionate rebellion against the narrowly conceived idea that would restrict their role to that of protectors and feeders of women and children. They do not acknowledge and respect the same thing so readily in women. Perhaps until they do the world will not see the full creative relationship that life intends there should be between men and women.

As far as my mother is concerned, I was moved and reassured by this development so late in her life. For me her story is a source of unfailing confidence in the future. After many years in which the need to create must have been consciously forgotten, overlaid by a thousand anxieties of birth and death, war and peace, when it should, by all the dictates of reason, have vanished for good, then suddenly as an old lady my mother was able to turn round and find the same urge close beside her . . . After sixty uninterrupted years as a wife and mother she turned confidently to the authentic and original vision of her life, and was at once enabled to pursue the dream of her African girlhood.

from : Laurens Van Der Post, *Venture to the Interior*

10 Women of Upper Canada

Ontario, Canada, early nineteenth century

The mere recital of the chores that fell to women in the early self-sufficient days of a community is exhausting. They grew their own hops to make their own rising to make their own bread. They saved ashes to make their own lye to boil with collected fat to make their own soap. They made their own candles. They spun wool, they made clothes, cutting up old garments for patterns. They had complete responsibility for the dairy, the milking, the butter-making, and the cheese-making, for which they made their own rennet from a calf's stomach. They took part in the butchering of beasts, in the making of sausages, the smoking of hams, the salting of pork. They did great laundries, which they finished, in spite of protective bandages, with bleeding wrists. They stood through the long nights keeping the fire going under the huge potash pots and stirring the hardening mass. In the cold spring nights they tended the fires under the maple syrup. Such tasks fell to women because the men needed sleep for their hard days . . .

The vegetable garden too was the woman's care, as well as the putting down of berries, pickles, fruits and preserves; the making of substitutes for tea and coffee from dandelion roots, sumach leaves and parched grain; the dyeing of wool and knitting; the care of the poultry; the dressing and curing of fish and game. And, of course, there were three meals a day to prepare.

They were married early, at about seventeen, and by the time they were twenty-five they were emaciated and dejected. Child-bearing, scanty food, and a hard life made them old at thirty. Neglected and frequently left alone while their husbands were away hunting or carousing, they accepted the solace and company of any hunter or traveller who happened by . . .

Under these circumstances, chastity was not expected of girls, and since children early shared the burden of scraping out an existence, a young woman with one or two of them had a better chance of marriage than one with none. Courtship was intensely practical. A young man left home at an early age, taking up a grant of land and preparing to live as his father had. A woman was needed to take on the drudgery of the cabin while he cleared an acre or two. He would seek one out among the forest settlements and present himself to her family, telling them who he was, how much land he had and where it was. After he had eaten a meal with them, if he was acceptable, he was invited to come again for another meal on a specific day. That occasion would see a big supper, after which the girl's family withdrew to the loft, or even simply to the other side of a blanket hung from the roof, leaving the young couple the rest of the cabin and a bed. Here they passed the night. In the morning the girl, if she wished, asked the man to come again; the man could accept or refuse, as he pleased, and was under no obligation to return. However, considering the high value, or rather the necessity, of women as partners, or at least as labour, the girl took no great chance of being left. In any case, there would always be another man. Such customs were shocking to the immigrants who began arriving in numbers in the late 'twenties; yet this form of courtship was common in rural communities throughout the world.

from : W. H. Graham, *Tiger Dunlop*

11 Emigration to Scotland

Ireland, nineteenth century

My father's people farmed a piece of stony land on the side of Brague mountain, and in between the men travelled to the Scottish harvests . . .

There was little or nothing in Ireland for him, but if he had been fairly prosperous he would have gone just the same. It was a sign of virility, of awareness, of adventurous spirit, that a young fellow should be away from Granemore by the time he was twenty-one, after that only the cabbages remained. Some, especially those who went to America, never came back, but many did return to tell their experiences and to stir the blood of those who waited to go. They told of no ease and fortune but of hard physical effort, that was often dangerous too, but there were pay packets for doing it, and that was enough.

He had known my mother from when they were both very young, and they married in Ireland during one of his periods home from Scotland. They were of an age, twenty-five at the time and I'm sure he hankered after a home of his own after years spent in model lodging houses, farm bothies and cramped tenements. The one they rented in Cowie's Square could not have been smaller, and their first child died in it before I was born . . .

Five of us in one room was a bit cramped, but the builders had spaced it out cunningly enough. The two beds were the hole in the wall kind, and curtained off from the room proper. The sink, with cold tap only of course, was under the only window. We had a wooden chest in which my mother stored blankets, and which made an extra seat, two chairs, and a table, and some shelves along the wall. That was the lot and it was enough. If we had owned the classiest furniture in all Scotland we would still have lacked space. When the two chairs and the chest were in use the rest of us sat on the fender in front of the fire.

The terraced buildings in Cowie's Square were not all one-roomed homes like ours, 'Single-Ends' was the Craigneuk term for them. Just one flight above lived the aristocratic two-roomed families. They reached their homes by flights of stone stairs at the back of the buildings. We single-enders reached our doors in the close that ran from the main street to the back. In each close there were four families living, and their pride of home and caste were indicated by bright brass plates which announced their names. To have a nameless door was to have a shameless life. There were quite a few nameless ones for we were tough in the square . . .

The miners made revelry on their Friday paydays and the steel workers on their Saturday paydays. My mother used to lock the door to shut out the sounds, while outside my brother Peter and me, and all the kids thrilled at the sight of the big policemen (mostly Highlanders) carting off the disturbers of the peace. Sometimes we aided the police by fetching the drunk's barrow from the station. This was a flat affair on which the violent were spreadeagled and tied, and trundled off to the cells. It was a most degrading sight, especially when a woman occupied the barrow. I watched in fascinated horror as she lay there dishevelled, sodden, beaten by life, and shrieking obscenities.

I should have been in bed, and so should my brother Peter, but there were no strict child-rearing rules in our home.

Sometimes as if we weren't crowded enough, my mother would take in a lodger. Her idea was not for profit, not with the sort we had, but to tide them over a rough period. They were always Irishmen, newly landed, and seeking work. If they managed to find it they paid their way and moved out. If they were unlucky then so were we, for they hung on eating what there was and paid nothing. Sometimes in desperation my mother had to gather up something pawnable to get them their fare back to Ireland.

At times like these my brother Peter and me especially were often hungry. We'd be like hawks watching the lodgers at meal-times. If they moved or turned their backs for a moment we swooped on their plates. It was desperately disappointing each time the lodger learned to hold fast to his plate.

Every time a boarder entered Peter and me had to sleep on the floor. It didn't disturb us much, in fact I used to sleep better that way. Every night on shutting my eyes I pursued my unfailing ambition to keep awake until I finished my night prayers. I even managed once. However, I frequently achieved another ambition, to go to sleep with jujubes in my mouth and find them still there the following morning.

My parents got on very well together, although they didn't express affection outwardly. They hadn't the training, vocabulary, or desire to do so. I never heard them quarrel or raise their voice in anger, and I could hardly have missed it in our one-room home. They displayed no effusive affection to my brother and sister and me. There was no kissing, no hugging, no wrestling in fun, and we didn't miss it; their huge fount of good will towards us was enough. We took that for granted as our natural right, which it was. We took their serenity in each other's presence for granted too, when really it was a great piece of good fortune for us.

We grew up without the least hint or training about sex. Nor did we ever mention it to one another, for we inherited the vast reticence of our parents. The result for me at least was a groping of my way through adolescence that almost tortured and bewildered me out of my mind. I think my brother and sister escaped more lightly, for they were always more stolid and stronger nerved than me.

from : Patrick McGeown, *Heat the Furnace Seven Times More*

12 Australian outback life

Australia, 1954

After every sandstorm Mrs. Johnson must bring the wheel-barrow indoors and shovel the sand up. It comes in everywhere for many of the windows are merely covered with mosquito netting instead of glass . . .

'Better bring your things inside,' she called. 'You won't be able to travel any further today. We're in for a good sandstorm.'

We were to spend nearly two days in Bulloo Downs with Wattie Johnson and his wife Ella, waiting for the storm to cease, and those two days were to be a revelation to me of just what the life of a housewife in the outback can mean.

The Johnsons have six children, ranging from eleven years to eleven months. In the rather primitive kitchen is a large wooden table—you need a large table—to seat six children. But, in addition to that, leading off from the kitchen is a dining-room, the furniture of which consists of an even larger wooden table and two long benches. Here, three times a day, Mrs. Johnson sets the table for five hungry men— her husband and the stockmen. Their work is strenuous, so they have steak for breakfast, steak for dinner and steak for supper.

In the middle of the morning and of the afternoon there is 'Smoko', which means cakes to be baked. There are no bakers within a hundred miles so Mrs. Johnson also has to find time to bake enough bread for twelve people, not to mention several men who are employed looking after the bores . . . She bakes their bread too.

She eats her meals in the kitchen so that she can look after the children, which means that she rarely, if ever, has meals with her husband. The size of the washing up pile after each meal has to be not seen, but tackled, to be believed.

from : Beryl Miles, *The Stars my Blanket*

13 Seeking a new way of life

Israel, nineteen-sixties

In the beginning there was not much else but the land, some of it unpromising stony soil, and so these early fathers of the gathering in would have had in any case to turn themselves from professional men and traders, urban dwellers in ghettos, into rural farmers tilling the soil. But they did not do this in a spirit of mere necessity, they did it with a positive exaltation. To go with this union of the people and the soil there must also be a new way of living, freed from the trammels, the hypocrisies and the deceits of the old life which they had left behind. A way of life which released to the maximum the common spirit which each man felt to flow so strongly within him, which liberated all his energies for the tasks in hand, and which gave every soul an equal stake in the life of the infant settlements and in their defence in time of trouble. All material goods were held by the kibbutz and distributed to its members as their need required. This was true also of all money. Services were common to all, food cooked and eaten together, children cared for and taught in their own special home so that the women, equally with the men, were able to give the full eight hours daily of work on the land. Life was hard, simple, austere, but the compensations were also very great. Within the kibbutz a spirit grew up of interdependence and of a depth of reality which made the urgent individual preoccupations of the outside world appear vain and trivial. What mattered was the community, and submerging their separate identities in the group they found strength and satisfaction.

This was pioneering, treading a path both physical and sociological which had not been trodden in quite this way before. The standard of education and culture in the kibbutzim was very high; it was an élite who had elected to follow their ideals in this fashion, a second choosing of a chosen people. The ground that they broke, whether it was the actual soil of Palestine or in the realm of social custom, was fresh ground. The buildings they erected, whether the houses in which they lived or the ramifications of group living, went up where there had not been such structures before. The crops that they harvested, whether the growth was vegetable or spiritual, grew where no such crops had ever grown. The kibbutzim looked outward and saw that what they were doing was good and could set a pattern for a new nation.

But in time there grew a second generation for whom the kibbutz was not an exciting pioneering experiment but home—safe, established, cosy, and on the whole not something they much wanted to share with other people . . .

The Army was the nation, and the nation was also the Army, for in an emergency it would take only a very short time for every single man and woman to report back to their units, ready and under arms ... After a year in normal training a group of young people, both men and women, who had come to know each other well and to work well together as a unit (it was possible that they might even have originally come into the Army together from a youth movement) might elect to go, as an entity, to start a new Nahal on some barren hillside where no cultivation had taken place before. Many of this group would be young people whose background was in any case rural, but not all; some would be from towns, going off with a light in their eyes and a gun over their shoulders to till the soil in the old pattern that had been pioneered by their parents before them. Undoubtedly there was still a strong pull for many of the young people in the cultivation of the sacred soil, and not just simply in its cultivation but in the knowledge which was implicit in the role that the Army played in this. Every extra yard of Israel which was made fertile and eventually settled was one more acre embattled against the possible encroachment of an enemy.

from : Mora Dickson, *Israeli Interlude*

14 Medicine Bow

Wyoming, U.S.A., eighteen-seventies

I have seen and slept in many like it since. Scattered wide, they littered the frontier from the Columbia to the Rio Grande, from the Missouri to the Sierras. They lay stark, dotted over a planet of treeless dust like soiled packs of cards. Each was similar to the next, as one old five-spot of clubs resembles another. Houses, empty bottles, and garbage, they were forever of the same shapeless pattern. More forlorn they were than stale bones. They seemed to have been strewn there by the wind and to be waiting till the wind should come again and blow them away.

Medicine Bow was my first, and I took its dimensions, twenty nine buildings in all—one coal shute, one water tank, the station, one store, two eating-houses, one billiard hall, two tool-houses, one feed stable, and twelve others that for one reason and another I shall not name.

from : Owen Wister, *The Virginian*

15 Thompson

Manitoba, Canada, 1961

This place is on the border line of arctic and subarctic. In many places it is impossible to dig down below a foot or so, because of the permafrost which extends down into the earth to various depths depending on the nature of the clay or other soil, and more particularly on the nature of the ground cover; if the cover is composed of muskeg moss, or leaf mould or other insulating material, it prevents the sun's rays from thawing out the ground in the short summer, and so permanent frost remains—and you just can't dig through it. So now they are clearing the topsoil off the places that they intend to build on next year, and the sun does the trick during the summer. But for those places where they intend to build now, they just build a fire of logs, soak it with oil and keep it burning for about four days. Then they get the big diggers working. In this way, during January and February they dug down for the foundation of the shopping centre, then, covering the places with tents of neoprene plastic, and heating the inside, they poured in concrete for pylons and sills. (In January at 50 degrees below zero!*) Now a big crane is feeding steel eye-beams to men who are bolting them together to form the floors and walls of the shopping centre. They are at it right now—Sunday morning. The telephone men are digging a deep trench in which they are laying four plastic 3-inch pipes containing in all 800 telephone wires for the new houses that are growing up like mushrooms. These are for the families of some of the 2,000 men working in the nickel mine, mill smelter or refinery. There are about 2,000 people in all at present living in the township proper including women and children and the people engaged on building and general services.

What a place! The usual spirit of optimism and comradeship seems missing. Every one seems glum. Perhaps this is because there are so many foreign languages spoken, and people are not sure whom to trust. Many of them have been displaced from their homes in Europe and have brought an atmosphere of fear, hate and suspicion with them that will no doubt take some time to dispel.

from : A letter from Jack Jones, Great Falls, Manitoba

* Centigrade

16 New towns in the North

Canada, 1966

I flew from Edmonton to Hay River, mostly over virgin forest and bush. The mining engineer in the seat beside me pointed out one block of forest where a particularly rare bear could be found; later through the clouds he showed me the Mackenzie Highway with the new railway running parallel to it, cutting through the dense forests. It was pioneer country all right.

Hay River came as a shock. A journalist had warned me that it was a 'dump', but the Chamber of Commerce leaflet had urged tourists to 'take the Mackenzie route to Hay River, hub of the North'. Hub it certainly is. It lies at the head of the Highway and the Railway, and is the jumping-off place for planes going north and for barge traffic to the Arctic down the Mackenzie River. But I was not prepared for its untidiness and shoddiness. Dust lies thick in summer, for the roads are not surfaced. When it rains, the mud is everywhere, up to your knees. Boardwalks are often broken or non-existent. The new railway sensibly runs right through the old town to the docks, but it does not add glamour. Many buildings seem as bleak as any 'Western Movie' town—shabby barber's shop, poolroom, Chinese restaurant, one-horse stores with few goods, virulent mosquitoes buzzing everywhere. Everybody is too busy to be tidy, and the garbage and rubbish is just thrown out anywhere. The hotel, a long wooden prefabricated building beside the Great Slave Lake, is not unattractive from the outside, but to enter you have to run the gauntlet of drunken men and women—white, Indian and Métis—who lean over the rail all day.

When you have wandered round for a few days, however, something catches the imagination, you feel the excitement of growth and enterprise. In the old town, built on an island and terribly damaged by the flood which took Hay River onto the world's front pages in 1963, there is the aluminium Igloo Movie Theatre shining round and silver in the light northern evenings; there is a new hospital, a new school. The Hudson's Bay Store is large and well stocked.

By the docks activity begins early in the mornings and often goes on all night. The Northern Transportation Company must shift its cargoes down the Mackenzie in the three short ice-free months. If they fail, oil exploration companies in Alaska will go short of rigs and machinery; Eskimos and government officials in remote places like Tuktoyaktuk, will be without prefabricated homes; empty oil drums will not get back to Norman Wells for refilling; household goods, groceries, canoes, jeeps, snowploughs, precious lumber will not arrive before freeze-up in Arctic settlements where stores have to be ordered a year ahead. Transporting heavy freight by air is exorbitantly expensive, although the population use planes like taxis to get themselves about . . .

The pay is so good that many crew and shore staff could live the whole year on what they earn in three months. But, except on beer in the hotel saloon, they do not spend it in Hay River; they take it out of the Northwest Territories to their homes in Alberta, Manitoba or British Columbia, or to glamorous holiday places like Mexico. That is what worries those who want Hay River to grow on a permanent basis, and not become just another short-lived boom town.

from : Barbara Wace, 'Pioneers in Canada's North',
The Geographical Magazine, April 1966

17 The race for land

Oklahoma, U.S.A., 1889

All that there was of Guthrie, the now famous 'magic city' on April 22nd, at 1.30 p.m., when the first train from the north drew up at the station and unloaded its first instalment of settlers, was a water-tank, a small station-house, a shanty for the Wells Fargo Express, and a Government Land Office—a building twenty by forty feet, hastily constructed five hundred feet from the depot . . .

I remember throwing my blankets out of the car window the instant the train stopped at the station. I remember tumbling after them through the self-same window. Then I joined the wild scramble for a town lot up the sloping hillside at a pace discounting any 'go-as-you-please' race. There were several thousand people converging on the same plot of ground, each eager for a town lot which was to be acquired without cost or without price, each solely dependent on his own efforts, and animated by a spirit of fair play and good humour.

The race was not over when you reached the particular lot you were content to select for your possession. The contest was still who should drive their stakes first, who would erect their little tents soonest, and then, who would quickest build a little wooden shanty.

The situation was so peculiar that it is difficult to convey correct impressions of the situation. It reminded me of playing blindman's-buff. One did not know how far to go before stopping; it was hard to tell when it was best to stop, and it was a puzzle whether to turn to the right or the left. Everyone appeared dazed, and all for the most part acted like a flock of stray sheep. Where the boldest led, many others followed. I found myself, without exactly knowing how, about midway between the government building and depot. I accosted a man who looked like a deputy, and asked him if this was to be a street along here.

'Yes,' he replied. 'We are laying off four corner lots right here for a lumber yard.'

'Is this the corner where I stand?' I inquired.

'Yes,' he responded, approaching me.

'Then I claim this corner lot!' I said with decision, as I jammed my location stick in the ground and hammered it securely home with my heel. 'I propose to have one lot at all hazards on this town site, and you will have to limit yourself to three, in this location at least.'

An angry altercation ensued, but I stoutly maintained my position, and my rights. I proceeded at once to unstrap a small folding cot I brought with me, and by standing it on its end it made a tolerable centre-pole for a tent. I then threw a couple of my blankets over the cot, and staked them securely into the ground on either side. Thus I had a claim that was unjumpable because of substantial improvements, and I felt safe and breathed more freely until my brother arrived on the third train, with our tent and equipments. Not long after his arrival, an enterprising individual came driving by with a plough, and we hired him for a dollar to plough around the lot I had stepped off, twenty-five feet in front and one hundred and forty feet in depth. Before dusk we had a large wall tent erected on our newly-acquired premises, with a couple of cots inside and a liberal amount of blankets for bedding. Now we felt doubly secure in our possession, and as night approached I strolled up on the eminence near the land office, and surveyed the wonderful cyclorama spread out before me on all sides. Ten thousand people had 'squatted' upon a square mile of virgin prairie that first afternoon, and as the myriad of white tents suddenly appeared upon the face of the country, it was as though a vast flock of huge white-winged birds had just settled down upon the hillsides and in the valleys. Here indeed was *a city laid out and populated in half a day.* Thousands of camp-fires sparkled upon the dark bosom of the prairie as far as the eye could reach, and there arose from this huge camp a subdued hum declaring that this almost innumerable multitude of the brave and self-reliant men had come to stay and work, and build in that distant Western wilderness a city that should forever be a trophy to American enterprise and daring.

from : Hamilton S. Wicks, 'The opening of Oklahoma',
The Cosmopolitan, September 1889

18 The Klondike Gold Rush

Canada, 1898

For many people today the entire story of the Klondike gold rush is evoked by a single scene. It shows a solid line of men, forming a human chain, hanging across the white face of a mountain rampart...

All winter long, from Sheep Camp to the summit of the Chilkoot Pass, for four weary miles the endless line of men stretched up the slippery slope, a human garland hanging from the summit and draped across the expanse of the mountainside. From first light to last, the line was never broken as the men who formed it inched slowly upward, climbing in that odd rhythmic motion that came to be called 'The Chilkoot Lock-Step'. As on the White Pass, all individuality seemed to end as each man became a link in the chain. Even separate sounds were lost, merged in the single all-encompassing groan which rose from the slow-moving mass and echoed like a hum through the bowl of the mountains.

This was no Technicolour scene. The early photographs render it faithfully in black and white : the straining men in various shades of dun limned against the sunless slopes. For two months of perpetual twilight the Chilkoot was without tint or pigment.

To an alpinist, even an amateur one, the ascent of the pass would have seemed child's play, for it was in no sense a difficult or arduous climb. But the men of '98 were not mountaineers. Poorly attired in heavy furs and wools, rather than in the light hooded parkas which were far more practicable, the novices sweated and froze alternately. Unable to disrobe or bathe, seldom free of the winds that were the terror of the trail, bent double under their packs by day and by the need to curl up for warmth at night, half nourished by cold beans and soggy flapjacks, plagued by the resultant dysentery and stomach cramps—filthy, stinking, red-eyed, and bone-weary, they still forced themselves upwards...

Whisky and silk, steamboats and pianos, live chickens and stuffed turkeys, timber and glassware, bacon and beans, all went over on men's backs. If a man was too poor to hire a packer, he climbed the pass forty times before he got his outfit across...

And on arrival men moved from their fetid cabins by night into murky, constricted mine shafts by day. Mining in the sub-Arctic is unique because the permanently frozen ground must be thawed before the bedrock can be reached; it is this bedrock, ten, twenty, and even fifty feet below the surface, that contains the gold. At first the miners let the sun do the work. This was a long, laborious process : a few inches of thawed earth were scraped away each day, and an entire summer might pass by before the goal was attained. Soon, however, wood fires replaced the sun. The gold-seekers lit them by night, removed the ashes and the thawed earth in the morning, then lit a new fire, burning their way slowly down to form a shaft whose sides remained frozen as hard as granite. This method allowed miners to work all winter, choking and wheezing in their smoky dungeons far below the snow-covered surface of the ground as they tunnelled this way and that seeking the 'pay streak' which marked an erst-while creek channel. The paydirt thus obtained was hoisted up the shaft and piled in a mound, known as a 'dump'. In the spring, when the ice broke on the creeks and water gushed down the hillsides, the miners built long spill-ways or sluiceboxes to counterfeit the ancient action of nature. The gravel was shovelled into these boxes and, as the water rushed through, was swept away. But the heavier gold was caught in the crossbars and in the matting on the bottom, as it had once been caught in the crevices of the streambeds. Every two or three days the water was diverted from the sluicebox as each miner panned the residue at the bottom in what came to be known as a 'clean-up'. The various stages in this process had been arrived at by trial and error over the years, since the days of '49 in California; in the Yukon Valley they reached their greatest refinement.

from : Pierre Berton, *Klondike*

19 To the mines

South Africa, eighteen-seventies

But the search for diamonds, the finding of diamonds went on. From Hopetown to the Vaal river crossings and back to the dry diggings; and then, of a sudden, at Vooruitsicht, the richest find of all, on which the hungry myriads swarmed and settled and burrowed like ants that pick the bones of a carcass.

So Kimberley came : a pitted camp of tents and tin shanties set up in a treeless desert and girt by leagues of knee deep sand, where a man could earn more in a week by bossing-up natives than the shrewdest farmer could drag out of the land in half a lifetime...

[And after Kimberley, Johannesburg.] It lay there, that small plot of ground, on the open veldt, five thousand six hundred feet above sea level, encompassed by marshy land on three sides and bounded on the fourth by a barren ridge : a desert of dust and red earth, on which the shape of the city to come was but vaguely foreshadowed by lines of wooden pegs defining its unmade streets and the central space of the outspan where the converging trails of coaches and carts and wagons off-loaded their burdens—rusty machinery, boilers and galvanised sheets; crockery, furniture, forage and produce—incontinently dumping them there in the dust and the sun.

As yet there were no buildings more permanent than the mud and reed hut called Walkers Hotel; but already the traffic in 'stands' had begun. Corner lots on the pegged enclosures had become gambling counters to be sold and resold half a dozen times in a month. Everywhere there were tents. Reaching forward from the congested nucleus of Ferreira's camp, their fat scattered tilts, bleached by the sun, resembled, when seen from a distance, a litter of paper scraps strewn haphazard, or a flock of white egrets come to rest on the shoals of a sandy estuary.

In these tents, without water or sanitation, dwelt men—three thousand of them, drawn not only from the backwash of Berberton but from Kimberley, from the Cape, from Natal, from the uttermost corners of the earth to which the rumour of easy wealth had penetrated. Here were skilled miners from Colorado and Ballarat; Hebrew capitalists from Kimberley; mining engineers from America; builders and blacksmiths, hucksters, panders, saloon-keepers; casual labourers, down and outs—every imaginable sort of human riff-raff washed on to the barren ridge like jetsam cast up by the tides.

To these thousands was added an even greater concourse of natives : Malay drivers from Capetown, whose carts plied from one end of the reef to the other at exorbitant fares; Griquas, Hottentots, Cape-coloured folk, and outnumbering all these, the hordes of raw Kaffirs, who, tramping to and from Kimberley, were snatched up like metallic particles by the magnet of Johannesburg and swept, naked, underground—to have their lungs eaten away by sharp crystals of powdered quartz—or flung on the tented streets to rot their bewildered brains with Cape Smoke and *dagga*, or raw potato-spirit laced with tobacco juice. Sometimes in the crowded kraals where these were herded, tribal affrays broke out in which black men were killed; and that was a pity—for, even with this vast influx, labour was scarce, and the stamps must be fed and the pockets of their owners filled.

There were high wages (or pickings) for every man, black or white, who had the strength to move. Never before in the history of this impoverished land had money flowed so lavishly, or been of so little value, as that when the mines of the Rand poured forth in their sluggish rivulets of grey-green slime. Money to waste . . .

There would be money enough to pay through the nose for everything, if only the miners were given the power to dig and crush their gold. Wages, prices, the hungry mouths of men counted for nothing, provided the stamps were fed.

There were hundreds of these rising and falling now : the batteries filled the air with an incessant clatter and thudding. Primitive wooden headgear and hauling-winches driven by wood-fired steam were hurriedly being erected on every side—not only in the centre of the town from which Captain Ferreira's canvas camp had been shifted to uncover the gold beneath it, but on every sky line save the rocky ridge to northward. They ringed the remaining horizons until the township was girt by a broken circle of fires that glimmered by night and plumes of white steam that blew away on the wind by day. The gleaming dumps rose beside them; they too, shone white in the sun; and the surrounding veldt was scarred by pits and trenches such as are hurriedly dug about a beleagured city.

from : Brett Young, *The City of Gold*

20 Speeding for iron ore

Western Australia, nineteen-sixties

The wild but beautiful country in which vast resources [of haematite] are known to exist is singularly unattractive to the prospector. It is very hot in summer, and, during the three months of The Wet, it is humid as well as hot, with periodic cyclonic rains. The three winter months provide a most welcome respite; for the rest of the year the rugged Hamersley and Ophthalmia ranges, with their deep slashed gorges and rocky outcrops radiating heat, were best avoided. They were literally thousands of miles from anywhere.

... Residents were stunned by the speed and scale of the operations. Access roads and buildings—mining plant, offices, mess halls and houses—appeared as if by magic on the desolate scene. The country was alive with bull-dozers, giant mechanical shovels, huge cement mixers and trailers, and bitumen roads spread like a tangle of typewriter ribbons across mountains and through valleys.

The railway link [to Dampier] cost $A50,000,000 and was completed in one year and fifteen days—a feat which previously would have been deemed impossible. It carries the largest trains in the world.

The township of Dampier seemed to spring up overnight. Eighty-four constructed houses arrived and were dumped on prepared sites, most of which have wonderful views over the Indian Ocean and the Samper Archipelago. They were built with maximum insulation on a raft of concrete, to withstand possible cyclones. All houses in Dampier are air-conditioned and possess every possible convenience and amenity for tropical living. The hospital is new and well equipped and the off-duty nurse can choose between shell collecting, fishing, swimming all the year round or even eating oysters off the rocks. More and more buildings are being erected and the town is continuing to grow apace. It is expected ultimately that an iron and steel mill will be situated there, using oil from nearby Barrow Island.

Perhaps the greatest problem yet to be contended with is that of social integration of the iron workers. Their rapid education in modern methods and amenities is likely to set impossible standards to other employers of small labour forces. The handful of station-owners look on the iron companies as intruders. Manpower is being lost to them and even the aborigine is becoming expensive to employ.

from : H. H. Wilson, 'Australia's Modern Iron Age',
The Geographical Magazine, January 1969

21 Prospecting for nickel

Western Australia, 1969

No fewer than fifty companies are competing to carve up adjoining tracts of bushland. And hundreds of fly-bitten, sweating prospectors are frantically pegging claims wherever they can.

They're not particularly worried if the ground has already been pegged. After all, the Mining Warden's court will take months to sort out the conflicting rights, and meanwhile even the flimsiest claim may mean hard cash.

The rush was triggered off by Poseidon's nickel strike only seven miles away. Since then, cattle and sheep drovers, business men, clerks, ladies of easy virtue, diplomats and widows have all shared with Laverton's inhabitants in the sudden fortune, even the local policeman, Constable Griffith became $A24,000 richer overnight...

He used to know everybody by their first names; after all there were only eighty whites and a few dark-skinned, easy-going aboriginals in the township. A couple of weeks ago the arrival of Sunday papers from Kalgoorlie or Perth was a major event. Today up to a dozen light planes a day land in Laverton's dusty main street (there is not even a hint of an airstrip) and tourist coaches, taxis and private cars keep pouring in. Prospectors ride in on horse-back or in Land-Rovers.

In the evening Laverton is ringed by blazing campfires and the night is loud with lusty songs...

The great nickel fever is on; and the boom is feeding on itself. Pessimists are simply shouted down and run out of town. Everyone wants a nickel strike. A few weeks ago Poseidon was only one of many barely known mining companies listed in Adelaide. But ever since Western Mining Corporation made its first nickel strike on the

223

long-abandoned old goldfields at Kambala near Kalgoorlie, the whole
of this baking, dusty bush-covered area has been nervous with appre-
hensive tension.

from : Colin Chapman, 'Nickel fever hits outback',
The Observer, October 19, 1969

22 After oil on the permafrost

Alaska, U.S.A., 1969

The temperatures in winter often go below minus 70°F, in the summer
they rise to a steady 60° and 70°.

But in summer the movement of lorries or even the footsteps of
workmen can break up the surface, reducing the ground below to a
gluey swamp-like consistency. If roads are built—and they must be—
a seven-foot layer of gravel has to be used for insulation. When the
summer thawing is at its peak, there is constant and rapid erosion.
A track that was made by a caterpillar vehicle eroded quickly into a
56-foot gorge. If a pipeline were laid on the surface, it would sink
and eventually create a rushing summer river that would wash away
the pipeline. Soil conservation becomes of paramount importance.

There is no darkness during the height of the summer, and the men
never have any real opportunity to rest. As a result, some of the
operations were suspended until the winter when the ground was
firmer and more reliable, although human survival conditions were
at their lowest. Now that oil has been discovered, however, work is
carried on all year long . . .

The men who responded to the Arctic call fell into two categories :
those who wanted to make a lot of money in a short time, and those
who liked living in remote places away from civilisation—the same
kind of man who would be just as happy working in the hot solitude
of the Sahara, few of the men are under 30 . . .

Despite the lucrative pay and the amount of time off, the routine
is not easy. There are two drilling teams at each rig, and they work
alternate shifts. They live, eat, and relax in a thermostatically controlled barracks, and sleep four to a room. When they are not working
there is not very much to do. Because of the temperature outside in
winter they are voluntarily confined to the barracks.

They read, play shuffleboard, and watch 16 millimetre versions of
Westerns, epics, and old Doris Day movies which are brought in
regularly by the aircraft that services the sites three times daily. The
freezing temperatures take their toll on the men's hands, causing them
to split and bleed easily, which is accepted as part of the business.

There is no staff doctor; anyone injured is flown immediately to the nearest hospital. No drinking is allowed, although, says one crewman, 'No-one minds if you have the odd nip now and then.' Fairbanks is the nearest metropolitan city; it takes 28 days for the caterpillar supply train to travel the 360 miles to Prudhoe Bay.

The intense cold, like a tropical climate, creates mental and physical apathy. Combined with the winter confinement and the lack of recreational facilities, this is the biggest complaint of the men. When they have finished their four-week stint, they are able to fly to any place they want to go. Most of them choose Los Angeles 3,000 miles away. After four weeks of nights which last 22 hours, the sun of California is like a long-lost friend.

With only two hours of sunless twilight each day, visibility is restricted in all directions, and at times the snow and sky blend together so perfectly that there appears to be no horizon. For the aircraft which supply the camps, this is a constant hazard : the snow reflects lights and shadows and can play fatal tricks on even the most experienced pilots.

from : Donald Wiederman, 'Hot millions under ice',
The Daily Telegraph Magazine, May 16, 1969

23 Land of pioneers

Siberia, nineteen-sixties

Siberia excited his emotions as had no other part of the land. I found then that a great part of his youth and early middle age had been spent working all over Siberia. Before Siberia could be properly developed, he said, it had to be surveyed geographically and geologically. When Soviet scientists first began their gigantic task, it was fantastic how little organised scientific knowledge there was of the region. They had a terrible time for famine and civil war challenged Russian resources almost to breaking point. He had friends among geologists who could not get boats or trucks to help them on their scientific reconnaissances of the unknown and had actually gone out into the tundra of Siberia using reindeer and mules as pack-horses. Even today it was a problem getting transport for geologists because of the incredible size of Siberia, more than twice the size of western Russia, twice that of Europe and bigger than Australia. Did I realise that from East to West Siberia was more than four thousand miles, and from South to North close on two thousand miles? More than three million square miles of it was covered with forest, or '*taiga*' as he called it. In the *taiga* the summers were hot and short, the winters long. In winter the temperatures would easily fall to 70° below zero*. Yet they were easily borne and healthy because the climate is dry and on the whole windless. Like all Siberians he was inclined to boast of the cold winters yet he said that one Siberian summer was worth nine winters. However, surely I could imagine the difficulties of surveying so vast a country in so extreme a climate? The amount of unbroken forest in Siberia alone covered over three million square miles. From above it was a sea of green that swept over plains, descended into valleys and broke over the mountains with equal intensity. Pines, cedars, silver-firs, larches and spruces nearly shut out the sky. Many of the cedars were 250 feet high and nine feet in diameter. The moment a cloud covered the sun the forests were dark and even in summer a poor geologist had a job finding his way around. The worst forests were the Urmans or Cherns, the black, damp coniferous ones on hilly and marshy ground. The trees among them grew in an odd way at all angles from the earth, not all straight and the space between them was littered with fallen branches, tops broken off by lightning and whole trunks uprooted by some high wind. Working in these forests how one longed for the great Siberian steppes, the southern plains or even the bare, cold and windy tundra in the north. Yet once out of them one experienced a powerful nostalgia for the sound of a great tree exploding like a bomb from the frost and the tense wintry silence rushing in to wipe out the sound. Forced on one occasion to winter on a mountain of solid metal not far from Ilymsk, hard by the Angara, he told me of the delight he had enjoyed watching the natural life, from smaller species like the marten, ermine, kolinsky, weasel, glutton, squirrel, chipmunk, and the wonderful sable up to the badger, otter, wolves and bears. He told me of encounters with bears coming out of their sleep in hollow trunks whence their breath sometimes rose to hang like smoke above the stumps. He said there were thousands of them as well as wolves, foxes and lynxes. He told me of another winter in the north where the *taiga* declines into the open tundra and how the reindeer and polar foxes in their thousands moved from the open into the *taiga* fringes for food and cover. Siberia has two-thirds of the world's reindeer population, all now collectivized and much more profitable than ever before. Already the reindeer's enemy, the wolf, is being eliminated, hunted down by helicopter and radio-telephone and he himself had participated in such a hunt over the tundra. He told me of a summer by the shore of a forest lake, and of long evenings fishing for his supper. The woods around were full of mushrooms, the shores red with huge bilberries and raspberries and the earth around his camp a metre deep with pine-cones and dry moss.

from : Laurens Van Der Post, *Journey into Russia*

* Centigrade

24 Pioneers (or exploiters) of the Mato Grosso

Brazil, 1969

Long ago the government sold off the entire state, at peppercorn prices of a penny or two [½p-1p] an acre, and an ownership map of the area looks like a patchwork quilt. The patches vary in size, but most are rectangles with sides from 10 miles to 50 miles long. Most of these areas used to be miles from anywhere, and nobody could do much with their possessions, except perhaps sell them at, say, twopence or threepence an acre. With estates of a million acres or more even such a modest deal had its rewards. Nevertheless the big returns, the exploitation of these areas, had to wait until the Indians had gone and the government road had come sufficiently near.

This has now happened to a huge portion of the Mato Grosso state which until very recently had been quite untouched. Of course it had been the hunting grounds of various tribes, but the final solution to that problem had been successfully administered. Disease, inter-tribal war, and inter-tribal encounters, all played their part. The remaining Indians were gathered into one national park, several missionary encampments, and a few other dwelling places with much less control and patronage. Quite suddenly a vast area had no one living in it, and through this area a road was carved—with both skill and speed—for some 400 miles from a small frontier town called Xavantina to another on the banks of the Araguaia. The hinterland to the south and west of São Félix had suddenly become accessible.

So had a large number of the million acre patches ... Even so it is hard work. The forest is difficult enough to walk through, and harder still once it is half cut down, but the method of turning it into foreseeable profit is a splendid mixture of crude destruction and solid cunning ... They use nothing fancier than an axe to cut down the trees, and it takes one man ten days to turn an acre of basic forest into his own jungle of fallen timber. As after some artillery barrage a few trees are left standing, solitary sentinels of the former army, to look down upon the chaos at their feet. Once a year in the dry month of August, someone puts a match to this mile after mile of former forest and it burns very well ... The following August with half burnt boles lying about in every direction, the destroyer sets fire to it again, and again the smoke hangs heavily over the ground. Then, for a third year, having pulled the remains together into heaps, they burn these heaps and the giant forest has almost gone. When the rains come, a couple of months later, a tall kind of grass is scattered and sown wherever there is soil. This grows well, and it is time to move in the cattle ...

It is unfortunate that these big ranches are giving employment to so few people. Even the biggest of them, with 20,000 cattle and its own aircraft and hotel, has only 120 families on the estate. For further forest destruction 250 clearers are hired from April to August then, after the biggest annual bonfire of them all, dismissed. At least some work for some people is better than no work for anyone.

No attempt is made to sell the timber, but it is used to build up the ranch ...

It is men, axes, belts, planks, nails, steam and dust, a well worn combination from the past.

The cattle, mainly from zebu stock, with their unsightly lumps and folds of flesh, are entirely right for this world. They pick their way over the forest ruins, they suffer the local form of tsetse, a tabanid that packs a similar punch. They eat the tough and wiry 6 feet grass. They stand out in the midday sun then withstand 5 feet of water falling in the rainy season. They probably walked to the fazenda for several hundred miles, and they are rounded up by skilful men on mules. Those cowboy films have it all wrong; they never show shirts clinging with sweat, or feet with spurs but without shoes, or clouds of biting flies. Nor do they suggest smell or dirt.

The vultures have learnt long ago where the slaughter house stands, and they sit on the Passchendaele trees savouring the stink. Cow killing is still a rare event, mostly for home consumption, but stocks have to be built up so that hundreds can be killed a week, and frozen, or tinned, or dried, for those necessary profits.

from : Anthony Smith, 'Carving farmland from the
Brazilian forest', *The Times*, October 25, 1969

25 Mountaineer prisoners of war

Kenya, 1942

I was shaken out of my sleep by Umberto : 'Quick. Get up. Come and look at Mount Kenya !'

'What does it look like?'

'You shall see. The shape recalls Monviso viewed from Turin, but this is far more imposing.'

Owing to the rainy season we had so far had no opportunity of seeing anything of the mountain but the huge forest-clad pedestal. I was so anxious to see it that I almost got entangled in my bootlaces while dressing.

'Hurry up', shouted Umberto from the door, 'otherwise the peak will become covered with clouds again.'

I emerged at last, stumbled a few steps in the mud and then I saw it : an ethereal mountain emerging from a tossing sea of clouds framed between two dark barracks—a massive blue-black tooth of sheer rock inlaid with azure glaciers, austere yet floating fairy-like on the near horizon. It was the first 17,000-foot peak I had ever seen.

I stood gazing until the vision disappeared among the shifting cloud banks.

For hours afterwards I remained spell-bound.

I had definitely fallen in love.

Day followed weary day and the mountain remained blanketed under a pall of mist and cloud. The one glimpse I had of it days before seemed like the memory of a dream. Prison life fastened on me like a leaden chain. Future prospects were not even considered and only the present existed for us, dark and dismal.

For three months I had had no news of my family and to add to my anxiety there were rumours of a fatal epidemic of measles raging among the children in the vacation camps of Ethiopia. Nerves were near breaking point. The maddening worries about which one could do nothing, the passivity to which we were condemned, the deadly monotony of the rains and above all the communal life one was forced to lead in a small barrack with twenty-five or thirty similarly irritable people seemed likely to drive one mad . . .

The night sky was clear. There was a smell of good earth in the air such as I had seldom noticed in Africa. I was thinking 'The future exists if you know how to make it' and 'It's up to you', as I turned the corner of my barrack at the exact spot from where I had seen Mount Kenya for the first time, and from which I had **always** since then cast a look in the direction of the peak.

Now it was visible again and in the starlight it looked even more tantalising than in daylight. The white glaciers gleamed with mysterious light and its superb summit towered against the sky. It was a challenge.

A thought crossed my numbed mind like a flash . . .

In order to break the monotony of life one had only to start taking risks again, to try to get out of the Noah's Ark, which was preserving us from the risks of war but isolating us from the world, to get out into the deluge of life. If there is no means of escaping to a neutral country or of living under a false name in occupied Somalia as many have done, then, I thought, at least I shall stage a break in this awful travesty of life. I shall try to get out, climb Mount Kenya and return here.

I realised from the start that I could not do this single-handed; I should have to find companions. As a proof that we had reached the summit—if ever we did so—we should leave a flag there . . .

The more I considered the idea of escape, the more I realized the magnitude of the task I had set myself. Should we be able to climb without a long period of acclimatization in the thin air of 17,000 feet? How should we make the actual climb? Whom should I ask to accompany me? How could we get out of camp and in again? These and other problems kept my mind fully occupied. I found it fascinating to elaborate, in the utmost secrecy, the first details of my scheme.

Life took on another rhythm because it had a purpose...

Never, I imagine, have mountaineers approached the mountain of their dreams—a colossus of 17,000 feet at that—under such conditions; not at least in this century with its highly organised methods of collecting information. Our ignorance proved an insuperable handicap from the point of view of material achievement; but from the spiritual point of view, which is of far greater importance to the true mountaineer, it was in the nature of a gift from God. Every step led to new discoveries, and we were continually in a state of amazed admiration and gratitude. It was as though we were living at the beginning of time, before men had begun to give names to things.

from : Felice Benuzzi, *No Picnic on Mount Kenya*

26 Gentlemen explorers

Africa, nineteenth century

Nothing is more intriguing in African exploration in the nineteenth century than the casualness with which it was often undertaken. A group of friends meet and discuss a trip abroad. Shall it be Vienna, Naples, or the Canary Islands? Or possibly Africa? Yes of course Africa. They know nothing about Africa, no shipping lines exist, no one can tell them anything very definite about the climate, the kind of medicines required on the journey, the local languages, the food, the money or the inhabitants; and maps are unobtainable. But presumably, they argue, these things will be made clear as they proceed along their way. The gunsmith in the Strand supplies them with firearms, the banker gives them a draft on Cairo, the hatter furnishes sun-helmets with flaps at the back, and off they go as lightheartedly as if they were setting off for the South of France to avoid the English winter.

from : Alan Moorehead, *The Blue Nile*

27 Prospecting beneath the sea

Ireland, 1969

One's hands are occupied working under the sea, but one's mind is free, and all the time I was humping stones around I was thinking: 'I'm here at last, at last there is nowhere else I would rather be, nothing else I would rather be doing. This is the life for me. No time for eating or sleeping. Exhausted when I get up, and even more tired when I go to bed. That's what I like. I enjoy it all, including the discomfort, the exhaustion, the cold, the wretchedness of sea-sickness.'

I moved something yellow. A gold coin? No, just a shell. One was easily fooled. I examined it closely so as not to get caught like that again. It wasn't a shell, it was a gold medallion. It had a cross on it, the cross of the Order of Alcantara. On the other side there was an engraving of a saint with a tree. But to which knight had it belonged?

In and around the front of the cave, under a layer of rocks, stretched a dense compound or magma of round stones and cannon balls, and an agglomeration of wreckage, which at first I thought was ballast. I realised it wasn't the following day when I picked up one end of a superb gold chain, and found that it went right down into that black magma, and came out the other side.

There would have been a risk of breaking the artefacts if we had tried to prise them free from their crust of magma under water. So, we spent the first month dislodging chunks of the sea bed from the pitted rocks, putting them in slings and hoisting them up. Foreheads dripping with perspiration and backs aching, we heaved them on board. Once on land, in the evening we very carefully chipped away at this crust, stone by stone. From out of this vile magma came piastres and reals, escudos and ducats, copper buckles, gold chains, pieces of pottery, lead bullets, leather straps, fragments of cartridges, knives and forks, spoons . . .

There were days when we had to dive blind, when the water was so black that we couldn't see our hands in front of our faces, when we got lost in the most familiar places. Great black masses would seem to hurtle towards us, moving aside at the very last minute, or else the blackness above would become even more dense. We were just playthings for the swell, which threw us towards rocks or hurled us into the cave at will . . .

In calm weather the operation is easy enough. You put a steel sling around the boulder you want to move—if it's that kind of shape —or if it's egg-shaped you spin a web of steel around it. Then you link the lifting bags by their shackles to the steel sling and inflate them from a spare aqualung . . . But heavy swells make everything difficult. You have to grab some seaweed with one hand just to try to remain near your boulder and work the sling into place with the other. The sea takes the huge heavy rubber bags where it pleases while you try to fight your way towards the work site with the aid of two helpers. You are out of breath and exhausted by the time it is finally shackled up. Then you stick the inflating hose into the mouth of the bag and try to get a look at what happens, each time the swell throws you near it.

When it starts to lift off it becomes crazy; waves pushing the bag take the eight-ton rock just jumping towards you, then away. You try to keep out of harm's way but you have to watch what's happening. Of course it's about now that thick clouds of sand obscure the scene, big drops of sweat get in your eyes, and seaweed blacks out your face mask with every wave.

Then you are thrown against a nearby rock which catches the buckle of your lead belt. So there you are, the spare aqualung under one arm, the other around a stump of seaweed struggling with your belt, one eye on the buckle, the other on the mad, jumping rock which keeps bumping around you with thunderous tremors.

Often the swell will throw the rock around until the sling is shaken loose and between two clumps of waving seaweed you catch a glimpse of the bunch of huge balloons rocketing towards the surface. If the sling holds them you will be forced around at the mercy of the waves until you let the boulder down anywhere rather than be carried to Scotland or dashed against the cliff.

Such manoeuvres carried out half blind in the chaos of the wild waters seem frighteningly dangerous. In two years, however, we have had few accidents, and nothing worse than a couple of crushed fingers ... We are proud of our 8,000 hours of work. After our ten months here the whole area is gutted, chipped, turned over, unrecognisable. We have scraped deep furrows in the rock. One by one we have learnt all the tricks of the sea and dragged out of it the secret of four centuries. Soon we shall have to deflate the boats once again. I shall recount the lead bullets, photograph the last jewels, polish all our gold coins and the 600 silver ones.

Then it will be back for another winter in the libraries. Until next spring calls us like sea-swallows to Ireland and its many Armada wrecks. And I look forward to it for again it will be a patient labour of love.

from : 'The amazing story of the discovery of
Spanish Armada Treasure', *The Observer
Magazine,* September 21, 1969

28 Pioneer northwest passage by oil tanker *Manhattan*

Arctic, 1969

'General progress considerably slowed by ice six to nine feet thick, freezing solid round hull. Also hard snow and ice collecting on prow, thereby increasing friction with highly concentrated flows' ...

Manhattan's soaring, flaring bow, designed and built to slice and smash the ice, looking in its power and elegance, like the whim of some eccentric multi-millionaire yachtsman with a taste for the biggest kind of sport, had come through unscarred. The great hull, specially protected within during a rushed summer rebuild by the most slender yet impregnable casing of steel, and without by a nine-foot wide belt of the same, had cracked the pack ice with something of the certainty, the inimitably American confidence that had put men on the moon.

And the comparison is deliberate. If the knowledge and techniques which have made space travel a reality had not been available, *Manhattan* would not have moved a sea mile beyond Baffin Bay. But a satellite photographed the ice ahead; another gave the ship's position; lasers measured the ice depth; radios hundreds of times more powerful than those provided for mere warm water tankers defeated the lures of the magnetic pole, computers consumed and digested the raw material ...

Just two weeks ago *Manhattan* was returning to the Delaware, a round trip completed, a triumph by any standards, rational or emotional, of man, his courage and skills, over an environment totally hostile to his efforts.

from : Anthony Verrier, '40 million gamble', *The Daily Telegraph Magazine*, November 28, 1969

29 Exploration made easy

Western Australia, nineteen-fifties

The story of how Hancock discovered Mt. Tom Price at Hamersley almost qualifies for legend status back home, but in this country it is surprisingly little known. Although he refused to talk about his current trip [to London] Hancock did relate to us the story he had told many times before.

For many years, he said, he had flown his own plane, and back in

1952 he was running his wife into Perth 'to get away from the flies and the dust' from a small, white asbestos mine he was working up country. 'The conditions were very bad with the cloud base right down on the mountains. I did not want to turn back, so the only thing I could do was to follow a gorge which I thought would take me through. We had flown for some while when I realized that we were passing almost over what looked like a massive outcrop of iron ore.'

'I could not stop on that trip, but the next winter I went back and landed close by. I thought that the ore looked low quality but I took a couple of pieces back for assay and found that there in the natural state was untouched ore of a quality two per cent higher than the average blast furnace feed used in the United States.'

It was a discovery which Hancock knew would eventually make him a rich man and indeed he has now received royalties on his find worth hundreds of millions of Australian dollars.

from : The Times, July 13, 1970

30 First American to take off into space

Florida, U.S.A.

'Fear? Have you ever seen a rocket taking off? It stands there, so big that the men around it look tiny, like flies, they light a little spark, and a great bellow tears the air to shreds, a white cloud spreads, and it lifts off, up into the infinite, and you blaspheme : God, we've caught you by the coat tails! And as you utter this polite blasphemy, you no longer fear the rocket because you remember that it was man who built it, it was man who lighted the spark that fired the rocket. The rocket without man is a glove without a hand ...'

Four hours are a lot when you're shut in a steel nutshell that's swaying and vibrating ninety feet above the ground and you don't know what's happening because no one has tried it before, you're melting with the heat, nervousness constricts your throat, impatience wrings your heart. Deke, what's up? It's because visibility isn't good, the Control Centre couldn't follow the first stage of the flight because of the clouds, it'll clear in half an hour. O.K., half an hour has passed, Deke, what's up now? It's a valve that's overheated, Al, we'll have to change it, how do you feel? I feel fine, Deke, will you ring Louise and tell her I'm fine? O.K., Al. How long will it take to change the valve, Deke? Thirty or forty minutes, Al. O.K., Deke. Ten minutes, twenty minutes, thirty minutes, forty minutes, fifty minutes, sixty, seventy, eighty, eighty-one, eighty-two, eighty-three, eighty-four, eighty-five, eighty-six minutes to change the valve, well, are we ready, Deke? Yes, Al, starting countdown again. Deke, countdown has stopped again, what's up now Deke? It's the technicians who want to check an electronic computer on account of the trajectory, Al. Well, it's done now, this time we're all set, far from it, they've stopped again, what is it now, Deke? It's the fuel pressure that's too high, keep calm, Al. I'm calmer than you are, by God, why don't you sort things out and light this candle, for God's sake?

It was 9.23 when they started countdown again. The sun had dried up the last drop of rain.

'Are we ready, Deke?'

'Ready, Al.'

'Freedom Seven calling. Fuel is go . . .'

'Oxygen is go.'

'One point two G. Cabin at fourteen psi.'

'Go! Go! Go! Go! Go! Go!'

'Final count, start!'

'Ten . . . nine . . . eight . . . seven . . . six . . . five . . . four . . . three . . . two . . . one . . . zero . . . lift-off!'

'Ignition. Lift-off!'

'You're on your way, Jose,' said Slayton's low calm voice.

from : Oriana Faliaci, *If the Sun Dies*

31 Dangers of space flight

Outer Space, 1962

As we started to heat up on re-entry, I could feel something let go on the blunt end of the capsule behind me. There was a considerable thump, and I felt sure it was the retro-pack breaking away. I made a transmission to Al Shepard to this effect, but he apparently did not hear me. By this time, the capsule was so hot that a barrier of ionization had built up around it and cut off all communications between me and the people on the ground. This was normal, and I had expected it to happen, but it left me more or less alone with my little problem.

I saw one of the three metal straps that hold the retro-pack in place start to flap around loose in front of the window. Then I began to see a bright orange glow building up around the capsule. 'A real fireball outside,' I said into the microphone. The loose strap burned off at this point and dropped away. Then, right away, I could see big flaming chunks go flying by the window. Some of them were as big as six to eight inches across. I could hear them bump against the capsule behind me before they took off, and I thought that the heat-shield might be tearing apart. As it turned out later, these were parts of the retro-pack breaking up. It had not fallen away after all, and the heatshield itself was coming through in perfect shape. This was a bad moment. But I knew that if the worst was really happening it would all be over shortly and there was nothing I could do about it. So I kept on with what I had been doing—trying to keep the capsule under control—and sweated it out.

I knew that if the shield were falling apart, I would feel the heat pulse first at my back, and I waited for it. I kept on controlling the capsule. It was programmed to do a slow, steady spin on its roll axis at the rate of ten degrees per second to equalize the aerodynamic flow around the capsule and to keep it from exceeding the limits that we had estimated were maximum for re-entry. The automatic control system was normally supposed to handle this procedure but I kept control with the manual stick and did it myself. Pieces of flaming material were still flying past the window during this period, and the glow outside was still bright and orange. It lasted for only about a minute, but these few moments ticked off inside the capsule like days on a calendar. I still waited for the heat, and I made several attempts to contact the Control Centre and keep them informed.

'Hello, Cape. *Friendship* 7. Over. Hello, Cape, *Friendship* 7. How do you receive? Over.' There was no answer.

from : (John Glenn) Seven Astronauts of
Project Mercury, *Into Orbit*

Notes on Section 5

The bold figures indicate extract numbers

1 The Donner party of whose tragic journey Virginia Reed writes were making for land in California, and unfortunately had to face the Sierra Nevada in winter (1846). Most settlers aimed at getting over in summer. Two years later the trail was followed by adventurers seeking gold (discovered in California in 1848). Others went from the eastern seaboard perilously round the Cape in all sorts of craft. The fastest time by clipper was eighty-nine days, but it could take five months by brig or side-wheel steamer. Equipment and stores went this way. Others took any ship available—regardless of its condition—to the Isthmus, and went overland by jungle track to Panama, there to await with 4000 others a passage on a ship going to San Francisco. The eating of human flesh is referred to also by earlier settlers in Virginia and in Eskimo stories as late as 1926. The last words of the letter show the spirit of the pioneering young.

2 The Bantu, Dutch and English became the basic elements of southern Africa's people.

3 Alexis Creek (52° 0′ N, 123° 20′ W) is on the River Chilcotin and the road to Bella Coola.

4 The nuns responded to a plea for help as teachers in the prairies.

5 The flowing wheat (which came later) has been said to have physical effects, amongst them a feeling of sea-sickness!

6 Emigrants were not only ignorant as to the nature of the journey, but also as to the nature of the country. (Even as recently as 1967 some families returned to England because they couldn't take the unexpected heat of Sydney.) Apart from first-class saloon passengers, emigrants 'did for themselves'. Some children died on every voyage for want of proper food and from disease.

7 Loneliness seems to have been the big problem in early outback Australia. Outback wives are still hard to come by. The Australian of today is an urban dweller in the main.

8 Flies are a constant menace to men and animals in warm places all over the world. This ranch would undoubtedly have refrigeration today.

9 A special tribute to the author's mother, and a philosophical look at creativity which is often stifled by everyday routine.

10 Compare this with Section 3, extract No. 13. The work is much the same; the century and the atmosphere different. In 1820 life was hard for women in Western Europe also, unless they had servants. In the mines, factories and workshops and on the land women were exploited and debased. The form of courtship described still occurs in some peasant communities where the bearing of children is regarded as essential to the continuance of the family unit.

11 The quality of life possible in these conditions is revealing. By present-

237

day standards in Britain, this would be regarded as sub-standard property. In many parts of the world it would still be considered as more than adequate for family life.

12 This is fairly typical of the struggling years of young settlers. The dust and the hard-eating persist, but light planes have improved access and mechanical help makes housework easier.

13 The second-generation pioneers have been stimulated by war and the constant threat of war with Arab neighbours. They also face social problems arising from the languages and traditions of the people who are coming into Israel from all over the world and collecting in their several cultural groups. They have to be taught a common language and assimilated.

The kibbutzim have adopted the principle 'to each according to his need—from each according to his ability'. The kibbutzim vary. They own land communally, farm intensively on modern lines, and may have processing factories in which they may employ outside labour. Only three per cent of the Israelis live in kibbutzim. In border zones the kibbutz may be a Nahal, or have a Nahal attached, manned by young men and women soldiers between eighteen and twenty-two years of age. In some kibbutzim children live entirely separate from parents, in others they come home at night and for weekends, and in others the child is part of the family. As well as kibbutzim there are moshavs, or co-operatives. Some of these have individual land and private family life; others have communal land and run the farm and plant as a business. Half the people of Israel live in the four main towns.

14–15 These extracts have features in common, despite their differing dates. Medicine Bow (41° 56′ N, 106° 11′ W) has never grown much. Now the population is only around the 400 mark. Thompson and Hay River (extract No. 16) are equally stark as new towns. Thompson (55° 50′ N, 97° 34′ W) developed during a rush to find nickel for steel-making. A branch of Churchill railway was thrown out to its site by the Burntwood River. The climate is severe, though the latitude is that of Copenhagen approximately, and the social problem of displaced persons (who are often content to accept conditions of work unacceptable to older-established workers) is a complication.

16 Hay River, on the Great Slave Lake and railway to Edmonton, has an airport and a road to the south, and planes visit outback settlements. As in extract No. 15 an attempt to establish settled life is being made, but there remains the problem of money going out rather than people coming in to settle down in prosperity. The general mess and muck that accompanies fast development is illustrated here.

17–19 These are complementary and show the scramble for land and the hardship which men were content to endure in the desire for big rewards; certainly not 'money for nothing'. Guthrie (extract No. 17) in fact is still small.

20 Emphasises the speed and scale of operations in the context of modern technology and the big company. The speed of change is greater than ever before. Social problems are as acute as in Thompson, Manitoba, 1961 (extract No. 15). See also extract No. 29.

21 Nickel again, as in extract No. 15, this time in Laverton, where in 1969 they were pegging claims, just as they did in Kimberley and the Rand nearly a hundred years before. Today's 'peggers' do not intend to work the land or mines themselves, but to sell out to companies at fantastic profits. They also invest in shares which, in the case of one company, rose from 7s (35p) to over £100 sterling in a matter of weeks in 1969, owing to stock market buying all over the world, and then dropped to below half that value in 1970. No doubt a desert mining town on the lines of Broken Hill will develop if the promise of nickel-mining on a large scale is fulfilled. Otherwise there will be a slump and yet another ghost town.

22 Men who come to work the oil-rigs because they like solitude are likely to be disappointed. The harsh climate dictates for them conditions almost as crowded as for the earlier gold-rush miners, though there are of course more amenities. The short spring, as in Siberia, no doubt has its moments (see extract No. 23 and also Section 10, extract No. 2). Wages are fantastically high for the men working on the drills, and even for those (the majority) engaged on road works and general maintenance in this area of special difficulty. After a stint of work the men are more than ready for a change of scene, hence the visits by plane every few weeks to Los Angeles and elsewhere. An oil pipeline is proposed from the oil-fields to the south coast town of Valdez in the earthquake zone. See also extract No 28.

The Eskimos of the area come off badly, although new houses are provided for them. They have come suddenly into contact with modern technology and experience many pressures they had not met before. They have lost their hunting grounds, and are not compensated in the big deals being made for their land. In Barrow, the most developed Eskimo base, they work in the less well-paid jobs and live in civilised squalor despite the supermarkets, piped fuel and white man's charity.

23 Early Siberia was opened up, in cruelty, by forced labour; today by volunteers, who do in fact find more freedom than in other parts of the U.S.S.R. They also get more pay. The plane is invaluable, as railways are rare, roads few and bad, and rivers navigable only for part of the year.

24 Xavantina is on the River Mortes at approximately 15° south, and is about 100 miles (160 km) west of Aruanã. The road runs parallel to the River Mortes and joins the River Araguaia at São Félix, which stands at the confluence of the two rivers. It has been suggested that the rights of primitive man should be more carefully preserved (see Section 6, extract No 10). Note 'quite suddenly a vast area had no one living in it.'

25–26 These passages have certain elements in common. They express among other things the desire to explore for its own sake and to stretch the mental and physical powers. The casual nineteenth-century gentlemen's expeditions have been followed by a growing number of traveller writers to whom we are indebted for much of our knowledge of wild places; by large numbers of students 'roughing it'; and by sponsored, well-equipped and well-planned expeditions. Hence our respect and admiration for the attempt by Italian prisoners of war in Kenya to climb Mount Kenya without maps, and with primitive apparatus collected secretly and stored with meagre food from their rations. They escaped; they climbed (not to the top but a long way up); they suffered; they returned to camp—the whole expedition bringing refreshment of mind and spirit.

27 The author refers to this exciting work as underwater archaeology rather than as treasure hunting. Skin-diving is becoming increasingly important in ocean recovery of astronauts, in the camera tracking of whales and other creatures, and in other scientific work, as well as in inspecting and servicing underwater installations and ships.

28 The U.S. oil tanker *Manhattan*, 118,000 tons, made her pioneer journey of 4500 miles (7240 km) from Delaware to 20 miles (32 km) off Point Barrow in the hope of opening up a seaway for 250,000-tonners to make the round trip in forty days (with the purpose of cheapening Alaskan oil in the States). She was assisted eight or nine times to break through by a Canadian 6000-ton icebreaker. Her route was via Thule, Cape Clarendon, and Sachs Harbour, to Point Barrow. On board were 126 experts.

29 Hamersley, 22° 0′ S, 117° 45′ E. This is the only extract added after the compiler's death. It seemed well worth including as a complete contrast to the conditions under which prospecting for minerals was carried on in the nineteenth century. The article tells us nothing, however, of the conditions under which the ore is actually worked. See also extract No. 20.

30–31 Both extracts highlight the bravery of astronauts, which we may be beginning to take for granted.

6

Spoliation of environment: what now?

These extracts are from the writings of people who feel strongly about what is happening to the earth and its treasures, about the physical environment in which we live and about the quality of life we enjoy. Among the subjects raised are: the mistakes of developers, amongst whom one may recognise pioneers in their struggle to survive; exploiters, careless of waste; some of the forms of pollution resulting from the development of overpopulated affluent societies, whose peoples have now the power to ruin the earth; and some of the aesthetic problems of maintaining and managing decent conditions in town and country places for man's work and recreation. The last extracts highlight positive action. Most pieces are short; the long extract 9 is included as it is a classic exposition of fast degeneration of land under man's hand in a temperate humid climate.

'Quit thinking about land-use as solely an economic problem. Examine each question in terms of what is ethically and aesthetically right, as well as economically expedient.'

Robert Arvill

'There is virtually no form of environmental pollution that we do not know how to control. It is just a question of economics. At the heart of the problem lies the question: How much prosperity, and for whom, shall be sacrificed for how much environmental purity, and for whom?'

Lord Kennet

'Landscape equals habitat plus man—the natural environment

changed by a creature who is himself constantly changing
... to achieve good landscapes for our new ways of
living we must deliberately design new settings to suit our
new land-uses. And the past cannot help us. There are no
traditions for industrial landscape ... nor for any of our
other new land-uses.'

Nan Fairbrother

1 Destruction of sugar maples

New York State, U.S.A., 1793

A deep and careless incision had been made into each tree near its root, into which little sprouts, formed of the bark of the alder, or of the sumac, were fastened; and a trough, roughly dug out of linden, or of basswood, was lying at the root of each tree, to catch the sap that flowed from this extremely wasteful and inartificial arrangement . . .

'It grieves me to witness the extravagance that pervades this country,' said the Judge, 'where the settlers trifle with the blessings they might enjoy, with the prodigality of successful adventurers. You are not exempt from the censure yourself, Kirby, for you make dreadful wounds in these trees where a small incision would effect the same object. I earnestly beg you to remember, that they are the growth of centuries, and when once gone, none living will see their loss remedied.'

'Why, I don't know, Judge,' returned the man he addressed : 'It seems to me, if there's a plenty of anything in this mountaynious country, it's the trees. If there's any sin in chopping them I've a pretty heavy account to settle; for I've chopped over the best part of a thousand acres, with my own hands, counting both Varmount and York states; and I hope to live to finish the whull, before I lay up my ax.'

from : James Fenimore Cooper, *The Pioneers*

2 Changing the vegetation pattern

North America

The grasslands were hunting grounds, the home of bison. Indian fortunes could be improved by extension of grasslands. To help themselves, the Indians deliberately set fire to the dry grasses along the forest edge. Repeated scorching often killed back the woodlands, enlarging the prairies and the potential supply of meat. Today no one knows how much of the long-grass prairie stretching east of the Mississippi was in trees before the Indians began changing the landscape.

When viewed in modern perspective, most of man's activities are seen to affect plants in this same direction—inducing successions toward vegetation tolerating more and more arid conditions. Forest becomes prairie. Prairie becomes chaparral or thorn scrub, or outright desert. Indeed, the recent invention of reforesting land is almost

243

unique in pushing plant successions the other way—toward types requiring more moisture.

from : Lorus J. and Margery Milne, *The balance of Nature*

3 Land hunger

Kenya

Looking out from the small yellow aircraft ... one could see how different theory was from practice, here as elsewhere. In a forest reserve no one is allowed to fell trees, cultivate, start fires, or graze livestock. In less than half an hour I counted seventeen active fires and saw the shambles created by innumerable others. Whole ridgebacks of the mountain sticking up like black spines, were as bare as slag heaps and already runnelled and creased by gully erosion. Older fires were still smoking in some of these devastated areas; one could see the forest being eaten into like a great fur belt attacked by moths.

As sure as fate, one day, there will be no more water for cattle in the streams below.

from : Elspeth Huxley, *A New Earth*

4 Fires, goats and nomads

Turkey

We entered a broad valley with *yaylas** on either hand, and beyond them the spurs of the mountains. Between some of the spurs villages were huddled, showing like small green buds in the clefts of a twig in early spring : for the spurs themselves were utterly barren ... In southern Turkey, I was told, the greatest scourges are fires, goats and nomads, and as I drove along the roads I was constantly seeing signs let into the hillside in the whitewashed stones telling people to preserve and protect their forests. Erosion and natural beauty apart, these trees are of immense value, not only for their timber but also for the resin which in certain areas is tapped exactly as rubber is tapped in Malaya.

from : Michael Pereira, *Mountain and a Shore*

* High-pasture settlements

5 Search for fuel

Sahara

Women without any protection carry camel loads of wood on their shoulders. You would see them filing over the dunes in the heat of the noon bent beneath their burdens. In search of fuel, these women will trek for weeks across the deserts. When they find an old tree or a clump of bushes they will hack them and destroy them. Then they go on with the search until all of them can return together to their lords and masters with their back-breaking faggots. They have to find fuel to keep their families warm in the bitterly cold nights and to do their cooking. But every time they destroy a tree or pull up a bush the desert wins another victory. That soil, which the vegetation has been holding together, breaks up and is snatched away by the wind to become drifting sand to add to a dune and to bury what had been a fertile garden.

from : Ritchie Calder, *Men against the Desert*

6 Overstocking and drought years

Australia, nineteen-forties

On treeless plains grass and shrubs hold the earth : and on vast tracks of sandy soil the salt and blue bushes grow. On both these there is good feed for sheep and cattle. So flocks and herds increase, and great fortunes are made. Comes a drought, small creeks and water-holes dry up, and the animals surround those that remain. Soon grass and shrubs are eaten up, and around the watering-place is a bare circle of baked earth. At its circumference there is herbage, and the animals come in to drink and walk back to the feeding ground. The bare circle is widening. Soon it extends in a radius of three or four miles from the water, and the animals begin to fear the journey. Until driven by thirst they do not leave the herbage, and until driven by hunger they do not leave the watering-place. Soon they are dying by thousands and hundreds of thousands. Had they been less numerous the radius of the bare circle would have been smaller and they would have survived the drought. The rabbits die by millions. On the waterless side of the vermin-proof fences their dead bodies accumulate like a sand bank and the survivors thus reach the top of the fence and contiune their search for water.

Comes the rain and in a week or so the bare earth is once more

245

green. Seeds in the ground have sprouted. More stock is bought, and the young shoots are eaten up before the herbage has seeded. The rabbits ensure that not a blade is overlooked. These droughts are recurrent, and so also became the practice of restocking until, in some areas, there was no new growth after the rain because there were no more seeds in the earth. So the baked soil crumbled and was blown away. In place of the station or sheep run there is a desert. In recent years the lights of Adelaide have had to be turned on in the middle of the day, so dark the sky when the soil of Australia is passing out to sea.

from : Halliday Sutherland, *Southward Journey*

7 Destructive agriculture of the New World

U.S.A.

They ploughed the land, planted the crops in long, straight rows, cultivated between the rows, and developed the most destructive type of agriculture the world has ever known.

Our people are mechanical minded. The 2,000 tractors of 1910 grew to $3\frac{1}{2}$ million faster moving types by 1950. The horses and mule-population fell from 25 million to $7\frac{1}{2}$ million. Fences—the Maginot Line against erosion—were torn out to make more room for the tractors. This gave the wind and water a longer sweep. As a result millions of tons of good topsoil were carried down the slopes and dumped into the rivers. Mud clogged the harbors. Silt poured into the reservoirs, reducing their storage capacity from 1 to 3 per cent a year. And, beginning in early 1934, dust storms tore the soil loose from its moorings in Kansas wheat fields, spread it over the country to the east, and carried some of it on out to sea.

The handwriting of erosion was plain for everyone to see. People in high places began to be cognizant of the damage that was being done. Public sentiment was aroused . . .

The Soil Conservative Act was passed in 1935, and the Soil Conservation Service came into existence. Strip-cropping, contour-farming, and the planting of forests got under way. Farmers began to realise that it was necessary to take greater advantage of roots as a means of sewing the soil to the earth. But millions of acres of good land had been ruined before this came to pass.

from : Firman E. Bear, 'The Earth and the fullness thereof',
Journal of the Franklin Institute, Vol. 254, No. 2, July 1952

8 Changing pattern of the fields

Norfolk, England, 1968

We walked through a sea of barley. It stretched as far as the eye could see in all directions, surging up to the path and round the feet of occasional elm trees, last vestiges of the former hedges. 'This could be Canada', we said to one another, 'these great fields.'

They were starting to harvest. Machines swept past, unimpeded, taking up the crop and leaving behind them the tightly baled straw to be collected later. We looked around. Nearby they were ploughing already, and in the hot dry air a faint haze of dust was rising, as the wind swept, soil-ladened, across the vast bare fields.

A special contribution by J. James

9 Classic sequence of destruction of the land

New Zealand

The Maori was not an accomplished agriculturalist. His efforts to grow the Kumara (sweet potato) and the Taro were his only real adventures into the realms of farming. In view of this it is interesting to note that he was always careful to choose the richest soils and he saw to it that several years of fallow followed the growing of each crop. To prepare the land for the crop he first of all burned off any rough vegetation; and after the first rain he broke up the soft surface with the *ko*, a primitive wooden hoe. Such cultivation as he did was necessarily shallow and in the long run his farming activities in no way impoverished the soil . . .

For the *Pakeha*,* to work the land, something more effective than the *ko* was required. It was necessary to import machinery from the home country. As more land was opened up the need became pressing. Once cultivated, the land yielded wheat, potatoes and barley, which helped to feed the settlers; but history has shown that man is ambitious beyond the stage of a full stomach. Even the simplest of needs—kerosene for the lamps, glassware, paper, pots and pans and the hundred and one household essentials—had to be imported. In other words, it was necessary to trade with the homeland if the people were to attain the better life they had dreamed of and for which they were striving.

The main item for exchange was wool, from the backs of the

* White settler

hardy merino-sheep. There was a demand in England for the raw wool and in New Zealand a market for the manufactured cloth. Before long all the easier flat land was settled. The newcomers were forced to move back into the foothills and soon even beyond into the high country, to seek pastures for their sheep. But the going wasn't easy! The way was barred by a seemingly impenetrable barrier—the bush. It is well to pause here and reflect that the bush was not, as the name seems to imply, an area of scrubby growth. It was in fact a dense forest of tall timber trees forcing their way upward through a vast twisted mass of creeping vines, tree ferns, small shrubs and young growth. Its only inhabitants were the birds, a rather sombre-hued population, some slow in flight, some quick, but all living together in a natural sanctuary, silent save for their own unique music. This was the barrier to an expanding industry. To the men and women who had braved 12,000 miles of stormy seas to build a new home, the barrier resolved itself into one of time. It was the time taken for the axe to fell and split; the time taken for fire to consume; the time taken to clear and plough and sow. In all it was but a short time.

True there were some who saw the worth of the timber and were quick to realise that here was a ready-made source of wealth. Throughout the country, but more particularly in the kauri forests of North Auckland, timber mills sprang up. The timber trade was profitable and compared with sheep-farming the returns were much quicker . . .

The constant urge to produce wool soon led to the grazing of the highland tussock stands which flourished above the bush on the steep mountain-sides. The merinos didn't eat very much of the tussock plants but they thrived on the grasses and herbs which grow in their shelter.

Huge tracts of land were grazed and the sheep wandered at will. Fences were almost non-existent, the only boundaries being those that nature provided in the form of rivers and ranges.

In course of time the price of wool started to drop and to keep pace with the falling returns the numbers of sheep were increased. As prices continued to drop the numbers grew beyond the normal carrying capacity of the land. To the runholder, the first indication of this state of overgrazing was a falling off of condition in his flock. Unfortunately the deterioration in the animals lagged behind that of the tussock pastures. The inevitable result was that the cover was seriously impaired before the runholder became aware of it. The tussock was still there in most cases but it was much weaker with little in the way of grasses or herbs growing around it.

Faced with reducing his stock or producing more feed, the worried runholder played his last card—a trump! Unhappily it was a small trump rapidly countered with a joker, for this hardy pioneer resorted to the use of fire. Thousands of acres of tussock were burned off and through the blackened hillsides there appeared as if by magic a veritable sea of young grass. The hungry sheep crowded the new pastures and in short order the succulent shoots disappeared. The green sward that had appeared so providentially yesterday had completely vanished today. Given time Nature could probably have recovered from this blow, but the runholder repeated the offence, often in the drier summer weather when a hot fire not only burnt off the top hamper, but also destroyed the grass-roots completely. But this was not the end. The heavy rains of the mountains whipped down on the bare unprotected soil and sheered it off the steep slopes. There was only a thin layer of soil in the first place and very soon the large stones beneath were exposed. Deprived of the binding action of soil and roots, the stones began to move. Avalanches of shale and debris gathered momentum, swept down the faces and plunged into the forests. This was the joker to which the runholder had no answer . . .

Once invaded by screes and gullies, the floor of the bush was disturbed to the extent that the trees, which relied for their very existence on the well-being of the carpet of litter, were substantially weakened. Every here and there a tree died and others were undermined and fell by encroaching gullies. The leafy canopy was opened up, letting light and warmth penetrate to the exposed roots. Finally, through the ever-increasing gaps came the wind. It swept right into the heart of the bush, dessicating the mossy floor and laying low hundreds of thirsty shallow-rooted trees. Thus was initiated a slow but steady cycle resulting in the ultimate destruction of the forest.

The effect of the sheep in the forest was indeed indirect and of rather minor importance when compared with the ravages of certain other animals that the Pakeha saw fit to introduce. Within the bush are to be found many species of deer. The red deer, the fallow deer, the sambur deer and the wapiti or elk, to name the most important, have each their own domain in the bush. In addition to deer there are goats, pigs, wild cattle, chamois and thar. New Zealand had originally no grazing and browsing animals and given a little forethought it should have been obvious that the introduction of such creatures would bring about far-reaching changes. The problem might have been approached more sanely but for the outcry of sportsmen and curiously sentimental folk who were determined to convert this new land into a small replica of their homeland . . .

The lower tussock-lands initially weakened by sheep-grazing, seemed to attract the rabbits.* Before long they were competing with the sheep for every bite of green grass. The arrival of the stoat and weasel did little to discourage the rabbit. These bloodthirsty little

* Introduced 1838

creatures seemed keener to concentrate on the unwary native birds. Living in such a land devoid of predatory animals the birds were unprepared for such attacks and consequently great numbers were killed.

This may sound a far cry from the story of forest destruction, but in fact it is singularly important a feature for the New Zealand native bush is almost completely dependent on its birds for its very existence . . .

In the higher country, where the forest was removed or partially removed, the bare unprotected soil was rapidly washed into the rivers by the naturally heavy rainfall. On the site of the forests, screes and actively eroding gullies appeared. Vast quantities of stones and boulders found their way into the rivers and very soon the beds were raised above the surrounding country. At this stage any rain heavier than normal resulted in flooding on the flat lands. As the building-up process continued the peak floods slowly increased. But the raised beds were not the primary cause of these disasters. The answer was in the time it took for all the run-off waters from one heavy rain to reach the river. In the days of the forest much of the rain soaked into the soil, and that which did run off took relatively longer to do so. The river could usually cope with this flow and seldom overtopped its banks. Once the bush was removed, however, little water soaked into the soil and the bulk of it reached the streams and rivers in a very short time. A surging peak flow was the inevitable result.

. . . The help of science has now been evoked in combating the soil erosion that affects nearly a quarter of the entire country. Farmers are being taught new techniques, including contour-terracing which retards the downward flow of rain and soil. A vigorous government-sponsored afforestation programme has also been put into effect.

from : C. R. Stanton, 'The vengeance of Tane',
The Geographical Magazine, September, 1949

10 How do we feel about primitive people?

Almost everywhere, where primitive peoples occupy exploitable lands or other resources they tend to be treated as vermin.

This devastation of peoples is taking place despite the seemingly fair or even protective legal codes which exist in most countries. It is rare for primitive peoples in any country to have any legal ownership of the lands they have occupied for generations . . . What is needed urgently is a powerful independent body able to act inside each country—something like a World Wildlife Fund for primitive peoples.

Without the help of some such fund it is doubtful if any primitive peoples will still exist in fifteen years. At the best they will have been 'integrated', transformed into daily labourers at the lowest level of local employment. At the worst they will have been hunted down and killed by professional murderers . . . They are often, in fact, of the highest intelligence, originality and creativeness within a framework utterly different from our own. Each tribe destroyed is like a library burned and lost forever.

And there is something else—primitive people are also humans who live, work, hope and love. They are our brothers. By any moral standards whatever, we must help them . . .

from : Francis Huxley and Nicholas Guppy, 'A wild life fund for humans is needed', letter in *The Sunday Times*, June 9, 1969

11 Living space for man

It is pointed out that intelligent protection and controlled cropping of wild species can assist the protein-starved populations in certain parts of the world. While this is perfectly true on a short-term basis, the long-term picture is more gloomy. If our numbers continue to increase at the present frightening rate, it will eventually become a matter of choosing between us and them. No matter how valuable they are to us symbolically, scientifically or aesthetically, the economics of the situation will shift against them. The blunt fact is that when our own species density reaches a certain pitch, there will be no space left for other animals. The argument that they constitute an essential source of food does not, unhappily, stand up to close scrutiny. It is more efficient to eat plant food direct, than to convert it into animal flesh and then eat the animals. As the demand for living space increases still further, even more drastic steps will ultimately have to be taken and we shall be driven to synthesizing our food-stuffs. Unless we can colonize other planets on a massive scale and spread the load, or seriously check our population increase in some way, we shall, in the not-too-far distant future, have to remove all other forms of life from the earth.

If this sounds rather melodramatic, consider the figures involved. At the end of the seventeenth century the world population of naked apes was only 500 million. It has now risen to 3,000 million. Every twenty-four hours it increases by another 150,000 ... To put it another way, the densities we now experience in our major cities would exist in every corner of the globe. The consequence of this for all forms of wild life is obvious. The effect it would have on our own species is equally depressing.

from : Desmond Morris, *The Naked Ape*

12 The empty woods of Ohio

U.S.A., early nineteenth century

Every place she went, nothing moved. The river stood still with ice. Not even a snowbird did she lay eyes on. The whole wilderness stood empty, deserted and forlorn.

Oh, down in her heart she knew what was the matter. It wasn't the drought that had done this. It was the big hunts. It wasn't the Lord, but the humans. The men claimed they would clean the game and vermin from these woods. Well, they could be satisfied now. They should be glad her pappy wasn't here to curse them. Couldn't they leave enough game to breed for next year, he'd a yelled at them. More than once she heard him sneer at men and women back in Pennsylvany for wasting pigeons. They'd knock them down by the thousands from their roost, salt them away in hogsheads for trade, and shovel the rest to the hogs. But what made him cruel as death when he told it, was the massacre of Pennsylvany's buffalo. The Wild Bulls' Last Stand, he used to call it. Up in the White Mountains. They had broke down some haystacks, and the settlers vowed they'd get those wild bulls. They drove them up in a high mountain valley where the herd could go no further for the deep crusted snow. Then they shot them, first and last, big and little, cut out their tongues and a few humps and let them stand while they went back to their farms singing hymns and whooping themselves hoarse as crows. Worth had seen it his own self.

... Sayward hated to come back to the cabin at nightfall without anything. Oh, she hated to face those hungry little ones empty-handed. When she opened the door she felt glad they lay asleep, all tumbled together in their mammy's bed with the yarn blankets pulled over them. She would let them sleep all night if they would, for bodies dead to the world didn't know that their little guts were empty.

from : Conrad Richter, *The Fields*

13 What chance have the whales?

Antarctic and tropics

Only Japan and Russia still continue the cruel hunt, but even they may abandon it ... The early harpooner, creeping up on feeding whales, thought them rather stupid. He had learned to guess where they would surface and rarely failed to manoeuvre his craft into position for a shot.

To him whales were little more enterprising than cows. The odd one that acted unpredictably was considered 'crazy'.

Whales began to go 'crazy' in increasing numbers, and it became clear that their 'craziness' was a reasoned attempt to escape ... Changes which whales have made after having been hunted intensively in the Antarctic for less than 30 years, have done little to arrest their mortality because modern fleets could kill far more than their quotas. They have, however, made it necessary to buy faster catchers and better navigation aids.

Few people realise what efforts whales make to survive. Each year they travel to the Antarctic to feed on the plankton they need to produce their heat-conserving layer of blubber. They return to the tropics to give birth to their young, born without blubber. As the baby emerges, it is rushed to the surface by other whales so that its first breath will consist of air and not water.

from : Richard Lambert, 'What chance has Moby Dick?',
The Daily Telegraph, November 28, 1968

14 Twentieth-century squalor

New Mexico, U.S.A.

Unhappily, in New Mexico much of the handiwork of modern man is both ugly and squalid. All the places where he lives, whether considerable towns like Albuquerque or small settlements along the highway, are appallingly untidy, probably the untidiest places in the world. For this is not the humble, yielding squalor of poverty, but the squalor of a people possessing ample material wealth and an abundance of steel. Individuals lightheartedly fling discarded equipment outside their houses—gas-stoves, pots and pans, petrol tins or whatever it may be—while the community as a whole does just the same thing, making vast, steely middens round their towns formed of rubbish which will deteriorate horribly, but never rot away. Nor will any blade of grass grow to soften or screen it. We English hardly appreciate the kindness of our grass in mitigating urban ugliness and adding finish to our roads. It is the great tidier and softener. Here instead of grass there is only dust.

To my eyes there can be nothing more dismal than a disused car dump in a setting of dust. The large, haphazard second-hand car marts surrounding many towns do nothing to add to the amenities, but the outer ring of dumps where the once-adored automobile finds its last ungrateful resting place is an abomination and disgrace. A dump may occupy several acres. Cars, vans and buses are chaotically tumbled, rusty, surrounded by broken glass, and with parts torn savagely off—wheels missing, bonnets left gaping after the plundering of some part of the engine—the victims of base mechanical violations. I believe in fact that these dumps are run as commercial investments and that the violaters actually pay for their loot. This makes it all the more surprising that in several small highway settlements (I cannot bring myself to call them villages) I saw cars which had simply been abandoned by the wayside, pushed on to a piece of waste ground or a vacant building plot and left to decay. I found myself trying to imagine in just what moment of boredom, irritation or sudden fortune a man might decide to leave his car by the road, much as in Europe a tramp will cast off an old boot.

from : J. B. Priestley and Jacquetta Hawkes, *Journey down a Rainbow*

15 Nineteenth-century Manchester

England, 1861

Everywhere are marks of manufacturing life; the cinder heaps form mountains; the earth is seamed with excavations; tall furnaces belch forth flames. We are nearing Manchester. In the bronzed sky at sunset a strangely-shaped cloud hangs over the plain; under this motionless covering are hundreds of bristling chimneys, as tall as obelisks; a huge and black mass is next distinguishable, then endless rows of buildings, and we enter the Babel of bricks.

Walked through the city; seen close at hand, it is still more dismal. The air and the soil appear charged with fog and soot. Manufactories with their blackened bricks, their naked fronts, their windows destitute of shutters, and resembling huge and cheap penitentiaries, succeed each other in rows . . . One of these buildings is a rectangle of six stories, in each of which there are forty windows; it is there that, lit up by gas, amid the deafening noise of looms, thousands of workpeople, cabined, classified, immovable, mechanically drive their machines every day from morning to night; can any form of existence be more opposed to, and at variance with, the natural instincts of man?

from : Hippolyte Taine, *Notes on England*

16 People of the steel country

South Wales, nineteen-sixties

In all the valleys of the South Welsh mountains we find the power and turbulence of men, dedicated to making their world stronger, more reliable and dirtier . . .

After a man has handled molten metal, treating it as casually as a boy would a glass of pop, life must be a bit of a let down. I seem to see in the faces of steel-workers, when they are relaxing at the day's end, a grave melancholy as if they had seen it all, as indeed they have.

Ebbw Vale stands at the head of the valley. It is a confined place. To the south you will pass through towns that sprang out of the writhing need for coal and steel, towns like Aberbeeg and Cwm, where the streets are like a petrified meringue, twirled out of plumb by the twists and turns of the hillsides.

But to the north there is an astonishing other world. Down from the moorland come the wild ponies, creatures that roam the streets of Ebbw Vale in a democratic brotherhood with the citizens. And sheep dogs foxed by living in a world half-pastoral, half-industrial, trapped by their neuroses into not knowing exactly what they are supposed to be rounding up . . .

The men of the valleys live in two worlds. They know on the one hand, the noise, disfigurements, the failures of industrial man, and just over the ridge, a pastoral calm that has never seriously been breached.

from : Gwyn Thomas, *A Welsh Eye*

17 Legacy of neglect: coal

South Wales, 1966

A man-made mountain of lumpy black treacle collapsed into itself last Friday and slid down upon the school at Aberfan 'just after morning prayers'.

The collapsed slag heap looks wierdly, wickedly voluptuous as you see it from a distance, for it sprawls into the village like a reclining female monster, a wanton negress shifting awkwardly on smelly hams. The sense of outrage and impotent disgust seems to coil itself into the very walk of those who approach the defilement, their gumboots slip-slap-slopping on the slime.

Everywhere, too, is the stench—something like a mixture of mouldering bread and wet coal. Newcomers lift their heads, like gundogs, to sniff momentarily at the foul air. The cringing brown houses are splattered with mud up to the tiny top windows, where curtains are drawn to keep in the grief. Filth is everywhere sucking at your feet and working into the corners of your eyes. It is the dirtiest, nastiest and most evil conglomeration that I ever wish to see . . .

As the rain came again, thickening and darkening the sky above the surrounding mounds of black, brown and grey-green, anxious eyes turned once more to the gigantic conical slag still towering so malignantly above the village. All hope had gone by now, but the tip might still slide further into the beleaguered houses, might yet scatter the busy yellow machines and shovelling men. It was then, especially, that one felt the enormity of the dead slag's power, and the disgust that such gargantuan waste should have been piled at people's backyards. Why should it be? Why is it thought necessary to be so loathsomely uncivilised?

The past is piled all around one here, and the bad, mean-minded, short-sighted methods of the past have not yet been discarded. Hence the fatalistic language and the half-formulated idea that some God has cheated. 'If only . . .' people kept saying at Aberfan. 'If only' it had collapsed earlier in the morning. 'If only' it had fallen after mid-day, when the children would have dispersed in noisily happy throngs for their half-term holiday. 'If only' it had stopped raining a day earlier. 'If only' someone had rung the Coal Board the night before. 'If only' the powers that be had taken the slightest notice of all the earlier fears and warnings about the tip. If only . . . If only . . . If only . . . the inevitable, tragic punctuation of any disaster.

from : Dennis Potter, 'Aberfan', *New Society,* October 27, 1966

18 Gold town in the desert: Kalgoorlie

Western Australia

Let's look at Kalgoorlie and its satellite Boulder. You've all seen it a thousand times. It's the T.V. Western small town, with stores, sidewalks, saloons, and two-storeyed commercial buildings : the town where the sheriff walks slowly down Main Street, guns low, in a white hat; only here he is watched by wandering aborigines instead of lolling Indians. There are a surprising number of women about, for many of the miners are married, and streets and shops are full of housewives, grannies, mothers and teenagers. The women are good-looking, usually tall and level eyed. Many of them walk with a peculiar but attractive pacing motion kicking the leg slightly forward at each step.

This, the bustling centre of town, is surrounded by a belt of small tidy houses, where hibiscus flowers grow in the hedges and fig trees drop ripe fruit on to the pavement. The houses are often walled, and almost always roofed, with corrugated iron. There are small, neat gardens afire with poinsettia. Beyond the tidy houses begin the untidy shacks. Here corrugated iron is universal, and it is rusty, but still the bougainvillea and plumbago grow wild, to remind you that this is not a northern slum but a tropic camp. The bush begins at the last hovel's back door—huge white dumps of gold slime, salt pans, scrub desert, a few gum trees, red laterite soil scattered with black ironstone gravel : and everywhere like the aftermath of a hurricane, the debris of 70 years of laissez-faire mining—jagged sheets of rusty iron; bolts, screws, boilers, pulleys; wire and chain and wood; chimneys, wheels, bars—miles and miles of it. Erect among the fallen and decayed debris a few tall headframes, the great wheels turning, mark the mines now in operation. There are not many of them.

from : John Masters, 'Gold, camels and wise men, frankincense and myrrh', *The Daily Telegraph Magazine*, September 29, 1967

19 Industrial wastes: Rhine tributaries

West Germany, nineteen-sixties

A student of Heidelberg may still sing of how he has lost his heart in *Heidelberg, am Neckarstrand,* but the song was written long before the manufacturers of detergents had begun their fierce struggle to make their own products more foamy than those of their rivals. Today one is more likely to lose one's life than one's heart, for the locks are so filled with film-star foam shampoo that a deck-hand falling overboard will almost certainly be smothered before he can be located below the mass of froth and hauled out. People have in fact been drowned in the Neckar precisely in that way.

The river itself, fortunately enough, is not entirely decked in foam, and the trouble arises only at the locks, many of which are very deep . . . The *Commodore's** saloon hatch is more than five feet above the water line, but on the Neckar we were sometimes obliged to close the doors to prevent the foam spilling over the sill and down the steps into the saloon . . .

The Main terminates in depressing fashion as a black stain of filthy water disfiguring the cool steely grey of the Rhine far below the confluence opposite Mainz, for this magnificent stream which carries away the water from the Franconian hills and forests suffers a worse fate than its sister the Neckar. It is not mere telly-bred detergent which is added to the Main, but the most revolting products of industries at Frankfurt and Aschaffenburg, among them the effluent of paper mills. These mills somehow manage to produce a material which resembles chewed blotting paper (and may well be precisely that), but which coagulates, sinks, decays, and rises to the surface again as a stinking mass of corruption seething with methane and strangely resembling sewage.

from : Roger Pilkington, *Small boat to Bavaria*

20 Price of progress

Japan, 1969

Not long ago I was watching waves breaking on a beach near Tokyo during a typhoon. These big waves, surging upward in brilliant blue, turned red just before breaking and frothed around one's feet in primrose yellow.

Pollution was the cause of this odd phenomenon. During a typhoon the waves disturb all the charming and not-so-charming things that have settled on the bottom of the sea, and hurl them back at the land. Hence the weird colour effects.

It may be said that industrial pollution, including pollution of the

* The author's boat

skies (above all in Tokyo), is just one of the many problems to which the Japanese are giving much more attention these days. One may cite other problems : crowded trains and jammed city roads; small and often poky housing; sewage systems which use open channels rather than pipes.

To say this is not to deny that much has been achieved. Japan is now the number two economic power in the free world, bigger than West Germany, much bigger than Britain. The Japanese have been expanding more rapidly than any other nation in the world for the past 10 years, and there is at least a fair chance that they will continue to do so for the next 10 . . .

This is not always an easy country to live in, for the Japanese. Above all it is crowded, packed together, too public. The problem is at its worst in housing. The average living space in Tokyo is no more than four *tatami*, about 70 square feet. It is surprising that human beings get by in such spaces, when one considers the sale of light electrical goods—how do all the washers, stoves, refrigerators, and television sets fit in?

Where do people put their books, for instance? The Japanese buy books as keenly as any people in the world. A best-selling author may easily hope to sell 500,000 copies of a new work in a few months. The collected works of leading Japanese writers are being published as soon as the writers reach their early thirties. Where does one put, say, half a dozen volumes of *Oe*? Certainly not on the coffee table, because the coffee table is also the dining table.

It is not only that housing is so small, but that the price of anything of reasonable size is so high . . . Average Japanese city dwellers must resign themselves to living in hutches. Meanwhile, it becomes harder and harder to buy land and build a little house. Given the recent level of land prices, most families must rule out the possibility of having their own place, unless they inherit.

Housing, then, is a major problem, but so is getting to work. Tokyo has long been known overseas for the 'pullers' and 'pushers', the station attendants who, at the rush hour, are responsible for packing the trains—and also for emptying them, if the doors simply will not close. This over-packing is no joke in summer, when temperatures are regularly in the nineties*; and the trains are rarely air-conditioned. The little, white-bloused office girls and their besuited bosses have sticky rides into work.

What is worse is that the roads have become just as bad—and more dangerous. The number of private cars being sold has increased tenfold since the beginning of the 1960's, and there is no sign of a decline. Commercial traffic has also greatly risen, and the dump-truck has become something of a synonym for a murder weapon.

* Fahrenheit

What is serious is that there is no end in sight to the escalation of the traffic problem. It has hit the authorities so fast that they have not had time to make provision for the future. The number of vehicles on the roads goes on increasing, the population of the cities grows by leaps and bounds, the Tubes get more and more choked (in spite of new construction), and the jams get worse all round.

These are problems all over the world but what makes the situation worse in Japan is that the scope for expanding road systems in the cities is so limited. Land has become too expensive, or it is just not for sale; it is probably as high priced in Tokyo as anywhere in the world. Even a tiny housing plot on the outskirts of the capital would scarcely cost less than £5,000.

Again and again it is a problem of space. There is only just enough room for 100 million prosperous Japanese. This is visibly as true when the Japanese try to get away as it is when they stay at home. The beaches in summer are as crowded as the Ginza shopping centre in Tokyo. For the first time this year the authorities have given a warning against pollution on almost all major beaches within range of Tokyo. There has even been a notice that most swimming pools in Tokyo are contaminated.

from : 'The high price of progress', *The Times,* September 24, 1969

21 The Great London Fog, December 1952

London, England, 1952

By Friday morning a heavy, wet blanket had closed down. You could just see your own feet. The streets were a queer, unfamiliar world. As you groped along the pavement, blurred faces without bodies floated past you. Sounds were curiously muffled : motor-car horns, grinding brakes, the warning cries of pedestrians trying to avoid the traffic and one another. This was a real 'pea-souper', a 'London particular'. The main arteries leading into the centre of town were clogged with buses moving at two miles an hour. The conductors walked ahead, calling directions to the drivers . . .

As the day went on, the fog changed colour. In the early morning it had been a dirty white. When a million chimneys began to pour coal smoke into the air it became light brown, dark brown, black. By afternoon all London was coughing.

Even then most Londoners weren't seriously worried—except the weather forecasters. Fog occurs when a body of moist air is cooled and condenses into tiny droplets which attract and hold particles of soot and smoke. Ordinarily fog is dissipated by wind—the lightest current of air is enough; or the fog rises into the cooler layers of air that usually lie above it.

Now there was no wind, and no promise of any. Worse, the layer of air above the fog was not cooler but warmer. Meteorologists call this rare occurrence an 'inversion roof'. The upper, warmer air acts as a lid, holding the fog down. And hour by hour its content of smoke and soot grows denser.

On Saturday morning thousands of Londoners began to be frightened. They were those people, mostly over 50, who had a tendency to bronchitis or asthma. In a long black fog such people are in acute distress. Their lungs burn, their hearts labour, they gasp for breath. They feel as if they are choking to death—and sometimes they do.

By Saturday noon all the doctors were on the run. Even with normal transport they couldn't have reached all the patients who needed them. Some of them stayed in their surgeries and tried to help sufferers by phone . . .

Towards noon on Monday the fog lifted a little, then came down again. Then it rose a little more. Finally all was clear.

Londoners rubbed the soot out of their eyes and saw a city covered with dirt.

from : Edwin Muller, 'The Great London Fog', reprinted with permission from June 1953 British *Reader's Digest*
© 1953 The Reader's Digest

22 Smog in Los Angeles

California, U.S.A., 1969

At last our 3,000 miles journey across the American continent was nearing its end. We left the El Cajon Pass through the San Bernardino mountains and started the descent into the Los Angeles Basin. Having driven through many miles of desert on a hot September afternoon we wound down the windows of the car in search of a breath of cool air, and immediately we were aware that the air smelt of ozone; yet we were still many miles from the sea. As we continued down the pass observing the mist obscuring the expected views of the valley, we discussed this phenomenon, and as we did so, our smarting eyes began to water and we suddenly realised—*this* was smog . . .

Seen from the window early in the morning the nearby San Gabriel Mountains made a spectacular view, crowned by the shining domes of Mount Wilson Observatory, framed by a brilliant blue sky. However, as the morning wore on and the heat intensified, the irritation to eye and nose increased and the distant view and azure sky were blotted out by the acrid chemical-laden mist. On days like this we used to envy those who lived or worked in air-conditioned buildings. However, such envy was mostly unjustified, for though air-conditioners can effectively filter particles out of the air, the troublesome gaseous contaminants which cause the smog (ozone, nitrogen dioxide, sulphur dioxide, etc) pass through unhindered and the effect of the air-conditioners was merely to circulate the smog throughout the building.

Weekend trips to the mountains provided welcome relief and fresh clear air. The intensity of the smog down below, always seemed to increase on Saturdays and Sundays because of the exhaust fumes issuing from the extra cars which crowded onto the roads.

The number of bad smoggy days depended entirely on the weather conditions. When the breezes blew, the air was crystal clear with only occasional smoggy days. However, when the sort of weather prevailed that prevented the basin emptying itself, the smog remained; one smoggy day relentlessly following another with only the evening cool providing some relief. When this happened, tempers frayed and the constant irritation to the eyes and running nose caused tiredness. At times when the intensity of smog reached more than a certain level, the first of the smog alerts sounded on the radio requesting us not to burn fires or rubbish or take unnecessary car journeys. This occasionally was followed by the second-stage alert, banning all unessential traffic and fires, with a third alert, so far as we know not yet put into effect, which would ban all moving traffic from the road.

With the coming of autumn the smoggy days lessened and the blue skies and sunny days for which California is so famous returned.

A special contribution by Janet Smith

23 The car-culture

California, U.S.A., nineteen-sixties

If the original industrial revolution was inextricably linked with the development of the railways then the present technological and social revolution is linked with the car. California has over nine million cars spread among a population of 17.3 million people. If the cars were laid bumper to bumper the line would stretch round the equator. The two car family is commonplace : a three car family is not at all rare. Los Angeles is quite incomprehensible unless it is remembered that it is the first American city to have taken rapid shape *after* the invention of the car. Whereas most cities have adapted themselves to the car, the reverse is true in Los Angeles where the car has determined the development of the city and suburbs. The huge number of vehicles has led to the construction of vast lengths of state highway (145,000 miles) and to the intricate freeway system around Los Angeles. On these freeways surrealist signs nudge each other : "This stretch is being spotted by aircraft". "It is an offecnce to travel at less than 50 miles per hour". The famous Camino Real has been rechristened the Pacific Highway. When Father Junipero Serra blazed the Californian missionary trail two hundred years ago he did not envisage cars, bumper to bumper, loaded with teenagers carrying surfboards leaping towards the beaches.

In the place of the traditional relationship between man and horse —that impressive partnership which helped to open up the West over a century ago—there is a new relationship between a family and its cars. The implications of the car revolution are staggering. Whole streets exist for nothing else but satisfying every conceivable whim of the driver : garage after garage, drive-in cinemas, drive-in restaurants, drive-in banks and drive-in churches ... In the few empty spaces left around Los Angeles it is common to pass car cemeteries heaped high with crazy patterns of jagged steel that were once moving machines. These miniature mountains of rusted junk spiral desperately into the air like some setting for a German expressionist play.

The cheapest way of living for kicks available to the bored Los Angeles citizen is a dash along one of the freeways. With anything up to eight lanes of traffic, the freeways resemble a giant escalator that has got out of control. It is an unnerving sight to glance around and see three other cars nose to nose at 75 miles per hour. A journey along the freeway at night is like a descent into a hell of technological power : the cars seem involved in a stampede of enormous dimensions. Ahead, nothing can be seen except the silhouettes of cars with their lines of red rear lights. On the other side of the freeway four lanes of glaring headlights dazzle you and the whole picture is a chiaroscuro of red and white. Accidents of gigantic proportions occur on these freeways. There is the story of one freeway where seventy-five cars collided in a great chain-reaction that took an hour just to happen.

from : Richard Gilbert, *City of the Angels*

24 Non-walking America

California, U.S.A.

Nowhere along their length did the highways seem to contract, confine themselves, centre themselves for a community round them. There were no parks along the highways, no statues, no plaques commemorating notable events; there were no vistas, no streets that radiated from this point or that; there was nowhere that one could turn and look back the way one had come. As for walking along the El Camino or Bayshore Highway—there is no point in even mentioning the possibility . . .

When you walked in the suburbs the chances were that there would be no one else in sight who was walking; and this in itself was enough to make you feel uncomfortable. Then, the pavements and the roads and the gardens were all on one flat level with one another, and the houses had no fences; so that when you walked you were not only singular, but totally exposed in your singularity. Householders working in their gardens stopped to watch you go, and people in the passing cars turned their heads to stare in surprise at you. And you had to walk briskly and look neither to the right nor to the left, to avoid giving the impression of being either a prowler or a Peeping Tom. For all those fenceless houses were open to your gaze.

from : Dan Jacobson, *No further West—California visited*

25 Anarchy of the road

Europe, 1967

We are just home from a 5,000 mile drive slantwise across Europe to the southern tip of Greece and back. We return, devoted European motorists though we are, more than ever horrified by the environmental problems raised by the growth of motor traffic. The motor has opened every place up, and every place seems on the way to being ruined.

The things in towns which used to attract us are no longer worth the agony of battling through the mêlée . . .

The motor camp sites are the new concentration camps of Europe —so concentrated that from July onwards you cannot find a square yard of unsoiled ground to pitch a tent, even supposing you wished to stay in this new kind of seasonal slum. The Gross Glockner Pass —a solid queue of vehicles up and down . . . Driving long mileages, hot day after hot day along the autoputs and the autobahns we were subjected for hours to shattering noise, piercing horns and continuous envelopment in fumes from huge trucks.

Our lives rested precariously between the skill of our own hands and the hands of thousands of barging Germans, irritable Italians, frantic French, desperate Dutch and others nurtured in the anarchy of continental motoring, all crazy to get the better of the man in front and free to do it at any speed. Parking places are filthy, though in Germany some effort has been made to improvement. Behind many lay-bys is a new kind of sylviculture—sanitary woodland. Blood plasma depots, with red bottle signs, along the autobahns . . .

These are kaleidoscopic impressions. We could add many more. They make us ask : Where are we heading with motor traffic? Is any nation even beginning to get a grip of these problems, whether in terms of capital investment, controls or behaviour?

from : Sir Colin and Lady Buchanan, letter to *The Times*,
August 25, 1967

26 Urban blight: lack of heart

U.S.A. and general

The thing that the traveller in the United States misses most in cities outside New England is a heart, a focal point. It can be a green or a fountain, or a monument as in Indianapolis. Most European cities have their lovely Arc de Triomphe or Piazza San Marco, which gives a sense of delight and majesty to their entire city. In most American cities the heart of the city is simply the street intersection where the biggest department store and bank face each other. And walk five blocks away in any direction, and you are deep in slums, warehouses or used-car lots.

The challenge of tackling urban blight in the United States does not necessarily mean tearing down miles of buildings and replacing them with thirty-storey concrete slabs jutting up from fenced off grassland. Inhabitants would be happier if they could simply have their old neighbourhood homes and streets spruced up, with some pleasant open spaces added . . .

Most urban areas are desperately short of the kinds of places where people can relax comfortably without spending much money : picnic groves, museums, libraries, public beaches, parks, ball parks for amateurs, golf courses, tennis courts, and gardens. Nothing seems to bring warmth and graciousness to brick and concrete surroundings more than splashes of flowers and rows of trees as the managers of New York's Radio City have learned. A number of cities such as New Orleans, Seattle, Cincinnati, and Norfolk are seeking to add new vitality and beauty to their cities, and one way they are doing it is by large-scale planting of trees and flowers.

... The national organization for civic improvement, ACTION, estimates that it would cost about one hundred billion dollars to wipe out United States slums. Billions more could justifiably be spent in general urban renewal each year and in cutting through the choking congestion brought by the automobile by developing swift public transit systems. This could help reunify the sprawling metropolitan areas.

from : Vance Packard, *The Waste Makers*

27 Progress and the bulldozer

London, England, nineteen-fifties

That was when it all began.

When what began? Nothing probably. Nothing personal. It was not going to affect them personally. The man said that. He said : 'If your house is half-way down Armstrong Avenue, it should be safe, according to the plan as I recall it.'

'Oh wonderful,' Martha said starkly. 'Nothing to worry about. Just everything I've ever known, every bit of pavement I've ever walked on, every shop I've been going to since I was too little to see over the counter—gone, disappeared, bulldozed under the earth.'

'Steady with the dramatics,' Guy said. 'It probably won't come to anything.'

'Steady yourself,' the man said, 'We're usually the last to hear anything in the Press Bureau, but this I do know ... It's Development Plan Four-O-Two Q Stroke Eight Four. That's the general plan for the whole project, as submitted to the Ministry. Now that they've agreed to put up the cash for property purchase and re-housing—that's about half the cost of the whole caboodle—the story can be told.

... "The Transurban Expressway," to name it in all its glory. A super-highway linking London with the northern arteries. Branches scything through the streets and houses and shops and modest squares to the western approaches. Flyovers and underpasses. A comprehensive development of marginal sites to provide for flats and office space and shopping concourses.'

266

'It's ghastly,' Martha said, and Guy went to the bar to get them all another drink.

'Why ghastly?' Robert P. V. affected to look hurt. 'I think it's neat. Don't you think it's about time somebody did something about getting traffic in and out of London?'

'Yes, but—why here? Why through here?'

He shrugged one narrow shoulder. 'That's what everybody says : "I'm all for progress, but just don't do it here." Two miles, approximately, of this triumphal avenue, slap through the anthill of Cottingham Park and other desirable districts, and all along the way, the ants crying out : "Why must you put it here?" '

'What if the ants object?' Guy set down the drinks '. . . Oh they'll get a chance, of course. There will be a Minister's public hearing, an inquiry on objections to the authority for compulsory purchase, right of appeal to the Lands Tribunal, and so on. Must strain every nerve to give at least the illusion that there is still some liberty of the subject.' Mr. Perigrine let out a grisly chuckle. 'God bless,' he said, and lifted the tankard . . .

'We'll build like mad, of course, if we can find any space to build. We'll shovel a lot of them out into the suburbs, protesting bitterly, and we'll get some of them out to the New Towns. But they can't get those houses unless they've got a job out there, and a lot of the types in town these days are almost unemployable, and from what I've seen, you've got 'em all here . . . One part of this extraordinary place is going up, and the other half is plunging downhill like the Gadarene swine. Incredible state of affairs.'

'But that,' said Martha sadly, 'is what makes it such a fascinating place to live in. Why here?' She asked again helplessly . . .

When it was time to tell her children that Guy was looking for a house outside London, and that they would be leaving Cottingham Park, Martha was afraid.

If they were unhappy about leaving, it would be her fault. She had brought them up to mirror her own love for these streets and curious little shops and sudden pockets of tree-filled gardens, this patchwork of houses in tones of grey and black and dirty white. It was like a village to them, and they were a part of all its life. They had clean desirable friends in the new painted houses in the converted streets, and hoarse ragged friends in the streets behind Armstrong Avenue where the Rise began its hopeless climb through shabbiness to squalor. Like Martha, they knew every inch of every pavement, knew everybody's dog and baby, and the fortunes and diseases of the proprietors and their relations in all the smaller shops.

Unlike Martha, they were not much disturbed by the devastation of the new road. The importance of it, and the excitement of something new to watch, the giant machines, and the masked men

267

kneeling with sizzling torches under little round-roofed shelters where watchmen crouched like tortoises at night compensated for the passing of the chocolate shop and the doll hospital, the cheap little cinema, the square with the jungle full of wild cats and zombies.

To Martha, Cottingham Park was being destroyed. To the children, it was merely being slightly changed, and the change was stimulating. One of the cranes on the office building site was over a hundred feet high and the driver climbed up the open shaft like a monkey on the Eiffel Tower. The crane and the bulldozers and the acetylene torches and the tumbling of bricks in clouds of ancient dust entered into their childhood to be recorded there along with the very childhood sights they were destroying.

'That's why they won't mind moving,' Guy said. 'They live from one new thrill to the next... They'll feel the same way about a new house. I don't know. They love it here... What is it you want, Martha? What is it you want us to do? God knows, I don't want the trouble and expense of finding another house and the nightmare of travelling into town and out every day if you don't even want it.'

'I'm not sure yet,' Martha said slowly. 'I want what everybody wants, but I think we should talk about it some more and not hurry to do anything. Why can't we just wait and see?'

from : Monica Dickens, *The Heart of London*

28 Defending urban villages from concrete and car

London, England, 1969

Odd, unbalanced and disturbing changes are taking place in my part of London, one of the many old villages engulfed by the metropolitan sprawl, as leases fall in and high rents and rates push out the socially valuable small tradesmen on whom the residents have always relied.

In five streets—most of them short, none longer than half-a-mile—we now have 26 eating places, 13 dress shops, nine tobacconists, eight pubs, seven estate agents, seven dry cleaners or launderettes and three betting shops. But only one shoe-mender, upholsterer, watch repairer, tailor and florist.

We can't buy inexpensive soft furnishings any more. Our last source of haberdashery and household linen is about to close...

268

Facilities for playing the horses have become more extensive than scope for buying fish, children's clothes, hardware and stationery . . .

Infilling of course, brings more cars for which no garage space exists and which often cannot be kept outside the owners' front doors because the streets are already choked. We therefore get another kind of application : to build garages on parts of gardens or abolish front lawns altogether and replace them with hard standings. The visual results are appalling. Endless lines of cars mill down the centre of the road; each side is lined with others already parked, then more are dotted about where trees, grass and flowers once refreshed the eye. It is death to any environment.

from : *The Daily Telegraph,* March 12, 1969

29 People versus planners

England

Architecture like painting or interior design is subject to fashion and the fashion at the moment is for massive council estates built with tower and slab blocks.

Largely because there is so little architectural criticism, such is the scale of visual illiteracy in this country, the layman often assumes that only by building high on a vast scale can the housing problem be solved and, in addition, can more and more people be crammed into the cities . . . Often the opposite is achieved. For example, in London in 1958 the population was approximately 8,220,000; in 1960 8,000,000; and in 1967, despite the addition of over 700 multi-storey buildings 7,880,000.

Meanwhile, apart altogether from essential slum clearance, the disfigurement of our cities proceeds at a rapid rate on a vast scale. The sadness and insensitivity cannot be measured.

So long as a new estate is built on a modest scale, the consequences are usually good; but when it extends as far as the eye can see, with block after block stretching into the distance, the result is almost certain to be dull and oppressive to look at and socially disastrous. And one cause of the trouble surely is the tendency of the architect to see in a shabby district no more than meets the eye. He can spot a building of historical interest, but rarely has any feeling for the rich texture of metropolitan life. His passion for tidiness encourages him to demolish street after street like an over-zealous housewife clearing her attic, and in the process much of real value is thrown away with the refuse. . . . Entire streets of well-kept houses, where the occupants wish for nothing more than a bathroom, are also demolished when money might have been saved had it been spent on improvements rather than new buildings. In London, if not the provinces, young couples eager to purchase a house of their own move into these districts and by their example send a road on its way to reclamation. Only after a strenuous fight and united action by all the residents can such a street be saved ...

... In many parts of London and in provincial cities, architects are busy robbing districts of their spice and variety. In place of a bizarre, if not beautiful mixture all that is left are buildings of one age.

from : The Times, September 14, 1968

30 Slums of the future: Glasgow

Scotland

The slums of the future stand high on the skyline, monuments to the folly of treating people and houses as bloodless statistics, and not as families and homes.

Glasgow has built the tallest residential flats, a soaring 31-storey block 300 feet high at Balornock's Red Road site ...

A special issue of the Architectural Review on 'Housing and the Environment' states that community life has been thoughtlessly destroyed and been replaced by a sterile segregated pattern of living to which people may take generations to adapt. It describes the Red Road flats as totally lacking in individuality, 'their nightmare sublimity of scale—seems to result from too much model making'.

Glasgow's skyscrapers are littered with notices banning children from playing; the lifts are small, inadequate, and often do not work. They are not even big enough to take a stretcher. Play space at the foot of these great blocks is usually a pathetic acknowledgement that young children are energetic. Even so, swings and chutes are often locked up before teatime. Loneliness is intensified by the fact that mothers dare not let their three or four year olds downstairs unaccompanied. Children, when they first go to school, are sometimes withdrawn. They do not fit in; the seeds of isolation and mental trouble have already been sown.

from : Michael Grieve, 'The vicious circle',
The Illustrated London News, December 9, 1967

31 The new industrial age

British Isles and general

In the present influx of gigantic constructions and power lines, the landscape of the British Isles faces the greatest crisis of its history. There have been vast changes in the past; the gradual clearance of the forests; the enclosure of open landscape into hedged fields, and the sprawling urban development of the last century. But although the areas covered by these changes were enormous, never before has the country-side been invaded by so many objects, nor by constructions comparable in size to the modern power stations, hydro-electric schemes and airfields. Not only are the erections we are dealing with far greater in scale and number than their predecessors, but they are scattered over the whole land, whereas the desolation of the first industrial revolution was at least limited to certain areas. Industrial expansion which in the nineteenth century followed the railways and the coalfields, today runs foot-loose along the roads and power-lines. The country's life, which only a century ago was mainly static and rooted in the soil, is increasingly one of movement and mechanization. Travel once concentrated on the railways, now not only chokes the road system but takes vast areas of land for airfields and requires the erection on coast and hill-top of various forms of radar mast and navigational aid. Communication is served not only by telegraph posts and wires but also by the masts of television and broadcasting services.

Because the sites of the new power sources, nuclear fission, water and oil, are widely distributed over the British Isles, the evolving pattern of power in the landscape is unrelated to the old industrial map of Britain. The new map consists of the immense constructions of the oil refineries, the nuclear reactors and power stations, and, radiating from them, the great latticed towers and overhead lines of the electricity grid, forming a network which covers the whole country and spreads even to the most remote rural areas.

This comprehensive network of power opens up a prospect of future wealth for the country, of clean industry and more efficient agriculture. Its construction is a triumphant answer to a challenge to our technical skill, but it also presents a second challenge, which so far is not only unanswered but barely recognised.

Our generation blames the industrialists of the nineteenth century bitterly for having destroyed so much of the landscape and left us a legacy of thousands of acres of ugly and derelict land, but this is nothing compared with the havoc we shall leave to our descendants unless we take avoiding action now and find a means of reconciling our need for power with our need for a landscape fit to live in.

from : Sylvia Crowe, *The Landscape of Power*

32 A monstrous apple refrigerator

Kent, England, nineteen-fifties

The farmer was not surprised when I complained to him about the hideous effect of the huge apple-refrigerator which he had put up bang in the middle of the exquisite view from my windows and terrace ... I spoke next about the beauty of the landscape. He looked blank, just as I should look if shown a formula representing an aniline dye, or the love-making of a neutron. I tried to demonstrate how that huge erection, built in biscuit-coloured asbestos corrugations, dwarfed everything else along the valley.

He scratched his head, thrusting his cap over his eyes. 'Well ...' he said, slowly : 'Would you like to see inside?' As though that might give us something mutually comprehensible ...

He swung back the sliding door, and we entered the building. It was lighted by glass panes in the southern roof. I stood awed by size, as one stands in the Olympia, or used to stand in the Crystal Palace. The interior almost had a nobility, a character accentuated by the swallows shadow-skating in the heights round and about the girders. Patiently, as though explaining in words of one syllable to a mentally defective, my neighbour demonstrated the three great refrigerating chambers and gave me the figures of how many tons of apples could be stored in each for an indefinite period of time. Then we examined the machinery for sorting the apples; rather like assembly belts, at which women (all of whom I knew, for they were the housewives of the cottages dotted about the valley) stood, during the apple-harvest time, sorting the fruit as it bobbled past them at lazy-river pace.

I was duly impressed, and we became really chatty, the farmer's self-confidence enhanced by his pride in this new acquisition. 'All the same', I said, 'from the outside, the monster is an eyesore, and I wish you would undertake to camouflage it as you would have done during the war. It would then settle down comfortably and harmoniously into the landscape.'

It was the word *landscape* that still eluded him. The blank look in his eye reminded me once again that men and women who get their living from the soil seldom have time, or sufficient ease of mind, to look up from it towards a wider contemplation. My neighbour chuckled at last. If I had been less foreign to him, he would have dug me in the ribs. Instead, he raised his stick and pointed at the Olympian shed. 'Take a ton of paint to cover that,' he said. 'And you know the price of paint nowadays? Why, it's mortal! It's mortal!' Then he added—and now the eye was twinkling mischievously—'Tell you what. You plant a row of poplars along your bottom fence. They'll soon hide it.'

from : Richard Church, *A Country Window*

33 We know; we must decide what to do

General

Although much remains to be understood, we do have a sufficient basis of knowledge and ideas to make it possible for us to create a new fabric for man and his physical environment. All the time we must remember that man is both part of nature and yet able to influence its processes; that he, like other animals, needs space and repose; and that all his actions have far-reaching effects on other living creatures.

Man had made vast changes on the earth with relatively primitive tools and limited knowledge. What is he going to achieve with the vast power now at his command and the explosion of knowledge under way? Here it is important to note that while between 1840 and 1940 man created better food, clothing, housing and hygiene for millions, he also contaminated the land, air, rivers and sea and eliminated much wild life. Now we believe that he need not have done so, that in the next century greater progress can be achieved without the accompanying despoliation, and the old dereliction and waste can be cleared away. Such a creative approach requires perception of the significant and lasting features of the national inheritance. These are, of course inter-related. As understanding increases, more values will be identified and cherished.

People must know the implications of their tastes and preferences : for example, that consuming vast quantities of newspapers and magazines imperils the forests; that veneering furniture requires the chopping down of certain trees; that growing speck-free fruit and vegetables needs the use of chemicals; that using certain types of indestructible plastic involves special methods of refuse disposal; that an open-coal fire leads to air pollution; and so on. People cannot both demand a product and oppose the means of getting it and the damage it may cause. Knowing what lies behind the chosen product is not, in itself, enough. People must be helped to develop some criteria so that they can demand alternatives and can judge what shortcomings may be due to plain mismanagement. Such levels of perception demand an alert, educated and participating citizen, responsive to the environment and conscious of his responsibilities to others and to posterity.

from : Robert Arvill, *Man and Environment*

34 Philosophy of a naturalist

Tanganyika (now Tanzania), 1959

If we had died that night nobody could have made sense out of our many notes on the life of the herds of animals in Serengeti. Nobody else could have edited and cut the seventy thousand feet of coloured film intended to produce *the* film of our dreams. The chances of survival of the Serengeti inhabitants would have been lessened.

This probably seems unimportant to most people, to the people who would say : 'Those two didn't deserve any better. Why did they risk their necks for zebras and lions?' Men have other ideals for which they are willing to die : freedom, glory, politics, religion, the rulership of their class or the expansion of national borders. But in the long run Michael and I will be proved right . . .

Men are easily inspired by human ideas, but they forget them again just as quickly. Only Nature is eternal, unless we senselessly destroy it. In fifty years' time nobody will be interested in the results of the conferences which fill today's headlines.

But when, fifty years from now, a lion walks into the red dawn and roars resoundingly, it will mean something to people and quicken their hearts whether they are bolshevists or democrats, or whether they speak English, German, Russian or Swahili. They will stand in quiet awe as, for the first time in their lives, they watch twenty thousand zebras wander across the endless plains.

Is it really so stupid to work for the zebras, lions and men who will walk the earth fifty years from now? And for those in a hundred or two hundred years time . . .?

MICHAEL GRZIMEK
12.4.1934—10.1.1959
He gave all he possessed for the wild
animals of Africa, including his life

from : Bernhard and Michael Grzimek, *Serengeti shall not Die*

35 Making the Sahara green

Algeria and Sahara

The United States should be deeply interested in the reclamation of the Sahara. As in their own Dust Bowl, the weapon in this great task is ever more trees.

Trees fix the soil and replenish it. For millions of years trees have provided shelter for man, bird and beast; they absorb impurities in the air and give off the breath of life, oxygen. Trees are an essential link in the water cycle, and restore the balance of nature. They also provide building material, paper, films and even clothes. Fruit and nut-bearing trees give shelter for other food crops.

Pilot planting schemes in Algeria and Morocco have proved successful. Tunisia and Libya have progressive planting programmes and a million acres have been reclaimed on the west bank of the Nile by Colonel Nasser.* Conservation in Nigeria is keeping the desert at bay. These beginnings show what can be done on a grand scale.

Eucalyptus *camaldulensis* is perhaps the most widely planted in Algeria and Morocco : but many other strains of eucalyptus will do almost as well. Another native of Australia, the casuarina, will tolerate saline soils and impregnate the ground with nitrogen and thus improve it. Tamarisk grows to a large tree near the centre of the Sahara . . .

With the development of electronic apparatus and an elaborate mathematical formula, devised by two Austrian professors, it is now possible to locate water at depths varying from 400 to 4,000 feet with minimal error. This has put an entirely new complexion on Sahara reclamation, allowing us to chart accurately the position, extent and pressure of subterranean water . . . In Tripolitania seedlings of Eucalyptus *camaldulensis* planted three years ago and never watered have reached a height of 30 feet on pure silica. Immediately after planting during the short rainy season the site was sprayed with an oil product which fixed the sand and prevented loss of moisture . . .

On our first Sunday evening in Algeria we met foresters returning from supervising the planting of olive trees by 1000 volunteers round the barrage at Arba'atache. A week later in Constantine we saw lorry loads of cheering enthusiasts go by on their way to plant trees on the hills.

Everywhere we have encountered the opinion that the greatest bottle-neck will not be money, but skilled workers and supervisors. The race is between education and disaster.

from : Richard St. Barbe Baker, *Sahara Conquest*

* Egyptian President 1956–70

36 A creed to preserve our natural heritage

*Part of President Johnson's message
to Congress, February 1966*

To sustain an environment suitable for man, we must fight on a thousand battlegrounds. Despite all our wealth and knowledge, we cannot create a Redwood Forest, a wild river, or a gleaming seashore.

But we can keep those we have.

The science that has increased our abundance can find ways to restore and renew an environment equal to our needs.

The time is ripe to set forth a creed to preserve our natural heritage—principles which men and women of goodwill will support in order to assure the beauty and bounty of their land. Conservation is ethically sound. It is rooted in our love of the land, our respect for the rights of others, our devotion to the rule of law.

Let us proclaim a creed to preserve our natural heritage with rights and the duties to respect those rights :

The right to clean water—and the duty not to pollute it.

The right to clean air—and the duty not to befoul it.

The right to surroundings reasonably free from man-made ugliness —and the duty not to blight.

The rights of easy access to places of beauty and tranquillity where every family can find recreation and refreshment—and the duty to preserve such places clean and unspoiled.

The right to enjoy plants and animals in their natural habitats— and the duty not to eliminate them from the face of this earth.

These rights assert that no person, or company or government has a right in this day and age to pollute, to abuse resources, or to waste our common heritage.

The work to achieve these rights will not be easy. It cannot be completed in a year or five years. But there will never be a better time to begin.

Let us from this moment begin our work in earnest—so that future generations of Americans will look back and say :

1966 was the year of the new conservation, when farsighted men took farsighted steps to preserve the beauty that is the heritage of our Republic.

I urge the Congress to give favourable consideration to the proposals I have recommended in this message.

(*signed*) Lyndon B. Johnson

37 If the nation wants a lovely land it can have it

England

A thousand years of work and wisdom has gone into making this English landscape. You can't really call it 'natural' : men planted the trees, shaped the fields, planted, pruned and wove the hedges, quarried and cut stones, and built the farm-house. They sowed and reaped centuries of crops; they wore the paths; they watched the land and dug the ditches which drained and watered it.

... We need the landscape, and we need it whole and healthy. It is not just a matter of keeping a few patches of Green Belt for picnics. The landscape is a whole living thing, and we must treat it so. The towns are part of it as much as the country. But what do we do? We make an evil mess of both.

... Think what a city ought to mean : a place to excite you, to challenge your thought and action, to talk and study in. And then look at the cities you know : dirty, smelly with petrol and hopelessly, hopelessly boring. Not a place at all, a no-place, a hole in thin air. Our towns are among the most densely populated in the world. Our island is extremely small. Our history is long, and is visible in town and country everywhere. You would think the conclusions obvious; plan carefully; keep what is good; shape town and country together; prevent waste; keep towns compact and firm; build beautifully. But no. Instead, speculative builders knock up their flashy Ideal Homes; property developers and local authorities butcher fine towns; bungaloid cancer eats up the landscape alongside the growths of caravans, garages, advertisements ...

Industry is essential, but it must be fitted into the landscape without ruining it. Slag-heaps and other masses of waste material can be made into welcome additions by planting grass or trees. Artificial lakes created by subsidence or excavation can provide pleasure and recreation. Power houses, factories, cooling towers—all can be impressive. But usually a sharp line of demarcation is needed; a mixture of industry and dying countryside is depressing and wasteful.

from : Fred and Enid Inglis, *Your England—Blotscape*
(Use of English Pamphlets No 1) 1967

38 Oil firms and landscape: what can be done

Milford Haven, Wales

The crude oil is pumped from ships to Milpaisan Farm, a mile away where eight 'bunded' storage tanks are half-concealed in a dip in the rolling countryside. No intermediate pumping stations are used on the pipeline to Llandarcy, and apart from the two stretches where it is exposed, as it crosses the main Swansea-Leeds railway line and inside the refinery boundary, there is, for the uninitiated, no evidence of its existence. A ten foot swathe of land was disturbed during the laying of the pipes but little can be seen of the disturbance a year later.

The British Petroleum Company is justifiably proud of its achievements, for Popton Fort has become one of the showpieces of the neighbourhood. The staff is tireless in its efforts to maintain the appearances of the place and there are no untidy corners. Every available space has been put to some useful purpose. Ladders and look-out points, some of which are shielded with glass, have been arranged so that visitors have a fine view across the Haven.

from : H. S. Bracey, *Landscape of Power*

39 Our roads need not be eyesores

England and general

One often hears it stated that most of our existing motorways are confoundedly dull. Only the M-6 as it sweeps northwards to Lancaster offers the traveller these superb and dramatic views of the kind that mark the broad highways of North America and Europe. Our failure here may prompt tourists to prefer the quiet byways, thereby adding to the congestion of the villages and hamlets.

Yet there are stretches of our own A1, or the Oxford By-pass, with broad grass verges and mature indigenous trees grouped to form focal points at bends, or the Mickleham By-pass, which curves around the wooded slopes of the intimate Surrey countryside, that show how modern roads need not detract from the splendour of the landscape. A motorway or a main class A road may appear entirely different in character from those winding lanes that perhaps owe their course to tracks first worn by badgers or deer or cattle, and broadened by the feet of early man; yet they can be just as much an integral and organic part of the landscape.

from : Gaston Christian, *Tomorrow's countryside*

40 An end to smoke: Pittsburgh

U.S.A., 1960

Fifteen years ago life in Pittsburgh was almost unbearable. The smoke was appalling, tainting everything, so that there was little relish in living. Throughout the States it was known as 'The Smoky City' and when its name was mentioned people would screw up their faces in distaste. The smoke came not only from a myriad factories and foundries, but from houses with coal fires, trains with steam locomotives, steam tugs and countless varied smoky machines. Almost all has now been eliminated. Fuels that made much smoke were banned by law, first in the city of Pittsburgh, then in the surrounding districts. There was naturally strong opposition. Some of the most vociferous came from laundry operators, who foresaw a serious drop in business, and sometimes insisted upon maintaining their own small belching chimneys, partly as a protest of principle, partly because (presumably) even a little laundry chimney dirties a few shirts. The railroads, after a show of reluctance, agreed to convert their trains almost entirely to diesel; to their secret delight, I am told, for they had wanted to make the change for years but had been prevented because the custom of coal-producers was so important to them. Stern penalties were imposed upon those who violated the smoke laws, and remarkably soon the place began to look up.

Indeed, some of the effects of the reforms were miraculous. Pittsburgh now gets 60 per cent more sunshine than it used to, and 60 per cent less dust and soot falls on the city. It is warmer, too, for the old horrible pall sometimes reduced the temperature by as much as 10 degrees ... The city's air is now sharp and clean; it is queer, like examining a half-cleaned picture, to look about you now in Pittsburgh and see, defacing old buildings, degrading trees, clinging to crevices and corners, blackening bridges and staling factories, engriming all the shores of the Ohio River, the dingy sediment left behind by the smoke.

from : James Morris, *Coast to Coast*

41 Tapiola: a planned settlement

Finland

To an outsider, the people of Tapiola appear to live in an unspoiled natural park. There are no traffic noises, no smoke or dust or soot. Except for the town centre, which is a shopping avenue for pedestrians only, there are no streets as other towns know them—just winding roads that follow the natural contours and curve round groves of tall trees. There is no parking problem, for Tapiola has plenty of car-parks and garages.

Houses and blocks of flats are set back from the roads, and all the gardens behind slope down or up to a forest path. Every dwelling, whether a flat in a tall block or an individual house, has at least one window facing forest, lake or sea . . .

In the centre of the embryonic town was an enormous and unsightly gravel pit. Architect Aarne Ervi, with two associates, designed a unique civic centre around it, converting the ugly hole into a lake with plume-like fountains spurting out of the water.

On one side of the man-made lake, Ervi optimistically envisaged a 13 storey office building with a spectacular sky-view restaurant. He planned an avenue with banks and shops. Near by would be a theatre and concert hall, public library and civic buildings. There, too, was to be an ultra-modern swimming pool.

. . . A committee chosen from local residents decides, usually with the advice of the State Housing Board, which of the applicants may buy the new houses. No offers can be made—prices are fixed. The selection committee implements Von Hertzen's* principle that in Tapiola professors, businessmen, office workers, craftsmen and labourers should live side by side as neighbours. Their children should go to the same schools and play together.

'Instead of a rich man's town, we've built a cross-section community,' he explains.

At present most of the residents are commuters who work in Helsinki. But this may not always be so. Many are finding local employment—in offices, shops, light industry. Tapiola's dwellings are planned for a population density of 24 residents per acre. This limits the town to about 16,000 inhabitants unless a high birth rate upsets the quota.

from : Frank Taylor, 'Finland's new town in the forest', reprinted
with permission from February 1966 British *Reader's Digest*
© 1966 The Reader's Digest

* Initiator of the scheme

42 Essential renewal in the back streets

Shanghai, China

The heat beats down like a palpable thing on the narrow stone-surfaced road through which the car can scarcely move because of the teeming mass of people.

I am seeing the most crowded quarter of Shanghai, I am told, with an area of 130,000 square yards. Here live 4,260 families comprising a total population of more than 18,000 . . .

'Before Liberation ninety per cent of the houses were made of matting,' Mrs. Tung begins, 'only ten per cent were of brick. Now, because of the improvement in the standard of living and the better wages we receive, sixty per cent are brick. In the past our streets were in a frightful condition. Only one road was surfaced, many were only running gutters and there was no drainage at all, the lower-lying areas and streets being ditches. There was a saying, "If it rains for one day you must wear overshoes for seven days" '.

'If there was a fire it swept through the place like a typhoon.'
. . . Out in the street it is hotter than ever. I see it all with new eyes. The neat brick houses with their clean-swept earth floors, the occasional matting shelter that houses a family—new matting, new furniture, new clothes. Orderly queues of people with buckets waiting their turns at the taps . . .

It is incredibly poverty-stricken by our standards, and yet so incredibly better than it was. Mrs. Tung presses my arm..

'You will see some of the people who used to live here at the New Housing Estate. They were the ones who lived in such appalling conditions that they simply had to be moved or they would have died!'

Everything is relative!

from : Dymphna Cusack, *Chinese Women Speak*

1 A fairly early example of pioneer waste. Clearings had been made by some of the Indian 'sauvages' (meaning forest dwellers), but the demands of white settlers in 1800 for fuel, potash (for soap making), charcoal, and ship and house building, were as much as 9 acres (3·6 ha) per homestead per year. Today 13 acres (5·2 ha) of woodland per citizen per year are needed in the U.S.A., especially softwoods which are still being cut faster than they can be replaced. As in Europe, some forest is maintained as leisure space and some is cropped systematically. A certain amount of softwood is imported.

In some tropical areas, in Malaya for example, pioneers are clearing forests for agriculture. It is to be hoped that flooding (likely to occur in areas of high rainfall when trees which transpire water are cut down), and leaching of humus and chemicals from the freshly exposed soils, do not ruin the land. The forests of the earth are rapidly decreasing at a time when carbon-dioxide from fuel-wastes is accumulating in the atmosphere, raising its temperature. Trees are valuable as they remove this gas and keep temperatures down.

2 Savana is also regarded as degenerated forest, and man's hand must be considered along with climate and soils as affecting the world vegetation pattern.

4-5 Nomadic people are the worst offenders in arid lands. Goats have split lips and are able to crop close to the ground and to strip trees. In their native habitats they contributed to the growth of deserts. When introduced into St. Helena (15° 55′ S, 5° 44′ W) by the Portugese, they multiplied in thousands and eventually turned a rich forest into a desert island. Dung is a desert fuel when no scrub is available.

6 Salt bush is grey and can be up to 8 feet (2·4 m) high. It takes in moisture from the air at night. Damaged pasture around wells is a world-wide problem. In Saudi Arabia today, a circle 47 miles (75 km) in radius has been ruined in ten years, by stock grazing and stamping around tapline water-pumping stations. Water on wheels has to be taken to the stock.

7 Destructive extensive farming, with a small labour force, machines and often mono-cropping. The extract refers first to the bad methods which contributed to the formation of a dustbowl in midwest U.S.A., and then to measures to retain or regain soil texture and fertility. These included contour ploughing (ploughing round a hillside rather than up and down it) in order to create miniature terraces to hold water and soil, and strip-cropping with a variety of crops, some of which will be holding down some of the ground during all the growing period. See also the Ukraine in Section 1, extract No. 28.

8 Specialised monoculture is becoming the fashion in eastern counties of England. Small farms are being swallowed by larger ones. Barley is the dominant crop because of subsidies. Rotation patterns have been discarded in favour of peas, beans and soft fruits, for freezing. Animals are going indoors. See also Section 8, extract No. 20. The mean rainfall is 18–25 inches

(450–635 mm). The Fens are losing 1 inch of top soil every year, and fears of a dustbowl have been expressed.

9 Taro is a 50 per cent starch root-crop whose tubers weigh 4–9 pounds (2–4·5 kg). Settlers probably did not know of the effect that exotic fauna had had in St. Helena and in the West Indies in earlier centuries. New Zealand birds were the forest seed-carriers and pest-destroyers. Winds are a constant feature and especially strong. Large-scale maps reveal the rugged nature of most of the country and the enormous number of streams eating into the land.

10 How do we feel about this? The letter was prompted by the recent herding of Amerindians in Brazil into reserves. See Section 5, extract N. 24. The grab for Eskimo hunting grounds by mineral prospectors in Alaska is amongst other contemporary acts that have certain parallels. See also Section 7, extract No. 13.

11 We have been warned not to waste our land and resources. It is likely that with the spread of birth-control the rate of population growth will slow down. Nuclear wastes from power stations and fall-out from atomic testing are thought by some scientists to be instrumental in causing infant mortality, abortions, and diseases which will substantially lower the expectancy of life, not only in the immediate environment but all over the earth. Desalination of sea water, and water discovered below the Sahara and Australian deserts by the oil men, will eventually allow the reclamation of vast areas of aridity. If ocean pollution can be prevented, foods are available there, and farming fish rather than hunting it offers a partial solution to the food problem. Intensive farming of animals is not the answer; even the broiler industry for chickens is wasteful, and said to involve a two-thirds loss in the conversion of fish (to fishmeal) to chickens. The Chinese early realised the value of plant foods, especially sprouted vegetables, as more economical than animal foods.

12 In 1800 the buffalo (or bison), a large wild ox, ranged over two-thirds of North America. It supported Indians in meat, fat, hides (for footwear, boats, clothes, tents), and sinews for thread. The buffalo was hunted unmercifully by settlers who feared for their crops and hated the Indians; and by some people, wantonly, for sport. The gun was its undoing, and by 1906 there were only 400 left, preserved on a ranch. From these, the present 10,000 in National Parks have been bred.

13 Whales have been hunted out of the Arctic, except for a few. Only Russia and Japan still hunt them in the Antarctic. Whale meat is liked in Northern Norway and in the Faroes where the *grindadráp* is still carried on. During the 1939–45 war, whale meat was eaten in Britain and whale oil used for soap and margarine. See also Section 9, extracts Nos. 27 and 28.

14 'Built-in obsolescence' of goods in the western world results from affluence, cost of repair labour, and advertising pressures on people to buy improved models. Discarded junk disposal is a big problem. New York is 13 per cent built on dumps, as it has 7 million tons a year to dispose of. Huge dumps are seen along the Hudson, and every town and village has the same problem. Cars can be compressed for scrap, and paper and old rags reconstituted. Plastic which will not rot is an eyesore in rural areas.

15 A flashback to England in 1861. The present population of Manchester is about three-quarters of a million. Today, the city is more commercial, and is ringed with varied industries, replacing the concentration of cotton mills. Note the *noise* of spinning and weaving, which still applies today. The texture of life in industrial towns in England is changing, with clean-air regulations and high-rise flats replacing housing packed round the mills. Former back-to-back dwellings (in 1969 there were 20,000 in Leeds for example) are being re-arranged so that two back-to-backs become one, and are being given bathrooms and individual sanitation. All the industrial towns have new housing estates on the outskirts, and many have good public buildings and activities in the city centres. The rivers are becoming increasingly polluted by industrial wastes and increased sewage output.

16 Ebbw Vale, Monmouth (51° 47′ N, 3° 12′ W). In South Wales the formerly beautifully wooded valleys are narrow, and are now followed by polluted rivers, canals, roads, railways, and terraced towns. Enormous quantities of water are used in steel-making, and increasing needs present a threat that reservoirs may be built, flooding parts of the valleys. Slag wastes and coal wastes from menacing tips (see extract No. 17, Aberfan). Chemical works discharge copper, zinc, arsenic and lead wastes in Swansea valley.

17 As a result of the Aberfan disaster this tip has been removed and others examined. The land is riddled with old workings and subsidence. Some tips near closed mines are grassed or wooded over. The introduction of light industry and the opening of new roads to the Midlands and South, are making the area more prosperous than it was.

18 The problem of waste and squalor in the midst of plenty is now world-wide.

19 The *Commodore* is a small boat with a crew of six to eight. In 1969 a bad scare occurred: millions of fish died in the Rhine below Bingen, in areas where drinking water is taken from the river. In Holland, sewage and chemical wastes from factories and farms have always to be removed by elaborate processes further downstream. This problem exists in all big rivers, lakes and seas where untreated wastes are emptied into them. The Hudson (U.S.A.) is unfit to swim in, the Great Lakes and Baltic Sea are badly affected, the English lakes are going the same way, and many coastal towns have been criticised for unclean beaches. Oil wastes from rigs, ships' bunkers and tankers in distress, and the discharge of chemically polluted rivers are killing vital food in the oceans. They are also reducing the amount of oxygen formation and the amount of carbon dioxide that can be absorbed. The prospect is warmer water and air, melting ice caps, and rising level of the seas to the present 400-foot (120 m) contour.

20 Along with prosperity the Japanese inherit the problems of the Western world (see above).

21–22 Two aspects of air pollution. After the scare of 1952 London introduced its clean-air policy, and only smokeless fuels were permitted. But over the British Isles as a whole one million tons of soot per year still fall, and offices and homes in Central London still rapidly become black and gritty if windows are opened. In London, Los Angeles and big towns everywhere the car adds considerably to pollution, emitting hydro-carbons and other poisons. Electric or steam-driven cars are forecast to supersede petrol-driven ones.

23-25 The car, a desirable instrument of mobility, takes its toll as a destroyer of environment, a sprawl-maker and a disfigurer of towns and country places.

26-28 Extract No. 26 deplores lack of heart in America. Nos. 27 and 28 show how places with a heart within the London area, as in so many other cities, are being sacrificed to ease traffic congestion—by building new metropolitan arteries, tower-block flats and speculative box-like offices. Traffic flows faster than before through the monotonous local-authority housing, despite the large number of 'one-man' cars and the goods traffic that still goes through—rather than round—the centre. As the number of cars increases, so the amount of exhaust pollutants rises.

29-30 These passages deal with several aspects of the social consequences and the contemporary attitude to housing people, and they are applicable to many parts of the world. High building is actually more costly and less space-saving than is commonly supposed. People are often unhappy in tower blocks; they may make stimulating places to work in as offices, but they cramp family life. When very high blocks overlook the parks, they are visible from them and spoil the illusion of *rus in urbe* that is so precious to the town dweller.

31 This was written in the late 1950's. Since the pioneer writers encouraged us to look at our landscape, amenity societies have fought many battles with insensitive developers. These confrontations are bound to increase in number and intensity.

32 Also looks at the landscape, but in an agricultural frame. Egg factories and broiler houses are other examples of what are really industrial buildings found in rural areas.

33-42 These extracts suggest that if we want to, we can put things right, but how are things to be set in motion? By pioneers, by climate of opinion, by governments, by industrialists? From necessity, opinion, education, fear?

33 A very positive attitude—we must accept change and industrial development. We must do this advisedly, choosing sites with care for the total environment.

34 Serengeti Plain, Tanzania National Park (2° 40′ S, 35° 0′ E). A scientific laboratory has been built in the Serengeti and named after Michael Grzimek.

35 Richard St. Barbe Baker, a pioneer in the work of tree-planting in Africa, founded the organisation 'The Men of the Trees' in Kenya in 1922.

36 Note that it was as long ago as 1935 that the U.S.A. Soil Conservation Act was passed, and some years since President Johnson pronounced his creed. Still pollution is continuing. It has become a political issue in the U.S.A.

37 The importance of a whole and healthy landscape is emphasised here, and some of the mistakes that have been made are pointed out. It is suggested that it is possible to shape both town and country beautifully.

38 This area was made a National Park about four years before the British Petroleum Company began to develop it as a deep-water terminus for giant oil-tankers.

39 This extract also suggests that, with planning, new developments can be made acceptable. Many battles over the routes of by-passes are inevitable.

40 Pittsburg has also been re-planned, a park and garden replacing crumbling railway yards, and a city of steel and glass replacing blighted areas.

41 Tapiola is a suburb of Helsinki. Tapio, the God of the Forest, is the name of a Finnish association of advisers on the use of woodlands. Finns like buildings to melt into the background.

42 As a contrast to the preceding extract, look at Shanghai's crowded quarter, where 18,000 people live at a density of 690 per acre (1725 per ha) and are thankful to do so. 'Liberation' dates from the end of the Kuomintang regime in 1949.

7

We don't all think alike

'The essence of civilisation is to respect the variety of life, and how few of us do so.' We have also to face very rapid change in social patterns. The extracts that follow cover such themes as differing values and standards, the stress of culture shock and the effects of culture contacts. While bearing in mind the dangers of generalisation, in this section we may find material to bring depth and immediacy to the study of current socio-political problems. 'I was a Southerner and they Easterners in behaviour and outlook . . . none of us Africans just because we were born such.'

1 All mankind is one great family

General

Not only religion, but unbiased common sense, as well as the accurate deductions of scientific research, lead to the conclusion that all mankind is one great family, of which the numerous nations and tribes existing are only various branches. Hence enlightened men in all countries must feel a wish to encourage and facilitate human intercourse in every manner, by removing as far as possible all impediments to it, in order to promote the reciprocal advantage and enjoyment of the whole human race.

Raja Rammohun Roy, 1772–1833

2 Indian Confederacy before the advent of the Europeans

North America, sixteenth century

'The Confederated chiefs now uproot the tallest pine tree and into the cavity thereby made we cast all weapons of war. Into the depths of the earth, deep down into the under-earth currents of water, flowing to unknown regions we cast all weapons of strife. We bury them from sight and we plant again the tree. Thus shall the Great Peace be established.'

The peace aims of the Confederacy were universal. Any Indian on the continent could enter the Confederation. The whole prospect was changed through settlements by the Whites and by their imperial struggles. Outside the Confederation were the Cherokees. After the creation of the United States the Cherokees wrote a constitution of the White Man's kind. They established a legislature, a judiciary and an executive branch. A free Press and public school system was set up and in their relations with the White Man they kept faith although the White Man consistently betrayed them. In the end they were expelled from their lands and driven into Arkansas. On that trek 4,000 Cherokees died.

from : Ritchie Calder, *The Inheritors*

3 Columbus writes to the King and Queen

West Indies, 1492

These people are without any religion, not idolaters, but very gentle, not knowing what is evil, nor the sins of murder and theft, being without arms, and so timid that a hundred would fly before one Spaniard although the Spaniard might be only joking with them. They, however, believe and know that there is a God in heaven, and say that we have come from heaven. At any prayer that we say, they repeat, and make the sign of the cross. Thus your Highnesses should resolve to make them Christians, for I believe that, if the work was begun, in a little time a multitude of nations would be converted to our faith, with the acquisition of great lordships, peoples and riches for Spain. Without doubt, there is in these lands a vast quantity of gold, and the Indians I have on board do not speak without reason when they say that in their islands there are places where they dig out gold, and wear it on their necks, ears, arms, and legs, the rings being very large. There are also precious stones, pearls, and an infinity of spices.

4 The puzzle of Christianity

Guinea

The most difficult obstacle for me in my progress toward civilisation was the obligation of trying to think of the Supreme Being as having human characteristics. My imagination could go along all too easily with the delineated picture, presented to us both in words and in paintings, of an enormous old man with a flowing beard, given to earth-shaking angers and terrifying revenges. He was the Great Police-man, having openings to the pits of hell handily in his back yard where the kitchen should have been. I could see the smoke and flames rising out of the pits, smell seared human flesh, and hear the screams of the tortured. They screamed through my sleep. As for the folk in the pits, their accents were clearly African.

My imagination would follow the descriptions and even embellish them with extra gruesome details. The imagination was willing, but the heart was not! Even while I quailed before the missionary-elaborated God, my heart remembered the Supreme Being of our Kofon religion. I was too filled with the tribal idea of the Supreme Being as the life force in all things to give complete credence to this outsize man kind of deity. I was afraid of Him even while I did not completely believe in Him.

I often thought about our days in the Bondo Bush when, after emptying our bodies of physical demands through an exhaustion of dancing and trying to empty our minds of all conscious thought, we willed for the Supreme Being to fill us with the life rhythms of earth. When this was achieved, and it sometimes was, one felt exhilarated and 'right'. It was difficult to feel 'right', difficult to feel anything but apprehension under the ever-watching eye of the Great Policeman with his arm tensed to swing, his club at the ready.

I felt guilty about making these comparisons between the Supreme Being of the tribes-people and the Jehovah of the Christians. I felt that this comparing was most likely the blackest of all things being tallied against me. Yet I could not make my mind leave off thinking about it.

Did the Great Policeman have special kind days, set aside with the regularity of market days, in which he showed another, and kinder side of his human nature? If not, how did white people get their fabulous wealth which was said to come as a blessing from their God? I was completely bewildered.

We were told about kindness as well as about wrath. Our primers were made up of Bible stories in which generosity and love and goodness were emphasised. There was the Good Samaritan. 'Which, now . . . was neighbour to him that fell among thieves?'

'The Samaritan! The Samaritan did right.'

'Yes, the Samaritan. Why?'

'Because he acted as one Sousou would act towards another.'

The answer is held right but the reason held wrong.

'No, no, Modupe! The Samaritan acted like a *Christian*.'

Why was every good act held to be exclusively Christian even when it had a counterpart in tribal life? All tribal things were denounced as bad—'the bad old ways'. Confusion sat on me. If the teacher had said, 'A Christian treats all men, everywhere, as though they were members of his own tribe,' that would have made clear sense. I would have gained some concept of the Christian ideal . . .

As I gained facility in reading and vocabulary, I found myself reading the Bible for pleasure as well as for answers to my confusions. Much of the Old Testament seemed to be about people who were a great deal more like Sousou than like missionaries. They made sacrifice, they considered circumcision a sacred ritual, they fancied gold bangles, they feared leprosy, their several wives came into palaver, one with the other. There was pride in children, there were tribal wars, curses were feared, diviners consulted, and just as in our Sousou stories, an animal like Balaam's donkey could reproach a man with human speech . . .

One day I was reading in Corinthians I, and none of the words seemed to make much sense or to be of special interest. The day was drowsily, dreamily hot. A fly buzzed around my head, distracting me. I was about to give up when a certain few words popped up at me as though they had been in bolder print, in blacker ink. They seemed to have no connection in meaning to any of the words before or after them.

'There is one glory in the sun, and another glory in the moon, and another glory of the stars. . .'

I stopped reading. I repeated the words over aloud to myself. Into my mind flashed the sight of my grandfather bending thoughtfully over the sundial he made by criss-crossing straws over a gourd. I saw him in my imagination as clearly as though my feet were in Dubréka. I saw every line in his good, kindly, noble face. I knew that he never looked at his home-made time device without feeling in his venerable bones the glory of the sun, that other glory of the moon, that further glory of the stars. He often spoke to me about these things. He meditated upon them.

A chill of excitement ran through me. I shivered with it as though in a fever chill, in spite of the heat of the day. *I had found my first clear answer to the confusions that devilled me! The Glory of God was not in an alarm-clock! The Glory of God was in the sun and the moon and the stars!* The Bible had carried God's mouth to me on that and I knew it for truth.

Perhaps I should have arrived at this sooner and with less mental anguish had not that first white man who came to Dubréka showed us mechanical gadgets as evidence of the power of God. Only one article in his 'juju kit' was of spiritual import—the Bible. Every other thing with which he tried to impress and convert our people was not an artefact of his religion but a representative item from his machine civilisation. He had led us to believe that white nations had guns and steamships and skyscrapers and mirrors and matches, while the black tribes had none of these things because the white God was more powerful. White men had credited their own brilliant inventions to their God in an attempt to enhance God's power. As though God needed an alarm-clock to be great! The greatness of God was in every stick and stone and star, just as we had been taught in the Bondo Bush. If God had a face, which seemed more improbable than ever now, that face bore more resemblance to my grandfather's when he felt the sun blessing his old bones than it did to the crafty visage of a spying policeman.

from : Prince Modupe, *I was a Savage*

5 Impact of Christian ideas

India

It is revealing to find, just after his return from South Africa, how Gandhi speaks of Christian, Western, simplicities with a new, discovering fervour: 'Before the Throne of the Almighty we shall be judged, not by what we have eaten nor by whom we have been touched but by whom we have served and how. Inasmuch as we serve a single human being in distress, we shall find favour in the sight of God.' The New Testament tone is not inappropriate. It is in India and with Gandhi, that one can begin to see how revolutionary the now familiar Christian ethic must once have been.

from : V. S. Naipaul, *An Area of Darkness*

6 Jamaican Christian in London

England, nineteen-fifties

Almost without exception the West Indian goes through a period of disillusionment when he starts life in England, and the disillusionment can be quite shattering amid the whirl of London's self-centred and often heartless activities. The West Indian is by nature deeply religious and coming from the profoundly Christian background of his own country he finds his faith faltering on arrival in his mother country. Even the most developed Christians have told me how their faith wavered when they found that Englishmen did not either believe or practice the Gospel that they had sent out to Jamaica ... the West Indian seeks out his nearest church and is once again shocked, for far from the crowded, overflowing churches to which he is used, he finds a few folk, who receive him politely, but without understanding and without that warmth of friendship to which the West Indian is accustomed in his churches at home ...

from : Clifford S. Hill, *Black and White in Harmony*

7 Leisure before the Europeans came

Africa

Before the European advent, most African tribes had so organised their lives that married men and elders had probably more leisure than any other people on earth. Wives looked after crops; sons herded cattle and fought wars; elders sat under trees, drank beer and either talked of local matters or dispensed judgement. Every man was a councillor and a magistrate, but attended to his duties more or less when he felt inclined, having to observe no hours or rotas.

A tree for shade, a gourd for beer, a horn for snuff, obedient wives, respectful sons, hardworking daughters; sun for warmth, milk, meat and millet for nourishment; a fertile soil, a perfect climate; the protection of magicians against the spite of spirits, and the schemes of evil-doers; it would be hard to imagine a life nearer than theirs to fulfilment of the hopes and dreams of the elderly male of any race or nation.

No life on earth is perfect, and it had its set-backs from time to time, but for everything there was a remedy and if the remedy failed there was a reason; for everything there was a purpose, for every man security within his tribe, his age-set, his clan and his family; and from this soil grew and thrived the blooms of dignity and contentment. Women did not come off nearly so well, but even so their work gave them pride, and no woman whatever her looks, age, or nature, was ever unwanted, lonely, or without the matrix of a family.

It becomes increasingly more difficult to sustain a conviction that the introduction of money, literacy, taxes, votes, the doctrine of work and the religion of materialism; that the suppression of cattle raids, magic, dancing, sacrifices and indigenous justice; that the end of contentment and the beginning of *angst;* that all these aspects of civilisation have made life happier and fuller for the tribesman.

from : Elspeth Huxley, *A New Earth*

8 Why hurry?

Papua

They don't look at life in the way we do. But does that necessarily mean that their way is wrong? For example, I took steel axes to them, one of the achievements of our civilisation. But the result was not always as overwhelming as one might have thought from our point of view, believing firmly as we do in the superiority of our civilisation. The Papuans certainly admired the sharpness of the steel axe and the high polish of its blade, and they were always quite proud to possess one. But my argument that with a steel axe you could do the same amount of work in half the time as compared with a stone axe —in other words, what is certainly for us the biggest advantage of the steel axe over the stone axe—made no impression on the Papuans at all. They are just not open to such an argument. Why should the thing be done any quicker? To what purpose and to whose advantage? I remember once telling my Tibetan friends that a jet plane would fly a certain distance much quicker than a piston-engined plane, and all I got for this, as it seemed to me, important item of information was blank and embarrassed silence. Finally one of the Tibetans asked uncertainly: 'But why?' And I must confess that there was no satisfactory answer I could give him.

from : Heinrich Harrer, *I come from the Stone Age*

9 A question of courtesy

Indo-Chinese border, 1942

I had committed the unforgivable crime of appearing to be in a hurry. That was enough for the shark to assume a blank expression and start fiddling about with some empty tins in the back of his shop, nodding his head with a sorrowful smile. I had seen his eyes glint when I mentioned petrol. There was a guaranteed profit for him in the deal. But profit was one thing, courtesy was another. The rules of Chinese courtesy, established and firmly fixed over the centuries, forbade him to strike a bargain in such an informal manner. He was shocked at my vulgarity and made no effort to conceal it. I should have embarked on a harmless conversation with him and, after an hour of commonplace chat, indirectly switched to the subject of the dearth of the fuel that makes motor-cars function. Having thus abided by the rules I could have ventured to insinuate that if someone had the extreme amiability to be good enough to let me have a little petrol, I should be eternally grateful to him. He would then have hinted that perhaps just to oblige him, one of his friends would consent to produce a few drops of the precious liquid. The ceremony would then have been prolonged by a ritual exchange of compliments. Finally I should have been entitled to slip him the agreed sum diffidently and with downcast eyes, a sum which he would have refused a good half dozen times before tucking it away in the pocket of his greatcoat. Then, and only then, should I have obtained satisfaction.

But I was a mere savage who didn't know the first thing about courtesy and I had stupidly enquired if it was possible to buy some petrol.

from : Pierre Boule, *The source of the River Kwai*

10 Tempo: the volunteer helper learns

British Honduras

One of the volunteers in British Honduras thought very poorly of that country when he arrived. Coming himself from a sophisticated and cultured background it seemed dead to the world outside, with a people who were idle and self-satisfied. He prepared for a miserable year . . .

A month later a hurricane hit Belize which brought all normal work to a standstill and created problems of such magnitude that there was no time to think of personal unhappiness. Houses were wrecked, thousands left homeless, food was short, disease probable, the town in chaos; the school in which he worked was virtually destroyed and over everything in the first days brooded a spirit of depression and fear.

Out of this experience, as work to put the town back on its feet gained momentum, the volunteer found that his whole attitude towards its people had changed. In their acceptance of the disaster and their attitude towards each other and himself he began to discover a kindliness and simplicity and friendliness which charmed him. The tempo of living, which in its slowness had originally annoyed him, was still there—but now he began to see it in a different light.

They are happy as they are, and surely that is better than anything. One has to realise that this is not England—obvious, but not all that easy. The people are accustomed to a much slower pace and are much friendlier.

from : Mora Dickson, *A World Elsewhere*

11 Masai contempt for civilisation

Kenya

Masai hearts are with their cattle; they desire no finer destiny for a son than to walk in the dust of a larger herd than his father's. The young man who dreams of glory sees fine white bulls and brindled cows and green grass knee-high, he does not see the stone bungalow, the shining motor-car, the well-cut suit, the framed diploma so alluring to his darker fellow countrymen. He likes to wear his hair in matted pig-tails smeared with red ochre and rancid butter, to stand with one foot against the other knee, to eat a compound of bullock's blood and curdled milk, to carry his long spear and to keep his women in their beads and coils and fly-infested mud burrow as his ancestors did—those ancestors whose lion head-dresses and painted shields filled the hearts of lesser breeds with terror, and won the right of conquest over the steppes of eastern Africa from their northern Somali deserts to their southern tsetse bush.

For the Masai have pride, and pride is a quality we recoil from in ourselves and half-admire, half-deplore in others . . . They *could* export fat steers and lambs, but have done next to nothing to improve the quality of their animals. This is because they do not need the cash. There are old men living in mud hovels with little but ear-rings, a spear and a blanket who could at any minute realize several thousand pounds for their cattle. Scarcely one of them could not afford a motor-car if he wanted one, probably a Jaguar at that. The plain fact is that they do not want motor-cars, or beds, or kitchen sinks, or radios, or refrigerators, or washing machines : they just want cattle, which they have, and which the processes of nature will increase for them without their having to do any disagreeable work.

It is an *impasse*. The whole machinery of modern society, modern trade, modern development, has been halted by the Masai's refusal to keep up with the Jones's or the Kamaus in this case. It is like a great Britannia aircraft grounded by a midge in the works. Modern civilisation runs on avarice as cars on petrol, and if there is no pump where you can fill up with avarice, you simply stay where you are. But even the Masai are not really free of avarice; it merely takes a different form. If they do not want bicycles and trousers, they do want more cattle, and this has led them into a great error. Instead of rejecting everything the West offered them, they accepted the hypodermic syringe of the vets. First of all the vets put an end to rinderpest, and then, rather less successfully, dealt with various other diseases that were keeping their herds in check . . .

No doubt it would have needed superhuman self-denial on the part of the Masai to have rejected this magical means of ending the periodic epidemics that had wiped out all but a rump of their cherished herds. Yet these were the means by which nature had kept herds and habitat in balance. Vegetation, controlled by constant factors like rainfall and soil structure, cannot multiply as creatures of the animal kingdom can, and do ... Anyway vets controlled diseases, livestock multiplied and their hoofs and mouths destroyed the precarious grass cover of the plains. The result is that except where the tsetse fly remains in control, the Masai are living in country poised upon the edge of deserthood. Some of it has gone over the edge, some hovers on the borderline, some has not reached it yet. And so pressure mounts upon those regions that are still protected by the tsetse fly.

The Masai way of life is certainly doomed. For a while it may continue, but nothing in the end can resist the pressures of Western materialism.

from : Elspeth Huxley, *A New Earth*

12 Rejection of Western life

Tristan da Cunha, 1966

In the West we have spent some four or five hundred years in proving a concept, at least, of the individual as a self-validating ideal. We pay constantly for its fragility in the hard coin of anxiety and tension; but it is even more distressing to have this ideal negated and indeed, assaulted by a living scale of values that sets our ideals at nought; where communication is oblique, using feeling, not words; but where no man goes in fear of his neighbour. For on Tristan there simply is no room, or provision, for the cultivation of exceptional individual prowess, nor for unique excellence of any kind, except good fellowship.

In England the Tristans' sense of corporate identity was undermined by association with a society antithetical in its aims and devices. So they voted to return home to Tristan, again subordinating individual preference, in uncounted cases to common unity. They felt, as a race, that there alone was where they belonged ... A man may still choose not to work for money; a family can still exist on Tristan, with its own house, its potatoes, meat, fish and chickens, on a couple of pounds a month for oddments from the canteen. But still they now have the means to make money. Not much by our standards, ten shillings [50p] a day basic wage, and a bonus on the quantity of fish caught. With this they may buy luxury foods (including tea and sugar) from the canteen, drink from the bar, transistors and clothes from Cape Town.

... Tristan now has the apparent freedom to choose whether it will join the twentieth century or not. The volcano simply forced Tristan to a reckoning with the wind of change, the siren song of increased complexity ... But once and for all, their visit has thrown into relief the problem of the individual, with whom all real culture, and with it, self-consciousness, begins and ends; the problem of 'making something more of one's life'. For many, perhaps the great majority, the question does not arise, and England was a forgettable interlude ... but a few have felt the unconscious promptings of complexity and are prepared to chance it in England a second time. As I watched them four months ago board the great Dutch liner that was to take them from their grieving relatives—the whole island population—on the beach, I felt that they hardly knew why they were going, that they were impelled by a force that had little to do with happiness and less to do with comfort.

from : Guy Brenton, 'Paradise regained', *The Observer Magazine, August* 28, 1966

13 Abhorrence of private land ownership

North America, eighteenth century

Among all the ways in which his values differed from the white man's it was between their respective attitudes toward land that there yawned the widest abyss. To the Indian the earth was a divine gift bestowed upon all men for their common good. That any one man should presume to claim personal ownership of any part of it was unthinkable. The narrow cultivated areas around an Indian town were apportioned among the community's families according to a rule of thumb by which each family used as much as it felt like taking the trouble to plant. The family gathered the harvest but nobody claimed the ownership of the land or raised more than each needed for the coming winter. In the adjacent expanse of wilderness the nation asserted the right to hunt and sometimes fought with neighbouring nations for the right but it was a right to use that was being disputed, not a title of possession. In practice the Indian hunter usually ranged as widely as he pleased. When an Indian nation went through the form, necessarily under duress, of selling tribal land to a white buyer it was the Indian hunting right in the area that was being relinquished, and each such successive transaction engineered by the white man but confirmed in the Indian's mind his immemorial right to use the land that still remained to him.

No aspect of the creeping advance of the white frontier, therefore, so profoundly disturbed the Indian as the preposterous assumption of private land ownership. The newcomers' insanity in tearing down the forest and killing off the game was an infuriating spectacle. But that they should then fence off areas of the land itself as parcels of private property struck at the heart of the Indian's conception of man's ordained place on earth. His abhorrence of the whole idea of land ownership lent an added zest to the perpetration of those inhuman atrocities which characterised his every attack on the settlements.

from : Dale van Every, *Forth to the Wilderness*

14 Primitive nature of communal loyalties

Russia and Africa

I had expected to find life in Russia utterly new and different from anything I had ever known. Yet I found it oddly familiar. I am forced to travel about the world a great deal yet this had never happened to me before. I have three times been in Japan yet my African past has not been much use in helping me to interpret the profound impact that that country and its people always makes on me. But at times in Russia without my upbringing and love of the primitive peoples of Africa I could have felt quite at a loss, and I suspect that it is a whale of a red herring to look to Marx for the origin and shape of Russian Communism. The claim of Russian Communism to be an 'objective absolute' is necessary in Russia, firstly to keep up appearances within the State; and secondly as a means of soliciting help from the outside world. But the claim to 'absolutism' is false. The Russians are naturally a communal people because they are basically a primitive people : and primitive man is naturally collective. I know a dozen or so tribes in Africa who without the technological dress of Soviet Russia, practise in essence a Soviet system, because it is their natural, primitive way. The collective value evolved in prolonged conditions of great danger is entrusted to a powerful central tribal authority who discharges it with a strange mixture of absolutism and deference to popular feeling, which it continually tests and consults without necessarily obeying it—just as in the Soviet Union. Change is imposed from the top against the inertia and resistance of the conservative whole who naturally feel safer with the customs and beliefs that have brought it safely out of the past. Possessions are owned not so much for the individual as on behalf of the tribe : property ultimately belongs to the chief on behalf of the whole. So the phenomenon of violent change brought about from the top against popular inclination because it is thought to be in the interest of the whole, is a familiar occurence in African history. Ivan the Terrible, Peter the Great and Stalin, complete with private obsession and personal mania, have scores of counterparts on the primitive African scene . . .

. . . The Soviet system struck me as extremely archaic and committed inevitably more and more to far-reaching change within itself if it is to survive in the emerging world. In its primitive concept too, and not in its Marxist pretensions lies the secret of its attraction for the developing peoples of Africa. They understand and sympathise with the Soviet readily because its way is so much closer to their own both in character and purpose than ours. It is not Marxist indoctrination which makes the new African States claim the democratic right to have a vote for each man—merely to use the votes to abolish democracy by eliminating all opposition to authority and instituting a one party State. It is because within themselves they stand at the same remote collective point in time as do the Russians. There is nothing primitive man fears more than a division within his community, within his communal self. All virtue is collective, all evil individual. What holds together is good, what divides is bad . . . The fear that my own countrymen to this day nourish in regard to the Africans who vastly outnumber them, is the same fear of being absorbed into a chaotic primitive horde which possessed all who shared a European frontier with Russia. One has only to travel along the Russian-European frontiers to find that the fires of these antagonisms still burn and to hear people use the same language about the Russians as a South African fanatic of apartheid will use about his black countrymen. A civilised and perceptive Pole will lose all these qualities at the mere mention of the word 'Russian', just as a gentle blue-eyed Boer will do when an African is under discussion. Many Poles speak of the Russians as 'cattle'; many Boers never speak of black Africans as anything but 'the creatures'. The parallel I find important because I believe there is unending danger ahead unless the world at large becomes aware of the existence of other kinds of 'apartheid' just as vicious as the South African variety, which is made unfairly to carry a censure arising out of an assumption that South Africa is unique and outside the forgivable of our comomn human fallibility.

So I could continue almost indefinitely with the list of primitive parallels between the African and the Russian way. In both there is a strange animism still found deep in the country, the superstitions among peasants about river, wood, earth and frost spirits—and their addiction, I was told, to archaic rituals and festive observances that are the despair of the bright commissars from the towns. There is the tendency, as in Africa, to be footloose and to be unable to endure for too long the cities and factories . . .

... But perhaps the most important parallel of all is the battle between the new and the old in Russia and the new and the old in Africa.

It is this internal battle in Russia which seems to me to be most significant and likely to increase in scale and intensity as in the emergent Africa. It is essentially a struggle of men who want to live individually and specifically rather than collectively and generally. This for me is the underlying meaning of the conflict raging in Russia between the intellectual and artistic worlds and the State. It is the meaning, too, of the battle in Africa between tribal authority and the new educated Africans and explains the hatred of the new generation of Africans for their chiefs and tribal traditions who, together, claim to be able to rule over and think for the tribe. It is a battle which once joined has to be fought to the end for there can never be any return to a state of collective innocence. It is a battle, moreover, which can only be legitimately fought from within by those whose lives are committed to the consequences ...

As important, of course, as the similarities between the Russian and African primitiveness are the differences. These are all implied in the fact that the Russians are European and primitive while in my country the native peoples are African and pagan. In Russia three generations of Soviet indoctrination has destroyed almost all evidence of religion, but one cannot travel through the width and depth of this country without being aware that in the behaviour and feeling of ordinary people something still remains of the primitive Christian concept. Authority daily and even violently denies it. But if the essence of Christian religion is, as Schwietzer put it, that 'Christianity is a reverence for life', then there are some signs of this in the new voices raised in art and literature in Russia. Today in the Christian world the awareness of what Christianity really was before the mind parcelled it out into systems is daily gaining ground and some years ago the World Council of Christian Churches meeting at Amsterdam perhaps recognized this when they define Communism as a 'heresy but a Christian heresy'.

from : Laurens Van Der Post, *Journey into Russia*

15 Tribal loyalty

General

'If Johnny had been a Gambian like those boys who set on me that evening, and of the same tribe as they were, he certainly wouldn't have helped me however close our friendship.'

'The more fool he.'

I restrained myself. 'There's another thing,' I went on. 'The family. We think our family ties are precious, or at any rate, that we should feel so. But they're nothing at all to theirs. Have you noticed, when an African makes a solemn promise, what he says to you?'

'I can't say I have.'

'He says, "I swear it on my mother's life." '

'And probably breaks his word.'

'Oh, no doubt! Just as we do when we swear upon our gods, or on our sacred books. The point I'm trying to convey, though, to the frosty heights of your Everest intelligence, dearest Theodora, is that there are entirely different moral concepts among different races: a fact which leads to endless misunderstanding on the political and social planes, and makes right conduct in you for instance, seem idiotic to Johnny Fortune, and some gesture of his which he believes is necessary and honourable to seem foolish, or even wicked, in your eyes.'

from : Colin MacInnes, *City of Spades*

16 Traditional family ties

India

That man is to be pitied who must stand alone against the dangers, seen and unseen, which beset him. Our families are our insurance. When a man falls ill, he knows that his family will care for him and his children until he is able to earn again. And they will be cared for without a word of reproach. If a man dies, his widow and children are sure of the protection of a home.

from : William and Charlotte Wiser, *Behind Mud Walls 1930–1960*

Nigeria

The struggle between the strong urge to cut himself adrift from his family and live his own life, on the one hand, and the wish to sacrifice his own comfort and happiness to fulfill deeply engrained family and communal obligations on the other has been a painful dilemma every wage-earning Nigerian has had to face.

from : James S. Coleman, *Nigeria: the Background to Nationalism*

China

Every family in China is really a communistic unit, with the principle of 'Do what you can and take what you need' guiding its functions ... A successful man, if he is an official, always gives the best jobs to his relatives, and if there are not enough jobs he can create sinecure ones ... It defeats any form of social organisation.

from : Lin Yutang, *My Country and my People*

China

The immense family loyalty shown by the Chinese—and unequalled by any other race in the world except, possibly, the Jews,—has for centuries handicapped China by preventing the growth of a larger loyalty, of a social sense in the Western meaning of those words. There are close observers of Chinese affairs who believe that Communism has developed in China partly because it is definitely in contradiction to this family loyalty, so incompatible with the tendencies of the modern world.

from : Vernon Bartlett, *Report from Malaya*

17 New social pattern

China, 1965

Western parents these days find it difficult to contain the undisciplined upsurge of their young. Imagine such a revolt actively encouraged by the highest authorities in the country. This is what Chinese adults have to face. The Mao regime, in its struggle to build the new China, has cast the family as the enemy—and with the family, religion, bourgeois culture, everything with a foot in yesterday.

The child is set in judgement over the parent. 'I say to myself that, while it is right for us poor peasants to show remembrance for our dead family members, the burning of joss paper is a superstitious act, and should be opposed. So I persuade my father not to do that, but he is very stubborn in his thought and insists on burning the joss paper. A dispute has thus arisen ... If he has incorrect thoughts, I will struggle firmly against him. I will make no exception, even for my own parents.'

from : Odile Cail, 'Mao's children', *The Observer*, December 14, 1969

18 On being a modern parent

Idakho village, Kenya

While in the past the more children there were in a Baluyia family, the more highly respected the parents were in the society, today a small but growing number of parents are thinking in terms of smaller families. The case for many children to increase a family's work-force is gradually losing ground as employment patterns change and parents realize how expensive it is to care for large families in modern times. Neither do so many parents think as in the past, of girls primarily as a source of wealth from bride price. A father with a large family, without reasonable sources of wealth to educate and to care for them adequately, is beginning to lose favour with the rest of the society.

Changes related to pregnancy and childbirth are also taking place. Now, as never in the past, there are expectant mothers who no longer undertake strenuous work right up to childbirth. Through increased medical care they are learning that to do so may affect the position of the child in the womb, and perhaps cause other serious complications. Husbands with some elementary education have become aware of the advantage of allowing their wives to have more rest during pregnancy. These women also are talking more freely, which was once taboo, about conception, pregnancy and childbirth, not only among themselves, but with their husbands and, above all, with physicians and nurses. Many expectant mothers in or near the towns make an effort to visit a hospital or a health centre for pre- and later, post-natal examinations. In fact, there is pressure on the Government by the educated group of mothers to provide classes for expectant mothers especially where they can receive help from experts. Certainly the children of modern parents will be born at a maternity home or hospital since, in addition to services there being free, the Government now requires that all children be registered and that the registration certificate bear the name of the place of birth and the medical staff in attendance. In my own case, our three young children were born at a hospital and have certificates of birth, documents which the parents of neither their mother nor myself would have reason to know when we were born in the thirties.

These new requirements mean, in effect, that both parents will have to make early preparations for the arrival of the child, however contrary to tribal tradition. For example, they have to buy, in advance, articles of clothing adequate for the baby's needs. This practice has long been taboo in the tribe, of course, for fear of causing the child's death. The expectant mother, as has been said, will have to make frequent visits to the clinic and consult other experts. She will have to read books on child care, securing information about the right diet and conditions of rest. The father, too, will have to assume a different role from formerly, learning to create a comfortable, restful atmosphere for the mother both before and after delivery. Since our children must have a fair start in life, these things are imperative.

. . . It isn't always easy for modern parents to change from the old ways. My wife and I, for example, are trying to bring up our children in line with what Western books on child-rearing and child development advise. At the same time we wonder at the wisdom of thus trying to fit them into a life based on the Western culture when in actual fact a good proportion of their time as children will be lived with other children in the traditional Luyia society. This tends to create a feeling of insecurity in the parents—and perhaps in the children . . .

. . . We supplied our children with Western food in a Western manner in their early stages. Since that time they have also been introduced to the local food and the traditional way of eating it. Thus the whole process of learning to eat becomes complicated for them. Our children have to learn that there are certain times and places—and foods— when spoons are used for eating; others when knives and forks are the proper instruments; still others—as when eating the traditional *bushuma* or maize-meal—when the use of the hands only is the acceptable way. They must drink water from glasses at one moment and from traditional containers at other times.

Another typical instance can be cited. In naming our three children, we decided to differ from the customary Luyia practice. My children have taken my name, Lijembe, as a surname, in addition to their Christian names. From the traditional tribal standpoint this has caused difficulties . . . When my father visits us and plays with the children, as he loves to do, he rarely calls them by name. It is not within his experience or nature to refer to his grandchildren by his son's name. Neither would he refer to them by their Christian names.

To try to avoid such difficult situations by isolating ourselves and our children from the village life is a solution we feel we cannot afford, the traditional ties between us and our parents being still so strong. On the face of things, in fact, this is a simple and almost unimportant matter, as are the others just described. Yet each is the sort of thing that causes confusion and disappointment to the elders, and can set in motion feelings of indecision on the part of modern parents trying to rear our children in 'the valley between'. It is good that the children at least, because they *are* children, are far more flexible in these situations than we are . . .

. . . It is imperative that when our children grow up to become adults, they should have among other things a clear sense of balance. We recognize that the ties of traditional village life and kinship are still very strong, and that as cultural changes take place, there will be a case for future generations to retain, at least in part, those aspects of our culture that are worth keeping. We recognize, too, that the schools and other educational institutions have, as everywhere else, to assist the future Abidakho to appreciate what is good in both tribal and Western cultures, and that the future may discover some things better than either. To be able to help our children to achieve this appreciation, today's parents will need to be critical of the steps we take in the process of child rearing. Being educated ourselves, we hold positions of leadership in the society, and must act accordingly. Careful appreciation of Western methods of health and childcare, and critical retention of what is good in traditional methods, can help us modern parents to create the sense of balance in our children, enabling the future generation to work out, from the two cultures, a way of life more appropriate than either one of these, in line with what the people of Idakho, of Buluyia, and of Kenya will be wanting most.

> *from* : Joseph A. Lijembe, 'The valley between' in *East African Childhood: Three Versions,* edited by Lorene K. Fox

19 Impact of new ideas on a developing country

General

In the initial period of contact the recipient people may be antagonistic to changes suggested or imposed by outsiders, other than in the field of material goods of obvious utility. Adults are fearful of the changes they realize will come.

Subsequently there is increasing acceptance of the outsiders' ways, particularly by the younger generation, and growing enthusiasm to learn more. This leads to the rejection of a great deal of indigenous culture, to scorn for traditional ways, and to disregard of the advice of elders. The validity of earlier customs is denied, and people who cling to old ways are taunted as oldfashioned. In much of Africa, traditional songs, dances, and folklore were put aside, and hymns, drill, and school readers took their place. As a paramount chief told Dr. Reed, 'The white teachers taught us to despise our past,'—and for a time educated Africans did just this. There is a headlong rush to acquire foreign culture, and a desire on the part of the local élite to become like the economically dominant outsider.

This is followed by a period of disillusionment. It soon becomes apparent that the members of the less complex society cannot participate fully in the society of the more complex group. Restrictions imposed by the dominant power are part of the cause, but other deeper cultural and psychological causes are also involved. The dominated group feels that its own culture is threatened, but it has nothing to substitute; feelings of insecurity result. In some regions, in parts of Oceania, for example, depopulation followed, but more often, among tribal peoples the common reaction is the nationalistic manifestation of nativism. Several forms may occur, but the common element is a partial or complete rejection of the culture of the foreigner and an attempt to return to or restore the fundamental values of earlier days. ... Newly developing countries, which, in the twentieth century, are anxious to assimilate the material techniques, but, at the same time, to maintain indigenous 'spiritual values' find themselves frustrated in that changes do not come as easily as they wish. The élite, who a few years earlier eagerly sought to identify themselves with the ways of the West, in dress, education, food, and politics, and who often deprecated their own culture and its achievements, now lead their people in a search to discover the essence of their traditional cultural forms. The values inherent in ancient ways are recognised, and attempts are made to restore and perpetuate them. Identification of a way of life as peculiarly one's own and as a positive creation of the local group—the essence of successful nationalism—is accomplished through symbols. These symbols must have a high degree of visibility and they must stem from the traditional culture. They are focal points around which people rally, both to be convinced of and to reaffirm their faith in the vitality and uniqueness of their own culture.

The symbols of nationalism that reappear time after time, in Latin America, Africa, India, and Southeast Asia, are surprisingly similar; language, costume, dietary patterns, fiesta celebrations, an interest in archaeology (which gives the best possible evidence of past greatness) and folklore (to reconstruct music, dance, and popular arts) humor, and sometimes folk medicine, sports, and religion.

from : George M. Foster, *Traditional Cultures and the Impact of Technological Change*

20 What is real independence in a developing country?

Sierra Leone

'Look my friend, I made this trip with you because I wanted you to learn something for yourself, but it seems that you are likely to leave this country, perhaps even Africa, as uninformed about the realities as when you first arrived ... The thing which seems to concern you most is independence, and the way in which we react to its approach. You are clearly disappointed by what you have seen and equally by what you have not seen here. I think I ought to explain something about independence to you. Every African State wants to be independent of or from some colonial power or other. That is not too difficult in the present state of affairs; the difficulties involved vary only in degree. But there is another kind of independence, which, so far, very few African States seem to be able to appreciate—that is independence to grow, to build, to work, to achieve. Do you get my point? The first type is a kind of political charter. After receiving it and waving it around a while in the first flush of glory and excitement, many states discover that, in fact, their position has not really changed. Not only is the economic life of the country still fully controlled from outside, but that control penetrates in devious forms to the political and cultural life as well. The reason is simple. Some states immediately upon becoming, as is claimed, independent from a foreign power expect to blossom forth in all the splendour of advanced economic and social development—you know, universities, hospitals, blocks of flats, fancy government buildings, educational and social reforms, the lot. Those things cost money, so where is the money to come from? Well back they go to the former controlling power and the money is forthcoming as long as there is the right kind of collateral—either concessions in the development of that country's natural resources, if any, or concessions in terms of that country's strategic position in the event of the threat of war.'

He shifted his bulk to a more comfortable position, then said, 'Independence, like any other luxury has to be paid for, and the sooner we learn that the better for us. We cannot pay for it with our natural resources which lie buried in the ground, until those have been fully developed, but we can pay for it by putting ourselves to work. Look at Israel, my friend. Do you know what is the secret of Israel's development? Work, and more work, for every man, woman and child. Have you ever seen a group of Israelis? Well I have, and they are fine, strong, resolute and intelligent people, all proof of the fact that hard work is good for body, mind and spirit.'

'Independence will not mean a damned thing here or elsewhere until the children suck the fire of it from their mothers' breast and learn their responsibility for it with each school lesson. The people of Africa have more reason to make themselves into free independent entities than even the Israelis have, but they are too blind to the importance of first principles. We talk of Africans, but we don't know each other, we don't understand each other, we don't talk with each other. It is easier for you to fly from Dakar to Paris than from Dakar to Freetown. Our border is contiguous for three quarters of its length with

Guinea, the rest with Liberia, yet we have little contact with Guinea because they speak French and we speak English. Liberia is in an even worse position, literally surrounded by French-speaking Africans, yet having very little contact with them ... Sierra Leone is only a piece of Africa, a small piece. Try to understand us, and for the time being expect no more from us than we are able to give.' Saying this, he started the motor and we resumed our journey.

from : E. R. Braithwaite, *A Kind of Homecoming*

21 Culture shock

General

Everyone, when first stationed in a foreign country, experiences 'culture shock' to some degree ... He finds that he is irritable, depressed, and probably annoyed by the lack of attention shown him by his local technical counterpart. Everything seems to go wrong, and the technician finds he is increasingly outspoken about the shortcomings of the country he is expected to like. But it rarely occurs to him that the problem lies within himself; it is obvious that the host country and its unpredictable inhabitants are to blame.

Oberg defines the symptoms of culture shock as excessive preoccupation with drinking water, food, and dishes, fear of physical contact with servants, great concern over minor pains and skin eruptions, a hand-washing complex, fits of anger over delays and other minor frustrations, a fixed idea that 'people' are cheating you, delay and outright refusal to learn the language of the country, an absentminded faraway stare (sometimes called 'the tropical stare'), a feeling of helplessness and a desire for the people of one's own nationality, and 'a terrible longing to be back home' ...

... There is maid trouble, school trouble, shopping trouble—trouble everywhere. All the things about everyday living that were taken for granted at home now become insurmountable problems. The technician is now just another cog, as far as the bureaucracy to which he is assigned is concerned; he is no longer a novelty, and his national counterparts take him for granted. He is probably annoyed, too, because the gratitude he expects for his help is strangely lacking. This attitude is interpreted as indifference, or perhaps as an indication that the local people aren't friendly after all. At this stage the victim bands together with his fellow sufferers to exchange symptoms and to criticise the host country and all its citizens. The appraisal is derogatory, based on simple stereotypes which offer an easy rationalisation for one's troubles.

'These people can't plan.' 'They have no manners.' 'They ought to be taught how to get things done in a hurry,' and so on, the complaining runs. At this period the cocktail circuit becomes a convenient crutch, an easy and uninhibiting atmosphere in which to get a load off the chest.

This second stage represents the crisis in the disease; if it is successfully weathered, the patient will be restored to health. Passing the crisis ushers the patient into the third, or recovery stage. He now begins to understand some of the cues which orient him and perhaps enough of the language so that his isolation is not complete. Little by little the problems of living are worked out, and it becomes apparent that the situation although difficult is not absolutely hopeless, as it seemed only a short time earlier. A returning sense of humor is helpful at this point; when the patient can joke about his sad plight, he is well on the road to recovery. By now, he almost imagines himself to be an authority on the country, and he can bolster his ego by talking in a knowing fashion before awed new arrivals. It helps, too, to realise that other people are experiencing the same depression and to be able to help them by holding out encouragement.

The fourth stage represents full or near full recovery. By now, if ever, the technician will have made a relatively good adjustment to the situation in which he finds himself. He comes to accept the customs of the country for what they are. He doesn't wax enthusiastic about all of them, but he doesn't chafe. From time to time he experiences strain in his working relationships, but the basic anxiety of not being able to live is gone. Presently the technician realises that he is getting a great kick out of the new experience and that there can be real exhileration in the overseas experience. But however perceptive, no one realises fully the nature of his illness until he returns to the United States on home leave, or again to live in that country. It is almost embarrassing to realise how many shortcomings the good old U.S.A. seems to have and how frustrating and annoying so many experiences can be. Culture shock in reverse is much less serious than the original ailment, but it is surprising how many people can hardly wait through their home leaves to get back to the post which, only two short years before, seemed absolutely unbearable.

from : George M. Foster, *Traditional Cultures and the*
Impact of Technological Change

22 Teacher in Liberia

Liberia and general

I'd never before realized how American I was, not black American, just American. So many things I once took for granted now appear terribly significant, probably because I'm forced to do without them, newspapers, radio, novels, conversation, friends. Guess if I remained here long enough I would either forget about them or find substitutes. You know, you see something funny or read something and want to talk about it, and it's not easy to communicate the whole thing if there is no point of common reference, no understanding of the nuance which springs from an appreciation of mutually familiar circumstances. Guess these fellows feel the same way when they are in the U.S.A., even if they too are in a predominantly black group.

from : E. R. Braithwaite, *A Kind of Homecoming*

23 British residents: the Chinese point of view

China, nineteen-forties

He may be the son of a missionary, or a captain or a pilot, or a secretary in the consular service, or he may be a merchant to whom China is just a market for selling sardines and 'sunkist' oranges. He is not always uneducated; in fact, he may be a brilliant journalist, with one eye to a political advisorship and the other to a loan commission. He may even be very well informed within his limits, the limits of a man who can talk three syllables of Chinese and depends on his English-speaking Chinese friends for his supplies of information. But he keeps on with his adventure and he plays golf and his golf helps to keep him fit. He drinks Lipton's tea and reads the *North China Daily News* and his spirit revolts against the morning reports of banditry and kidnapping and recurrent civil wars, which spoil his breakfast for him. He is well shaved and dresses more neatly than his Chinese associates, and his boots are better shined than they would be if in England, although this is no credit to him, for the Chinese boys are such good bootblacks. He rides a distance of three or four miles from his home to his office every morning, and believes himself desired at Miss Smith's tea. He may have no aristocratic blood in his veins nor ancestral portraits in his halls, but he can always circumvent that by going further back in history and discovering that his fore-fathers in the primeval forests had the right blood in them, and that sets his mind at peace and relieves him of all anxiety to study things Chinese. But he is also uncomfortable every time his business takes him through Chinese streets where the heathen eyes all stare at him. He takes his handkerchief and vociferously blows his nose with it and bravely endures it, all the while in a blue funk. He broadly surveys the wave of blue-dressed humanity. It seems to him that their eyes are not quite so slant as the shilling-shocker covers represent them to be. Can these people stab one in the back? It seems unbelievable in the beautiful sunlight, but one never knows, and the courage and sportsmanship which he learned in the cricket field all leave him. Why, he would rather be knocked on the head by a cricket bat than go through those crooked streets again! Yes, it was *fear,* primeval fear of the Unknown.

But to him it is not just that. It is his *humanity* that cannot stand the sight of human misery and poverty, as understood in his own terms. He simply can't stand being pulled by a human beast of burden —he has to have a car. His car is not just a car, it is a moving covered corridor that leads from his home to the office and protects him from Chinese humanity. He will not leave his car and his civilisation. He tells Miss Smith so at tea, saying that a car in China is not a luxury but a necessity. That three-mile ride of an enclosed mind in an enclosed glass case from the home to the office he takes every day of his twenty-five years in China, although he does not mention this fact when he goes home to England and signs himself 'An Old Resident Twenty-Five Years in China' in correspondence to the London *Times.* It reads very impressively. Of course, he should know what he is talking about.

Meanwhile that three mile radius has seldom been exceeded except when he goes on cross-country paper hunts over Chinese farm fields, but then he is out in the open and knows how to defend himself. But in this he is mistaken, for he never has to, and this he knows himself for he merely says so, when he is out for sport. He has never been invited to Chinese homes, has sedulously avoided Chinese restaurants, and has never read a single line of Chinese newspapers.

from : Lin Yutang, *My Country and my People*

24 Pakistani expatriate woman

England

Obviously it is foolish to generalize : a Hungarian political refugee will have patently different problems to face from a Punjabi village-girl. But even so, it is remarkable with what tenacity, conscious or otherwise, women of all backgrounds cling to their traditions and culture . . .

Nasima Madni was brought up in an orthodox fashion. 'Before marriage', she explained, 'I used to wear *burqa*.* But after marriage because my husband, he is not so orthodox that he likes to cover his wife, so I had to leave *burqa*. But I use always to wear a coat, because I don't want to be very attractive for the people who are walking on the roads.'

She is a gentle, soft-voiced creature, very eager to be friendly and helpful. Her marriage to her cousin was arranged when she was 19, in 1960, as soon as she'd finished college. So she went straight from her parents' home to her mother-in-law's. Before coming to England she had learned to cook but never practised it—her mother-in-law fussed her, 'she didn't like me to work'—never run a home. As a woman in Pakistan, one is always aware of this invisible curtain of protection, a feeling of being cherished.

England in 1964, predictably brought problems. On one level there were the already well-vented difficulties of accommodation. Then, where work was concerned, 'It was really quite *horrible* time for me. Because I never wear Western dresses, and they always say if I wear Western dresses then they give me the job. As a sales girl, I had to do it—but then I could stand behind the counter. I used to go in my dresses and change. But I felt very shy. Western dress is quite attractive, but, I mean, it can't *cover* you.'

A solution was found in starting her own dressmaking business at home, making in particular sari blouses and *shalwar-kameez* (the trouser and tunic) for Indians and Pakistanis. But although her husband considered this new employment more 'respectable', there were others who failed to. 'You see, in Pakistan they are mostly low-class illiterate persons, the tailors. So they try to talk to me in typical manner—just like a servant . . .'

As a Muslim—and her religion is dear to her—she is enjoined to try and pray five times a day, hard to achieve in office or shop. The dictates of Islam itself guide and influence both hers and her husband's lives to a considerable degree. In Nasima's attitude towards family and marriage, she is equally faithful to her upbringing. Early marriage she deems desirable, and much freedom before it unwise—'because the

* Long covering garment with face veil

girl will have something in her mind, what she would like after marriage, what type of husband and house. If she can't get these things she will be upset and it won't be a successful marriage. For example with me, before marriage I knew only my college and house and some friends, and *nothing* about other world. So whatever my husband liked, I did it and liked it, because I didn't have anything in my mind.'

Understandably, she wants to go back eventually. For a Pakistani girl, missing her family's protective care, life in England can be a harsh exposure.

from : Naseem Khan, 'How the immigrant woman sees Britain', *The Times*, July 18, 1967

25 African contrasts

Uganda

I frequently noticed luxurious cars parked by the banana trees that drooped over pathetic-looking mud buildings; these were rectangular huts, very perfunctorily thatched and obviously unfinished, for you could see the reed or elephant-grass framework poking through the red mud smeared on them for walls. I asked, 'But why, when the cars are such good quality aren't the garages built in more permanent form? They look more suitable for sheltering farm jalopies or the worn out Cape carts or sledges that Uncle Cecil uses for moving his grain harvest.'

'What garages?' from my sister and her brother-in-law.

'I mean these,' pointing, 'these we keep passing.'

'Those aren't garages. They are the people's houses.'

'People's houses?' The South African native in me was flabbergasted; I nearly fell off my seat. 'You must be joking! People can't live in those things. Why, they haven't any windows, or only those wooden shutters that are always pulled to. Besides, you can see how the plaster isn't finished off smoothly as it would be for a dwelling place. Or the thatch, it would be sewn up, not left straggling in this way.'

My sister did not answer. William did not speak either. I looked at the buildings anew and saw that what they told me was right; people were living there. I saw some sitting by them on the red ground. And there were clumps of canna lillies planted near, and petunias, poinsettias, bougainvillaea. I remember reading how the Baganda loved flowers. But I was surprised because I had expected

314

the dwelling places they built would be of a piece. I was about to say so, contrasting them with pagan people's huts at home in South Africa but didn't. I was confused because I now realised I had so far seen no pagans, only 'dressed' people as we would say at home, meaning, not that pagans went naked (on the contrary they are well covered in their ochre-smeared blankets and shawls) but that people in Western-style clothing had adopted Western standards. I was too startled for the moment by the apparent confusion in standards to ask my sister and her brother-in-law to elucidate, so instead I said, 'Would you show me where the pagans live, then?' pulling my eyes away from the expensive cars and the houses they stood by.

My sister hesitated, finally murmured, 'It's—it's different here. There are no pagans as against "Westernised". Everybody "dresses", is "civilised".' I looked at her, about to demand what on earth she meant; but because she was giving me a curious imploring kind of look I bit my tongue and was silent, not knowing what to ask. Questions pressed forward in my mind forcing my mouth open but I shut it again without speaking. There was a constrained atmosphere now in the car; or rather I felt in a difficulty for I couldn't help comparing what I saw with the impressions we had received years before from the East Africans who had stayed with us. I realised I had rather expected the expensive cars I saw would be parked by 'mansions' as they had said. Were these 'dressed' people who were clearly better off than us in the South not of the class the students had come from? Yet with us at home the resources of people of the same kind were spent on the house and home first, on motor cars later.

That drive from Entebbe to Kampala was the first of the surprises to come. For, on the one hand what Southerner would not be impressed, indeed breathless at the visible signs of wealth which was on a scale I had thought Africa incapable of? Yet in this short space I saw discrepancies that greatly disturbed me.

We drove on and climbed over the brow of another hillock and now Kampala appeared and spread before my eyes. It was a sizeable town. Its white houses were dotted over hills neighbouring one another. They had galvanised iron roofs painted red or green, some of aluminium colour gleaming in the sunlight, others were tiled. A splendid modern sight; wonderful to see it practically on the Equator in fabulous 'Darkest Africa' as I had first at Nairobi, then Entebbe, now Kampala. My spirits lifted as I contemplated what our fellow Bantu were capable of . . .

I did not yet appreciate that Kampala, like Entebbe with its modern streets, lighting, drainage, telephones, mosquito gauze and such things was Europeans' and Indians' work.

from : Noni Jabavu, *Drawn in Colour*

26 Italian children in a new land

England

The real barrier is not colour, or even language, though that is much more formidable : it's a barrier of outlook, culture, values, way of life. Language is a part of it, but not all ...

At first they came in driblets at all ages and all stages of the school year, as ignorant of the language as so many stuffed owls. Like the Caribbeans, they came from peasant families. Uprooted from the poorest parts of southern Italy, including Sicily, they had lived in extreme poverty, without a clue to any of the material furnishings we take for granted. They had never used a water-closet, a knife and fork, a handkerchief, let alone a blackboard, a book, a traffic crossing, stairways or electric light. They had run wild on barren hillsides herding goats, without shoes.

'Their background was so different,' remarked the headmaster, 'it was another world, another outlook, a completely different pattern of ideas. Life had made very few demands. Punctuality meant nothing. Time flowed on. They had no idea of discipline, their parents had no ambition as we understand the word. They'd never even seen a book. They'd come and gone as they liked and sat in the sun. They understood nothing and our sort of life was totally strange.'

And here they were, deposited by mothers on their way to work on the doorsteps of teachers cut off from all communication by the language barrier. If the teachers wanted to explain how to open a cupboard door or hold a pencil, they had to do it in mime.

'We start', said the Bedford headmaster, 'with a simple proposition, that each child is not a problem but an individual—an individual we welcome and want. Not an outsider. We try to make each child feel that we are interested in everything about him—his mind, his body, his teeth, his hair, the way he uses the lavatory. It's a question of social training. That comes first. Making every one of them feel he's part of the community' ...

Children will pick up a language very quickly; the social habits, the outlook, of a strange community takes much longer, especially when you only have the children six or seven hours a day for five days a week. For the rest of the time they're back in their own tight, warm, transplanted family, speaking and hearing nothing but their native tongue, eating their own kind of food, living their own kind of life. They're pitched to and fro between the two worlds like a shuttle and no wonder some of them express their bewilderment by what is now called anti-social behaviour, but used to have blunter names ...

In the long run it is the English custom, habit, way of life that must set the pattern. It's the immigrants who will be absorbed. This, Italian parents resent, even while they know it to be inevitable. Even if they themselves return one day to Italy, most of the children will stay behind. But probably few parents *will* return.

Meanwhile, they feel their children being sucked away, adopting values they don't understand and often disapprove of—the freedom of the young for instance, their independence and their sexual laxity. These Italians have a strong family cohesion. Frugal, hardworking, sober citizens—their crime record is considerably lower than the 'natives'—they go home at night, draw the curtains, and stick together. Now their teenage children are going off to cinemas and cafés and dancehalls, throwing away money on pop discs and even motor bikes.

from : Elspeth Huxley, *Back Street, New Worlds*

27 The Irish start life in the New World

U.S.A., nineteenth century

The Irish have, in fact, always been a highly social people, gregarious above everything; their virtues are hospitality, good humour and wit. With an immense relish for the company of other people, they depend to an exaggerated extent on human intercourse, especially with other Irish . . .

The immense majority of the Irish sought employment in towns, and economic conditions in the United States cities at the time of the famine emigration did not favour the Irish. Immigrants of other nations were pouring in, and employment for the unskilled was difficult to secure. The Irish were advised, warned, implored by newspapers, officials, philanthropists, to leave the cities and go west; but they remained, or if they did leave one city they moved to another, to engage in the lowest type of labour, earn the least wages and live in the worst conditions. Within a short time, almost a few months, the Irish had created a world in New York, and for that matter in every other city in which they settled, that was exclusively Irish. 'They love to clan together in some out of the way place,' wrote the New York Association for Improving the Conditions of the Poor, 'are content to live together in filth and disorder with a bare sustenance, provided they can drink and smoke and gossip, and enjoy their balls and wakes and frolics without molestation.' The Irish emigrant arriving at New York, or going to cities in the interior of the United States—Albany, Utica, Cincinnati, Louisville—went straight to the Irish quarter, called 'Irish town', 'Paddy town' or 'The Irish Channel', where he associated exclusively with his fellow-countrymen and had no contact with

American culture or American ideas. 'He is lost in the crowd of his countrymen, who encompass him in such numbers that his glimpses of American manners, morals and religion are few and faint', wrote an American journalist. There was, moreover, a bond which held Irish to Irish which no other nation shared, Irish hatred of England, the burning sense of injustice, resentment, and the feeling of dispossession with which nine out of ten emigrants left their native land. 'They feel they have been wronged in their own country,' wrote an American observer; 'they feel amongst themselves the tie of bearing one common wrong.'

from : Cecil Woodham-Smith, *The Great Hunger: Ireland 1845–9*

28 West Indians in English cities: clash of cultures

England, nineteen-sixties

Most people of the English urban working-class think in terms of rent, not ownership; increasingly they tend to feel the council owes them a house; and of course, council rents are heavily subsidised. To buy through a building society costs a lot more, and sub-letting is regarded as a separate occupation. Owning and sub-letting what are known as 'houses in multiple occupation' isn't part of our natural habit. And then we lack the strong incentive of the immigrant... If there's one thing on which all immigrants agree it is that almost to a man, they mean to buy a house; and to this end they save and save. A house represents the very thing they've left home to find—security. ... 'Their whole life is centred in the family', an observer said. 'Their children don't get on their nerves as ours do if we're tightly packed. They like sharing things. The women share their cookers, pots and pans, storage cupboards, everything. *Our* wives wouldn't be on speaking terms in those conditions, but not the West Indians; to them it's congenial; they have a different outlook from ours.' This outlook the Italians share. 'Unique in my experience', said a public health inspector in Bedford, 'they're quite prepared to use the same cookers and sinks at the same time without falling out.'

In warm climates, you don't shut yourself up inside four walls, light the fire and close the door against draughts and strangers. You have the open-sided shed, the outdoor cooking fire, people coming and going; you observe an ancient, deep, universal tradition of hospitality. To refuse a stranger, let alone a relative, food and shelter is a heinous crime. Now the immigrants are in our houses, built to meet a different need and match another outlook : and yet they haven't left their own outlook, their own traditions, their own customs and beliefs behind . . .

Basically, this situation has prevailed ever since a world of cultivators began to take to towns . . . They come to cities, pack into slums, wander like babes in the wood through forests not just of brick and concrete but of different ideas. The adjustment's always painful and difficult.

from : Elspeth Huxley, *Back Street, New Worlds*

29 To the city

Johannesburg, South Africa, nineteen-forties

From Ixopo the toy train climbs up into other hills, the green rolling hills of Lufafa, Eastwolds, Donnybrook. From Donnybrook the broadgauge runs to the great valley of the Umkomaas. Here the tribes live, and the soil is sick, almost beyond healing. Up out of the valley it climbs, past Hemu-hemu to Elandskop. Down the long valley of the Umsindusi, past Edendale and the black slums to Pietermaritzburg, the lovely city. Change here to the greatest train of all, the train for Johannesburg. Here is a white man's wonder, a train that has no engine, only an iron cage on its head, taking power from metal ropes stretched out above.

Climb up to Hilton and Lion's river, to Balgowan, Rosetta, Mooi River, through hills lovely beyond any singing of it. Thunder through the night, over battlefields of long ago. Climb over the Drakensberg, on to the level plains.

Wake in the swaying coach to the half-light before the dawn. The engine is steaming again, and there are no more ropes overhead. This is a new country, a strange country, rolling and rolling away as far as the eye can see. There are new names here, hard names for a Zulu who has been schooled in English. For they are in the language that was called Afrikaans, a language that he had never yet heard spoken.

—The mines, they cry, the mines. For many of them are going to work in the mines.

—Are these the mines, those flat white hills in the distance? He can ask safely, for there is no one here who heard him yesterday.

—That is the rock out of the mines, umfundisi. The gold has been taken out of it.

—How does the rock come out?

—We go down and dig it out, umfundisi. And when it is hard to

319

dig, we go away, and the white men blow it out with the firesticks. Then we come back and clear it away; we load it on the trucks; and it goes up in a cage, up a long chimney so long that I cannot say it for you.

—How does it go up?

—It is wound up by a great wheel. Wait, and I shall show you one.

He is silent, and his heart beats a little faster, with excitement and fear.

—There is the wheel, umfundisi. There is the wheel.

A great iron structure rearing into the air, and a great wheel above it, going so fast that the spokes play tricks with the sight. Great buildings, and steam blowing out of pipes, and men hurrying about. A great white hill, and an endless procession of trucks climbing upon it, high up in the air. On the ground, motor-cars, lorries, buses, one great confusion.

—Is that Johannesburg? he asks.

But they laugh confidently. Old hands some of them are.

—That is nothing, they say. In Johannesburg there are buildings so high—but they cannot describe them.

—My brother, says one, you know the hill that stands so, straight up, behind my father's kraal. So high as that.

The other man nods, but Kumalo does not know that hill.

And now the buildings are endless, the buildings, and the white hills, and the great wheels, and streets without number, and cars and lorries and buses.

—This surely is Johannesburg? he says.

But they laugh again. They are growing a little tired. This is nothing, they say.

Railway-lines, railway-lines, it is a wonder. To the left, to the right, so many that he cannot count. A train rushes past them, with a sudden roaring of sound that makes him jump in his seat. And on the other side of them, another races beside them, but drops slowly behind. Stations, stations, more than he has ever imagined. People are waiting there in hundreds, but the train rushes past, leaving them disappointed.

The buildings get higher, the streets more uncountable. How does one find one's way in such a confusion? It is dusk, and the lights are coming on in the streets.

One of the men points for him.

—Johannesburg, umfundisi.

He sees great high buildings; there are red and green lights on them, almost as tall as the buildings. They go on and off. Water comes out of a bottle, till the glass is full. Then the lights go out. And when they come on again, lo the bottle is full and upright, and the glass empty. And there goes the bottle over again. Black and white, it says, black and white, though it is red and green. It is too much to understand.

He is silent, his head aches, he is afraid. There is this railway station to come, this great place with all its tunnels under the ground. The train stops, under a great roof, and there are thousands of people. Steps go down into the earth, and here is the tunnel under the ground. Black people, white people, some going, some coming, so many that the tunnel is full. He goes carefully that he may not bump anybody, holding tightly on to his bag. He comes out into a great hall, and the stream goes up the steps, and here he is out in the street. The noise is immense. Cars and buses one behind the other, more than he has ever imagined. The stream goes over the street, but remembering Mpanza's son, he is afraid to follow. Lights change from green to red, and back again to green. He has heard that. When it is green, you may go. But when he starts across, a great bus swings across the path. There is some law of the place that he does not understand, and he retreats again. He finds himself a place against the wall, he will look as though he is waiting for some purpose. His heart beats like that of a child, there is nothing to do or think to stop it. *Tixo*, watch over me, he says to himself. *Tixo*, watch over me.

from : Alan Paton, *Cry the beloved Country*

30 A great city—a great solitude

England, nineteen-sixties

I came to London. It had become the centre of my world and I had worked hard to come to it. And I was lost. London was not the centre of my world. I had been misled; but there was nowhere else to go. It was a good place for getting lost in, a city no one ever knew, a city explored from the neutral heart outwards until, after years, it defined itself into a jumble of clearings separated by stretches of the unknown, through which the narrowest of paths had been cut. Here I became no more than the inhabitant of a big city, robbed of loyalties, time passing, taking me away from what I was, thrown more and more into myself, fighting to keep my balance and to keep alive the thought of the clear world beyond the bricks and asphalt and the chaos of railway lines. All mythical lands faded, and in the big city I was confined to a smaller world than I had ever known. I became my flat, my desk, my name.

from : V. S. Naipaul, *An Area of Darkness*

31 Culture contact is a two-way traffic

East Africa

We hear a great deal about the devastating effect that the European has on the native in Africa, but no one has ever stopped to inquire into the effect of the native on the European. The interplay of forces set in motion by that vast concourse of black, primitive people living so intimately with a small handful of white people ... For it is by no means a one-sided business. Some of us who were born and bred in Africa are well aware of it.

People like myself, whose first memory is of a large, black, smiling, crooning, warm, full-bosomed figure bending over his cot and whose friends for years were naked black urchins, know that contact between Europeans and Africans is, whether the individual wishes it or not, a significant, almost measureless two-way flow of traffic. The traffic can, with proper understanding and tolerance, enrich as well the life of the European. Or he can, with his blind intolerance, divert and disorganise it to his own impoverishment and embitterment.

from : Laurens Van Der Post, *Venture to the Interior*

32 Racial contacts in the South

U.S.A., 1969

'I don't know anywhere that a Negro is treated better than around here,' Mr. Seward was saying to the three of us on the spring morning when I visited him with my wife and my father. 'You take your average person from up North, he just doesn't *know* the Negro like we do. Now for instance I have a Negro who's worked for me for years, name of Ernest. He knows if he breaks his arm—like he did a while ago, fell off a tractor—he knows he can come to me and I'll see that he's taken care of, hospital expenses and all, and I'll take care of him and his family while he's unable to work, right on down the line. I don't ask him to pay back a cent, either, that's for sure. We have a wonderful relationship, that Negro and myself. By God I'd die for that Negro and he knows it, and he'd do the same for me. But Ernest doesn't want to sit down at my table, here in this house, and have supper with me—and he wouldn't want me in *his* house. And Ernest's got kids like I do, and he doesn't want them to go to school with my Bobby, any more than Bobby wants to go to school with *his* kids. It works both ways. People up North don't seem to understand that.'

from : William Styron, *The Confessions of Nat Turner*

33 Eskimoes looking at the white man

Northwest Canada

'They are like new-born children in our country, and it would be below one's dignity to contradict a senseless child.' So they did not contradict the white man and his willful spirit, but let him think and judge wrongly as he pleased. But Eskimoes also feared white people because of their power and riches and concealed their deeper reasonings from them, especially when whites scoffed at their beliefs and traditions or tried to change them overnight without trying to understand the circumstances that conditioned them.

from : Peter Frenchen, *Book of the Eskimoes*

34 Looking at Europeans

Nigeria, nineteen-thirties

When I think of Europeans I notice that they differ, not only in complexion but also in manner, habits and speech. Some are good, kind, patient and strong in judging what is right and trying to understand us and our customs. Others are hot-headed and will not take the time to seek to know us. Possibly it is because they are new to us and are worried by having so many things to do.

The white men are great in their fashion of doing things. They like to do everything in order. They are not like some black men who jump from one thing unfinished to a fresh one, and by so doing may be unable to finish both. They trust very much to writing. I do not think they can remember anything properly if they do not write it down. I have gone many times to meet them for business. Whenever I went they had to write some words before they could remember to do my wish. Sometimes twenty and more men would go and lay complaints before the white man and he would not forget any. They were all written in a book.

They spend much time in arranging things in their offices and

323

houses. In the house one would always see some servants brushing the floor and clearing away something hanging from the roof. At the end of the month these servants go and receive a heavy sum of money. I consider this is a waste for such small work. Why, they could have done such for themselves.

I like very much the way they keep their premises. But it would be impossible for me to grow flowers and leaves in places where I should plant yams and other crops for food. They seem to take interest in what cannot feed them. I wonder why they like to satisfy their eyes rather than their belly. I think they do not know the right use of money. They spend their money for those who cook their food, of which they will also have a share. This is very ridiculous when a man has got a wife, a brother or sister who can cook for him.

The white men love their wives more than anything they have in life. I have been acquainted with some of them for over twenty years but I have never seen them quarrelling or fighting with their wives. It is a surprising thing to me to note that they are all rich, but they would be seen with only one wife.

In speech they are different from us. They do not all speak together. They have patience and speak one after another without any interruption. But they do not use parables to illustrate their judgement when they want to decide any case as we do. I do not always enjoy meeting them when they come new from their country. They have so many different manners. Sometimes I go to the office or house to meet them. If there is no interpreter present they try to satisfy me with the words: 'Obon, Ndewo! (Chief I salute you!)' They would have to call the interpreter before they could say more. They speak very rapidly and I praise the men who have to interpret such a stream of words.

from : 'The story of Udo Akpabio' in *Ten Africans,*
edited by Margery Perham

35 African food and the European: social contact

West Africa

The Europeans who live in West Africa, business-men, officials, technicians, teachers, missionaries, even 'old settlers' with decades of so-called Africa experience, unanimously declare African food uneatable. They have never dared try to get used to it; after the first shy nibbles they shudder, give up and stick to the routine of having

European tinned food cooked for them by trained servants. Even anthropologists, ethnologists and linguists, who visit and investigate tribal groups in remote regions and who are dependent on a good relationship with the population, are inclined to cram their jeeps with tinned food and avoid partaking of African dishes.

This dependence on tinned food limits mobility or else leaves the traveller dependent also on his own vehicle. True human relationship is blocked, for how can uninhibited confidence develop when one side despises the other's food, calls it uneatable or even dirty? Discrimination against what our fellow men eat means discrimination against our fellow men, and no one should think the African misses the point.

... Any dish which has been prepared according to traditional African cooking has been so thoroughly boiled or roasted that even the toughest microbe will be destroyed; and what you eat uncooked, like the fruits, are in a secure casing of shell or peel.

African food has always agreed with me very well. Probably it is more suited to the damp heat of the climate. After eating European meals I was usually tired, after African food I found it no effort to walk or cycle several miles even in the heat of the day. Presumably the vitamin-rich red pepper stimulated the circulation and helped to balance the body's water content.

Admittedly changing over to African food is trying, though a return to European food is equally unpleasant. When the body has grown accustomed to strong spices, European food seems terribly insipid, it is as if you were chewing paste and mortar; and at your first meals, you are overcome by nausea which it is very hard to keep down. But you can lessen the discomfort by adding plenty of condiments.

Because of the transition difficulty I tried to arrange on my travels that I had to change my eating style as seldom as possible. I tried to accept my European invitations on consecutive days wherever I could, and kept eating African food as my normal diet. Thus I got to know many new dishes. Tree-worms are a delicacy, the huge African snail tastes very succulent, baked ants are as crisp as the skin of a roast goose. African food is simply a habit like many others, and once you feel at home with it you can afford to express special preferences without offending your host. After the first meals, for instance, I was allowed to eat with knife and fork : because when eating with my fingers I never succeeded in maintaining that lack of messiness which the African takes for granted at his meals ...

A walk through one of the big markets offers the housewife a rich choice of foods. Long alleys are formed by the rows of stalls under shady palm matting or corrugated-iron roofs. The market-women have their wares in front of them on low tables and boards, behind which they sit, on low stools or on the ground. There are alleys of palm-oil, being sold in bottles and bowls and gourds and tins and buckets, red palm-oil with or without spices, with a mild, medium or strong dose of pepper, cold or hot; alleys of red Capsicum pepper—Chili pepper—in fresh fruits and half dried fruits and dried fruits, ground coarse or fine, again as weak or strong as anyone could require; alleys of yams, vegetables ten or twenty times bigger than our potatoes, irregular in shape but mostly longish, and dark in colour. It is not easy to assess their weight, you buy without scales, and the housewife needs a practised eye to pick out the best values from all these irregular shapes. There are yams too in dried slices and ground to flour, mashed and pre-cooked and pressed into round flat cakes. As with our potatoes, there are many ways of preparing them; and this applies also to other tuber vegetables of the most varied sorts unknown to the European; alleys of meat and dried fish, big and small, whole fishes and half fishes and fishes in spicy sauces. When I saw these golden-brown dried fishes for the first time, at the Dakar market, covered with flies and giving off a pervasive smell, I could not have believed that a few weeks later I should be eating them straight from the stall. You break open the skin and nibble off the white inside, which is dry and well cooked, for the sun is an excellent cook.

There are alleys of all the fruits which grow in tropical climates; pineapples, pumpkins, tree melons, plantains, bananas—five big bananas cost a penny—and shining yellow oranges which look like lemons and are as sweet as honey. The market-women have a knife lying by them, with which they readily cut these oranges open and peel them for customers. You cut out a little round hat at the top, cut the yellow peel off the upper edge, put it to your lips and squeeze the juice into your mouth. Plantains are like big bananas with reddish flesh which is firmer than a banana's. The housewife usually slices them, then dips them in red pepper and deep-fries them in palm-oil, a juicy, crispy appetising dish, pungent and sweet, to go with the yams. It can be used in place of meat and is admirably filling.

There are alleys of live hens and chickens in big hand-woven baskets, alleys of game and animal carcasses, and then the alleys of special titbits : huge snails which climb up the walls of big tin barrels, with shells bigger than a man's fist; white tree-worms thick as a thumb with tiny black heads; crabs, rodents, locusts and snakes.

So the housewife has plenty of choice, and the traveller too is catered for everywhere. At many stalls in the markets he can get food already cooked, and in any settlement where car or train may stop, women will come dashing up to offer the foods they carry in big round trays on their heads : *akara* (bean-flour doughnuts stuck with pepper); *eko* (maize pudding) wrapped in big green leaves; dried fish or a leg of chicken dipped in pepper and fried; and all sorts of fruits and vegetables—enough for a meal of several courses. In Africa, in fact, whether staying with a family or travelling round, you need not worry about getting enough to eat.

from : J. Jahn, *Through African Doors*

36 Who am I?

India

And for the first time in my life I was one of the crowd. There was nothing in my appearance or dress to distinguish me from the crowd eternally hurrying into Churchgate Station. In Trinidad to be an Indian was distinctive. To be anything there was distinctive; difference was each man's attribute. To be an Indian in England was distinctive; in Egypt it was more so. Now in Bombay I entered a shop or restaurant and awaited a special quality of response. And there was nothing. It was like being denied part of my reality. Again and again I was caught. I was faceless. I might sink without a trace into the Indian crowd. I had been made by Trinidad and England; recognition of my difference was necessary to me. I felt the need to impose myself, and didn't know how.

'You require dark glasses? From your accent, sir, I perceive that you are perhaps a student, returned from Europe. You will understand there what I am about to say. Observe how these lenses soften glare and heighten colour. With the manufacture of these lenses I assure you that a new chapter has been written in the history of optics.'

So I was a student, perhaps returned from Europe. The patter was better than I had expected. But I didn't buy the lenses the man offered. I bought Crookes, hideously expensive, in a clip-on Indian frame which broke almost as soon as I left the shop. I was too tired to go back, to talk in a voice whose absurdity I felt whenever I opened my mouth. Feeling less real than before behind my dark glasses, which rattled in their broken frame, the Bombay street splintered into dazzle with every step I took, I walked, unnoticed, back to the hotel, past the fat, impertinent Anglo-Indian girl and the rat-faced Anglo-Indian manager in a silky fawn-coloured suit, and lay down on my bed below the electric ceiling fan.

from : V. S. Naipaul, *An Area of Darkness*

327

37 Reflections of a hybrid East African

Tanzania

I climbed to the top of a small volcano overlooking the stretch of farmland along the side of Kilimanjaro. The sides were steep, and when I reached the rim my breath came in long gasps. Turning I looked back at the patchwork of corn and ploughed land, the beautiful ordered pattern of crops and waiting soil.

A minute lorry, loaded high with sacks of wheat, trundled down the precipitous road, the drone of its engine carried in the hot air to where I stood. I watched it, tipping to one side and the other, making its way down to the ramshackle village of Ol Molog. To a stranger the village might look squalid enough but to us it showed a promise of the new Africa. A new 'hotel' stood on one side of the open bowl of dust that was the village centre. In one shanty the trade union and the political National Union had their offices. There was a beer shop, a grocer and a butcher, though they probably did no more than eke out a meagre existence. There was a bus that carried bags of mail and sweating crowds of passengers; there was even a tiny mud 'post office', its roof poles sticking out like the quills of a frightened porcupine. The mail bags were delivered there and horsemen from the different farms rode down each evening to collect them. A school, a church, a dispensary, and a village post completed the amenities of the village. And on the outskirts there was a large cement tank where Masai watered their huge herds of cattle.

The village was the social centre of the district. On Sundays it was filled with workers from the farms. Dust-covered and fly-ridden, it was a growing-point of the new Africa, still uncertain of its direction but breaking through the ground of ancient custom.

The lorry gathered speed, I could just see it ahead of its cloud of dust. It sped on into the wastes of the plain below—into the Africa of geological time.

I felt myself to be in some way a strange hybrid between the two Africas. Born in primitive Africa, sharing even my christening with eight African babies, inevitably I have strong African roots. I am with the African of the present day in his struggle to emerge into the modern world and yet allow his past to have meaning and status. But I have been schooled in England, and brought up by English parents so that I find a renewal of some of the deepest things in myself when I return to the source of my own civilisation.

The individual identity of which we are each aware within ourselves is made up of reactions and adaptations to our environment and experience. We can hardly imagine being without the ideas and customs we accepted in childhood. They become part of ourselves.

They may range from brushing one's teeth, giving presents at Christmas, killing a sheep when a child is born, to views about life and behaviour. It is the sum of these that makes every race carry its distinguishing features through several generations, and makes us Englishmen or Africans, Frenchmen or Americans. These habits and attitudes are persistent and go much further than the colour of skin. ... I remembered a discussion I had had with Michael* as to whether it was possible to live as a liberal in either white or black Africa.

'I don't think it matters where you live,' Michael had said. 'It's how you live that matters. It's our job to live as a bridge in Africa—a living bridge between two worlds, two races and even two times in history.'

That seemed to me to sum up our position and our purpose.

from : Susan Wood, *A Fly in Amber*

38 'There is just civilisation'

General

There is no such thing as Western civilisation, there is civilisation. It happens that in this century there is an eager desire in every part of the world—even in Communist countries—to copy the way of life of Americans and Western Europeans, but Western civilisation has its immense debts to the Chinese, the Indians, the Persians, the Greeks and so many other races remote from Western Europe and the United States. And these various contributions to civilisation have one essential feature in common—they are based upon the initiative, the independence of mind, the experience of individuals.

from : Vernon Bartlett, *Report from Malaya*

* The author's husband

Notes on Section 7
The bold figures indicate extract numbers

1 Raja Rammohun Roy—philosopher, religious and educational reformer, and member of the East India Company. He represented Indian affairs in England.

2 'One of the most enlightened institutions probably that the world has ever known.'—Ritchie Calder.

3 Mixed motives—mixed blessings.

4 This extract is concerned with lack of communication. How does one express in simple words the abstract ideas of faith, to a people whose culture one does not understand or respect?

5 Mahatma Gandhi was assassinated in 1948. He taught and practised passive resistance in India, and the acceptance of all, including the untouchables of Hindu society. Gandhi has been described as a colonial blend of Hindu and Christian, of East and West.

6 The West Indian of this extract is a product of ancestral slavery on European-owned plantations, mixed stock, basically African in origin, and mission schooling of undoubted sincerity.

–9 These passages show different aspects of the 'pace of life'. This can be observed in a small country like England; city life compared with small town and village life, for example. River Kwai, Quai or Noi (extract No. 9).

10 Voluntary Service Overseas is undertaken by young people before a job or university, or by retired people. The aim may vary from seeing the world, or doing something 'different', to the desire to 'do good' in an adventurous framework. The young are generally accepted more easily; their energy is welcomed; their faults forgiven; they are often 'fathered' by the men they come to help, and develop a wholesome respect for the community they are working in, especially if they take the trouble to learn its language.

11 'The Masai have won respect by their contempt for civilisation and all that it offered them.'—E. Huxley. Some Masai have of course come to terms with the modern world.

12 The island of Tristan da Cunha in the South Atlantic lies 1800 miles (2897 km) west of Cape Town in South Africa and 1200 miles (1931 km) southeast of Rio de Janeiro in South America. In 1961 the volcano, which was believed to be extinct, erupted and caused the islanders to evacuate to nearby Nightingale Island, a tiny uninhabited island 18 miles (29 km) away. From there they were taken to Cape Town and then to England. After a stay of over a year their problem was whether to remain in England or return to Tristan and to the isolated life and its cultural structure. The 260 people are interrelated, but the original garrison of 1816 has been infused with new blood from time to time. Some work is available with a deep-freeze (crayfish) company, and about £25,000 is earned annually by the community from the sale of postage stamps.

12 This is about the eighteenth century, but it expresses ideas still held by some primitive peoples. A similar situation was experienced in the settlement of New Zealand. The Maoris held the land jointly as tribes and maintained that it could not be alienated; fierce wars were fought as a result. The Maoris are now a respected section of New Zealand society and their position can be contrasted with that of the less fortunate Indian in the U.S.A.

14–16 Mr. Van Der Post's insight (No. 14) is supported by extract No. 15 (the conversation took place in England). Extract No. 16 takes a look at family ties. The extended family, clan or tribe, is a world-wide concept, ensuring that no orphans or widows are alone and no elderly without family support. Western civilisation, with its emphasis on individual rights, has well-nigh killed the system; hence the increasing need for state and voluntary services for the poor and lonely, and the vast problems of longevity and stress.

17 To the Chinese, communism brought an end to anarchy. The present Maoist development, to ensure continuance of the system, seems to demand from the people a conception of character (a subject with which the average Chinese is said to be obsessed) entirely different from the traditional one taught by the family. According to Lin Yutang, author of *My Country and my People*, '... of zeal for reform, public spirit, sense of adventure, and heroic courage, the Chinese are devoid ... They have indomitable patience, indefatigable industry, a sense of duty and that unequalled genius for finding happiness in hard environments, which we call contentment.' One has the impression that most of the older peasants have adopted the collectives and communes by compromising to suit themselves and preserving many of the old traditions; hence the contemporary re-focusing on the young, particularly the very young, and the inevitable family tensions.

18 This expresses not only the problems of sensible African parents but those of all societies where children are educated to a greater extent, and in different patterns from their parents. It is particularly marked when the young university student emerges from a village environment, to which it is hoped he will return the benefit of his experience.

19–20 These two passages deal with some of the problems faced by developing and newly independent countries. After the Second World War there was an increasing demand from colonies for independence. Sierra Leone was amongst the first British Protectorates in Africa to be granted independence (1961) but has remained a member of the British Commonwealth.

21 This is strangely applicable not only to expatriates but to everyone at some stage in life. Cultural shock is experienced by all whose pattern of life is forcibly disturbed so that they are living in violently changed circumstances.

23 The experience of this black American in West Africa illustrates the importance not only of a common language but also of general cultural background.

24 The fear of integration is also felt by some educated Hindu women, who fear the moral climate of contemporary Western society, despite the fact that they like to work and study in the West.

25 Noni Jabavu is the daughter and grand-daughter of educated people. Her love of South Africa is evident, despite personal humiliations which she discloses elewhere in the book from which this extract was taken.

26 The problem of integrating immigrant children is now being dealt with in varying ways. These depend on individual needs of a particular area but include lessons at special reception centres, additional language lessons and individual attention

27 A flashback of about 120 years to when, after the failure of the potato crop, famine was rife in Ireland and large-scale emigration to Britain and the U.S.A. took place, the great majority of the emigrants seeking town life. Skill with the spade has persisted to this day among working-class Irishmen, many of whom are engaged on tunnel, road, pipeline and other industrial excavation work. Compare with extract No. 28.

28 Immigrant peoples are eventually accepted in Britain. As they become more at home, and especially if their standard of living rises, they tend to disperse more widely.

29–30 The draw of the cities, now world-wide, at first builds individual tensions, especially for those from unsophisticated backgrounds.

32 This passage highlights the complexities of the racial situation in the southern states of the U.S.A.; forced integration seems unlikely to be a happy or successful solution. The farmer's attitude is 'leave well alone'; how strong is his case?

33 Lack of understanding—and often the will to understand—have underlain the tensions between races throughout history; apathy on one side and contempt on the other is a situation of total non-communication.

35 Mr Jahn emphasises the importance of food in the social contacts between people. The variety of foods used in West Africa is of special interest.

8

Labour on the land

The aim of this section is to emphasise the attitude towards the job and the effect of the job on the worker, starting with the simple jobs and leading on to the effects of increasing mechanisation. Man's relation to the soil and his humanity—and sometimes inhumanity—in the treatment of animals is illustrated. In many of the extracts, though the work is hard, there is a sense of satisfaction, a feeling for the soil and for animals, a sense of rhythm and of companionship in teamwork.

The earlier extracts are concerned with the hard work of cultivation; of ploughing, harvesting, and irrigation. There follow some accounts of modern methods, and of working with flocks and herds.

1 A titbit on food

West Coast, South America

Let us remind ourselves once again that all civilisations derive from agriculture and that more than half the food the world eats today was first cultivated by the Indians of the Andes. From that region came maize, in twenty varieties; sweet potatoes; yams; squash; many types of bean; maniocs; peanuts; cashews; pineapples; chocolate; avocados; tomatoes; pepper; papaya; strawberries and blackberries. Some of these may seem surprising because they have been domesticated for so long or have run wild in other parts of the world that we forget their American origin. Yet it is not really strange that the lands of the West Coast of South America should have been the plant nursery for most of the world. Latitude is compensated for by altitude. That is to say, climatic conditions vary from the torrid lowlands to the high cold slopes and plateaux of the Andes, so that the plants at varying altitudes could be acclimatised in countries of different latitudes. The universality of the potato is an example. In Peru potatoes grow, in differing varieties, from the blistering coastal lands to as high as 15,000 feet. Thus, in terms of temperature-adaptation, they can be grown in countries from the Equator to the Arctic.

from : Ritchie Calder, *The Inheritors*

2 Love of the earth

China

. . . . and he himself took a hoe and broke up the soil into fine loamy stuff, soft as black sugar, and still dark with the wetness of the land upon it. This he did for the sheer joy he had in it and not for any necessity, and when he was weary he lay down upon his land, and he slept and the health of the earth spread into his flesh.

from : Pearl Buck, *The Good Earth*

3 Walking on one's own land

Victoria, Australia

The great thing about clover and grass is that you can, without being bored, without feeling that it would best be left to another day, wander over the fields that occupy you all the week, and yet enjoy a holiday walk through a fine patch of your own pasture.

It is, of course, often wearying to walk across the pasture to close a gate, inspect a fence, or pull a sheep from a channel; but to stroll for miles with friends, jumping channels, dodging water, climbing through fences, looking at pasture, talking about grass and everything under the sun is a never-ending source of delight.

from : Humphrey Kemp, *The Astonished Earth*

4 Carting mangolds

East Anglia, England, 1920

The carts went up the rows. Three men went with a cart, one behind to deal with the two rows that the wheels spanned, and one on either side. The method employed was this; you grasped the leaves of the mangold with the left hand with much the same motion as a cow's tongue makes encompassing a bite of grass. You pulled the mangold out of the ground, swung it upwards, and at the right moment slipped your knife-blade through the leaves where they joined the root. Then, if you had judged correctly, the mangold flew into the cart and you were left with the leaves in your hand. You dropped them, and stooped to pull another. The whole process took the labourer one second.

The men showed me by example how to do it. I took up my position at the side of the tumbril. But my first mangold flew right over the tumbril and hit the man on the other side.

'You are too strong, sir,' he smiled.

The next mangold hit the wheel, and the next the shaft. For five minutes I bombarded the tumbril in vain. It shook and rattled. I could not judge the right moment at which to sever the leaves from the root. Sometimes the globe fell at my feet, sometimes even it hit the horse, who did not seem to mind, but stood unmoved. I grovelled about picking up my misses and putting them in the tumbril. My hands were muddy. The men were highly amused. I felt hot and impotent, as though the whole thing were a practical joke at my expense.

At last I got one in, and there was a cry of, 'Well done, sir; now another.' By a stroke of luck the next one went in also. I began to smile. I discovered that the whole thing was a matter of rhythm, and by dinner-time I was getting four out of six into the tumbril.

As I was very slow, the man at the back gave me a hand with my two rows besides pulling his own. This hurt my pride, and by the time we knocked off at one o'clock I managed to keep up with the tumbril unaided by working twice as hard as they.

At dinner Mr. Colville asked me how I was getting on.

'Mind you don't cut your hand,' he warned me. 'That is what everybody does the first time they pull mangolds.' He showed me a scar on his finger. But I smiled, for I was beginning to feel expert, and said I should be particularly careful.

However, the afternoon was not far advanced before the knife slipped and my finger bled. It was, luckily, only a scratch; I bound my handkerchief round it and continued. I was beginning to enjoy the work. The rhythm was restful after my early struggles. It was pleasant to feel the mangold's weight vanish at the jerk of the knife, and see the globe, rosier for the sinking sun, go bounding into the cart. The big ones thundered in, the small ones pattered.

Near the gateway of the field the clamp was set, and thither the loads were taken. A man was stationed there, building up the clamp, and every now and then there would be a deep rumble as he tipped a load down and covered them with straw, so that the clamp was as steep and smooth as a cottage roof.

Sometimes, between loads the men would slice a mangold, exposing the juicy saffron flesh, and eat it. They found it refreshing. I tasted a slice; it was sweet and cold and crisp. The mangolds in this field were of a kind called 'Golden Tankard', one of the men told me.

There was a glow upon us all. The sun grew large and red, became the king of mangolds there on the horizon. The air turned frosty, the coarse leaves crackled in our hands, and, trampled, gave up their odour. Twilight came on, and horse and tumbril moving clampwards became a silhouette of toil.

We stretched. That was all for to-day. Matches were struck, illumining faces, and pipes glowed. A minute's contemplation of the sky.

'Rain? No, bor, that won't rain.' A word to me. 'You done wonderful well, sir, considerin'.' And the group toiled homeward over the fields.

from : Adrian Bell, *Corduroy*

5 Skilled enjoyment: vines and wine making

Gironde, France

Michel Rachelet, sitting at the table, raised his tired grey head and looked thoughtfully at the vineyards sleeping in the moonlight. Vines were mysterious. He had given his life to them, and having learned enough to be modest he would not have dared to say that he knew all about them—although he certainly would not have admitted that any man knew more. Here on the gently sloping ground which faced south-eastward they had the ideal exposure and soil—a soil in which no other crop would have grown well, for it was thick with pebbles as large as a child's fist. That was another aspect of the mystery of vines. But besides a particular soil they needed also good weather and proper care. God attended to the weather and he, Rachelet, to the care. God had done them well this year—enough rain, then ample sunshine. And Rachelet, although the strain of daily work and constant responsibility had grown almost unbearable, had seen to it that nothing was lacking on his side.

As soon as last year's grapes had been picked and their leaves had fallen, the ground had been ploughed up, weeded and manured. Rachelet did not trust the new composite fertilisers which it was claimed did everything for the minimum of effort. Chemicals were to be used as a doctor uses medicine but the staple diet was farmyard manure, well dug in. It was a saying of his that land needed a top dressing of human sweat. In his mind's eye, the old man could see the scene in front of him as it had been in the brisk autumn weather eleven months ago—the well-trained horses with the special ploughs designed to work along the metre-wide corridors between the rows of vines, the men and women with their hoes and spades piling the soil up in waves to protect the roots from frost. The smell of the newly turned earth and of rubbish fires was in the air. The distant poplar trees were like a row of brooms and a sparkling mist hung over Gironde.

Then had come the pruning, *la taille sèche*. His team of horticulturalists had worked slowly down the rows, cutting away the unproductive wood. They worked bent almost double so that from the distance they looked like some strange species of animal—except when now and then one rose to his full height to ease his aching back. It was a long pilgrimage, the pruning—many kilometres for each man to travel at a snail's pace. And the fences themselves had often to be renewed. There was enough work for everybody in the winter-time.

As Spring approached, Rachelet's problem had been the timing of

337

the first green pruning. If the canes were cut early no sap would be lost but the quickly growing shoots would be liable to damage by frost. If the pruning were done late the vines would bleed. By a combination of experience and instinct Rachelet had learned to pick his time, and this year he had got it exactly right.

The extent of pruning called for imagination. Rachelet had trained his men to look at the almost bare canes and picture the plant as it would be when it was fully grown. Then the quantity of leaves and branches must match the root area yet this must be adjusted by pruning before an eye had turned into a bud.

The *bourgeonnement* had always fascinated him. It was not only the joy of seeing every morning from one's cottage doorway that the vineyard was painted a stronger shade of green; it was the detail of the change. When one looked closely at a particular cane one noticed that the sprouting eyes were larger than when one had seen them last. Soon after this the brown scales fell from the eyes and the woolly buds became visible. Then came the stage which used to excite him so much as a child—and still did. The tiny leaves became separated on their little stalk, even the cluster of minute flower buds was distinguishable. It was a vine branch in miniature.

It would be a real branch soon enough, and meanwhile there was plenty to be done. Each shoot was examined and every one which was imperfect was cut away. And later, when the remaining shoots had grown a little, the ends of some of them were snipped to make them bunch well.

Then the flowering started. This too was a lovely thing to watch in detail. The green hats which the buds wore fell off and the delicate members of the flowers were seen. It was like a conjuring trick. But it was an anxious time for the *vigneron* looking for symptoms of *la coulure*, the disease of barrenness.

The fertilization had gone well this year. When the tiny grapes were forming, the clusters were examined and the least promising removed. And finally, just before the vintage, the old leaves which had done their work were cut away to give more light to the ripening grapes— yet not so much that they would be sunburned.

That covered the plants' development and discipline by pruning. But there had been, besides the active watch for fungoid and insect pests, the passive watch for late frosts and devastating hail. That had been the outdoors round which Rachelet had known for fifty-four years as a qualified *vigneron* and for much of twenty more as a child and apprentice, excluding his years of military service.

But most of his work recently had been in the *chai*—he felt a sudden longing to visit the *chai* before he slept—to walk among the hogsheads of young wine, to go down to the cellar beneath and browse among the thousands upon thousands of bottles which were for him so full of interest and experience. He thought of all those wines as friends whom he had known since birth. It was his fancy that wine passed through childhood and adolescence in the fermenting vat. How well, at what rate, and for how long a wine continued to mature depended principally on what it was born with.

from : J. M. Scott, *The Man who made Wine*

6 Peasant wheat harvest

Sicily

The mother who has made the bread puts it, when it is not on the table, under lock and key; it is a precious thing, to be used sparingly —a sacred thing, too, for it is considered an unpardonable sin to throw out even a mouldy crust among the other household garbage. If stale or mouldy bread is ever found in a house—and that is seldom— it is put to immediate use, boiled in onion and tomato water to make what is called *pani cottu,* or added to soup. If the bread is treated with disrespect the harvest will be bad next year.

*   *   *

As soon as the grain can be broken in the fingers the *contadini** begin to prepare for the harvest. They prepare cords of *disa* to bind the sheaves; they sharpen their scythes, get out their old broad-brimmed hats, and wait for the word to start to be given by some wise elder. The next morning they set out at dawn, and even if the forecast has been pessimistic there is an atmosphere almost of *festa*†.

The peasant paterfamilias who owns the ground organises the crew. If there is much grain to harvest he invites his relations, but in a bad season only the immediate family takes part, and the father assumes the position of foreman. Before they leave the town he lectures the party, in particular he threatens terrible penalties for smoking, or for leaving on the field so much as an ear of corn, for each one of these might go to make bread, and thus is holy in itself.

In the early dawn the gang passes through the streets of the town with an almost military tread; with their dark clothing and their wide hats, their haversacks on their shoulders and their sickles at their sides, they might, indeed, be mistaken for some guerilla band setting out for battle or a clash with rival partisans. Some member of the gang will

* Peasants
† Holiday or festivity

whisper to his neighbour, or another, passing a friend's house, will call
him to make haste; the footsteps and voices are brittle and magnified
in the silence of the dawn.

Sometimes two parties will meet, and there ensues a ritual for all
the world like the exchange of passwords appropriate to the fantasy:

'Greetings! Today we harvest but tomorrow we shall eat,' recites
the leader of the first gang, with strange intensity, and the other
replies:

'That is our life as always.'

When they reach the harvest field each man puts his haversack into
the bamboo shelter; then with much bustle they shed their jackets and
prepare for work. The old men are dressed, as befits their dignity and
authority, in trousers and long-sleeved shirts, with a handkerchief at
the throat and a red head-cloth as a symbol of their wisdom, but the
young men and boys are stripped to the waist. Drawn up before the
standing corn they watch their leader, silent and expectant. Suddenly
he shouts: 'Let us go forward in the name of God, boys,' and each goes
down upon his knees to grasp an armful of stems with his left arm,
bending his sickle to slice through the tautened golden stems an
inch or two above the ground.

They work silently and swiftly, while the sun is not yet scorching,
laying their swathes at their sides. An old man or a boy moving up
and down the line gathers six or seven swathes together to form a
sheaf, and ties it with grass twine. Gradually, as the sun climbs and
sweat begins to pour from the naked torsos, the pace slows and the
songs begin by which the southern peasant supports almost intolerable
labour. One man sings a ribald verse and another responds; their
voices ring out across the pale sheets of grain motionless under the
molten sun. Every now and again they are interrupted by the voice
of the leader, who intones, rather than sings:

> Your hands and not your mouth's the thing
> Today you sweat, tomorrow sing.

Often there are other harvesting gangs nearby, who reply to the
sung verses in an exchange that becomes ever more bawdy ...

*   *   *

Their voices drift clear and melodious over the still, parched countryside; but for the distant braying of an ass, they are the only audible
sound under the baking sun and sky. No breath of wind stirs the trees
or the ears of corn. A boy goes round the kneeling ranks with a big
earthenware jar of water, and as each man drinks he mutters 'Oh
God be praised.'

The hour allowed for eating is announced with another ritual shout
from the leader. The men rise slowly, stretching aching backs and

limbs, shaking the sweat off them as a dog shakes water from his coat. They leave their sickles where they lie and make for the little bamboo shelter that is the only oasis of shade in a desert of sun. Inside, they sit in a circle, and each takes from his haversack the hunk of dry bread that is the habitual midday meal of the Sicilian peasant. He cuts pieces from it with a knife and eats with infinite relish; (something to eat with the bread is a rarity, and has a special word, *cumpanaggiu*, deriving from the latin *cum pani**). Between mouthfuls he drinks copiously from the big earthenware jar, holding it away from his mouth so that the water trickles in and the whole mouth is washed by it; Sicilians learn to make even water go a long way.

After the meal the heat is so intense as to make work almost impossible. The ground is burning under foot, the corn stems are like red-hot wires to the touch. Usually the leader allows his men to sleep for a while if they can; some cannot, for there are burnt shoulders and blistered hands, especially among the young boys who still have tender skins. These make for some olive tree at the edge of the field, and in its shade or high among its branches they sit and sing, slow monotonous tunes like dirges; some of the treble voices are as pure as nightingales', but the sound is as sad as a hunting horn in the deep woods.

When the leader gives the order to start again work begins with the same concentrated enthusiasm as at the beginning of the day, and to the accompaniment of songs and obscenities it goes on without pause until after the sun has set. The gang sets out for home in a body, as it left in the morning, but one man remains behind to stand guard over the harvested sheaves.

The harvest may last many days. They are not paid, these peasants who toil in the sun, for payment is unheard of between relations, and the work they do is thought no more than a fitting tribute to the head of their family.

After the harvest comes the threshing. This too is an affair of tradition, and the threshing floors have been used for century after century. Each grain-producing district has its old traditional place, and to these each *contadino* brings his harvest to be threshed as his father did before him.

*　　*　　*

The sheaves are spread on the threshing floor early in the morning, and from the moment when the sun is over the mountains the scene takes on all the characters of ritual. At the centre of the ring stands a young man dressed in a long white habit, with a kerchief knotted at his throat and a red band around his head. In his right hand he holds the joined reins of two mules, and in his left a long whip. He

* With bread

341

raises his whip and brings the lash down upon the mules; as he does so he calls out to them in a great and musical voice : *'To the threshing, oh black ones'*.

The mules begin to move, round and round the narrow ring, and as they circulate the young man sings to them.

* * *

If the song should stop the mules become fractious and difficult; hour after hour it goes on, and sometimes within earshot is another *aia** where another young man with the reins and whip is singing the same song to his mules, so that it becomes a chorus for two separated voices who keep exactly the same time, and sound as one.

With an occasional halt for man and mules to drink, and an occasional reversal of direction to avoid dizziness, the *pisatura*, or turning of the mules, goes on until the beating hooves send the bright grain dancing in the air and a hand thrust among the straw can feel it loose among the stems. The mules make their last lap, the young man invokes the saints to witness the splendour and valour of their work, and the *pisatura* is over.

from : Gavin Maxwell, *The Ten Pains of Death*

7 Fun of the coconut harvest

South Pacific, nineteen-thirties

The coconuts were husked in no time by the men, who passed them to the women, who with quick swings of their heavy butcher knives cut the shells into perfect halves. Then they scooped out the spongy center and put the *utos* into separate clean baskets for eating. The shells were later carried to the beaches to soak a day or two in the sea, so that the meat would be tougher and less liable to rot during the drying process.

I remember diving into the clear sea, hunting for baby *utos* left in the coconut shells and liking the taste of the salted, marble-size things. And sometimes we children took tiny bites of coconut meat, intentionally leaving the marks in the meat for the men to swear about later . . .

Two days after being put in the lagoon the coconut shells were taken from the water and laid on the high wooden racks which had

---

* Threshing place

been erected on the beaches, where the sun was strongest. The meat faced the sun, and when rain threatened all hands helped turn the coconut shells upside down to prevent them from getting wet and losing their precious oiliness. At night they were automatically turned upside down.

It took several weeks for the coconuts to dry completely without losing their oil. Then the meat, curling inward, away from the shell, was spooned out with wooden spatulas, cut into small pieces, and stored in copra sacks. There is no reason to think that this ancient method of making copra has been improved upon today in Puka-Puka.

While nature was curing the coconut meat—the people found time to enjoy the festival. Groups of them would practise the singing of hymns and play the American games Papa had taught them, like baseball and poker. The children however had to combine school, learning to read nursery rhymes and to add four and six, often using dried coconuts to illustrate the problem.

from : Johnny Frisbie, *The Frisbies of the South Seas*

8 The olive harvest

Sicily

The following passage comprises a selection of extracts from a first-hand account by a Sicilian peasant, Toto Castello, which was translated by Gavin Maxwell and included in his book The Ten Pains of Death.

'For a peasant family it's a tragedy to be without oil. No matter how poor they may be, they always have, besides their little granary, their jar of oil.

*   *   *

'We used to finish picking up the olives in the evening after sunset. They were all put into a sack which my companions took in turns to carry on their backs. I never carried it, because I was landlord. Coming home you saw the same scene everywhere; peasants coming back from the fields with sacks of olives on their backs; women sitting on carts with their hair soaking wet, and the marks of exhaustion and pain on their faces; mules walking slowly in Indian file; tired, breathless old men who trailed along behind everyone else. An atmosphere of melancholy hung over them all; they seldom spoke, and only the children would give raucous shouts which broke the evening silence. Today everything is just the same as it used to be then—nothing's changed.

'So the Sicilian olive harvest begins; not the real harvest, but its first phase : the proper harvest will take place in a few days, when the olives begin to fall more quickly. Those which have been picked up from the ground are put in large baskets and covered with plenty of salt, and left there until the harvest is over. There are more olives to salvage on windy or rainy days, and then everyone is mobilised; grown-ups, and children, women and old men.

'It's really as soon as the peasants have finished the grape harvest that they make a start on the olives. Here it takes place in November. In Sicily the olive harvest isn't at the same time of the year as elsewhere—each region is different. In Calabria it goes on into January, in Campania they even wait for the spring, while in Catania they often finish gathering the olives at the end of January. But in the west of Sicily, where the rule is poverty and destitution, the olives are harvested very early, because the peasants can't wait for them any longer. This is not traditional; many old people have told me that in the old days the olives were abundant even in this area, but that times have changed and the curse of God lies heavy upon them and their families.

'The olive harvest is a very complicated thing; above all it needs men who can do the various different jobs. There are four types of workers.

'First there are the *cutuliatura*. These are the men who shake the olives from the tree and are nearly always very strong and fearless young men who have gained a reputation for this work in their own village. They're entrusted with the most dangerous tasks; they have to climb up the highest branches of the trees in groups of two or three and shake the branches loaded with olives. Often they are provided with long sticks which they use to poke at the branches they can't reach.

'Then there are the *cugghitura*, those who pick up the olives from the ground; they're mostly women and children. Usually they're in groups of five, six, or seven, according to the size of the tree.

'Next are the *passulunara* (*passaluni* is the word for the olives which are kept under salt for eating), who are for the most part old men of experience; they separate the ordinary olives for crushing from those which will be preserved and then either sold or kept at home to eat with bread. They also select the olives for salting which are green in colour and larger than the ordinary ones. They are preserved with salt and vinegar and will keep for a very long time.

'The *arrisciuppatura* are women and children who at the end of the day go over the ground under the olive trees a second time in search of olives overlooked by the *cugghitura*. The rich farmers take

344

up most of these workers. There mustn't be one single olive left on the ground, or else there will be crowds of people under these trees later on looking for olives of any description which may have been left behind. There used to be *trappitara*, people who worked the mills which crush the olives, but today there are modern implements even in the tiny villages.

'The *cugghitura* are most important, particularly the children. Children work more quickly; they're given only small wages, and they give more in return for their money. Only the richer children go to school, but at the time of the olive harvest you won't see any children in the streets.

'The children rise at dawn, and go off to work, shivering with cold, and without breakfast; the farmer gives them nothing to eat in the morning. After half a day bent double over the ground they get a piece of bread and salted olives from the farmer. They go on working till late at night; often they sleep out in the fields on a bed of hay. Often they sing as they work; it's hard to keep a boy's spirits down.

*　　*　　*

'And so the olive harvest ends, a sad, dismal harvest. The oil is nearly always used for family needs—it's very rarely sold, except where there's enough to do both. It's the last of the three principal harvests of the year, and so the whole season ends on a note of pessimism which you can see in the eyes of every peasant. And they say once more :

We poor must suffer
If we want to live. . . '

from : Gavin Maxwell, *The Ten Pains of Death*

9 The young rice planters: a meditation

Southeast Asia

Hands pull on their shoulders, shake them awake in the dark. Hustle of preparation as they start out for the fields—a crowd of them walking together to set out the rice plants.

Morning mist and dew—cool—then sudden light. The chill of the first step into deep mud !—ankle deep—knee deep, and alive with who knows what—strange creeping, sliding sneaking things that live in the soft slime !—'Don't think.'

A faint sickly smell all-pervading, and growing stronger with the

345

growing strength of sun—human excrement, collected with care, fermented, mixed with mud—spread on the fields. No waste ever—for centuries and centuries.

Sun-up, beating fierce and hot as you work, hour after hour, bending, stooping, setting, scooping, stamping, sweating, thrusting,—sideways, backwards, backwards. Rhythmic movement—pacing one another, singing,—for joy, for company, for need to keep going.

Sun high,—sun hats—broad and light. Wet feet, wet thighs! aching backs. 'Keep going—not too fast now—harbour your strength, don't drag back.' Not looking. Down the field and up again.

And then eat. 'Sink in the shade if you can find any, and eat and drink, and laugh, and rest as long as you can.'

And then, on and on again till sundown. And the same the next day and the next, and again, till the job is done.

'Raise your head with pride.' The rows are straight, the plants are firm, and sprouting already, the lone pump is pulsing, the buckets passing. The channels are unblocked and a shining trickle is spreading fast between the ridges.

The fields reflect the light of the moon.

A special contribution by Eleanor Lowe

10 Irrigation furrows

Australia

No matter how new tools and equipment improve means of carrying out agricultural tasks, the homely shovel or spade will never become superfluous. In irrigated areas of Egypt and the Middle East the heavy versatile Biblical model hoe takes the place of the spade and is often the only agricultural implement used.

In Australia the irrigator attends his flood or furrow irrigation with a shovel. Water intended to flow in the direction and manner desired is at some stage or other confined within earthen banks or ridges which, eroding by the natural action of moving water, necessitates repair and maintenance . . .

Most of our water was conveyed, checked, controlled and delivered, by the fairly skilled unimproved drudgery of handling the ancient material, mud, with a shovel.

Banks to stop and then release water were made day and night, with ordinary mud, sticky mud, in fact, mud of all kinds.

Channel banks that gave way to yabbie* and mouse-hole penetration
* Worm

needed more mud for repair; everywhere mud was used to block, stop and let go. No Persian or Arab could tell us anything about mud and its application.

from : Humphrey Kemp, *The Astonished Earth*

11 Intensive use of the land

Egypt, 1966

Since the beginning of historical time a large proportion of the energy of the Egyptian people has been devoted to the harnessing of . . . flood water to provide them with the means of life—to the digging of canals to distribute it, to the digging of ditches to drain it, to the building of walls to contain it, to the invention of machines to lift it, to the erection of dams to store it, and latterly, to the devising of means to turn the water's flow into electric power. The landscape of Egypt seen from the air, with the network of canals directing the water by a series of infinite gradations from the dammed-up river to the smallest fields, is evidence of this continued pre-occupation. In Egypt the Nile is hardly ever out of sight, hardly ever out of mind . . .

Under perennial irrigation the fields are not inundated during the Nile flood. They are cultivated all the year round and the water is brought to them all the year round by canals. During the flood, when the canals are full, watering takes place every day and the water is led onto the fields by gravity along hand-hoed channels from the full canals which, at the points at which they serve as irrigators, run slightly above the level of the surrounding land, being retained by earth banks. For the rest of the year watering takes place perhaps ten times a month, the water being lifted from the partially empty canals by mechanical pumps or by the shadoof, the Archimedes screw or by the saqia . . .

There is little mechanisation and the implements used by the cultivator are few and rudimentary.* The simplest, and most universal is the 'fas', which is a large hoe, of which the triangular iron blade is fitted at an angle of about 120 degrees to the wooden handle. The 'fas' is used for weeding, for making the little irrigation furrows along which the water from the canals is led onto the fields, for breaking up large lumps of earth, and for a hundred other purposes. The 'mihrath' or plough consists of a pointed iron socket fitted onto the bottom of a stout wooden bifurcated shaft standing about three feet high with double handle-bars at the top. Fitted into and hingeing onto, the point

* Except on a few large estates

347

of bifurcation, is a wooden shaft about four yards long, fitted with a double wooden yoke designed to pass over the shoulders of two beasts —sometimes two gamus (buffalo), sometimes a gamus and an ass, and sometimes a gamus and a camel. The cultivator, leaning on the double handle-bars, presses the iron point into the ground while the animals drag the machines forward to make a shallow furrow. In this way it is possible for one man and two beasts to plough from one-third to one-half a feddan* in a day. The 'zahhafa' or harrow, used to cover the furrows over after sowing, usually consists simply of a length of palm-tree trunk dragged transversely across the furrows by a couple of beasts attached to the trunk by ropes. By this means about four feddans can be harrowed in a day. The zahhafa is also used to level the soil after picking and clearing. Another levelling instrument is the 'kassabia' which is simply a heavy, shallow, rectangular wooden frame, like a box, without top or bottom, which is fitted with handles and which the cultivator pushes over the soil. Cereal crops are reaped with a hand sickle (mehasha), threshed by wooden cart (norag) with circular iron blades for wheels which is drawn by an ass and driven in circles round the village threshing floor on which the reaped ears are laid. The winnowing is done with a winnowing fork (garouf) with which the threshed corn is thrown up into the air and the corn separated from the chaff. Cotton is picked by hand, usually by women and children. Bersim† is either cut with a sickle or eaten *in situ* by the tethered animals for whom it is grown . . .

Work on the perennially irrigated fields is heavy and continuous. There are three ploughings and three harvests a year. There are the irrigation furrows to be hoed and maintained and the water to be led into them. In the two months approximately of the flood the watering is done every day but the water flows in by gravity, and it is simply a question of directing it. For nine other months, when watering takes place about ten days a month, it has to be lifted from the canal and it is a matter of constant vigilance for each cultivator to ensure that he gets his share. For one month January, during what is known as the 'gaffaf', no water is let into the canals, which are left dry in order to enable them to be dredged and weeded, a process which keeps the cultivator busy with his 'fas' and 'guffa' (small straw basket). The heavy cropping involves the necessity for heavy manuring, which is done with animal and pigeon manure to the extent available and with manufactured nitrates or superphosphates.

Where land is so scarce and living so sparse, nothing is wasted. Every square inch of land is utilized, every available drop of water applied. Maize stalks after being harvested, cotton plants after being picked, weeds after being dried, are used for fuel. Wheat and barley

* One feddan is 1 acre (0.4 hectacre) approximately
† Clover

348

straw (tibn) is used as summer feed for domestic animals and for mixing with earth to make bricks for building . . . everywhere . . . the methods of cultivation and the crops cultivated,* are very much the same. The villages too look very much the same wherever they are located.

from : John Marlowe, *Four Aspects of Egypt*

12 Irrigation in Peruvian desert

Peru

The dark, reedy lanes of irrigation ditches quartered the meagre-looking fields and golden vineyards. The tall maize, softly mellowing, waved its tassels in the breeze that blew up from the Pacific; in the groves of bananas, winter was turning the leaves into ragged flaps of brown paper. Ox-carts dawdled along roads lined with yellow mud-block walls, and in many of the fields it was ploughing season. The ground was being tilled partly by massive American tractors, partly by oxen slowly dragging those cumbersome wooden ploughs which the Spaniards brought four centuries ago; and in the cotton fields women bent over the rows of young plants, cultivating them with that back-breaking, short-handled hoe which has survived all over Peru from the earliest days of agriculture, changing its blade from stone to bronze, and later from bronze to iron, but never changing its essential form . . .

The hills stood in sharp relief, defined by shadow and light, their steep sides rising to blunt and rounded tops over which the pylons marched like black skeletons from the power stations in the mountains. They were the most barren hills I had ever seen, more barren than Mexico, more barren than the burning deserts of Arizona, where one sees at least the scattered cacti that keep alive by storing the moisture of rare rainfalls. Here there were not even cacti. The slopes of shaly stone were unrelieved by the least shoot of green and their extraordinary aridity emphasised the narrowness and vulnerability of the fertile lands beside the river. A few years' neglect of the irrigation ditches which the generations of Indian and Spanish farmers have used for a millenium, and the desert would return, as it has returned in other Peruvian valleys once cultivated by prehistoric peoples, lapping in its desiccating tide down to the very cane-brakes along the river banks.

from : George Woodcock, *Incas and Other Men*

* Except in the remaining areas of basin irrigation

13 Riding a tractor: satisfaction

Norfolk, England, nineteen-thirties

Bob gave me my first lesson in setting-out a field for plowing. First he and I paced out the field, setting sticks where the single-furrow plow was to set-in. Then he drove his plow across the field. I followed on the Ferguson tractor, steering in the furrow, and feeling an immense satisfaction when I looked over my shoulder, to watch the swede and mangold tops being turned under in two furrows, and the new earth lying on top. At last I was plowing my own land!

I reflected that, ten years ago, writing of such a scene, my inclination would have been to describe a pair of great horses plodding before poor old Hodge, the swingle-trees* swaying as the traces or chains tautened; the wave of earth rearing up and turning over, the soft shear of the share, the bright breast of the plough gleaming like a curved silver sunflower petal. Behind white gulls would wave and fall, uttering cries of the wild seashore. And all day Hodge, an old sack over his shoulders against driving rain, in broken boots, a bit of bread and cheese his only dinner, toiling there against the elements. And twenty years ago I would have scorned to mention even an iron horse-plow; my Hodge (by way of Hardy and Jefferies) would have driven a plow of wood, apple-tree wood. As for writing about a tractor, that snorting, fume-making, craft-killing ugliness, I would have scorned such things of civilized decadence. (I would conveniently have forgotten my racing motor-cycle in this connection.)

Now for a truthful picture. This plowman's shoulders were protected by a leather flying-coat, with collar. There *was* a sack; it covered the iron seat of the machine I was steering. No, that isn't quite true; the machine was steering itself. I merely sat on a covered iron seat, and was carried across the field by the power of twenty synthetic horses. My feet and legs were inside rubber boots, warmed by the torpedo-like body of the tractor. My hands were warm in thick leather gloves, of horse-hide, bought at Wanamaker's Stores in New York eight years before, and still in good condition, after constant use.

To start the first furrow of our new venture, the steward had worn his new buskins, with six overcoats. Even so clad, the polar wind was so cold that his face, as he walked behind the horses, steering the plow, was blue and shrunken. I was well wrapped, wearing a pair of poplin pyjama trousers under my flannel trousers, and over them, a pair of blue dungaree overalls. These three layers kept the air warm around my legs.

The job seemed easy. All I had to do was to let the tractor steer itself up **the** straight trough whence the previous furrow had been

* Cross bars (holding ends of traces)

turned, to the other end of the field. Then I pulled a lever, and the twin ploughs, controlled by automatic oil-pumps, were lifted by three steel arms out of the earth. My tail up, as it were, I steered along the headland to the next marked furrow, and, pushing the lever forward, began to plow down another marked-out stretch . . . Half-way down my fourth furrow, I heard, above the subdued roar of the engine, a noise like an ungreased axle. It became a jingle, then a jangle. Looking round, I found myself staring into the brown eyes of a white bird less than a yard from my face. Behind its spread whiteness other birds were dipping, cutting, interweaving, alighting on the earth with upheld wings, scrambling, pecking, flapping, jostling, about the dark brown furrows. My first gulls!

from : Henry Williamson, *The Story of a Norfolk Farm*

14 Mechanised farming in East Africa

Tanzania

At harvest time the farm is a patchwork of colour—gold, rich red brown, a late crop of maturing green, turning later to amber and yellow, and the dark brown of forest soil already ploughed for the next sowing. The giant combine cuts like a battleship through the flowing straw sea.

. . . At harvest time the combines cut all day and the rumble of wheat lorries, coming up the hill to take the loads of grain to the railhead, is incessant. The first lorry would leave at four in the morning and the last bag would be humped at eight o'clock at night. While one crop was being harvested the next planting would be under way and while this was going on great lumbering clouds would hover overhead threatening rain. At times like this when a breakdown in combine or tractor could cause a delay worth a great deal of money and trouble, the workshop becomes the nerve centre of the farm. Machinery rumbles in and out, refilling at the diesel pumps, being checked, greased and despatched again. Bags of grain are piled ready for loading, and the gunnies and twine are assembled for transfer to the working combines. Instead of the gleaming row of spanners hung symmetrically in their sizes, there are gaps on the wall. On the large table in the centre a tractor engine reduced to small cogs and ball-bearings lies in orderly rows. Each part, cleaned in petrol, gleams waiting to be fitted hand to glove, socket to sleeve, bearing to ball race. The marvel and intricacy, the logic and order of the machine combined with the miraculous renewal of nature, achieved a yearly crop which made about three million loaves.

from : Susan Wood, *A Fly in Amber*

15 Scientific farming

Alberta, Canada, nineteen-sixties

The Westersund farm is large, even by Canadian standards. It takes up four and a quarter sections (2,720 acres) of rich grain land some 50 miles south of Calgary. The farm is completely mechanised and, except for a brief period during harvest, is operated entirely by the Westersunds themselves. Besides Varno there is his wife, Juanita, and two teenage daughters.

Westersund's methods are based on the maximum use of modern farming machinery. One such machine is a six-cylinder four-wheel drive diesel tractor bought in 1959 that can cultivate or seed 30 to 40 acres an hour in a one-man operation. Last year he bought a double swather. This piece of equipment lays a 16-foot swath, and on subsequent rounds lays a second such swath on top of the first. The resulting 32-foot swath increases the capacity of the farm's two combines.

A third useful piece of equipment is a special cultivator* which allows the residue and surface trash from previous crops to remain in place on top of the land to prevent soil erosion.

Westersund uses aerial spraying as the most economical method of weed control. He contracts from a flying farmer at 50 to 70 cents an acre (about 3s 6d to 5s)† plus the cost of chemicals. He is himself a 'flying farmer', owning a low-wing, four-seat, 205 h.p. aircraft which the family flies some 250 hours a year or 40,000 miles. Operating costs are no more than those of a car.

At present the farm has two combines and in the autumn two men are hired to help with the combining. The Westersund farm averages 20 to 40 bushels of wheat per acre and 10 to 20 bushels of flax.

Although the farm lies in rich grain country, the Westersunds have varied their crops according to economic conditions and prospects. From time to time they have raised wheat, oats and barley, grass seed and flax, and kept a few cattle, pigs and chickens.

As scientific farmers, they keep crop, rainfall and production records. They keep their own books and have them audited by a chartered accountant each year.

* Cuts the plants off below the surface
† 17½p to 25p per 0.4 hectare approx.

Varno Westersund belongs to the community of prosperous and enterprising farmers of Canada who, making full use of modern aids and techniques, have established their country as one of the world's great granaries.

from : 'One man and 2,720 acres', *Commonwealth Today*,
No. 109, 1966

16 Big farms: family enthusiasm

India, 1968

Until a couple of years ago by far the greater part of India's crops was grown by peasants—illiterate, chronically short of capital, and wedded to traditional methods. Today gentlemen farmers drawn from the higher castes may be found within driving distance of practically every Indian large town. For them agriculture has become a hobby, sometimes even a passion. They see themselves as patriots acting in the national interest to help to liberate India from dependence on food imports. At the same time they have found that farming can be highly profitable.

Last autumn in Karnal district 100 miles north of Delhi, I called on the local agricultural officer. Just as I started to ask him which cultivators I could visit, in walked a short, chubby, grey-haired man in his fifties. Although he had all the external characteristics of a businessman, he turned out to be the prize cultivator of the entire area.

As I later saw at his 65-acre farm, he achieved splendid yields from Mexican wheat, Taichung paddy, hybrid maize and hybrid bajra. Using the dwarf Mexican wheat he got more than two tons an acre, while from the Taichung paddy he got more than three tons an acre. He had two tubewells, a tractor, a wheat-threshing machine and an old car.

This model farmer told me straight-forwardly that he had been a commission merchant and a moneylender . . .

It is characteristic of the agricultural scene in India today that I should have come upon these families of merchants, ex-moneylenders and advocates who were investing heavily in the land. Another group who have begun to sink funds into farming are the industrialists. The great cities of Delhi, Baroda, Bombay, Hyderabad, Bangalore, Coimbatore and Madurai are being ringed with poultry farms, fruit orchards, vegetables and spice gardens. Some of these are registered directly in the names of industrialists or of members of their own families; others are in the names of the company, of a cooperative, or of friends.

Even where the farm is called an orchard (a *bagh*), it is quite common to see fields of the latest varieties of paddy, wheat, or one of the hybrid millets. Owners take pride in their understanding of scientific farming. They, their wives and their sons rattle off with astonishing speed the combination of ammonium sulphate, superphosphate, potash, green manure, farmyard manure, pesticides and treated seeds which they believe to be best suited to their particular soil and water supply.

An outstanding feature of the new agriculture is its reliance on power, as embodied in the tractor and the well with motor, of which there are various kinds—pump-set, tubewell, bore-well with engine, or, in Madras, filter-point well. Properly handled, the tractor ploughs better and quicker than the bullock team, and reduces the peak season demand for hired labour. In parts of the Punjab the bullock has already been displaced by the tractor and in central Gujarat its days are numbered. I found in Gujarat that after using tractors in their own fields, the richer cultivators had organized a regular system of ploughing other people's fields at fixed charges.

Just as the tractor reduces dependence on human and animal labour, so the well with an electric pump or oil engine makes agriculture less of a gamble on monsoons or the vagaries of over-burdened irrigation networks. Since 1967 the Madras State electricity programme has outstripped the rest of the country. In Madras alone there are now 280,000 electrified wells at work. In districts like south Arcot the goal of the more alert farmers with resources to invest is continuous cropping.

The point has been reached where prestige symbols in the Punjab are now mechanical. In marriage negotiations when the representatives of the two sides come together, a common opening gambit of one party may be: 'Do you have tractor?' To which the likely reply is: 'Do you have tubewell?'

It used to be said that agriculture in India was less of an occupation than a way of life. This is not the case today with those cultivators who use modern equipment.

from: Daniel Thorner, 'Gentlemen farmers—the new rich of India',
The Times, September 9, 1968

17 Co-operative farming

North Vietnam, nineteen-fifties and sixties

With independence came land reform. I had a fifth of a sao. I was given another fifth to build a house on, and two saos for growing rice. My wife and I had to turn the new land over with spades and forks, for we had no buffalo to pull the plough. It made us so happy to own a plot of land for the first time in our lives. Sometimes we even worked at night, and we reaped good harvests. I worked really hard on my land for four years, and we reaped good harvests every year. Early in 1956 I began to build a new house, converting the old cottage into a kitchen. I gradually scraped the building materials together . . .

By 1958 people were beginning to join the co-operative, but I wasn't keen. I wanted to be free to sell my rice, for I was doing well out of it. At that stage there were only twenty-eight families in the co-operative. Early in 1960 I changed my mind and joined. I'll tell you why : it was getting harder to sell my rice, for controls had been brought in, and I was having to operate on the black market. Previously, I had made more out of buying and selling other people's rice than out of growing my own. When converted into paddy, my earnings as a dealer were sufficient to feed us throughout the year—and there were usually a couple of hundredweights left over. On the other hand, the rice we grew at home was only enough to cover sundry expenses like family ceremonies and a few new bits and pieces. After the controls were introduced, I began to smuggle the rice to market, displaying only a portion of my wares in one basket. My other basket was full of rice, but I covered it over with banana leaves. This extra rice escaped detection, and so I managed to sell more than I was officially allowed to. I kept it up for two years, until 1960.

I had my own fruit trees, and a small pond for breeding fish, and I felt there was no point in becoming a member of the co-operative. But officials came to see me and said : 'Join, and you will enjoy a better standard of living. You may be comfortably off now, but you'll do even better in the co-operative.' They kept on and on about it, and in the end I joined, thinking it would benefit me. There was a good harvest in the summer of 1960, but the returns were poorer than those I'd had in previous years. So I asked permission to leave the co-operative. The officials in charge didn't like this at all. Yes, they said, the harvest was a good one, but not as good as it ought to have been, for the rice had yellowed; our co-operative would do better in future; when times were bad I would enjoy the benefits of mutual aid, and at the Lunar New Year I would receive my share of fish from the co-operative. 'In this way,' I was told, 'you are helping to make the country stronger. You must be patriotic.'

But I saw how my earnings had fallen off, and I thought : 'I don't need a share of their fish. I've a pond of my own, and with the fish I breed I can buy more rice—to say nothing of the rice we grow on our own land.'

I realized that everyone was joining the co-operative in an effort to build a strong nation, and I could see this was a patriotic thing to do. But it was the idea of collective ownership that bothered me; for private land yielded sufficient, whereas co-operative land yielded less. So I kept on pressing them for permission to leave, and after a few months they said : 'Very well—you may leave since you are so keen to.' But I only missed one harvest. Early in 1961 I asked to be readmitted, for the following reasons. My trading activities kept me so busy that I had to pay other people to work my land and catch fish from my pond; but all these people were now working in the co-operative, with the result that labour had become more expensive and they were no longer willing to work at the old rates of pay. This meant I didn't make enough profit. Besides, all the time I was out of the co-operative I didn't get any meat coupons, for they were only distributed to co-operators. I asked my relations what they thought I should do, and applied for readmission. Returns had been good that year. There had been two harvests, thanks to the new dikes.

At first I was turned down and told : 'It was all thoroughly explained to you, and yet you left.' But I didn't give up, and after a fortnight they accepted me. 'There must be no more quibbling, though,' they said. 'We told you before : the idea is to achieve a higher standard of living by pooling our resources' . . .

In 1962 the returns were adequate, though there was a smaller surplus than in previous years—a hundredweight of rice from the first harvest and four hundredweights from the second, plus fifty dongs for the fish. But I managed to acquire items which other co-operatives were allowed to sell at state-controlled prices (which are far lower than the prices on the free market) : sugar, beans, tobacco, clothing materials and oil. We built a large defensive dike around our village, and we've been able to reap two harvests a year ever since. I didn't do much towards building the dike, for I suffer from elephantiasis and am not allowed to wade about in the water; but I made up for this by helping with tasks on dry land.

Nowadays I work in the fruit-tree plantation, while my wife works in the fields. I plant longans and orange trees. There are sixty people in my working party, including twenty old men and thirty old women; the rest are children between the ages of ten and fifteen. The work is shared out so that the weakest do the light jobs, while the strongest do the digging. Work begins at seven and goes on until eleven, with a short break at nine. One of us does the watering, another does the weeding, and a third plants new shrubs. In the afternoons we work from two till five, picking fruit and so on. I'm given rice in the fifth lunar month, and again in the tenth. Since 1962 I've been able to afford a cycle (275 dongs), a pair of blankets (100 dongs), two flower vases (sixty dongs), and a mosquito net (twenty-five dongs). I'm contented and I love living in this village. My family has lived here for generations : in accordance with ancient custom, my umbilical cord was cut off and buried in local soil, and my father's body is buried here too.

How can anyone leave his native village without regrets? We live surrounded by our kith and kin, and we can always turn to relations when times are bad. And there is always plenty of helpful give and take between ourselves and the neighbours : we grew up with them, and in the old days we shared food with them when it was short, and we have borne heavy burdens together. There is nothing to stop us from earning our living elsewhere, but it wouldn't be the same.

from : Gérard Chaliand, *The Peasants of North Vietnam*

18 Pattern of a modern farmer

England

I am a lazy man and especially allergic to repetitive toil. Most of the farm work when I was a boy on my father's farm was extremely dull. On most jobs there was no need to be alert; all that was necessary was to be able to bear weariness and extreme boredom ... What I hated was walking monotonously behind a horse-drawn plough, roller or harrow, driving a horse-rake or horse-plough, and above all, keeping my back permanently bent at hoeing. I believe many old farm workers suffered that sort of uncomfortable boredom by keeping their minds quite blank ...

Farming is a reliable, certain way of making a living, and yet almost every popular thought about it is the reverse of truth. The slow sequence of seedtime, growth, ripening and harvest is actually a race against time. How many days are there when it is possible to sow seed? How quickly can weeds smother a crop? How long can a sheep remain alive if it does something as simple as lying on its back? The whole thing is a much wilder rush than what has been described as the weekend dash from London to the sea. In addition it is a gamble which makes the Stock Exchange seem no more exciting than a church whist drive. This way of living which I have called reliable is so chancy that it is quite impossible to insure against many of its hazards. A liner can be covered against the perils of the sea but not a crop of turnips in a safe English field.

Then there is the belief that farming practices are permanent and enduring. The lowing herd winding slowly o'er the lea must surely remain, and yet hardly a word is true. Lowing is associated with hunger or the desire to return to a suckling calf. No valuable cow is allowed to be hungry. Calves are now removed at birth and fed on complicated, scientific diets, so that their mothers, having never seen them, do not suffer any maternal yearnings. The herd does not wind slowly o'er the

357

lea because the lea is now a ley.* The old lea was a tough bit of permanent pasture which treading would not damage. The ley has been grown expensively on ploughed earth, from seeds, with the help of chemical manures. It is too valuable to be soiled and trodden by insanitary cows. Instead, a large machine cuts the herbage and blows it into a trailer, which is hauled to the cows who are waiting in a clean concrete yard. All the winding they do is for exercise rather like human prisoners in gaol.

Sometimes I have felt that there was a permanence in the way farming tends to return to old methods, and perhaps that is partly why I think of it as one of my certain things ... The old idea of keeping cows permanently indoors was practised in the town dairies of the great cities. Very often the sheds used were in cellars and were highly insanitary and unhealthy. It was necessary because milk had to be delivered fresh twice daily since it would sour in under twelve hours. Hygienic production, cooling and bottling lengthened the fresh life of milk to well over thirty-six hours. Railways, and later motor transport, made it possible to bring milk in from the country from distances of a hundred miles; and finally pasteurisation stopped souring for at least four days. Today milk from Wales could easily be sold in London : there is no longer any point in shutting up cows in expensive city premises. In the old days no attempt was made to breed in town dairies. The cows were bought in the country in full milk. They were fed on a generous diet so that when they dried off they were fat enough for slaughter. The fact that they were not pregnant meant milking for several months longer than they would have done on a farm, but it was still wasteful to buy cows at the peak of production, and to use them only for one lactation.

The modern housing of cows in the country dodges most of the town dairy problems. Their bulky food such as hay is near at hand. An open yard with a slatted floor is more hygienic than a dark cellar. There is no question of space to limit breeding and rearing, whilst, more important, modern knowledge of nutrition makes it possible to give rations which keep the animals healthy. One snag to indoor cow-farming still remains. The town dairyman got rid of manure to local market gardeners, many of whom still survive near our great cities, but he had to buy straw, and cleaning out was expensive. The modern country cowman on a grass farm also finds straw for bedding expensive, so he tries to cut costs by laying slatted floors and by washing down concrete to turn solid excreta into slush. To get rid of slush he must pay for a sewage disposal plant, which means wasting fertility, or go to considerable trouble with tanks, pumps and pipe lines for irrigation with liquid manure.

The other old idea, which seems to have returned in connexion with

* Sown pasture

permanently housed cows, used to be known as 'soiling'. It was a system of growing a succession of green crops such as vetches, trifolium, kale, cabbage, rape and maize, to be cut and carted to the cows. Our forefathers were very proud of this plan and I have a vague recollection of my first farming reading being a book called *Farming on Factory Lines*. It died out because the process was not mechanised; growing, cutting, loading and carting were a very expensive business. Its only advantage was that much heavier crops of herbage could be grown on arable land than on permanent pasture. Today grass is treated as a crop. In many cases it is temporary pasture grown under arable conditions, but even when it is left as a collection of perennial plants it is fertilized to yield three or four grazings a year. This would seem to mean that there is even less reason for cutting and carting herbage than there used to be. A cow is perfectly equipped for cutting, elevating and transporting her own food. The reasons for the 'wheel returning' are new. Grass is now such a valuable crop that we want to be able to ration it with accuracy. It is wasteful to trample it in wet weather, to have animals lying on it, and dropping fertilizer on it in a highly patchy and unorganized manner. More important is the fact that few dairy farms are remote from roads, and driving cows on roads is a modern nightmare. We are aided in our attempt to manage on 'factory lines' by the new machines. A forage harvester not only cuts grass; it chews it up to some extent, and blows it into a trailer. The labour of removing, loading and carting herbage is reduced to a few hours by one man. The machines cost something in fuel, but we need not reckon their capital cost because we should have to buy them anyway for the old job of preserving winter food as hay and silage. They are now used from April to November instead of for three months only, and a machine in constant use is one of the aims of agriculture. Far too many of our machines are idle for most of the year. I imagine thousands of farmers have implements such as corn drills which do not do twenty days' work per annum even on fairly large holdings, and for the rest of the time take up a lot of valuable, covered storage space.

It may be that what I am suggesting about the certain thing of farming is that just as all seasons return in a different form, so do the systems. We built farm buildings to keep animals comfortable in the days when a man's time cost twelve shillings [6op] a week for sixty hours or more. Then we built to produce hygienic milk with no reference to the comfort of man or beast, so that we spent our time in cold water and draughts. Now for some animals we have come back to a standard of comfort which is far above standards for humans. Many farmers have artificial heat in piggeries and poultry houses, whilst they and their wives still sleep in freezing bedrooms. Insulation in fattening houses has reached a far higher standard than in council houses. We have returned to the old idea of making animals comfortable but often in strange new ways, and for new reasons . . .

The latest type of house for poultry fattening has no windows at all. It is found better to be able to control the light with absolute precision so that we can govern the periods of eating and sleeping. A shaft of strong sunlight makes particles of dust look like flies, at which a bored bird might peck—which is one step from pecking another bird and cannibalism.

I admit that housing humans who are expected to breed, and to live for a very long time, is slightly different from housing a bird whose only function is to grow to slaughter weight in ten weeks. Yet it is an amazing development to have gone back to overcrowding, to darkness, and to a floor a foot thick in litter and droppings without utter disaster. We seem to have gone back to the very worst mistakes of our ancestors, but, in fact, the wheel has not returned to the same place. We have antibiotics for disease control. The essence of the system is that a strictly isolated house only contains one age of chickens, so that they do not catch diseases by contact with older hens. They are all brought in on one day and all go for slaughter on one day, and between batches there is a break of a fortnight for disinfection and cleaning. Their diet contains every known combination of proteins, vitamins and minerals. Their growth is hastened with hormones.

from : Ralph Wightman, *Abiding Things*

19 'We are only producing what the public wants'

United Kingdom and General

'We don't ill-treat them,' said a broiler manager, a likeable young man with a great capacity for hard work. 'They live in a nice warm atmosphere out of the wind and the rain, and have *ad lib.* food. Rather like a club.'

The day-old chicks are installed, 8,000 or 10,000 at a time, sometimes more, in long, windowless houses punctuated only with extractor fans in rows along the ridge of the roofs and air intake vents along the side walls. Inside a house the impression is of a long, wide, dark tunnel disappearing into the gloom, the floor covered with chickens as far as the eye can see. There are lights down each side, hoppers for food hang from the beams, and pipes keep a constant supply of water. The houses are sprayed regularly with insecticides to keep the chickens free of pests.

For the first two weeks the chicks are kept under warm brooders at a steady temperature of 90 degrees (that of a mother hen) in a constant, round-the-clock, bright light. Thus they are encouraged to eat and grow quickly. After two weeks the lights are changed to amber and go on and off for two hours round the clock. So the birds eat and sleep, eat and sleep, eat and sleep.

At six weeks they are big enough to feel the intensity of crowding, and too much light would mean too much fighting, so the lights are changed to 25 watt red—virtual darkness—and these go on and off round the clock every two hours. So they exist for the last four weeks of their short lives, almost immobile, their only function to put on weight.

Many broilermen have their chickens de-beaked to avoid feather pecking and fighting in the later stages . . .

On a visit to one packing station, an innocuous-looking, factory-like building, we were issued with white overalls and wellington boots to protect us from the blood in the slaughter room. Then we went into the shed. Crates were stacked up the inside wall, 12 birds to the crate. The birds are starved for 12 to 16 hours before they reach the packing station and they are apt to spend the best part of a day in their crates after they reach it, before their turn comes. During this time they get neither food nor drink, because any undigested food is waste and can impair the keeping quality of the carcase in the deep freeze.

Taken out of their crates, the birds are suspended by their legs on a moving belt, gently because they must not be frightened or they would not de-feather so well. The time taken to reach the slaughter-man varies between one and five minutes according to the layout and speed of the conveyor belt. As they move along their beaks open and shut, mutely, in what has all the appearance of fear, but I was told that chickens are dim creatures and have not the slightest idea of what is happening to them . . .

In 1961 some 28 million laying birds—nearly half the total—were housed in battery cages.

In the battery unit automation is exploited to the full. The cages are ranked one above the other, three, four, or even five tiers high. Food is supplied by a conveyor belt and water is laid on.

The bird stands on a wire grid which has a one-in-five slope from back to front, so that the egg rolls away into a rack in front of the cage.

The droppings fall on to a tray which is automatically "squeegeed" off at intervals.

For a long time only one bird was housed in each cage, then two were tried together. Mortality was no greater, and the birds even seemed to enjoy the companionship. Then three birds were tried to a cage; some even tried four to the ordinary 15- or 16-inch cage.

One firm is making production comparisons with 'one bird to a

361

nine-and-a-half-inch cage, two to a 12-inch cage and three to a 16-inch cage. Other possible combinations are four to a 16-inch cage or four or five in a 24-inch cage.'

from : *The Observer*, March 1, 1964

20 Time and motion farming

St Osyth, near Clacton, England, 1969

Early on this routine day, four years after his start as a farmer in his own right and a good bit after St. Clere's Hall was carved out of the wilderness for the Saxon Earl Godwin, Tom Grantham, with immediate duties tidied up and the milk collected by the tanker, walked with me across the frozen slush, which crackled like potato crisps underfoot, to review his progress while filling his pipe before the log fire . . .

'I had also been studying the general situation and I'd realised that we were still too diversified. Costs were still soaring. Capital was becoming scarcer. I was in danger of keeling over. Agribusiness was everywhere demonstrating the scale and style that had to be followed. I could see that the small farm was doomed in another 15 years unless it forced itself up into another league by doing a ruthless time-and-motion scrutiny of itself.

'This meant either doubling up on everything, cows, pigs and arable crops, or, alternatively, concentrating on one unit only. After all, I went for cows. I had machinery scattered rusting for 11 months in the year. I sold the lot—the combine and everything. This is heavy land and you need pretty potent machines to deal with it. Let contractors blunt their tools on it. I allocated 110 acres for wheat and barley, 30 acres for grass, and then gutted the big building, turned it over to cowyards and milking parlour, installed the machinery and cut right back on staff. I started with 60 animals and I shall be up to 130 next autumn and 150 in 1970.

'I believe I've now got the formula. I've got a target of four cows per acre, which is very intensive. The break-even point is 500 gallons a year. If you get that from a cow your costs are covered. Fifteen of mine are producing 1,000 gallons and a few over 1,200 gallons—it averages out at 800 gallons per cow, 50 above the national average for the Channel Islands. You have to reckon this out to the last penny. It costs 14 pence* per gallon to feed a cow on silage and 15 pence* to feed it on straw and balancers. That penny matters. You've got to make up your mind if it's worth spending or not.

'It's all a gamble. There are three cardinal factors in farming :

* Old currency

362

politics and the elements, and management—and management is how you control and cater for the first two. Of course you've got to know your land. You have to have know-how to sum up the risks. One small mistake and you're over the line. That's the danger of specialisation. If the government thinks it's too chancy for votes to hoist up the price of milk, you're lumbered. You either hit a bonanza or you don't—there's no mid way. But at last I feel I'm on the right track and forging ahead.

'Yet I get worried. This is the only viable way to operate today, but in Britain we are driving the land very hard. I don't say we're harming it but today's methods are, well, prodigal. Are we doing enough to replenish it? Are we replanting enough trees? Are we keeping up the humus content? Last spring the Fen country was practically a dust bowl after a spell of dry weather. I view the situation with a touch of apprehension. It comes down to how cheap the government wants its food. It doesn't matter a jot whether it's a Labour or a Conservative government—they want cheap food to stay in power, so the land has to deliver the goods. I just hope that in the long term we don't find that we demanded too much and returned too little.

'It frightens me at times. Yet farming is still a tremendous challenge. Sometimes it reduces me almost to tears and at other times it thrills me to bits. Mechanised though it is, and despite the hours you have to spend at the desk knee-deep in forms, it brings you back into direct contact with life.

'There are times—when the rain's pouring down your neck, and your trailer sinks up to its axles in mud, and you get a puncture in the pitch dark with a load of straw on top—when you wonder why you didn't go in for a nine-to-five job. Despite all that, you know inside that you're doing something apart from the world that's made up entirely of motor cars and concrete and money. How can I explain this? It may be that you're out in the fields and you see a sparrow-hawk attacking a rook, and you're aware of the fundamental contest of life. Or once again you have the tremendous thrill of seeing a cow calve successfully, and you have an indescribable sense of a new life being created. Or you watch the sun setting in a particular cloud formation. Or you have the pleasure of walking along a hedge and inspecting a nice crop of grass.

'They're satisfactions that are hard to explain, and which probably don't seem to fit in with the hard-headed accountancy and industrialisation that one has to come to terms with. But the real reward for me is to be able to walk this land with the knowledge that it's been grazed and cropped and cared for, with the Hall as its centre, for all these centuries, and that I'm able to extend its life. That's what matters.'

from : The Daily Telegraph Magazine, April 18, 1969

21 Cattle for blood and milk

Kenya

One day he showed me how he bled his cattle.

A Kikuyu seized the head of a brindled bull and twisted it over his thigh, gripping its neck with one hand so as to swell the jugular vein. Sammy took a bow from the boy's hand and, from a few yards' range, fired an arrow straight into the jugular. The arrowhead was ringed with a little block of wood so that its point could not penetrate more than about half an inch. Still with a casual air, Sammy plucked out the arrow and the blood spurted into a calabash held by the boy. Then Sammy closed the arrow-prick with finger and thumb and, to my surprise, it stayed closed and the bleeding stopped. The bull, released, strolled off and started to graze. I suppose this was no more harmful to it than bleeding human patients used to be—less so, in fact, as the bull was in good health. Sammy did not drink the blood in the calabash. The boy mixed it with milk and other ingredients, of which cows' urine was one, and let the brew ferment for a day or two. When it was ready to eat, its consistency was like that of soft cheese.

from : Elspeth Huxley, *The Flame Trees of Thika*

22 Droving in its heyday

Northern Territory, Australia

On the wall I noticed a complicated-looking schedule rather like a railway timetable. It was the Northern Territory's Droving Programme for twelve months—an astounding affair—giving a list of the ninety-two mobs of cattle varying between 1,500 and 1,200 head in each, which were scheduled to travel the Barkly Stock Route between March and August that year.

The whole thing was worked out in detail—from the dates they would be leaving their stations to the dates they would be arriving at such places an Anthony's Lagoon and Rankine, where they would be dipped for cattle tick before going on into Queensland . . .

At the next bore we came upon our first travelling mob of cattle. They were just beginning to move off from the trough after being watered and a long drift of dust was rising all round their hoofs. Seeing us approaching the drover wheeled his horse and cantered over.

'Good day,' he called, leaning down from the saddle to the level of the truck window. He was lean and sunburnt and had a black pointed beard. He was Drover Griffiths. It gave me quite a glow of satisfaction to consult my Droving Programme and find his name in black and white.

He had four other men with him. Three of them rode round the cattle continually, winging them, or keeping them on the stock route, if they were inclined to string out too far. The other men were the 'horse tailers', whose job it was to look after the mob of spare horses— three horses are provided for each man and ridden in turn. In addition to these riding horses there are night horses which are always kept saddled at night in case the cattle rush or break, which they usually do about 3 a.m., if they are going to.

One old fellow who had been with cattle all his life, told me quite a lot about this 'rushing'.

'When store cattle rush,' he said, 'it's the front ones what starts it. One starts running and the others chases after him, not knowing what's on. The ones behind sees them all rushin' so away they starts too. Well, once they starts, the ones in front has to keep goin' else the ones behind'll trample 'em down so they all keeps going. That's how it starts, see. All you have to do is race after 'em and try and turn the leader into the tail—ringing 'em its called. If you turn 'em and turn 'em, in the end they're just running round in a circle—only they don't see that see. They still think they're going some place.

'You have to be mighty smart when you're ringing and slip in at the side of 'em and out again quick—else they'll be right over on top of you.'

I asked him why they are said to 'rush' about 3 a.m. 'Well, you see, they're stillest then,' he replied. 'Takes but the smallest sound to set them off. So, if you've a mob of bullocks and dry cows, always shove a handful of cows with calves in among them. The calves'll keep bellowing for their mothers all night and the mothers'll keep bellowing back—and there'll be cows and calves movin' through the mob all night lookin' for each other. The mob never gets still enough to have a scare then.'

from : Beryl Miles, *Stars My Blanket*

23 A drover's life

Australia

Droving is not dead, or dying; nor is it the colourful romantic life that our literature suggests. To the drover, longing to 'blow' his cheque in town, life can be more lonely and boring than any office or factory job.

With the growth of road transport for stock in the outback, droving is supposed to be dying out. That may be so in some parts, but as a general assumption it is wrong.

Road trains are replacing droving outfits on long, arduous tracks through the bad country of the Northern Territory, Western Queensland and South Australia. On such routes as the Birdsville-Maree track, where water and feed is mostly scarce, often non-existent, walking stock lose condition. But as long as there are stock routes with good feed (most of the 'closer in' routes are in this class), there will be sheep and cattle walking them, attended by traditional drovers.

Many people probably don't realise that, at any given time, a goodly proportion of the stock walking the million-mile filigree network of stock routes over the Australian continent aren't going anywhere in particular. They are just 'following the feed', growing meat or wool, or both, in the process.

Undoubtedly, as their owners will tell you, they are on their way to market, but there may be some doubt about precisely which sale town they are headed for. If there is good feed on the stock routes, Queensland sheep may end up in Melbourne. There are instances of travelling sheep having been twice shorn while on the road before finally locating a new owner.

Today there are still plenty of 'graziers' who don't own an acre of land, yet have thousands of head of sheep or cattle eating their heads off on the better situated stock routes. So long as there is grass, edible burr or young saltbush there, these dealers will provide work for some at least of the 3,000 men still engaged in the droving industry.

Legitimate graziers, whose properties are sited in drought-stricken or fire or flood damaged areas are another source of employment for drovers. Not wanting to see their stock starve, and either unable or unwilling to sell them, they put their sheep or cattle 'on the road', ostensibly to a sale town. But more than likely the mob will find their way back, perhaps six months later, when the home paddocks are green again, or shearing time comes round.

Undoubtedly a lot more sheep and cattle, these days, are travelling by train and truck, and the men who look after them on these journeys are still called drovers. Nevertheless, most drovers still ride horses. Some of their outfits now run to a truck and perhaps a caravan instead of the traditional wagonette, but apart from this, droving today is much the same as it always was, except that fences make the job easier.

Most drovers still work and sleep in dusty clothes and high-heeled riding boots. Of necessity, many wear beards like their counterparts of yesteryear, because bore water is usually unsuitable for shaving, and there is still little need to keep up appearances on the track. A typical small droving turn-out usually includes the boss drover, a shepherd and a cook-horse-tailer. Drovers shifting large mobs of 5,000 or more sheep may employ two shepherds, a full-time cook and full-time horse-tailer.

Whether he is receiving £20 or £50 a week, the drover and his men have a lot to put up with. Out in poor country, where it takes 30 acres to feed a sheep, he may travel weeks between meetings with strangers with whom he can exchange yarns. In addition to the loneliness and boredom, there are heat, dust, flies, wind, worry about water and feed, lost stock, and personality clashes between the men in the outfit. At night, cattle drovers have the worry and work of keeping the mob quiet and contented, and must do their sleeping in shifts. The sheep man, where there are no existing fences, has the drudgery of erecting portable rolled-up wire fences, carried in the truck or wagon, to confine the flock.

This fencing is usually erected in a U or L shape, and after the sheep have been driven in, the outfit's dogs are chained to iron spikes driven into the ground at intervals across the opening. Out in fence-less country, unless a storm has brought a green pick, the standard feed is saltbush, poverty burr, barley grass and possum weed.

Along the outback stock routes there are bores and tanks every ten or twenty miles (about two days travel apart), but often a drover will find a tank dry. Worse, he may find some water, but not nearly enough for all his sheep or cattle. When this happens, the drover has to take his mob right around the bore, hopefully and at a fair distance, so that the stock will not smell the water. When sheep smell water, they stampede to it if they are really thirsty, packing-up, trampling and suffocating each other in their efforts to reach it.

City folk may think of droving as a carefree, romantic existence, but the daily routine in a drover's camp is as fixed as that of any city factory or office. But since drovers have no week-end breaks, they are likely to suffer not 'Mondayitis', but 'everydayitis'.

The usual droving day starts at 4 a.m. or thereabouts. At this hour the horse-tailer gets up, saddles the tethered 'night horse' and rides off into the darkness, listening for the tell-tale bells of the rest of the horses (there may be a dozen to thirty of them, spread over several square miles during their all-night graze). Next the cook rises and prepares breakfast for the camp. When the drover and his shepherds have eaten, they pick their mounts for the day from the horses the tailer has rounded up. Then they release the dogs required for work, saddle up and get the mob on the move. (Surplus dogs travel in the truck or wagonette, resting their burred and stone-cut pads ready for their next duty day.)

About an hour later, after washing up and breaking camp, the cook and horse-tailer follow the mob. The cook drives the wagon or truck, containing the outfit's bedding, food and worldly possessions. The horse-tailer, driving the spare horses, follows.

When the wagon passes the mob, a stopping place for lunch is agreed upon with the drover, and the cook and tailer go ahead to the pre-arranged rendezvous. When the mob catches up, the billy is already boiling and the inevitable chops sizzling in the camp oven. As a treat, there may be tinned peaches for sweets. After lunch, the wagon and horse-tailer move ahead, in the wake of the boss drover, who may have gone on to locate a suitable camp, or check that there is enough water in the next bore. At night when the mob has been watered and settled down, the evening meal is served round the camp-fire. Usually it is braised chops, rice and sultana pudding and, some-times, 'brownie' (a cake made in the camp oven, buried in the ashes of the fire). The meal is washed down with mugs of tea, cigarettes and pipes are set alight, and the inevitable campfire stories are told and retold.

At the end of a really long trip, most droving outfits live it up in town, until their accumulated pay is 'blued'. Then they saddle up for yet another long, lonely outback trek.

from : J. and M. Carter, 'A drover's life', *Walkabout,* June 1962

24 Dust and moving animals: nomadic discomforts

Mountainous country, eastern Turkey

Mounds of buried villages float above the mists like islands, and the horizon melts in dust to the south. Stubble blows loose in autumn over undulations whose wheat or barley once enriched the black-bearded Assyrians, and here the flocks move from morning to evening in their migrations, with one shepherd ahead of them and one behind them, under the clinging discomfort of their own dust. The dust creeps about the landscape above them to the height of a man's eyes, and reddens and weighs down their curled fleeces; and the sheep, plodding through the ages, nose the ground and bury their eyes in the coat of the one before it, kicking up their own troubles from their own soil, patient, unquestioning, and like mankind resolute to hide their faces from the goal of their marching, trusting to a shepherd that only their leader can see.

from : Freya Stark, *Riding to the Tigris*

25 Shepherd: a life's work

Scottish Highlands, 1969

Sheep are not easy creatures to love. Their white-woolly bodies are stiff, pale gold eyes unknowing. But a shepherd has to love his flock. James Maclean, who works in the Scottish highlands, says that a shepherd's instinct and skill has to be bred in him, and Maclean's father and grandfather were both shepherds. Maclean started when he was 13. He was taken away from school during the First World War to help with the lambing, because of the shortage of men on the farms, and he never went back.

Now he has charge of a flock numbering about 5,000, on a part of a large Inverness-shire estate. The sheep roam an area 25 by 30 miles, and Maclean manages alone, drawing help from other stockmen on the estate, and sometimes from casual labour, at the busiest times.

But the work is lonely, and shepherds become obsessed with their sheep, which are both their livelihood and their companions. 'The most treacherous time,' says Maclean, 'is the heavy winter.' Snow maroons the animals in drifts and the shepherds have to bring them in where it's safe. 'I've known men get lost like that. It's very exhausting, you can walk miles looking for sheep all over the hills, but there comes a point when you have to turn round so that you have enough strength to get back. But these men keep on going.'

Even in the lighter months much more of the work is on foot in the hills and mountains than it is in England, where a van or a Land-Rover can get the shepherd about. But Maclean looks wirily healthy on it all. Not a tall man, but he stands well upright and walks staunchly; his eyes are somewhat narrowed, but bright, and he looks determined, not in terms of ambition but in some private cause. He sees no acceptable hardship in his job.

After the winter months of protecting the flock from the weather, and preserving it from disease, the spring opens up the land and the lambing begins. Some of the best ewes in the flock are kept specifically for breeding—all Maclean's sheep are the same breed : blackface, a mountain sheep. There are about 4 breeds native to Britain, none of them, excepting those on a few islands off the Welsh coast, are wild sheep. The sheep was one of the first animals to be domesticated, and wild sheep only exist in primitive areas.

With the lambing over by the beginning of summer, the sheep are rounded up for shearing, branding and dipping. Extra labour is hired and, with Maclean, the three or four men deal with a few hundred sheep at a time. Maclean brings them in with Monty (named after Montgomery—an outburst of patriotism in the Scottish highlands), his black and white sheep-dog.

Over the 15 years Maclean has been on this estate, he has trained many dogs for sheepdog trials. Now he sticks to his own, and Monty's precision is a source of great pride.

The wool is sold at a standard rate per lb. and then, at the autumn sales, the sheep themselves are sold, bringing the numbers down to the basic winter flock. Maclean makes sure this is on good grazing land, and that the fences to keep them there are in good condition. Then he digs in for the winter. He says it is no good just knowing your sheep, you have to know the land also, and it can take years to know where the sheep may be safe, and where the land is being grazed in the best way.

'These days,' says Maclean, 'you get a lot of young men coming out of college thinking they know it all. A few, of course, are good, but they all need to work on the land before they know anything, and a lot don't see that. This work is not something you can learn from books.'

Maclean and his wife live in a cottage on top of a small hill, next to a quarry near the Moray Firth; their daughter has married and left home. Behind the house is a field with a small flock of 13 sheep. These belong to Maclean himself, and they are there ready for his retirement.

'I could never give it up. I shall need them for something to do.'

from : The Daily Telegraph Magazine, April 18, 1969

26 The man who disliked sheep

East Africa, early twentieth century

This business of looking after fourteen thousand sheep was no joke. I came to hate these animals, with their round woolly backs and obstinate selfish mouths. To prevent scab I was always having to dip them. At certain intervals they would be put through a long bath filled with a solution of Cooper's dip which, when first mixed, was a bright yellow colour, but could become a foul brown. I and two natives stood at the edge of the channel and with our plungers pressed the head of each animal under water as it passed.

The sun would beat down upon us, the dust from the yard would rise in clouds over the fences, and the procession of sheep as they clambered up to the dipping pens would seem endless. Once in the pens the animals would shake themselves, and as I counted them out with the round yellow sodom-apples, which I used as tallies in my hands, my nostrils would be filled with the fumes of the arsenic, sickly warm fumes mixed with the ammonia which rose from the steaming brown backs. On such occasions it would seem to me that I was under the influence of some strange hypnotic trance, and I would bitterly curse my fate, the miserable monotonous fate of a scurvy shepherd superintending the washing of his flocks.

It was better in the lambing season. This always took place in October, so that the ewes might have the advantage of the fresh grass springing up with the falling of the light autumn rains. I would arrange the lambing camps in different parts of the farm, and pleasant enough it was to come upon these centres of ovine life, with the anxious mothers fitfully nibbling at the creeping grass and the lambs snow-white, long-legged, long-tailed, frisking about on the open veldt. As soon as the lambs were six weeks old I could go from camp to camp ear-marking, castrating and tailing them. I made a point of doing this in the very early morning, so that the coldness of the air would lessen the bleeding. I became completely hardened to this occupation and would sear off the long appendages of these little symbols of salvation with expert deftness, and as I handled the red-hot copper instrument a long thin ray of light would suddenly come slanting across the blood-stained, scorched board at which I worked, and immediately the nervous barking of the impala would cease and the first birds begin to call. When the affair was over I would kneel down and count the lambs by the number of severed tails which lay in a heap at my side, recording the total in my notebook with bloody, sacrificial hands. A dozen or so of the fattest tails I would take back with me, and Kamoha would fry them and serve them up for breakfast like a dish of eels.

In January shearing would begin, and the long rough shed which for the rest of the year remained closed and empty, like a deserted church, would now suddenly become the centre of the farm work. Sheep would baa, natives would chatter, shears would click, the old wool-press would creak, and all would be stir and bustle. It was my business to class the wool, and as fleece after fleece was carried to me I would allocate them to the various bins according to the staple. There were bins for fleeces, for bellies, for first pieces, for second pieces, and for locks . . .

I would look out through the open door and see the wide African country stretching away, mile upon mile, outlandish, unkempt, to where the high mountains rose, upon whose terraces the heavy-limbed marauders slept, their gibbous, gently heaving, obscurely spotted bellies warm in the sun.

And so the long years passed slowly by. I saw little of the neighbouring settlers. My life became reduced to one unending struggle with the material world.

from : Llewelyn Powys, *Black Laughter*

27 The lambing: care of animals

North Wales, 1931

Some mornings we wake to the barbaric music of a gale that lashes at the squat stone house until the bed shakes. It is an effort to open the back door against the thrust and vacuum of the wind, and the rain blinds the eyes with stinging blows, so that one walks bent double, leaning against the storm, tottering like an old man. Luck's long coat is blown to each side of him. A parting is made along his spine, and the hairs are plastered to his sides in an instant by the deluge of water.

On these stormy days I go down to the low ground first, to see whether the sheep are clear of the flooded river. The ewes lie behind every hillock and rock and bit of wall. Their long, broad tails, left uncut for just such weather, are curled against the storm as some sort of protection. The mothers have their lambs crouched up under their chests, and wait in stoic patience for the ordeal to end.

I may stumble on a dead lamb, born quite recently. He could never have risen to his feet, and must have been at once flattened into the soaking earth by the gale, for his mother has cleaned the upper side of him, but when I turn him over the under-side is untouched. The ewe hovers near by, the afterbirth just breaking free. It is no time for delicacy, and I send Luck for her. He ranges round her, just a neck ahead, and turns her in tightening circles, until I am able to spring and grab her. I put her on my back, and carry her with her dead lamb to a building.

As we stumble into shelter the diminution of noise and violence is abrupt, and one hears the storm at a little distance as it swoops and screeches round the shed, like a harpy balked of her prey. Suddenly a figure darkens the doorway. It will be John Davies. He is wearing oilskins over an old overcoat. He has oilskin leggings over knee-high rubber boots, and on his head is a sou'wester over an old felt hat. He is wet to the skin. From under his coat he drags a puling lamb, an uncleaned, newborn morsel, in which the spark of life, still vigorous, would speedily have been quenched outside.

'His mother will not be worth potching with,' explains Davies. 'She haven't no milk for him.'

I turn over the ewe whose dead lamb I have brought in with me. Her swollen, unsucked udder is full of milk.

'She'll make him a proper mother,' I tell Davies, and draw a little of the thick first milk for him to see.

'Wait till I do make the little flamer a raincoat,' says Davies. And he will pull out his knife and skin the mother's dead lamb. We fit the skin over the live lamb and put him near the bereaved ewe who

372

backs away suspiciously at first, but she speedily smells her substance on his new coat, and trots back, whickering, to make much of him.

I hold the ewe for a minute or two, while Davies puts the lamb to a teat. As the lamb sucks he strengthens quite visibly. He rises on to his back legs, waggles his tail, then rises to his front legs, unsteady but triumphant, and pushes with ever increasing emphasis at the udder. It will not be more than a day or two before the adoption is complete and the skin can be removed.

Sometimes we come across a ewe whose lamb has disappeared. Perhaps he has been swept away by a stream, or has tumbled into a hole, or has been carried away by a fox. But we can now and then manage an adoption without the skin of the vanished offspring by rubbing the new lamb under the ewe's tail, so that her own smell is on him . . .

If the rain drives down all day, by nightfall every building will be holding couples. Many of the lambs will be too weak to trust outside, and many of the mothers will have been so buffeted by the gale that they will not feed their offspring. Lambs will lie in the cottages and in Dyffryn house. These are the really bad cases which have not the strength to suck at a ewe. Some are brought in chilled right through by the cold rain, and are revived in a basin of warm water and given a little gin. Others are fed drop by drop with a fountain-pen filler. There may be one that has been almost drained of blood by a weasel, his body so flaccid that when picked up he drapes over the hand like a white cloth.

The gale may last a fortnight. If it is prolonged the work gets out of hand, and we have to leave the old stagers in the *ffridd* to look after themselves while we concentrate on the bottom land. In the buildings the family distinctions become impossibly complicated. The skin belongs to that ewe's dead lamb. This lamb has been deserted. Is that lone ewe with milk in her udder his mother? Or is her son represented by this skin? Then Davies says, 'That flamer have come to her senses. I be going to let her out with her lamb into the stackyard.'

And when two or three indifferent couples are under observation in the stackyard, wrongly paired, the confusion becomes worse confounded. And we dare not keep a ewe in for long, or her milk will dry up, for it is almost impossible to persuade her to eat artificial food. Yet if the couple are turned out prematurely the ewe may desert her lamb.

John Davies and Thomas develop an open hostility to Providence. They curse the careless mountains. They are working eighteen hours a day. Their clothes are used up faster than they can be dried, and they are always wet and cold. But they do not grumble at the work. They grumble about Dyffryn's tragic trouble.

But, as in Genesis, there comes a day when the floods subside and the quaking ground becomes firm again. For many days the mists have veiled the hills, and now the sun woos the filmy clouds and lifts them to his embrace, so that they die in the warmth of his kiss. And the mountains seem to shake their streaming flanks like monsters rising from the deep, and they lie a-sprawl as they dry visibly in the sunshine.

The ewes come forth from every sort of sheltering-place and begin to graze again phlegmatically, some with lambs at foot who wrinkle their noses at the world which has been so hostile to them, others heavy, their ordeal still to come. John Davies and his son begin to smile, and daily John Davies comes to me to say some such thing as, 'That ewe in the pen by the top building have come to her senses. I have let go the flamer.'

We begin to look through the *ffridd*, and find that the wily older sheep show little sign of the hard times they have been through. Here and there a lamb is wedged between two boulders in a stream, drowned while following his mother. Where we can we put slate slabs as bridges, but these have to be exactly on the sheep tracks, or they are not used. In one place is a lamb, dead now, whose living eyes have been plucked by crows. A carrion crow will feed on a lamb but partly born.

But soon we forget the losses of the storm. Each day new lambs come, forty or fifty of them. The percentage of deaths shrinks. Soon the whole valley seems filled with contented couples. The lambs become stronger, and the ewes leave them asleep while they graze farther afield, always to return unerringly to where their lambs lie. And now the lambs themselves are showing initiative. Groups of them dispute the sovereignty of a hillock. They chase one another, losing themselves and bleating pitifully, until their mother recognises their voice and calls back as she trots in search.

No miser with his hoarded gold can feel the pleasure which comes to Esme and I as we stroll now through our doubled flock. The farm has given birth, and we identify ourselves with its labour. We have shared many of the pangs. There is no greed in our eyes as we survey the teeming land; rather are we humbled before the courage, persistence, and simplicity of nature. We have been privileged, for the gods have performed before us the great play of life. A gigantic orgasm has been succeeded by a gigantic birth. The fluid of fertility has been poured over our hills and valleys by firm hands whose generosity shames humanity. We feel that we have assisted at a miracle. And, of course, we have.

from : Thomas Firbank, *I bought a Mountain*

28 Mustering in the mountains

New Zealand, early nineteen-sixties

We were to see most of them in the next few days, as we made camp with the musters on their lonely tracks through river valleys.

The muster is carried through with all the planning and precision of a military operation. Area by area, the back country is ransacked for sheep. No matter how high, how far they wander—sometimes way up toward the snow line, on rocky ridges or shingle slides without a trace of vegetation—they are retrieved by dogs and men and driven to the station. There they are dipped and mated, and held for the winter on warmer levels.

The musterers are men of a special breed. They pride themselves on their fitness for one of the toughest jobs in the world.

Limberly they scale half a dozen peaks, searching out sheep, all in a day's work. They may climb 3,000 feet up precipitous rock to bring down a mere three or four sheep. Soaked by rain, chilled by wind, they still crack jokes at the end of the day. They are awake again at four in the frosty morning, and out on the mountaintops before sunrise . . .

One day, in particular, stays fixed sharply in my memory.

It was toward the end of the muster; everyone was tired and looking forward to the station. I was walking the lower end of a valley with a tall and taciturn musterer named Ian, who had a thick growth of beard. On each side of us, musterers were working the 'tops'. We were to make sure no sheep were left in the valley, and we spent most of the long day without sight of one.

We lost touch with the other musterers; their whistles and cries, together with the faint barking of their dogs, receded into the great silences of the mountains.

Ian stopped, and looked up a steep mountainside. 'See them?' he said.

I looked. I could see only a mountain. Tussock merging into vast slides of shingle; rocky spurs beneath a ragged peak lightly sprinkled with snow; sheer bluffs and a lonely sparkling waterfall.

'See what?' I said.

'Look again,' he said.

'Sorry,' I conceded after a while. 'I can't see a thing.'

'Half a dozen sheep up there. Above the right-hand shingle slide.'

Baffled, I stared : I still couldn't see them.

With his dogs barking at his heels he went off to fetch the strays. It occurred to me that he could easily have forgotten about the sheep up there, and no one would have been any the wiser.

But that isn't in the high-country tradition. And so away he went,

LABOUR ON THE LAND

up a couple of thousand feet of mountain or more. We were late getting back to the hut that night, but there were half a dozen new sheep added to the mob. Ian didn't even think his effort worthy of mention.

Day by day small mobs of sheep, stringing out along the skyline, were brought down from distant places. The dogs became as weary and footsore as the men. Then, with the muster almost over, we were driving 18,000 sheep down to the station.

This is the last, most delicate of jobs. The big mob must be moved along slowly—one fright, and a couple of hundred might smother themselves in their own panic.

Sam Chaffey was waiting for us at the homestead, a grin on his face. 'Good muster?' he asked. 'Have a bath and a shave, and I'll send you both out on another one.'

We pleaded to be excused, very definitely, as we limped toward him.

Next day Sam, for light entertainment, showed us how he could move a mob of 2,000 sheep around with a single dog.

Standing on a hill, half a mile from the sheep, he sent the dog careering away. Whistling instructions, he had the dog spinning the sheep in a circle, then swinging in an oblong, then packed in a square. The patterns were almost perfect. It wouldn't have surprised us if Sam and his dog had persuaded the sheep to walk upright on their back legs.

'Only one thing I've never learned to do with my dog,' Sam confessed.

'What's that?'

'How to make it drive a tractor,' he said. 'Think of the labor it would save.'

from : Maurice Shadbolt, 'New Zealand—gift of the sea', *National Geographical Magazine*, April 1962

29 Sheep shearing

Australia

Halstead, the owner of Wattle Run, came into the shed and stood by the door. The men were all by their machines now; Quinlan, who did his own wool classing, was at his table under the big fanlight; the piece-pickers, roustabouts, and boys hitched up their pants and waited for the bell.

Everyone looked towards Quinlan as he raised his voice. 'Righto, men. Mr. Halstead wants good shearing, more than fast stuff. Some of the sheep are still picking up after the drought. Don't knock 'em around too much.' The shearers took no notice of this. Ocker Shand exaggeratedly cleaned his ear with his little finger as if he hadn't heard right. They knew how to handle sheep and didn't need to be told. 'Everybody ready?'

Then the bell went. Shearing was on again at Wattle Run. Paddy dived into the pen, his body in the crouch in which it would stay most of the day. He grabbed a sheep under the forelegs, sat it up, and dragged it out into the shed, on to the 'board'. With the sheep's fore-feet tucked under his left armpit, his left hand pulled his machine into gear as his right hand whipped up the handpiece. He worked with the automatic smoothness of one who knew his job and liked it now that he was doing it; he was no relation at all of the man who two days before had tried to dodge being signed up. He wore a sleeveless flannel singlet; his lean brown arms moved like thick striking snakes in the dust-flecked light.

The belly wool was thrown clear, then the wool on the left flank, then the neck. The sheep was moved between his knees like a sack : only an occasional bleat let you know it was alive. From the neck to the forearm the cutter ploughed, then the sheep was on its side and Paddy was beginning the longest cut, the 'long blow', from the flank to the top of the head. Then he propped the sheep against his leg and attacked the other side. Stab, punch, a long sweep, heave, every movement part of a beautifully co-ordinated whole, then the sheep was finished and was stumbling, Paddy's knee aiding it with a push, down the chute into the counting pen. Paddy had gained five seconds on the other shearers with his first sheep; by the end of the day he wanted to be the 'ringer' shearer.

from : Jon Cleary, *The Sundowners*

Notes on Section 8

The bold figures indicate the extract numbers

4 A mangold is a large kind of beet used for cattle food. Adrian Bell was a 'gentleman apprentice farmer'.

5 Gironde is a great wine-growing district in the Bordeaux area of France. Vine-growing calls for a measure of artistry as well as science.

6–8 Extracts Nos. 6 and 8 are set in Sicily, in a background of hard work and poverty, but they could represent the peasant attitude in many parts of the world. In contrast, extract No. 7 presents a much more leisurely view of labour on the land. Coconuts provide the main source of the world's vegetable oil. The largest area of production is the Pacific Islands where the coconuts are grown on smallholdings, but in the Philippines, the chief producer, these are being replaced by estates. The estates are more efficient and produce better-quality copra through the use of hot-air driers.

9 This extract is intended to typify rhythm, comradeship and hard work under uncomfortable conditions. Millions of people still plant out rice in this way.

10–12 These three passages deal with the work of irrigation and of farming on irrigated lands. Despite the speed with which mechanisation has grown in agriculture, the homely shovel and hoe are still very widely used. Sometimes modern mechanical methods are found alongside age-old ones (extract No. 12).

13 Mechanical ploughing is of course not such hard work as wielding a spade or hoe. Henry Williamson, a successful author, had hired help on his farm.

14 Here the work of harvesting the wheat crop is carried out by giant combines. It is sometimes forgotten that farm machinery needs maintenance and may break down.

15 Modern methods make feasible a drastic reduction in the labour force needed to work large arable farms. Aircraft facilitate spraying operations and permit easy surveillance of vast areas.

16 Here we have an account of farming in India very different from the conventional picture. It will be interesting to see what effect, if any, these 'gentlemen farmers' will have on the standard of living of the peasant masses. See also Section 4, extract No. 14.

17 The peasants of North Vietnam are endeavouring to improve their standards of living by co-operative farming under the influence of Chinese thought.

18 This extract refers to some of the effects on agriculture of modern methods—and yet perhaps not so modern, when we read of cows kept permanently indoors in the towns in Victorian times. Even today in some of the villages of Austria and south Germany cows are kept indoors. During

378

the day, cows pull carts laden with cut hay, clover, or grass, taking it to the cows indoors—no time to eat or spoil the meadows.

19 'We don't ill-treat them', said the broiler manager. Many people feel uncomfortable at the thought of living creatures being used merely as machines to produce eggs and meat. But this type of food production will continue until and unless enough people decide that they would be prepared to pay more for certain foods.

20 Kenneth Allsop gives us an insight into the way in which modern business techniques are being applied to farming.

21 Sammy is a Masai. On this farm there were both Masai and Kikuyu workers.

22-23 With very large flocks and herds, as in Australia, it is not really possible to help animals who get into difficulty during lambing or calving. By the end of a long journey between artesian bores there is considerable wastage in the animals' weight, and in a bad year there may be heavy loss from starvation and thirst. The use of planes to transport frozen carcases and of road-trains for live animals alleviates this problem to some extent. A road-train may carry a hundred beasts at a time in a lorry-driven assembly of linked-up trucks, but even this method of transport is expensive.

24 This short extract gives an idea of the discomforts of moving flocks in dry, dusty, mountainous country. Men who work with flocks and herds in dry places are not the only ones who have to contend with a dust-laden atmosphere. Those involved in hay-making and harvesting grain also have this problem.

25-28 These passages give detailed accounts of the hard work involved in sheep farming. Sheep demand more care and attention than cattle and are not suited to mechanised techniques. The resulting high labour cost is one of the major causes of the decline in sheep farming. Extracts Nos. 25 and 27 deal with sheep farming in Britain's uplands, the only effective use of the poor grazing pastures of these areas. Large hill-sheep subsidies from the government help to maintain these flocks which would otherwise be unprofitable.

29 It seems possible that the skill of the sheep shearer may become a lost art in view of the experiments taking place, particularly in the U.S.A., into what has become known as 'chemical shearing'. The sheep are fed or injected with a substance that causes the wool follicles to dry up and the fleece to be shed. Apart from the possible effects on human beings who may eat the carcases of sheep so treated, there is the disadvantage that while completely naked the sheep may suffer from sunburn and cold. Also, from the economic point of view, the temporary stoppage of the growth of the fibre means that something like a week's growth is lost every year. We may yet see the rearing of 'battery' sheep, however.

9

Labour in industry

This section is also concerned with Man's attitude towards his job and the effect of the job on the worker. In some cases is has been difficult to find workers who can describe what it is actually like to do certain jobs, and one has had to rely on the pen of a sympathetic and observant outsider whose experience may be of no more than a few hours.

The extracts fall into three main categories. First, those concerned with labouring, construction, mineral extraction and heavy industry. There follow some accounts of factory life, and then of certain outdoor jobs both on land and at sea.

A few extracts illustrating conditions in the nineteenth and early twentieth centuries are included to provide a comparison with those prevailing today. Conditions have of course much improved, but monotony and noise obviously have dire effects on large numbers of workers in industry. Though factories must comply with the law regarding temperature, adequate ventilation, lighting, space and so on, very many workers—including, for example, men who operate mechanical saws, coal-cutting machinery and road drills—must perforce be subjected to appalling noise at close quarters.

1 The labourer

General

There is more in labouring than just using a shovel, or in leaning on it. The labourer has an apprenticeship too, just as a prospective trades-man has one. In the labourer's case it is a private affair and there are no indentures. He gets no diplomas and he is scarcely aware of any skills, even when he has acquired them. The art is to bear the daily burden of tiredness and boredom equably, to know the right way to shovel, hammer, hold a wedge or a crowbar, carry loads, and to fill wheelbarrows. There is a rhythm in these actions which protects the heart and lungs, and brings serenity to the mind. Without that rhythm the muscles shriek, the chest is strained, and the mind infested with frustration and anxiety.

Sometimes an old hand will put a young one right, but more often it comes with observation and lengthening experience. It was Sanny Broon who showed me the way to use a long-shafted shovel. He showed me how to stand and how to dig the blade into the material, how much to lift, and how to swing it into, or from, a wagon. The tiresome way is to hold the shaft and haft rigidly from the beginning to the end of each operation. The lightsome way is to let the shaft pass through the loosely clenched lower hand in the act of swinging.

The same operation is ideal in hammer swinging too. Grip one hand firmly at the shaft end and the other low down, and as the hammer rises let the lower hand slide up the shaft until it grips firmly just under the other hand to take its part in the crash down. If a load is too much for one's strength, well that's simple, let some one get on the other end. A strained back is a vicious thing and there are no prizes for weightlifting or vanity.

from : Patrick McGeown, *Heat the Furnace Seven Times More*

2 Pick and shovel: working together

Oklahoma, U.S.A.

The three men walked out past the little whitewashed barn, and along a field edge. They came to a long narrow ditch with sections of concrete pipe lying beside it.

'Here's where we're a-working',' Wilkie said.

His father opened the barn and passed out two picks and three shovels. And he said to Tom : 'Here's your beauty.'

Tom hefted the pick. 'Jumping Jesus! If she don't feel good!'

'Wait'll about 'leven o'clock,' Wilkie suggested. 'See how good she feels then.'

They walked to the end of the ditch. Tom took off his coat and dropped it on the dirt pile. He pushed up his cap and stepped into the ditch. Then he spat on his hands. The pick rose into the air and flashed down. Tom grunted softly. The pick rose and fell, and the grunt came at the moment it sank into the ground and loosened the soil.

Wilkie said: 'Yes, sir, Pa, we got here a first-grade muck-stick man. This here boy been married to that there little digger.'

Tom said: 'I put in time (umph). Yes, sir, I sure did (umph). Put in my years (umph). Kinda like the feel (umph).' The soil loosened ahead of him ... His pick arced up and drove down, and the earth cracked under it. The sweat rolled down his forehead and down the sides of his nose, and it glistened on his neck. 'Damn it,' he said, 'a pick is a nice tool (umph), if you don' fight it (umph). You an' the pick (umph), workin' together (umph).'

In line, the three men worked, and the ditch inched along and the sun shone hotly down on them in the growing morning.

from: John Steinbeck, *Grapes of Wrath*

3 Head of steel

Labrador, Canada

It seemed a long time that I trudged across that desolate area of swamp, but at last I reached the shallow gravel rim that enclosed it, and round a bend I came on a gang of men working with drills and machine-operated spanners, bolting the rails together and driving spikes. The detached chassis and wheels of dismantled rail transporters lay beside the track, and up ahead were more men and machines, and beyond them the steel-laying train. Everywhere about me now there was a sense of movement, of drive and thrust and effort, so that Labrador seemed suddenly crowded and full of life. The track, laid on the bare gravel without ballast, like toy rails in a sandpit, had a newness about it that showed that it hadn't been there yesterday, and walking beside it, through all these gangs of men, I felt conspicuous ...

It was better when I reached the train itself. There were no gangs working there, just the wagons full of ties and plates and bolts which men threw out beside the track each time the train moved forward. The train was in a steep cut and I was forced to walk close beside it, so that when I reached the bunkhouse section I was conscious of men lounging in the open doorways of the coaches, staring down at me.

But nobody stopped me, and I went up past the engine and the rail transporters until at last I could see the steel-laying crane swinging with a length of rail. A whistle blew and the crane swung back, its claw empty. The train hooted and then moved forward a few yards. Another length of track had been laid.

There was something so fascinating about the rhythmic thrusting of this train into the unknown that for the moment I forgot everything else and climbed half-way up the side of the cut to watch it. Each time, before the train had stopped, the crane was already swinging, another length of steel balanced in its claw grip. A man stood signalling with his hands to the crane-driver and shouting instructions to the steel-laying gang, and as the rail came down on to the grade, they seized hold of it, thrusting it into place on the ties and spiking it there with the balanced swing of sledge-hammers.

This was Head of Steel and I stood and watched with a sort of awe. And then I saw the bare grade stretched out ahead, naked except for the few ties laid at regular intervals, and my gaze lifted to the black line of the jackpine. The yellow slash of the bulldozed grade ran into it and was abruptly swallowed.

from : Hammond Innes, *The Land God gave to Cain*

4 A visit to the coalface

England, nineteen-fifties

Suddenly we are plunging down at a dizzying, terrifying pace, into sheer, impossible blackness. Without my willing it my head jerks up, my eyes implore for the last sign of daylight. We appear to be dropping at a rate too fast to let us stop short of disaster. Sst. Sst. Dropping down, down and down, past seams whose lights blink at us several seconds after the cage has plunged past. Nobody in the cage speaks. I yawn to ease the pressure on my eardrums. I am stricken speechless. Then the cage slows and bounces to a stop, as precipitately as it was lowered. The folding metal gate is pushed back. I walk into the pit.

The first thing is the smell. Warm, oppressive, like a rank swamp into which cooking gas has seeped. We are standing in an enormous vault-like place, the walls curved and white-washed, bricked in. A small group of technicians and maintenance men squatting on a stone stage at a large black dynamo watch us. It's hot. I remove my jacket and carry it over my arm.

A well-lit, whitewashed tunnel leads down from the bottom of the cage head and we start walking along it . . .

We pass a large ventilator blowing out used air and the stench is powerful and putrid. Past the ventilator, I take a few breaths of air which only seconds before I had found heavy and offensive, and already it smells sweet and light to me.

This tunnel, well brightened, is twice as tall as me. I relax and begin to enjoy myself, observing, making mental notes. This isn't half so bad as I expected. It is, except for the artificial air which I cannot seem to get used to, fairly easy going ... There is a sharp decline and we are among several miners carrying tools. They are waiting to get into the paddy train, a string of small man-cars. Bolton, MacLane and I take a seat in one, facing the whitewashed wall. The operator, in the front car, rises and leans over to touch with a spatulate metal device the double strand of electrical wire which runs along the tunnel wall. A ring of bells and the string of tiny coaches sets off down hill.

Almost immediately the whitewash fades and is replaced by a greyish cement finish, and then bare rock, and we leave the lights behind and rattle into darkness. Along with the other men, I flick on the lamp hanging around my neck and adjust its beam. We seem to be bumping along each other's beams as we sweep into warm, hot, gritty air ...

We ride on for a long time. Then the paddy train slows up, the man in front leans out to touch the wires, the bells go off again, we stop. I get out with MacLane and Bolton. We pass miners totally un-recognisable, their faces black with coal dust. The tunnel becomes shallower. Walking and talking becomes more of an effort; it's not easy any more. We stop at the low-ceilinged intersection of several tunnels. Our voices do not echo; they carry but do not resound, like pebbles dropped into warm porridge, in and quickly covered over.

'Sleythorpe, Bolton?' asks MacLane.

'Sleythorpe,' says Bolton.

I dive into one of the tunnel roadways, after them, totally lost, bereft of compass points. This shaft too goes down, ever down, and is pitch dark. Miners coming up, picks on their shoulders, are illuminated by our torches and then disappear, mysterious black slow-moving pieces of sludge. Breathing comes harder.

Suddenly we are in an even lower tunnelway, dimly lit by far-spaced electric lamps in small wire cages. The walls on both sides consist of four to five feet of stone 'packing' built on each side of the road after the coal was removed. To walk is to walk stooped. I follow the sound of footsteps. After a hundred yards I find myself looking for the opening where I can straighten up again; instead, the tunnel narrows. This is the main highway for workers to get to the Sleythorpe seam, and it is necessary for us to walk doubled over completely. Sweat is pouring from me. I try to watch how MacLane and Bolton do it but can detect no discernible style. It seems to me they are racing ahead, stepping skilfully and surely between the wooden ties of the narrow-gauge tracks which constantly trip me up, and every time I stumble my head jerks up and slams my skull against the roof, sending my helmet either flying or jamming it painfully down over my ears. To avoid the tracks I adopt a kind of crouching, rolling gait, wasteful motion, but it helps me keep up.

Doubled over in the hot darkness, sweating, barely able to see my hand in front of my face, my ears humming with the depth (1800 feet plus what? I keep asking myself) and the ventilators and dynamos thrum, I stumble on. It seems hours since we left the luxury of the paddy train . . .

The several men nearest me, selected by our torches, are hacking away at the coal face, the wall of which seems to extend indefinitely in a sombre perspective composed of small teams of men, spaced several yards apart, working in a murky forest of steel and timber supports. This is the coal face, the work room. At no point is it higher than four feet nor wider than twelve. The men move about on knee-pads with the agility of war amputees. Their bodies are smeared with a mixture of sweat and coal dust, their faces are flat black except for the startling, almost accusatory, whites of their eyes which move about like captured moths in the dimness, and the unexpected sensuality of the redness of their lips and rims of their eyes. Every single one of them is naked except for a wide leather belt strapped across his waist from which hangs the box-like battery of his lamp and a strip of cloth . . .

The only way to work in this confined space is on the knees, and they are all on their knees. In teams of two and three they act in short, concentrated movements, one man with a pick, his mate shovelling away the loose coal into piles or on to the small conveyor belt which rolls on castors along the floor of the face. Most of this is normal long-wall coal-getting, with men in a long line working at the previously cut and blasted coal. The picks are used to hack down stubborn coal clinging to the 'cut' and the roof, but it is the shovel which is primarily used here; most of the men are shovelling very monotonously. In some of the other headings I heard pneumatic picks being used, but none here . . .

The thing that impresses me, again and again, down here at the face is the sinewy humour of these men. They are neither grim nor bitter nor angry. The point is, a visitor from the surface does feel all these things. These men are, however, tired; bone tired. You can see it in the way they start to work again, with pick and shovel; each man has his own little personal trick of conserving strength.

from : Clancy Sigal, *Weekend in Dimlock*

5 A modern coal mine

England, 1968

Note the neat surface buildings, the enclosed shafts, down one of which you drop smoothly by cage to the well-lit bottom. Take a paddy train along the narrowing roadways till you get within short walking and scrambling distance of the long wall face. As you are unaccustomed to mining conditions you find the noise at the face almost intolerable as most of the work is being done by machines. For example, there's the Trepanner, seventeen feet long, power-cutter-loader, gouging into the seam, and the armoured conveyor belts groaning as they shift the coal. All this in an enclosed space less than head-high. The dirt and heat and grit are there too, just as in the older pits. From time to time you see men with short-handled shovels clearing what the machine has missed. This mine is more mechanised than most. Even today, twenty out of every hundred tons of coal is got by hand-labour assisted by more primitive machines—heavy cramped work where the big machines haven't been able to go. Come back though, in a few years, and you may find that the machine has taken over, operated by remote control. There are likely to be only a handful of tough skilled men working below ground. The unproductive mines will all have been closed down.

A special contribution by N. Murray

6 Time and motion men in modern goldmines

Kalgoorlie, Western Australia

A hundred small companies have dwindled and amalgamated into four big ones . . .

At most of the mines they work ore containing only four pennyweight of gold per ton, or approximately one part in 170,000. The drives are hundreds or thousands of feet below the ground. You go down to them, fast, in a big cage. They can't fit as many miners into the cage as they could in Wales or Durham, for these are very big, burly men, full of incandescently obscene wit. Apart from the colour of the earth—it is a greyish-violet—you would think you were in a mechanised coal mine. There are the same long tunnels, rails on the floor, and trains of ore wagons being pulled about by small electric engines. The wagons are loaded by mechanical boggers, machines which scoop up the ore, raise the scoop back over themselves, and drop the load into the wagon behind. The only light is the round-rimmed beam from the lamp in your own helmet, or the irregular flash of another man's coming toward you. Flat plastic pipes slung along the roof line suck in fresh air to the roar of a Venturi nozzle.

Mechanisation does not reduce physical effort here, only changes its form. In the warm, humid atmosphere I watched big Frank Beccarelli, a machine minder, working at the face. He stood astride an air-leg drill, making holes where charges would later be placed. He had plugs in his ears, his teeth were set, sweat streamed down his forehead, his eyes glittered in the light from my lamp. The narrow space there at the head of the drive was like a cross between a boiler factory and a waterfall—Frank's drill stammered and shouted, the compressed air roared, a continuous jet of water went up the shaft of the drill to cool the bit, and poured out splashing at our feet.

At one mine they work a thick lode of even less valuable ore, not very far down, by hacking the whole lot out. This is not like a coal mine or a boiler factory, but an underground zoo, or an astrodome for bulldozer racing. Instead of single machine miners there are huge steel chariots drilling half a dozen holes into the roof simultaneously. Gigantic yellow transloaders growl and bellow at the piles of ore, and then roar backwards, lights glaring through the dust, to the unloading shaft. 'Keep close to the side,' our guide said. 'If you're wearing management's khaki overalls, they'll run you down.'. . .

In twenty years most men will get one or two 'dust tickets'—notations at the annual physical inspection, that their lungs have been affected by silicosis.

Above ground endless belts carry the ore through crushers, grinders, and roasters, gradually purifying it, until it reaches the final stage, the gold room. The gold room has barred doors and windows, and a large safe. The men working in it have worked for the company a long time, and they're all about six-foot-four and strong as cart horses. They move with unhurried steps as roaring oil-fired furnaces smelt the gold. They perform rites with steel trolleys, long tongs, conical buckets— the liquid pours out brilliant, blinding, slowly softens in colour until, before your eyes, it becomes gold.

After work, the pubs. Kalgoorlie has scores.

from : John Masters, 'Gold, camels and wise men, frankincense and myrrh', *The Daily Telegraph Magazine*, September 29, 1967

7 The large part played by luck

Australia

The mines are narrow vertical shafts dug down to the level where the opal is likely to be—usually between 12 and 80 feet. Each mine is the property of one man, a partnership, or a small syndicate. Sometimes there is a steel ladder. Sometimes the miner goes down in a bucket. There are no cages, no platmen, no books of safety precautions. All equipment is third-hand, patched, worn and rickety. The men work with daemonic energy for what they can find; for hope, not for salary . . .

Don's mine was 80 feet deep. I climbed down one night, the time when many miners work. The air in the shaft felt still and oppressive. The ladder was narrow, its rungs about 18 inches apart, made of several sections loosely wired together and somehow fastened to the side of the shaft. By half way I was cramped with terror. Don shouted up from below. 'Don't worry! You can't fall. There's nothing to stop you.' I got to the bottom trembling violently, my knuckles barked and earth in my hair.

There was the scene, just as Unlucky Miner had painted it—a low tunnel, boxes of explosives, wires, a few wavering lights. A little petrol engine put-putting on the surface to make 32 volt current for the lights and an electric drill. Another worked the winch. That was all the equipment. The staff consisted of a young navvy below and a winchman above.

The work is equally simple : drill holes; place charges in them; blow the charges; go home; come back tomorrow; load the debris you blew down yesterday into 12-gallon buckets; hoist it to the surface; drill holes . . .

It's simple, if you know where to drill the holes, or are born lucky. Everyone agrees that opal mining is 80 per cent luck, which is why as many amateurs as professionals strike it rich here. You also have to recognise the opal in the earth you've blown out, and make sure you don't miss it, or spoil it with your pick and shovel. And you have to be able to make it up the swaying, clanking 80-foot ladder to the surface in two minutes every night, from the time you light the fuse. Then the charges go off.

from : 'Opal mining in Australia,' *The Daily Telegraph Magazine*

8 The navvy age: hand-made railways

England, eighteen-forties

Thomas Eaton was one of the 1,100 navvies who made a railway tunnel three miles long through the Pennines. It took six years, from 1839 to 1845. No one kept an exact count of how many men died blasting through the millstone, or how many were buried by sudden falls of sandstone, or tipped out of a swaying bucket half-way up a 600-foot air shaft. But Eaton knew for sure that at least thirty-two men had died in one way or another, and the surgeon, whom he had got to know well seeing so much of him, said another 140 had been badly hurt. In the end things got so rough at the tunnel that Eaton could stand it no longer, and he left in the early winter of 1845, just before it was finished. The year after, he was one of the navvies who went to Westminster to give evidence before the Commons committee which was enquiring into the evils of the railway works . . .

In 1845 there were 200,000 men like Eaton working on about 3,000 miles of new line. In the eighty years from 1822 onwards, millions of navvies made 20,000 miles of railways in Britain, and thousands of miles more in Europe and the rest of the world.

The nineteenth century is not only the railway age but also the age of the navvy. The railway brought cheap, fast travel, encouraged commerce and ideas, and did a lot to create Britain's national prosperity and international ascendancy. But the railway was made by navvies, not by machines. A piece of engineering like the Great Western Railway from London to Bristol—known as Brunel's billiard table because the mean gradient is 1 in 1,380—was built with picks, shovels and gunpowder.

from : Terry Coleman, *The Railway Navvies*

9 Railway construction, 1968

London, England

Weary, damp and smothered in blue clay, five Irishmen, each with a fistful of £5 notes, popped out of a 75-foot-deep hole near the doorstep of the 'local' last night for a last pint before closing-time.

They are part of a band of 'human moles' who are digging a section of London's new Victoria Line extension from Victoria to Vauxhall and are due to start the most complex part of the tunnels under the Thames any time now.

Their nightly end-of-shift short-cut in the silence of the near-completed twin tunnels deep under Pimlico to their favourite public house near the Embankment takes them 15 minutes.

When the tube extension opens in 1972, automatic, silver trains will carry millions of office workers over this stretch of line in something like 90 seconds. But most of the white-collar workers will be earning less than one-fifth of the pay of this tough band of specialists who have made tunnelling their trade.

Only the strongest men can do the job, which frequently involves long hours underground, often in compressed air sections, wallowing in heavy clay and damp. As a result the 'mole men' are in short supply and take home pay packets of from £50 to £100 a week, or even more.

There are some 400 tunnel-diggers in the country and at the peak of work on the new line from Walthamstow to Victoria, coming into operation this autumn and in early 1969, some 300 were digging 60 feet and 70 feet below the streets of London.

Most of them are Irishmen.

In the shops and the public houses near Bessborough Gardens, at the south end of Vauxhall Bridge Road, the tills ring with the cash of the miners who have become among the highest paid manual workers in the country.

Most of the men can afford to be big spenders. Several I met admitted they spent up to £20 a week on drink, smoking and racing. But, they pointed out, that left plenty to send home to the family in Ireland . . .

Many have new cars they use for travelling to work or for touring during their days off. Others stack the money away for a 'rainy day', but most have not been out of work for years . . .

The men work strictly on a piece-rate basis and are paid by the footage of tunnel they complete in a shift which can be either eight or twelve hours. They work in gangs which compete to make the most money in a five-shift week . . .

Special shields protect the miners when they are tunnelling with fast-operating digging machines under normal circumstances. But much of the work under the Thames will be hand-tunnelling.

These last few words from the engineers in charge made up my mind that the 'human moles' earn, and are welcome to, every penny of those fat wage packets.

from : J. Mossman, 'Thames tunnellers and their reward',
The Daily Telegraph, June 7, 1968

10 Open hearths in Pittsburgh

U.S.A., nineteen-sixties

Not surprisingly, the greatest sight in Pittsburgh is her steel mills. Wearing a steel helmet, I entered a gallery of the open hearths with which Jones and Laughlin has replaced its old Bessemers. Rows of furnaces gave off blinding white light and roared like a hurricane. Screaming sirens cleared the way for overhead cranes, their loading hooks and magnets swaying like trunks and moving with elephantine deliberation. To protect my eyes I was given purple cobalt spectacles which turned everything to violet. Through these glasses my guide, a company press officer, determined by its colour the temperature of the metal inside—3,300 degrees Fahrenheit. The climax of a visit is the tapping, a spectacle familiar to television visitors of the U.S. Steel Hour; a steady-nerved visitor is occasionally invited to throw the firing key. Workmen in aluminiumized suits, silhouetted in the brightness like outer spacemen, took a sample of the incandescent liquid, like a housewife testing a cake in the oven. Then they put the *bazooka*, or jet-tapper, into place, a signal whistle blew and I pressed the key.

Whoosh! I was surrounded by a great explosion, as if I'd been caught inside a volcano. Fiery liquid spurted into a giant ladle, accompanied by the most marvellous fireworks I'd ever seen. Luminous metal cascaded like a fountain and spattered around us in a waterfall of stars coloured rose, orchid, purple. The molten metal swirled and churned in the 280-ton ladle like hot pink milk and the overflow gathered in glowing magenta lakes around its smoking base.

From the black ladle the metal was 'teemed'—poured—into ingot moulds by a muscular Negro named Jimmy Whyle, who my guide said 'Is the best steel pourer in the business and the best bartender at steelmen's parties.' We followed the ingots to the yards outside, where they would remain red for three or four hours, and then went on the 'blooming mill' where other ingots were reheated to a uniform temperature and, with great thunder and clatter, rolled and manipulated into shining ribbons of steel flying through space like silver demons. In two hours I had seen metal changed from ore to finished sheets and rolls, I emerged like a salamander from a shattering inferno.

from : Herbert Kubly, *At Large*

11 Disaster in the early days of iron making

South Wales, early nineteenth century

And Furnace Five split under blast.

With a shudder and a roar it split further, and we sat crouching at the table as fire leaped at the windows and iron rattled in drips on the roof. Transfixed, we sat, and Mari's feet drummed on the stairs and the door burst open and she stood there, shocked white and trembling.

'In the name of God what was that?' she whispered.

'A split,' I cried, and ran from the house, pulling my coat over my shoulders. The hollow was a bee-hive, with men running and others coming in from the tram roads, and crowds were already pressing around Furnace Five where my father was on shift. Women and children were screaming, men shouting commands, and a pump was already manned and buckets of water being passed down the line. Shanco Mathews came face to face with me, his hair smoking.

'Where is my father?' I cried.

'Three men are in the puddling shed,' he shouted. 'For God's sake fetch the Agent.'

'Away out of it!' I pulled him aside, but he tripped me, sending me sprawling. Up then, and I had two others down before I barged headlong through the men.

'Come back you fool!' shouted Caradoc Owen. 'She is split and will topple any minute.'

Free of them. I stripped off my coat and wound it around my head and shoulders and stumbled into the heat of the furnace. It was going like a pillar of fire, burning in quick, noisy flares that licked at the base of the cylinder and puffed up in balls of flame to the lip of the flue. Smoke was exploding in mushrooms from the wrecked puddling-house, weaving around the shattered roof and condensing in shafts of steam. Splintered timbers projected from the ruins where the roof slanted drunkenly, and beneath the roof a man was screaming, his voice as shrill as a child's, in short staccato cries, catching his breath to the torture of the scalding. The sand moulds were overflowing and the molten iron was running in little rivers of flame. The choked furnace was under pressure again, bellowing at the blocked shaft. Leaping past it I jumped the moulds and reached the door of the puddling house. The charred wood, shut by the blast of the split, went down like paper when I charged it, and I fell flat, gasping. It was strangely cool here away from the furnace, but the timber in the walls was coming alight as the glowing fingers of iron moved in. The man was no longer screaming, for the water in the steaming pits had dried, but I heard a low sighing that came from the overturned cauldrons where the metal was cooling on the floor. In darkness I stumbled forward, hands groping. Tripping over fallen beams and scattered ladles I lurched towards the sighing, and my path was lighted by the burning walls as the hot iron took them into a bonfire.

"Dada!" I cried.

No answer and the piled wreckage about me made shape in redness. The centre wall was down and with it the puddling flues, and the cauldrons that tapped from the furnace direct were on their sides or upside down. Ladles and tools were lying as the men had flung them, coats and gloves and eye shades were scattered about. Looking through the torn roof I saw the stars and racing white clouds sweeping over the moon.

...A man's face I saw then, in profile at my feet, burned black; a face of marble, drawn clean against the sooted walls of the house, and I knelt touching it. The flesh of the cheekbone was hot on one side. The other was melted into streams and the tips of my fingers touched jaw and teeth. Dead, this man, by iron scalding. Dead—but the ladle was still in his hand, gripped like a shepherd's crook. Dead with his legs and hips in the puddling cauldron, rigid to the waist where the forty gallons had caught him in its arms of molten iron, and cooling, gripped him.

'Blood of Christ,' said Shanco. 'Barney Kerrigan,' and he turned away his face.

Sickened, I raised myself, wondering what I would find for a father. The walls were well alight now, and the wind was sucking out the smoke in gusts through the roof.

'Over here,' cried Shanco, hopping.

'Iestyn,' said my father.

Under the arch of the furnace we found him; one leg and one arm thrusting out from the heaped bricks of the firebox lining, and the rest of him buried but safe from the iron.

'Iestyn,' he said and his voice echoed strong in his tomb.

'Dada!' I cried, and we went on to our knees and heaved the beams and bricks aside as men came flooding through the entrance.

'Faster!' I called to Shanco.

'Watch the wall!' cried the Agent, but I saw no wall. Only my father I saw, his buttocks arching as the weight of the wall was raised, and I heard no sounds but his gasping. A dozen men were working now, spitting, coughing, cursing in the smoke. The walls were roaring with flame as we pulled the last beam up and dragged him clear.

'Easy, for Christ's sake!' I whispered, but I knew we were too late ...

'Good little man,' I said, and kissed him.

'Eh, dear.'

I got up then, blinded, pushing them all aside. Steam was rising and the walls were smoking under the buckets. Through an avenue of men I walked, seeing nothing, until I came to the entrance where the women were waiting. My mother was before me suddenly, with Mari and Morfydd standing either side, and women were sobbing, but no sound came from mine. I raised my face.

'Finished, is he, Iestyn?'

'Aye Mama,' I said.

'In peace now my boy?' Her fingers screwed at her apron. I nodded choking.

The wind whispered between us then, bringing smoke. My mother lowered her face and clenched her hands, and weeping, said :

'Oh Hywel, my dearest one, my precious.'

I went from them shivering, cold.

from : Alexander Cordell, *The Rape of the Fair Country*

12 Creativity in steel making

England

In spite of the exhausting conditions steel making had a very attractive side. To the first-hand smelter there was great satisfaction as he watched the metal stream from his furnace into the waiting ladle. He had an awareness of creation; seven or eight hours previously this surging white-hot liquid had been one hundred tons of solid limestone, steel scrap, and hot iron. He had controlled the huge flame which played over the metal, saw that it did its work and that it didn't damage the furnace's brick roof or linings. Hour after hour he had tended it, watched for every change in the liquid, increased the slag contents with more lime, or thinned it out with iron ore. His junior smelters were every bit as interested as he was.

... At times, especially on the nightshift, I thrilled at the sight of it all. There was drama in the bright-lit noisy smelting shop, and the sweating men. It was there too when I looked across at the rolling mills and saw the bright ingots, fresh from the soaking pits, crunch in the rolls of the cogging mill. I'd tell myself that I had helped to make these ingots and I would watch the strip grow longer and longer, from bright heat to dull red, and I would listen for the swish of the saw as it cut through them like butter.

But an hour or so afterwards, when the sweat was pouring from me, and I was lashing manganese into a streaming ladle at 28 pounds a shovelful, then it was different. With my sweat towel covering my face to the eyes, to save me from scorching, and the dust of the manganese building a solid wall in my lungs, I saw little drama in steel making at all. I'd be asking myself what had gone wrong in my living that I should be there, while out in the world the bright clean clever men were asleep...

Instrumentation and progress in furnace building have bettered conditions and since this is so and the old skills are still necessary it is an even more interesting job as a result, and the smelters of today with their fair educational background should make the best of both worlds.

from : Patrick McGeown, *Heat the Furnace Seven Times More*

13 Woman steel worker

China

We go up a slippery track to the blast-furnace that looms black and enormous above us, a steady stream of molten iron flowing in an apparently casual fashion into moulds. As we mount we meet the first rush of hot air that comes from an intake where the naked fire is showing. Young workers are busy with shovels and sand near the aperture, all giving a picture of casualness as if in contempt of the giant that looms above them with such a potentiality for destruction.

We mount the steps, dodging a spray of water, one straying drop of which tells us its boiling temperature, into the control-room, where an attempt is made to explain a bewildering array of instruments...

A girl comes towards us buttoning her faded blue denim tunic that shows a striped shirt underneath. She is not more than four-foot-ten and less than seven stone and her heavy boots look disproportionately large. I imagine she is the secretary of the director I have come to see...

She speaks quickly, 'When I came my idea was to get a job in the chemical department. But there was nothing there and the manager said, "Well there are a number of other vacancies. Choose what you like."

'I chose the blast-furnace. Why I am not very clear.

'Everything about the steel works terrified me at the beginning; the noise, the heat, the danger. I was assigned to the planning section. I became fascinated with the processes and had a great desire to work on the furnace itself. So I did a special course in smelting and when I was successful at it was assigned to the blast-furnace and took over the job.'

from : Dymphna Cusack, *Chinese Women Speak*

14 Car building: birth of the assembly line

Detroit, U.S.A., circa 1913

The manufacturers of automobiles were confronting a problem. The more men they had working, the more time these men wasted moving from one job to the next, and getting into one another's way. At General Motors somebody had a bright idea—instead of sending the man to the work, why not bring the work to the man?

They began trying experiments; and very soon Henry's scouts told him about it. He couldn't afford to be left behind, so he tried it too. The work of assembling the flywheel magneto, a small but complex part, was put on a sliding table, just high enough to be convenient for the workers, who sat on stools, each performing one operation upon a line of magnetos which crept slowly by. In the old way, a man doing the work of making a magneto could turn out one every twenty minutes; now the work was cut into twenty-nine operations, performed by twenty-nine different men, and the time per magneto was thirteen minutes and ten seconds. It was a revolution.

They applied it to the making of a motor. Done by one man, it had taken nine hours and fifty-four minutes. When the assembling was divided among eighty-four different men, the time for a motor was cut by more than forty per cent.

Early in 1913 this revolution hit Abner Shutt, sub-foreman of spindle-nut screwing. One sunshiny morning he was ordered out to 'John R. Street', which runs through the Highland Park plant, to take part in an experiment in assembling a chassis, which is the car with its wheels before the body is put on. They had a platform on wheels, and a rope two hundred and fifty feet long, with a windlass to draw it. The materials to be used had been placed in piles along the route, and six assemblers were to travel with the platform and put a chassis together on the way, while men with stopwatches and note-books kept record of every second it took them.

By the old method of building a car on one spot like a house, it had taken twelve hours and twenty-eight minutes of labour to assemble one chassis. By this new crude experiment they cut the time more than half. So very soon they set to work to rip out large sections of the plant and build them over. A moving platform was installed, and the various parts of the chassis came to it either on hooks hanging from chains, or on small motor-trucks travelling up the aisles. Presently they raised the line to waist-height, and before long they had two lines, one for tall men and one for short.

A far cry from the days when Abner Shutt had travelled to the shed and rolled in two wheels by hand, and sorted out right spindle-nuts from lefts and screwed them himself. Now he oversaw a group

397

of men whose every motion had been calculated by engineers. The completed wheels, product of an assembly line of their own, came on rows of hooks, and descended to exactly the right height to be lifted off and slid on to the axle.

The man who did this did nothing else; another man put on the spindle nuts and started them by hand; still others finished the job with a wrench. Before the engineers got through with studying those operations, they had cut the time of assembling a chassis from twelve hours and twenty-eight minutes to one hour and thirty-three minutes.

Once this process was established, the irresistible tendency was to increase the speed of the "belt". Henry Ford might insist, as he continually did, that competition was wrong, and that he did not believe in it; but the fact was that he was competing at every moment of his life, and would continue to do so as long as he made motor-cars. In a hundred different plants scattered over the United States efforts were being made to beat him. In the long run, the successful ones would be those who contrived, by one method or another, to get the most out of a dollar's worth of labour. This was true from the first motion of the first hand which dug iron ore or collected the juice of rubber-plants in tropical jungles.

There was always a clamour from the sales departments for more cars. When the plant was turning out a thousand a day, those who had the job in hand knew that by increasing the speed of the assembly line one minute in an hour, they would get sixteen more cars that day. Why not try it? A couple of weeks later, after the workers on the line had accustomed themselves to the faster motions, why not try it again?

Never had there been such a device for speeding up labour. You simply moved a switch, and a thousand men jumped more quickly. It was an invisible tax, like the tariff, which the consumer pays without being aware of it. The worker cannot hold a stop-watch, and count the number of cars which come to him in an hour. Even if he learns about it from the man who sets the speed of the belt,—again it is like the tariff in that he can do nothing about it. If he is a weakling, there are a dozen strong men waiting outside to take his place. Shut your mouth and do what you're told!

from : Upton Sinclair, *The Flivver King*

15 Home industry: moving band

Japan, nineteen-sixties

In Gifu they make three things that children the world over associate with Japan : Japanese lanterns, fans and parasols. And they are all made by hand, by children's hands, women's hands, the wrinkled gnarled hands of old men and women. Every home in the town has things to cut out, glue, sew, pack or varnish, and this is all done within its four paper walls, while the family's rice cooks on the hearth and the baby is given the trimmings to play with, so that it can acquire the feel of the material.

If you want to see a whole parasol made, you must follow it from house to house, for each family has its special job : one splits bamboos to make the ribs, another cuts handles, a third makes the little black knobs for the end of the sticks, which are made in yet another place. The paper covering is cut in one place, oiled in another, glued, painted and adorned with flowers, butterflies, waterfalls and Fujiyama in still others. Every parasol requires the services of twenty or thirty specialists in as many homes. The streets of Gifu are like an everlasting conveyor belt, along which parasols in every stage move from house to house. On days when the sun is shining and the paper walls have been pushed aside, you can literally watch every step in the parasol's manufacture as you walk along.

from : Hakon Mielche, *Portrait of Japan*

16 Factory on the tea estate

Himalaya

The pluckers come in from up and down the lanes leading to the factory. I like all the colours of the head-shawls getting together with the pale attractive colour of the baskets and the bright leaf piled inside them. The coolies stop and take out a handful of leaf to show to W. They are proud of their work. Several of the women are champion pluckers and can pluck as much as one hundred to one hundred and twenty pounds a day of Assam leaf and fifty pounds of China.

When the leaf has been weighed, and the coolies paid a price per pound for anything they have plucked above the agreed amount, it is taken upstairs and the baskets emptied on the withering shelves and spread on their tiers to wither. Now the coolies are free to go . . .

They go away to their villages, smoking and laughing and talking through the late afternoon; and soon, in every hut, the smoke goes up and the cows are brought out and milked, the goats and chickens are fed, and the pumpkins are turned on the roof. Soon the firelight shines on gold skins and gold nose-rings, and turns the red-leeped walls to a deeper mixture of red and gold.

The leaf takes eighteen hours to wither; if it is very wet the hot air is turned on and swept by fans through the rooms. Withering leaf has a peculiar heavy rank smell. When it is ready, it is dropped down shutes in the floor to the rolling machines that roll it round and round to break the cells and give the necessary twist to the tea-leaf.

After that it is fermented on concrete slabs in a cool room, until it is the colour of tobacco; the coarser leaf goes back to be rolled again; it is separated on the jigger, a machine with wire-mesh trays that jiggles the finer leaf through.

Then it is fired. It is put on machines shaped like tanks and drawn backwards on caterpillar rollers into a cavern of hot air that rises from the furnaces; here are stokers and furnace doors clanging and a red-hot light across the floor. After twenty minutes' creeping in the inside of the machine the leaf falls out into troughs on the floor, the straight black tea we know.

It is not finished yet. Odorous and hot, it is scooped up with a shovel by boys and wheeled away in barrows. It is not quite cooked; if you crush it in your hand it feels spongy and it goes into a smaller fiercer cooker. Then it is cleaned, graded, sorted, and packed. This is all done by hand except that a gigantic jigger is used and the tea falls out on different sides in its different grades.

There are women sitting on the floor with flat scoop-shaped wicker trays sorting, sifting with a side-to-side motion that is skilful and impossible to copy; they can sift all the different sorts of tea to different sides of their trays without ever touching it with their fingers, they can toss an entire tray of tea to another on the floor two yards away in one flash of movement without spilling a leaf.

The colours are beautiful : the women sitting on the gold wood floor, the dirty colours of their working clothes—dull blue, mulberry, dull yellow, and the green bronze grasses they make into sweeping brooms, and the piles of black tea.

W. shows us some Flowery Orange Pekoe; some of its leaves are really gold.

W. 'You couldn't buy that for ten or twelve shillings [50p–60p] a pound.'

We see the leaf rushing down the valley from Rungjeli in sacks on the ropeway; we see the pack-ponies string in from Chinglam; we see the Munchi delving with his stick in the baskets to make sure there are no stones put in to cheat the weight. We see the day's production being weighed, black and redolent, in deep-sided wooden boxes that the boys wheel up on trucks.

The boxes are made in the factory since the war*; before, they were imported in pieces from Scandinavia and built in the workshops. When they are packed and shut and stencilled they go by pack-pony to the station in the forest to catch the little Himalaya train.

from : Rumer Godden, *Thus Far and no Further*

17 Why shouldn't a worker think?

General

As for the workman you are worrying about—let him think! Why shouldn't he? But not about where he put his hammer the day before; he ought to be thinking creatively, for instance about the complete elimination of manual labour and the transition to complete automation. Let him study the ultimate mysteries of his trade. Let him turn into a savant.

from : Vladimir Dudintsev, *Not by Bread Alone*

18 The machine shop

England, nineteen-fifties

The bright Monday-morning ring of the clocking-in machine made a jarring note, different from the tune that played inside Arthur. It was dead on half past seven. Once in the shop he allowed himself to be swallowed by its diverse noises, walked along lanes of capstan lathes and millers, drills and polishers and hand-presses, worked by a multiplicity of belts and pulleys turning and twisting and slapping on heavy well-oiled wheels overhead, dependent for power on a motor stopping at the far end of the halt like the black shining bulk of a stranded whale. Machines with their own small motors started with a jerk and a whine under the shadows of their operators, increasing a noise that made the brain reel and ache because the weekend had been too tranquil by contrast, a week-end that had terminated for Arthur in fishing for trout in the cool shade of a willow-sleeved canal near the Balloon Houses, miles away from the city. Motor-trolleys moved up and down

* World War II, 1939-45

the main gangways carrying boxes of work—pedals, hubs, nuts and bolts—from one part of the shop to another. Robboe the foreman bent over a stack of new time-sheets behind his glass partition; women and girls wearing turbans and hair nets and men and boys in clean blue overalls, settled down to their work, eager to get a good start on their day's stint; while sweepers and cleaners at everybody's beck and call already patrolled the gangways and looked busy.

Arthur reached his capstan lathe and took off his jacket, hanging it on a nearby nail so that he could keep an eye on his belongings. He pressed the starter button, and his motor came to life with a gentle thump. Looking around, it did not seem, despite the infernal noise of hurrying machinery, that anyone was working with particular speed. He smiled to himself and picked up a glittering steel cylinder from the top box of a pile beside him, and fixed it into the spindle. He jettisoned his cigarette into the sud-pan, drew back the capstan, and swung his turret on to its broadest drill. Two minutes passed while he contemplated the precise position of tools and cylinder; finally he spat on to both hands and rubbed them together, then switched on the sud-tap from the movable brass pipe, pressed a button that set the spindle running, and ran in the drill to a neat chamfer. Monday morning had lost its terror.

At a piecework rate of four-and-six [$22\frac{1}{2}$p] a hundred you could make your money if you knocked-up fourteen hundred a day—possible without grabbing too much—and if you went all out for a thousand in the morning you could dawdle through the afternoon and lark about with the women and talk to your mates now and again . . .

The minute you stepped out of the factory gates you thought no more about your work. But the funniest thing was that neither did you think about work when you were standing at your machine. You began the day by cutting and drilling steel cylinders with care, but gradually your actions became automatic and you forgot all about the machine and the quick working of your arms and hands and the fact that you were cutting and boring and rough-threading to within limits of only five-thousandths of an inch. The noise of motor-trolleys passing up and down the gangway and the excruciating din of flying and flapping belts slipped out of your consciousness after perhaps half an hour, without affecting the quality of the work you were turning out, and you forgot your past conflicts with the gaffer and turned to thinking of pleasant events that had at some time happened to you, or things that you hoped would happen to you in the future. If your machine was working well—the motor smooth, stops tight, jigs good—and you spring your actions into a favourable rhythm you became happy. You went off into pipedreams for the rest of the day . . .

It was marvellous the things you remembered while you worked on the lathe, things that you thought were forgotten and would never come back into your mind, often things that you hoped would stay forgotten. Time flew while you wore out the oil-soaked floor and worked furiously without knowing it : you lived in a compatible world of pictures that passed through your mind like a magic-lantern, often in vivid and glorious loony-colour, a world where memory and imagination ran free and did acrobatic tricks with your past and with what might be your future, an amok that produced all sorts of agreeable visions.

from : A. Sillitoe, *Saturday Night and Sunday Morning*

19 What's it all for?

England, 1969

The factory was on the industrial estate, built about 10 years ago when the collieries closed down. A white-coated young man met the girls—a dozen of them, all leavers—and myself, and we followed him into the factory.

'This', said the young man proudly, 'is one of the latest electronically controlled salt and pepper pot top moulding machines.' We watched dutifully as the steel strip went in at one end, the lights lit, the presses pressed, and the salt and pepper pot tops rolled out at the other end. The girls were not particularly impressed by this technological marvel, and were relieved when we continued past the automatic tea-vending machine (which did interest them) and into the assembly section. Two long tables faced each other. At one of them eight girls were putting powder compacts into boxes. They speeded up when they became aware of us watching them, but otherwise gave no sign of greeting. Another eight girls sat putting hinges into the powder compacts.

As we walked on past the presses, the chemical baths, the enamelling section, the varnish sprays, the polishing department, we saw about three dozen girls all told, mainly under 20, and some barely out of school themselves. I shall always remember the polishing machines. They droned noisily behind their metallic casings and each one had a large hole with a stool in front of it.

On each stool sat a girl with a box of unpolished compact lids by her left hand. The circular revolving table turned at a steady speed as each girl fed the rotating spindles with lids, which then passed into the hole, emerged gleaming, and were deftly removed by the girl, who put them in a box by her right hand. Layer by layer, the one box emptied and the other filled.

The noise seemed to grow louder as we stood there. Conversation was impossible. Afterwards, I asked the young man how long girls do this isolated and monotonous job. He seemed surprised : 'They do it all day—with two tea breaks.'

When we left the girls seemed to be relieved to be outside even though it was drizzling. As we walked along, I remembered the past four years. The girls aren't angels, nor are they particularly bright. But at least they'd done something at school. We had tried to arouse their interests in life, open up their minds and expand their horizons a little.

Many of these girls have little option but to go to a factory like the one we visited. It seems a criminal waste of ability on the part of industry that it makes such degrading demands on girls in particular. Every day since that wet Tuesday I have felt uneasy when I see those girls in school. 'What's it all for?' I ask myself.

from : John Carlin, 'With two tea breaks and all',
The Times Educational Supplement, October 31, 1969

20 Creative work and the machines

General

But it may be said, why not retain the machines *and* retain 'creative work'? Why not cultivate anachronisms as a spare-time hobby? Many people have played with this idea; it seems to solve with such beautiful ease the problems set by the machine. The citizen of Utopia, we are told, coming home from his daily two hours of turning a handle in the tomato-canning factory, will deliberately revert to a more primitive way of life and solace his creative instincts with a bit of fretwork, pottery-glazing, or handloom-weaving. And why is this picture an absurdity—as it is, of course? Because of a principle that is not always recognized, though always acted upon : that so long as the machine is *there*, one is under an obligation to use it. No one draws water from the well when he can turn on the tap.

from : George Orwell, *The Road to Wigan Pier*

21 Crop dusting by air

Australia

After a quick, purposeful reconnaissance of the paddock along the hill-side on the far side of the highway, looking for power-lines and skeletons of dead trees which could blend into dangerous anonymity against the hill, Sandy had side-slipped back down on to the operating strip and the day's work had begun. Chris and the Dutchman had worked well together. As soon as Sandy had taken off, loaded, on his six-minute round trip to the hill-side and back again, Chris would drive the front-end loader in towards the trailer where the Dutchman would slash open, in quick succession, four or five 122 pound bags and tip the fertiliser into the waiting maw of the loader. By the time Chris had backed away, ready for loading, Sandy would be side-slipping and fish-tailing down on to the strip again. As he finished his landing run at the designated loading point—a nice test of skill in an aircraft without brakes—the Dutchman would walk the aircraft to a halt with a grip on the port wing-tip, climb up on to the step of the port wing and flick open the catch of the fairing over the hopper in the front cockpit as Chris drove in towards the aircraft and lowered the loader-head over the open hopper. Simultaneously, Sandy would have produced a neatly folded plastic bag from inside his flying suit and drawn it over his helmeted head while the dust from the super pouring in to the hopper ahead of him blew back on the slip-stream. Bang shut would go the fairing on the hopper. Down would jump the Dutchman. Out would back Chris. Away would go Sandy on another six-minute haul over the undulating spurs of the hill-side paddock behind the quiet homestead. Six minutes later, the cycle would be repeated. Except for morning scones and tea, brought a mile from the homestead, which Sandy gulped down with his engine running, the work went on all morning. Lunch had been stew, potatoes, turnips and pudding, again brought over from the homestead. A solid, chunky farmer's meal eaten where you cared to stand or sit while the wind hummed through the rigging wires of the near-by Tiger and all hands kept an anxious eye on the weather.

Early in the afternoon, rain had come driving in from Bass Strait and Sandy had had to stay on the ground until the visibility improved and the turbulence ceased. Contour-flying up and over the spurs was tricky enough without having to fly against the weather, too. A farmer from a neighbouring property, meanwhile had bumped across to the strip and, in a shouted conversation with Sandy as he waited impatiently to take-off, had told him that he had a few tons of super just arrived at the railway station and could Agriavia spread that for him? Sandy had quickly calculated the hours left in the day, divided them by the tons of super to be spread, nodded in agreement, told the farmer to give Chris a quick map of his paddock and taken off again to finish the hill-side job. Later he had regretted this. Intermittent rain-squalls had reduced the available flying time during the afternoon and he had to fly hard to finish the second job before sunset. He had had the sense, though, to pause for a break when afternoon tea arrived in the back of a utility from the hill-side property. Cake, sausage-rolls, scones, and hot, sweet tea. It was black, strong tea he needed more than anything else to combat the fatigue he felt creeping upon him.

It was dark by the time both jobs were done and the pile of empty paper bags, that had held the superphosphate now spread on the hill-side and the low flats towards the coast, had burned like a bright funeral pyre as he and Chris had parked and refuelled the Tiger in the corner near the haystack. Once again they had raised the crude but efficient cattle-barrier and Sandy had been too tired to care when he cut his hand on a barb. He had almost fallen asleep in the jolting, uncomfortable bucket-seat as Chris had driven back to the hotel. After a shower and a meal, Sandy had fallen asleep by the fire with a Scotch-and-water untouched in his hand, and it had taken all his will power to change into pyjamas before he climbed into bed. He had refused another drink with young Chris. 'Grog kills more pilots than power-lines,' he'd grunted, 'See you at six.'

from : Geoff Taylor, *The Crop Dusters*

22 Striking oil

Canada

I don't know who noticed it first—the change in the note of the draw works' diesel. It penetrated to my mind as something different, a slowing up, a stickiness that deepened the note of the engine. Boy shouted something and then Garry's voice thundered out : 'The mud pump—quick !' His body was across the platform in a flash. Don and I had jumped to our feet, but we stood there, dazed, not knowing what was happening or what had to be done. 'Get the hell off that platform,' Garry shouted up to us. 'Run, you fools ! Run for your lives !'

I heard Boy say, 'God ! We've struck it !' and then we collided in a mad scramble for the ladder. As I reached it I caught a glimpse of the travelling block out of the tail of my eye. The wire hawsers that held it suspended from the crown block were slack, and the grief stem was slowly rising, pushing it upwards. Then I was down the ladder

406

and jumping for the ground, running blindly, not knowing what to expect, following the flying figures of my companions. The ground became boggy. It squelched under my feet. Then water splashed in my face and I stopped, thinking we'd reached the stream. The others had stopped, too. They were standing, staring back at the rig.

The grief stem was lifted right up to the crown block now. It was held there for a moment and then with a rending and tearing of steel it thrust the rig up clear of the ground. Then the stem bent over. The rig toppled and came crashing to the ground. The draw works, suddenly freed of their load, raced madly with a clattering cacophony of sound. And then in brilliant moonlight that gave the whole thing an air of unreality we watched the pipe seemingly squeezed out of the ground like toothpaste out of a tube.

It was like that for a moment, a great snake of piping, turning and twisting upwards and then with a roar like a hundred express trains it was blown clear. 'Garry! Garry!' Boy's voice sounded thin against the roar of the gas flare.

We splashed back towards the rig, searching for him. The light was lurid and uncertain. We stumbled against pieces of machinery, the scrap-heap of the rig. 'Garry!'

A shape loomed out of the darkness. A hand gripped mine. 'Well, we struck it.' It was Garry and his voice trembled slightly.

I'd been too dazed to consider the cause of the disaster. I still couldn't believe it. 'You mean we've struck oil?'

'Well, we've struck gas. There'll be oil down there, too, I guess.'

'It hasn't done your rig much good,' I said. I don't know why but I couldn't think of anything else to say. It was all too sudden, too unreal.

'Oh, to hell with the rig.' He laughed. It was a queer sound, violent and trembling and rather high-pitched against the solid roar of the gas. 'We've done what we came up here to do. We've proved there's oil down there. And we've done it in time'...

from : Hammond Innes, *Campbell's Kingdom*

23 On an oil rig in the North Sea

North Sea, 1966

To drill a hole in the bed of the North Sea you start by putting down a wide steel pipe. You hammer it into the bottom and send a diver to bolster it with sandbags. The top of the pipe rises some 30 feet above the sea. You pump the water out of it and then insert your drill.

For weeks, or possibly months or even years, you drill downwards, the flexible shaft snaking through the rock strata. It may go as much as 18 degrees away from a straight line. The bottom of the hole may be half a mile from directly under your feet. All the way down you line it with concrete.

At a depth of about one and a half miles you will, if you are lucky, strike a pocket of methane gas, the residue of plants and animals which flourished 260 million years ago. The gas, held under pressure by rocks, comes hissing up as from a punctured tyre. You analyse it and measure the flow. Then you plug the hole with concrete against the day when it will be connected to the mainland, 60 miles away, by pipe.

One of the dozen or so drilling rigs operating in the rush to exploit the North Sea is the Gas Council's Mr. Louie, a ponderous contraption of 7,000 tons. Five tugs pull her around. When she reaches a drilling site she lowers 12 legs so she can stand on the sea bed a hundred feet below. Even so, in rough weather she can shake enough to make people seasick.

... Everyone in Mr. Louie works like mad, the machinery roaring for 24 hours a day. She costs £5,000 a day to operate. For the actual drilling there are three shifts of 11 men, two of them working flat out for 12 hours a day and the third away on a week's leave. Supervisors, geologists, electricians, engineers and catering staff bring the total on the rig at any one time to about 40.

There is not much to do except work and eat. Four meat meals, served up at six-hourly intervals, punctuate the routine. Muse* sitting at table with everyone else. To manhandle steel drillpipes 90 feet long for 12 hours a day for a fortnight is exhausting. With their vast steaks and eight different kinds of vegetables, cooked in a mixture of American, British and German styles, the men swill down gallons of milk. They get no alcohol. The few who don't like milk get evil-looking fruit juices coloured mauve and fortified with vitamins. There are 23 different kinds of sauce and pickle on the table. The catering staff, whose sparkling cleanliness makes them look like different beings from the greasy drillers, work as hard as anyone ...

The atmosphere is friendly and egalitarian; Muse has just 'Bill' on his safety helmet and everyone calls him that. Anyone who fails to fit in gets replaced. The age range runs, roughly, from 20 to 40. The rig is a workplace, not a home. Men who are not working or eating are mostly asleep in their bunks, comfortable, but crammed closely together. On a sunny day they stretch out on the helicopter deck.

'We've British here, and we've got Frenchmen, Germans, a Hungarian and a Turk,' said Bill Muse. 'And, of course, we've got Americans —*and* Texans. We're a little United Nations.'

The key staff are mostly American—or Texan. They have the skill

* The drilling director

and expertise to pass on to the others. Each shift is headed by a driller and an assistant driller, who control routine operations. There is a derrick man who, secured by a safety belt, works on a platform 150 feet up. There are two men in charge of the machinery. Then there are six general labourers, termed 'roustabouts', who heave the drilling pipes into and out of position.

Muse supervises both shifts for 24 hours a day, his voice roaring over the machinery. He nips in to do manual work himself, hammering at a jammed thread, helping the roustabouts with a heavy load. All is hustle, everything done at the double in a bedlam of noise . . .

The main skill of his job lies in what bits to fit to the drill head and at what speed to revolve the drill. The softer the ground, the longer the cutting teeth on the bit and the faster the speed. For really hard rock Bill Muse uses a diamond bit, which is expensive. In tough conditions, it may be necessary to change the bit every three or four feet, heaving up a mile or more of drill shaft each time. To go too fast in hard rock can snap the shaft and it may take days to grip it with special prongs and grabs and get it working again. The good driller combines speed with economical use of his equipment.

The North Sea is the hardest proposition the drillers have ever faced. Rumour says that one rig, its operations blanketed in secrecy, has so far managed to get down only 18 inches. American drillers have been accustomed for 15 to 20 years to working under water, principally in the Gulf of Mexico, but the North Sea is much deeper than anywhere that has systematically been exploited before. When they move up to the northern part of the North Sea, where the water is 300 feet deep and much rougher, conditions will be worse still.

'We're killing the whale,' announced Bill Muse. This meant that he was sealing off the well. At intervals down the $1\frac{1}{2}$-mile shafts he placed five steel stoppers and on top of each of them 100 feet of concrete. He worked the concrete pump himself. At the top of the shaft he placed a concrete cap, containing a radioactive element so it can be located when the well is needed.

from : Colin Cross, 'How "Dry Hole Bill" got him a well',
The Observer, July 24, 1966

24 'Dressing down' cod on a fishing boat

Grand Banks, North Atlantic, eighteen-nineties

The shadow of the masts and rigging, with the never-furled riding-sail, rolled to and fro on the heaving deck in the moonlight; and the pile of fish by the stern shone like a dump of fluid silver. In the hold there were tramplings and rumblings where Disko Troop and Tom Platt moved among the salt-bins. Dan passed Harvey a pitchfork, and led him to the inboard end of the rough table, where Uncle Salters was drumming impatiently with a knife-haft. A tub of salt water lay at his feet.

'You pitch to dad an' Tom Platt down the hatch, an' take keer Uncle Salters don't cut yer eye out,' said Dan, swinging himself into the hold. 'I'll pass salt below.'

Penn and Manuel stood knee deep among cod in the pen, flourishing drawn knives. Long Jack, a basket at his feet and mittens on his hands, faced Uncle Salters at the table, and Harvey stared at the pitchfork and the tub.

'Hi!' shouted Manuel, stooping to the fish, and bringing one up with a finger under its gill and a finger in its eye. He laid it on the edge of the pen; the knife-blade glimmered with a sound of tearing, and the fish, slit from throat to vent, with a nick on either side of the neck, dropped at Long Jack's feet.

'Hi!' said Long Jack, with a scoop of his mittened hand. The cod's liver dropped in the basket. Another wrench and scoop sent the head and offal flying, and the empty fish slid across to Uncle Salters, who snorted fiercely. There was another sound of tearing, the backbone flew over the bulwarks, and the fish, headless, gutted, and open, splashed in the tub, sending the salt water into Harvey's astonished mouth. After the first yell, the men were silent. The cod moved along as though they were alive, and long ere Harvey had ceased wondering at the miraculous dexterity of it all, his tub was full.

'Pitch!' grunted Uncle Salters, without turning his head, and Harvey pitched the fish by twos and threes down the hatch.

'Hi! Pitch 'em bunchy,' shouted Dan. 'Don't scatter! Uncle Salters is the best splitter in the fleet. Watch him mind his book!'

Indeed, it looked a little as though the round uncle were cutting magazine pages against time. Manuel's body, cramped over from the hips, stayed like a statue; but his long arms grabbed the fish without ceasing. Little Penn toiled valiantly, but it was easy to see he was weak. Once or twice Manuel found time to help him without breaking the chain of supplies...

Down below, the rasping sound of rough salt rubbed on rough flesh sounded like the whirring of a grindstone—a steady undertone to the 'click-nick' of the knives in the pen, the wrench and schloop of torn heads, dropped liver and flying offal; the 'car-aah' of Uncle Salter's knife scooping away backbones; and the flap of wet, opened bodies falling into the tub.

At the end of an hour Harvey would have given the world to rest; for fresh, wet cod weigh more than you would think, and his back ached with the steady pitching. But he felt for the first time in his life that he was one of a working gang of men, took pride in the thought, and held on sullenly.

from : Rudyard Kipling, *Captains Courageous*

25 Mackerel fishing

At sea

'Mackerel!' called the lookout at the masthead.

The throb of the engine died away to a scarcely audible heartbeat of sound. A dozen men leaned over the rail of the mackerel seiner, peering into darkness. The seiner carried no light. To do so might frighten the fish. Everywhere was blackness—a thick and velvet blackness in which sky was indistinguishable from water.

But wait! Was there a flicker of light—a pale ghost of flame playing over the water there off the port bow? If there had been such a light it faded away into darkness again and the sea lay in black anonymity —a blank negation of life. But there it came again, and, like a nascent flame in a breeze, or a match cupped in the hands, it kindled to a brilliant glow; it spread into the surrounding darkness; it moved, a gleaming amorphous cloud, through the water.

'Mackerel,' echoed the captain after he had watched the light for several minutes. 'Listen!'

At first there was no sound but the soft slap of water against the boat. A sea bird, flying out of darkness into darkness, struck the mast, fell to the deck with a frightened cry, and fluttered off.

Silence again.

Then came a faint but unmistakable patter like a squall of rain on the sea—the sound of mackerel, the sound of a big school of mackerel feeding at the surface.

The captain gave the order to attempt a set. He himself ascended to the masthead to direct operations. The crew fell into their places; ten into the seine boat attached to a boom on the starboard side of the vessel; two into the dory that was towed behind the seine boat. The throb of the engine swelled. The vessel began to move in a wide circle, swinging around the glowing patch of sea. That was to quiet the fish; to round them up in a smaller circle. Three times the seiner circled the school. The second circle was smaller than the first and the third was smaller than the second. The glow in the water was brighter now and the patch of light more concentrated.

After the third circling of the school, the fisherman in the stern of the seine boat passed to the fisherman in the dory one end of the 1,200-foot net that lay piled in the bottom of the seine boat. The seine was dry, having caught no fish that night. The dory cast off and the men at the oars backed water. Again the vessel began to move, towing the seine boat. Now, as the space between the seine boat and dory lengthened, the net slid steadily over the side of the larger boat. A line buoyed by cork floats stretched across the water between them. From the cork line the net hung down in a vertical curtain of webbing a hundred feet deep, held down in the water by leads in the lower border. The line marked out by cords grew from an arc to a semicircle; from a semicircle it swung to the full circle to round up the mackerel in a space four hundred feet across.

from : Rachel Carson, *Under the Sea-Wind*

26 Fishing factory

North Atlantic, 1969

Sixty modern Japanese 'factory' fishing trawlers now operate off the West African coast of the Spanish Sahara under conditions more normally associated with military operations.

The vessels move out from their base—the harbour at Las Palmas in the Canary Isles—in strict formation : each squadron under the command of the captain of a radar ship. This has the capability to detect not only the movement of the giant fish shoals as they swim to the protected waters of the coral reef, which runs for over 700 miles parallel to the coast, but also warships of the Spanish Navy on patrol and Russian trawlers attempting to take advantage of the 'know-how' the Japanese have acquired during the past decade in fishing in the world's richest grounds.

The squadron leader, as he is called, gives the order to lay the nets generally at a speed of 16 knots, and for recovery at four knots. The catch is immediately processed on board and put into the deep freeze.

For superior fish, such as sole and hake, to be sold in European markets, a secret method is employed which seals the fish into plastic bags. Months later when the bag is opened the fish looks as though it had just come out of the ocean with large drops of salt water attached to the skin, while the smell of the sea hits the nostrils.

The major catches are squid or cuttle fish, which are transported in refrigerated ships back to Japan, where the people are extremely short of protein, to mix with their staple diet of rice and vegetables.

Soon after the 1939–45 war the Japanese realised the 'fish potential' of these waters beside the desert coastline where only a few Spanish trawlers worked. A private company invested large sums of money to produce a detailed survey of the ocean bed and the map which was eventually drawn not only indicated the route by which millions of fish move from the Atlantic to spawn in the sheltered waters of the coral reef, but it also showed rocks and other hazards to nets.

The value of the fish caught by the Japanese has, according to the consul-general in Las Palmas, Mr. Hiroshi Nagasaki, been reduced from £30 million a year to £20 million for two reasons.

First, the Spanish Government extended its territorial waters off the Spanish Sahara from six to twelve miles and, second, the Japanese have been joined by 30 Russian trawlers as well as some from Poland, Nationalist China, Korea, Bulgaria and Brazil. Spanish frigates and destroyers constantly patrol the area to prevent poaching.

The Japanese are trying to persuade General Franco to allow them to fish up to the six mile limit on the grounds that they are the only foreign fleet which is based in a Spanish port. They spend £2½ million a year in harbour dues and provisions, spend another £2½ million on cuttle fish or squid bought from Spanish fishermen, and Japanese sailors spend heavily on entertainment in Las Palmas. The Spanish Airline gets £400,000 in charter work for transporting 2,000 Japanese sailors each year from Frankfurt or Paris—which they reach on regular Japanese flights—to Las Palmas.

Initially, the sailors came from Tokyo for a tour of two years, but recently, as a result, this has been reduced to one year. When at sea they work for 16 hours and rest for eight.

In harbour, many amusements are especially set up for them. There are bars which serve Japanese drinks and eating houses with Japanese menus and music. There are, of course, brothels for the Asian seamen which are organised with daily medical supervision.

Big-game fishermen are deeply concerned that the Japanese and other trawlers are ruthlessly killing the tunny, sharks and other 'game' which were, according to experts, far more prolific around the Canary Islands than in Bermuda until the Japanese fleet arrived.

from : Clare Hollingworth, 'Japan's Atlantic Operation Fish',
The Daily Telegraph, August 12, 1969

27 Whaling ship

Antarctica, nineteen-forties

My guide had taken me first to the flensing decks. This is the centre of activity in a factory ship when the whales are coming in. There are two flensing decks—the fore-plan and the after-plan. And both looked the sort of charnel house you might dream up in a nightmare. Men waded knee-deep in the bulging intestines of the whales, their long-handled, curved-bladed flensing knives slashing at the bleeding hunks of meat exposed by the removal of the blubber casing. The winches chattered incessantly. The steam saws buzzed as they ripped into the backbone, carving it into star-shaped sections still festooned with ragged strands of red meat. Men with huge iron hooks dragged blubber, meat and bone to the chutes that took it to the boilers to be tried out* and the precious oil extracted. The noise and the smell were indescribable. And the work went on unceasingly as whale after whale was dragged up the slipway, the men working like demons and the decks slippery with blood and grease.

I followed one whale as it came up through the cavity in the stern. It was eighty feet long and weighed nearly a hundred tons. The men on the after-plan fell on it when it was still being winched along the deck. The flensers cut flaps of blubber from around its jaws, hawser shackle was rigged in holes cut in these flaps and in a moment the winches were ripping the blubber off the huge carcase, the flensers cutting it clear of the meat as it was rolled back. To clear the blubber from the belly, they winched the whale over on to its back, and as it thudded over on the deck urine poured out of its stomach in a wave and the pink mass of the tongue flopped over like a huge jelly. Stripped of its blubber it was winched to the fore-plan. The meat was cut away from the backbone and then the bone itself was cut up and sent to the pots. In just over an hour that hundred-ton monster had been worked up and absorbed by the factory ship . . .

She was a floating factory—a belching, stinking, muck-heap of activity two thousand miles from civilisation. Her upper works were black with grease and filth from the cloud of smoke that rolled out of her trying out funnel. And over everything hung the awful smell of whale. It was like a pall. It was the smell of decaying flesh, mingled with oil and fish, and lying on the air, thick and cloying, like an inescapable fog. But though her decks might present the appearance of some gargantuan slaughter-house, below all was neat and ordered as in a factory. There were the long lines of boilers, hissing gently with the steam that was being injected into them and with gutters bubbling with the hot oil. There was the refrigeration plant and machinery for

* Rendered down

cutting and packing and dehydrating the meat. There were crushing machines for converting the bone to fertiliser. There were laboratories and work-shops, sick bays, mess rooms, living quarters, store rooms, electric generating plant—everything. The *Southern Cross* was a well-stocked, well-populated factory town.

from : Hammond Innes, *The White South*

28 Harvest of whales

Faeroes, 1941

The afternoon of September 19th, 1941, three days after my arrival in the islands, was a phenomenon in Faeroe weather—a clear, warm, sunny day as good as any Indian summer day you would get at home. I was walking in the countryside near Hoyvik, between the froth-rimmed coast and the boulder-strewn hills. Around me, on the hard-won greenth of land which generations of Faeroemen had found it profitable to till, men and women were busy spreading grass to catch the drying sunheat, or were tying bundles of it to upright wooden posts to grow fit for garnering.

The scene was one of slow, peaceful, pastoral activity—until a solitary figure appeared in silhouette on the skyline, and the magic cry 'Grindabod!' swept like a sudden breeze across the fields. Its effect was electric. Instantly the farming ceased, and the men and women shielded their eyes against the sun's glare and looked out to sea. Then they hurriedly gathered up their implements and, whilst one of their number ran to the top of the next rise to pass on the call to other workers down below, they separated to their respective homes.

The green land was deserted, the farming forgotten. That cry which burns its way like wildfire through the town and the spacious country-side, driving along the fiords and the valleys and up over the stony hills, had set the life-blood of south Streymoy tingling with the promise of another harvest, borne to the people unexpectedly by the sea ...

The quayside was crowded. Adjacent offices and houses, the roofs of sheds and boat-houses, and even the backs of stationary lorries whose drivers had gone off to the hunt had been occupied by the early comers who wanted grandstand views. When the *grind* came into the harbour with the shepherding craft behind, and the people saw the sleek black bodies curving rhythmically under and out of the waves in a scurrying of white foam, they raised a full-throated, happy cheer. It was like some thrilling phase of a first-class sporting event at home in

415

the good old days, only one felt that the cheering had seldom reached such a peak of spontaneous joy.

Now there were men standing in the boats, and they had drawn the wooden sheaths from the keen-edged whale-weapons. Those on the edge of the quay stood ready with lances poised, and when the school was still some fifty yards from the harbour-head, some men, fully clothed and armed like Viking warriors wading ashore on some strange coast, leapt off the quay into three feet of water to get to close grips with the *grind* . . .

The whales were in dire trouble. In water too shallow for swimming they rocked and rolled without control. Their great tailflukes reared many feet into the air as some of them caught their heads among the rocks. The water roared and seethed, and was churned to an apple-green, ribbed and veined and crested with white foam.

The long whale-weapons did terrible work, and soon the water and the foam were gashed with crimson veins. Running rivulets and sordid pools of blood welled up from hidden bodies and trailed and spread over the surface of the sea. The backs of swimming whales broke the surface and their blood leapt in a steaming, crimson spout more than a foot into the air; blood oozed and flowed in the wake of the whales as they ploughed madly through the waves. They squealed in their agony beneath the reddening water, their cries—like plaintive, pathetic whimpers—only just audible to those watching from the quay . . .

An hour after the beginning of the *grindadráp* there were whales still swimming strongly in the red sea around the boats, but half-an-hour later the killing was virtually at an end. Nearly a hundred and fifty whales, cut and bleeding and all of them steaming and dead, lay side by side in well-ordered rows along the quay, so closely packed together that in some places you had to walk on their bodies to pass along the road. Only one craft had been sunk, a surprisingly small loss; it had been smashed to pieces by the tail-fluke of a desperate bull, and luckily its occupants had got off with nothing more serious than a good ducking and a few moments of apprehension whilst they swam to other boats. In the *melée* of a *grindadráp* duckings, bruises and cuts from mishandled knives and whale-weapons are of singularly little importance in face of the mounting quantity of meat . . .

The excitement was not all at an end. In the deepening dusk the people flocked down to the sea front once more, many this time resplendent in their national dress, and full of carnival spirits. In an ever-widening ring they danced at the harbour-head, the dead whales lying round about them in the gloom, and they sang verse after verse of monotonous and seemingly tuneless ballads, until their voices were hoarse. For hours the dancing and singing continued : those who grew tired (and despite the labours of the afternoon they did not tire easily) fell out, but always there were others to take their place.

To the casual observer from abroad the *grindadráp* must seem to be one of the cruellest forms of hunting in existence. The Faeroese, who are by natural temper a kindly, hospitable and well-educated people, admit this much themselves. But the *grindadráp* is the only method by which these whales can be killed successfully, and the conditions of life among the islands are such that the *grind*, like the seafowl, remains a vital source of the country's meat-supply. For the land is shockingly desolate over the greater part of its 540 square miles, and will never produce fresh meat in sufficient abundance to satisfy the needs of its 30,000 inhabitants. It is a land accursed, moreover, with a stormy and unproductive winter, so that the provision of a good stock of dried and salted meat must always be the primary consideration of the summer toil.

from : Kenneth Williamson, *The Atlantic Islands*

29 Whitecoats ahead, one point to port

Newfoundland, Canada, early twentieth century

A vast sigh came from the listening crew, then the captain threw out his hand, crying :

'Whitecoats, me sons! Bridgemaster, get the vessel to goin', full steam ahead! Six miles it says, an' one point on our port! Hump now !'

The men were recovering from the shock of a message from the skies. They fell to laughing and talking, shouting and bragging and planning, and scrambling past one another on their way below, to get their gear... Whitecoats were young harps, fattest and finest of seals, most desirable of all. And only six miles ahead! Though they were not yet within sight or hearing of the whitecoats, the men went wild with excitement. The seal hunters filled all standing space forward, burly rough vikings, eager to attack. Their ropes strung crosswise down from one shoulder gave them something of a military air; their tall iron-pointed gaffs might have been spears. Altogether they resembled an impatient, undisciplined army of mountain troops, prepared to fight on the ice.

Bob stood among them, shivering with excitement. Mentally he reviewed his outfit, fearful lest he had left some essential behind. Nunny-bag, ratline, gaff, and sculping knife, these were the necessary things, and he had them all. He turned up the sole of his boot, gazing thoughtfully. All set. The sole and heel of each boot were equipped with long heavy nails or 'chisels', as a guard against slipping on the ice. He had on his ice glasses. Compass—he did not need one. Only the watchmasters carried compasses.

The seconds ticked off while the men waited for the ship to get a little closer.

'Ye're not taking flags,' announced the captain. 'No markers. Haul what ye get to the ship. There won't be too many.'

The Old Man gave an order to the engine-room. They were slowing down. An instant more and the crew would be over the side. In that moment Bob Galloway had a clear sharp picture of the ice-fields on which he was to begin his career as a seal hunter. The sun was out, the ice glistening for miles on all sides. The sea was running a swell; no waves ever manage to build among the ice-floes, but at least the pans must heave up and down as the swell moves along. The chess-board of ice-cakes rose in a vast, slow, dizzying tilt, then slowly it sank, sank, until the *Ranger* seemed to be riding on top of the world, all the white frozen universe sloping steeply down and away from her. Then another long tremendous swell, knocking the floes together with a noise that sounded like strong teeth gnashing.

'Easy, easy,' cautioned the Old Man. The *Ranger* nosed up to a heavy pan, slower and slower. Whereupon the Captain let them go, shouting like a foghorn. 'All right, me hearties, go for 'em!'

And they went over, one hundred and fifty hunters fierce with excitement and the desire to get their share of the whitecoats, the precious young fat that meant money, food, clothing, medicine, comfort, and happiness to them and their families.

All that concerned the *Ranger's* men just now was the best route to the whitecoats. The best route was not necessarily the shortest however. Sometimes broad leads of open water blocked the way, in which case the straggling column went round, hopping and jumping with every step. Bob Galloway was about half way back, with Johnnie and the rest of the watch. The boy from Rocky Cove spent no time looking ahead : he knew he would hear of it as soon as a whitecoat was discovered, and meantime he wanted to make a good showing with the ice. He saw Mike Hallet ahead, stopping to test a floe with his gaff before he leaped on to it. Bob did the same, the chisels on the bottom of his boots crunching into the ice, the iron point of his gaff ringing as he tested places to put his feet. When he saw drifting snow on the ice, he grew wary, for there was no telling what was under it, likely as not it covered a hole, or a fissure between ice-cakes. The line of men rose and sank with the swell of the sea, and it was that very swell that presently laid Bob open to criticism. He leaped a ribbon of water and looked back to see that it was suddenly wider than he had thought.

'Lad, you're new to the ice' called Skipper Tom, from behind him, 'so I'll give you a bit of advice. Don't ever do what ye did a minute ago. The swell had started to pull the floes apart, so ye should have waited. In a minute they'd be coming together again, closer together and easier to jump. Eh?'

'I'll remember that', said the boy.

... 'Never batted a whitecoat, did ye?'

'No, sir,' said Bob, feeling miserably green again.

'All right, follow Johnnie—Johnnie you bat 'em and he can skin 'em. And don't hit 'em too hard Johnnie. I noticed you cracked a lot of head bones last year. That dulls the knife and slows ye' up. I'll show ye how to skin 'em b'y.'

'Right here, son,' called Hallet.

Bob ran up, and in a trice the watchmaster had the whitecoat out of its pelt.

'Like that,' he said hurriedly, and rose up.

'Follow Johnnie now, and skin his seals until you both get enough to tow. Don't cut any holes aft of the flippers. The owners deduct ten cents apiece for every hole like that. They take it out of the crew's share so be careful. Here, cut a slit forward, like this, and put your ratline through that. All right?'

'Yes, sir.'

The watchmaster hurried off, leaving Bob to take the pelt, or sculp, along with him. Tearing off his ratline, he threaded the pointed end through the slit that Hallet had made, drew the knot snug, and put the rope over his shoulder. Then he set out after Johnnie, pulling the pelt with him, while a crowd of gulls circled noisily over the carcass left behind.

All about him he could hear the cries of the young seals, calling the mothers who had deserted them. It was a queer indescribable sound, somewhat like the mewing of a cat, but also resembling the bark of a dog and the bleating of a lamb. Listening to it as he strode along, Bob was glad he did not have to begin his actual sealing by slaughtering whitecoats. They sounded so innocent and helpless.

'Ma-a-a-a-a-a-a-a !' they kept calling. 'Ma-a-a-a-a-a !'

The young seals sounded plaintive, and they looked plaintive...

'It's a shame to kill 'em', observed Bob, coming up.

'Yes, it is,' admitted Johnnie, 'but look at it this way. The seals eat two or three million codfish a day, to say nothing of other kinds. And we Newfoundlanders live on fish. Sure, and besides it isn't any worse than killing squabs and lambs. There's another one calling, off towards that hummock. I'm after him. We want to try to keep track of each other.'

from : T. Williamson, *North after Seals*

30 Sealers

Arctic

We raced across the ice at about 30 miles an hour; the komatic, to which I clung, yawed from side to side behind the Ski-doo, bucking over every ridge. A small flat-bottomed dory was tied to the back of the komatic. We could see the floe edge from a distance. At first it was like a solid wall stretching across the entire horizon, and then, as we came closer, the wall disintegrated into a thin grey mist rising from the open water. Ice merged imperceptibly with dark water that seemed viscous in the cold.

Owalook stopped the Ski-doo about 20 feet from the floe edge and, taking a boat-hook and his rifle, walked forward, probing the ice. Close to the edge he halted and began scraping the hook from side to side with a steady rhythmic motion. A few minutes passed and a small dark blob appeared in the water, then vanished. Owalook dropped the hook, sat down on the ice, raised his rifle and waited. The blob appeared again. It was a hundred yards out and barely discernible as the head of a seal. The rifle cracked; there was a flurry of water. 'Dead,' announced Owalook.

It had all happened so quickly and smoothly that I had hardly realised what had happened, and could not conceive that anyone could shoot so accurately, even with telescopic sights. Owalook had already unfastened the dory from the komatic. He pushed it gingerly on to the edge of the ice, rocked it once or twice to break the thin skin between him and the water, and pushed out in it.

Soon he was back with the seal in tow—it twitched a little and its brains flowed in a dark stream over the ice. I felt slightly sick and walked away, but felt ashamed, and forced myself to return. I had not been watching someone killing for sport; this was Owalook's sole means of livelihood.

from : Christian Bonnington, 'Where hunting is not a sport',
The Daily Telegraph Magazine, May 19, 1967

31 Man and bear

Florida, U.S.A., eighteen-eighties

Penny and Jody went to their room. They undressed on the side of the narrow bed.

There was room enough for the two thin bony bodies. The red faded from the west and the room was dusky. The hound slept and whimpered in her sleep. The moon rose, an hour past the full, and the small room lay in a silver brightness. Jody's feet burned. His knees twitched.

Penny said, 'You wakeful, son?'

'I cain't stop walkin'.'

'We went a fur piece. How you like bear-huntin', boy?'

'Well—' He rubbed his knees. 'I liked the trackin' and the trailin'. I liked seein' the saplin's broke down, and the ferns in the swamp.'

'I know.'

'I liked old Julia bayin' now and again—'

'But the fightin's right fearsome, ain't it son?'

'Hit's mighty fearsome.'

'Hit's sickenin', the dogs gittin' bloodied and sich as that. And son, you ain't never seen a bear kilt. But mean as they be, hit's someway piteeful when they go down and the dogs tears their throats and they cry out jest like a person, and lay down and die before you.'

Father and son lay in silence.

'If the wild creeturs'd only leave us be,' Penny said.

'I wisht we could kill 'em off,' Jody said. 'Them that steals offen us and does us harm.'

' 'Tain't stealin', in a creetur. A creetur's got his livin' to make and he makes it the best way he kin. Same as us. Hit's panther nature and wolf nature and bear nature to kill their meat. County lines is nothin' to them, nor a man's fences. How's a creetur to know the land's mine and paid for? How's a bear to know I'm dependin' on my hogs for my own rations? All he knows is, he's hongry.'

Jody lay staring into the brightness. Baxter's Island seemed to him a fortress ringed around with hunger. Now in the moonlight eyes were shining red and green and yellow. The hungry would dart into the clearing in swift forays, and kill and eat and slink away again. Pole-cats and 'possums would raid the hen-roost, wolf or panther might slay the calf before daylight, old Slewfoot might come again to murder and feed.

'A creetur's only doin' the same as me when I go huntin' us meat,' Penny said. 'Huntin' him where he lives and beds and raises his young uns. Hit's a hard law, but it's the law. "Kill or go hongry".'

Yet the clearing was safe. The creatures came, but they went away again. Jody began to shiver and could not tell why.

'You cold, son?'

'I reckon.'

He saw old Slewfoot wheel, and slash and snarl. He saw old Julia leap, and be caught and crushed, and hold on, and then fall away, broken and bleeding. But the clearing was safe.

'Move close, son. I'll warm you.'

He edged closer to his father's bones and sinews. Penny slipped an arm around him and he lay close against the lank thigh. His father was the core of safety. His father swam the swift creek to fetch back his wounded dog. The clearing was safe, and his father fought for it. A sense of snugness came over him and he dropped asleep. He awakened once, disturbed. Penny was crouched in the corner in the moonlight, ministering to the hound.

from : Marjorie K. Rawlings, *The Yearling*

Notes on Section 9

The bold figures indicate extract numbers

1–3 Wielding a pick and shovel may not be a very skilled job but the labourer does have to know how to handle them. In spite of the use of mechanical earth-moving equipment manual labour is still very widely employed.

4–7 Very few people apart from those actively engaged in mining have had the experience of seeing miners at work. Apart from the lack of daylight and the cramped conditions, there are always the smells and the heat, to say nothing of the dangers of fire, explosion and asphyxiation from poison gases. Mechanisation is, however, reducing the number of miners employed underground.

8–9 These two passages show the contrast between railway building and tunnelling in the middle of the nineteenth century and today. In the mid-nineteenth century not only were working conditions for the labourer often very dangerous, but, as the location changed from day to day, his living accommodation was of a temporary nature and standards were usually very low. The modern railway tunnellers are not only well paid but many are able to go by private car to their own homes when their shift is completed. See also extract No. 3.

10–13 The kind of tragedy that is described in extract No. 11 is unlikely to happen today, but things do go wrong occasionally; it is still no light job working with steel. The woman in extract No. 13 was a university graduate in charge of a furnace. She would have to do her share of scrambling about but no shovelling. Most of the heavy work on the furnace would now be done mechanically.

14 Henry Ford was a major pioneer of assembly-line techniques which are now used throughout the world. Ford's methods have helped to transform the motor-car from a luxury product for affluent people to a near-necessity within reach of many. But increasing car ownership has brought its attendant problems of pollution, traffic congestion and high accident figures. Wages in the industry are relatively high, but job-security is poor and production has been frequently disrupted by industrial disputes.

15 Japan has thousands of small family businesses as well as the enormous factories in the big towns. Having possessed such a parasol as a small girl the compiler found this passage of particular interest.

16 The Himalayas are one of the major tea-producing areas of the world. Physical conditions are particularly good, with a high rainfall (over 40 inches, 1010 mm), a warm, damp growing season, and a rich, well-drained soil, which the evergreen tea shrub needs. The tea leaf is still picked by hand, as no machine is able to match the skill of the tea pickers.

17–19 The question of whether a man is deadened by work in a factory or machine shop is debatable. Dudintsev said that a man is freed to think about things outside his actual job by the very fact that it is broken down into

423

simple repetitive actions and becomes automatic. Those of us who are fortunate enough to have jobs full of interest and variety are apt to think of repetitive jobs as soul-destroying (extract No. 19); perhaps we are wrong. 'Piecework rate' (extract No. 18) means payment according to the number of pieces of the same type that a worker completes in a given time. The rate per piece is fixed by agreement, and he can do as many as he pleases within reason, as long as he does not prejudice the work of others by going too fast or too slow.

20 'The tendency of mechanical progress ... is to frustrate the human need for effort and creation.' There is now a greater awareness of the dilemma of which Orwell wrote; automation brings shorter working hours and the problem of the best and most satisfying use of increased leisure. Technological advance breeds passivity in both work and leisure, and with it the hazard of boredom and frustration.

21 Crop-dusting with fertilisers or pesticides is becoming an increasingly important technique in modern farming. Compared with more conventional methods of application it enables a large area of land to be covered in a relatively short time. Strong or unpredictable winds, however, may blow insecticides where they may cause harm.

22-23 Drilling for oil involves heavy capital investment and is only under-taken where there is strong evidence—based on the geology and morphology of the area—to suggest its presence. Oil is found in a great variety of locations from the desert countries around the Persian Gulf to the ice-covered areas of Alaska—all bringing their particular problems.

24-26 Many fishing grounds, for example those of Iceland, are being overfished and the stock depleted. Intensive research is being carried out into the natural resources of the oceans which cover about three-quarters of the earth's surface but provide under 2 per cent of the world's food supply. Scientific 'fish farming'—fish breeding and catching under controlled con-ditions—makes it possible to increase the yield without causing a decrease in the stock.

27-28 Since the extract on commercial whaling was written, whaling fleets have become larger and are using increasingly sophisticated methods of searching and killing. These include radar, sonic devices, and explosive har-poons. As a result several sub-species, especially the blue whale, are threatened with extinction. Attempts have been made to curb the number of whales slaughtered, and for several years now a limit has been placed on the numbers permitted to be caught; but the annual quota has always been exceeded. A suggestion put forward at a recent conference in Stockholm, that all com-mercial whaling be banned for ten years to allow the whale population to breed and increase, seems unlikely to be accepted by the major whaling nations.

29-30 Sealing has become a rather emotional issue in recent years, because methods of killing are often far from humane. The seals undoubtedly re-present a threat to the livelihood of some people, by eating fish which would otherwise be available for human consumption, but the extent of that threat is disputed.

424

10

Harmony

A few extracts about man in harmony with his surroundings; about the pleasures of 'moments out of time'. Let us savour them. Let us not stifle the zest for life in ourselves or in others.

'There are collectors of days and hours and minutes, savouring the fine essence of each according to its season, storing in their memories its subtleties of light and shade, the quality of its stillness and movement.'

1 Alone in the mountains

Kashmir

The completely unbroken solitude and the absence of anything recalling the rest of humanity produce a unique feeling of liberation as one moves slowly through these tremendous gorges. Today the outside world and my own life—past and future—as part of that world seemed so utterly unreal that for a time I ceased to be aware of it and existed only in the present, acutely conscious of my surroundings and of physical sensation, but removed, in a dream-like way, from myself as a person. It was a strangely relaxing experience.

from : Dervla Murphy, *Full Tilt*

2 Summer madness

Siberia

Already the summer, some call from the forest, had infected us. Already without knowing it then, we were sliding back through the years to our boyhoods. Were they so very different, those English and Russian arcadian days of many summers past, when the sun shone strongly and time meant nothing beyond a yelp from the belly at noon? We tumbled out of the car and ran down a path, kicking stones and shovelling dust with our insteps, till we came to a group of weather-tanned fishermen by their canoes. With them everything was quickly arranged.

We spent that afternoon fishing on Lake Baikal from a canoe with an outboard motor. Dressed in faded blue, padded winter jackets, free at last from the dreary round of *Kolkhoz* and *Kombinat*, from the wearisome recital of statistics and record production figures and ideological argument, feeling relaxed in the company of men who were not Heroes of the Soviet Union and never hoped to be, we contentedly pulled fish out of the lake, only occasionally conscious of the fact that we were doing so 5,000 miles from home in the heart of a politically estranged land. We had become resigned to such incongruities.

When we had caught enough fish we returned to the bank and built a large fire of dead, dry timber inside the forest. The fisherman who was with us gutted the fish and spitted them on sharpened branches, sticking the branches in the ground in order to grill the fish. We drank vodka round the fire while the fish sizzled and in a little while, after the spirit had started to circulate round our systems we began to laugh. The clearing in the forest where we sat had become an enchanted glade, a dark green pool into which a grey evening light leaked through the cedar boughs and where bright flowers swam before our vodka-mesmerised eyes like tropical fish. We chortled with unaccountable happiness and I thought, 'Haven't I played this game before, in the woods of my childhood, swigging ginger pop and munching green apples in a den in the undergrowth?' The fisherman pulled the cooked fish away from the fire and we divided the portions, throwing them from hand to hand like hot potatoes till they were cool enough to eat. And when we had eaten them and the vodka was finished we got up and wandered around.

We wandered down to the edge of the forest, where the road was and where the flowers grew thickest and there was an elevated view for many miles across the thickly-timbered hills. I busied myself taking photographs . . .

I suppose because of my work as a photographer I have learnt to see as a camera sees, instantly to release a mental shutter and record in my brain a scene where all motion is frozen at the critical and significant moment; much of my memory consists of a file of such photographs, the action arrested in the lobes of my brain with all the kinetic stillness of figures on a Grecian frieze.

I first saw John. He was wearing Italian shoes, a blazer with Royal Navy buttons, and his Oxford college tie. At the moment I saw him he was hanging at arms' length from the lower branches of a solitary silver birch tree growing on a bluff of red earth above and away from the road; his left leg was bent upwards as if to find a foothold on the trunk of the tree, but his right leg hung straight down like a dead man's; though his back was towards me there was about his attitude a fierce, totally absorbed concentration that was wholly characteristic of him. I had not seen my friend dangling from a tree before, not in Siberia, or anywhere else, but when I saw Yuri I knew that the *cafard*, the spring fever, had not overtaken John alone.

Yuri was wearing a typically Russian grey raincoat and a typically Russian trilby hat—the walking-out uniform of any Soviet bureaucrat. . . . [He] was on the other side of the road and he must have spent the last few minutes busily rummaging along the roadside, for at his feet there was now a large pile of stones, each the size of a fist. As I saw him in that split-second of arrested time his squat mackintoshed form was leaning backwards, with his left leg braced forwards and his right arm stretched stiffly back. In his right hand he clutched a stone which he was about to propel with great vigour, as if it was a hand-grenade, towards the trunk of a birch tree some fifteen yards in front of him . . . The stone landed with a satisfying clonk against the trunk and Yuri quickly stooped down to gather another one. He threw stones as he played chess—swiftly, seemingly haphazardly, but to dire effect.

427

Nickolai, too, I transfixed with my beady camera eye during that brief and wholly absurd moment in the Siberian forest ... That afternoon he was very content, moving slowly among the bushes and between the trees at the edge of the forest gathering wild flowers to take home to his family; as he emerged, disappeared and re-emerged in the thickets he reminded me of some great, shy wild animal waiting in the African bush for night to fall before venturing to the waterhole, in the meantime gently and warily moving about feeding—on lilies. He held out his fist as if he was carrying a ceremonial sword, and slowly throttling in that massive paw was a bunch of very beautiful wild flowers ...

I called out to John and my voice shattered the stillness; the petrified figures in my mind's eye jolted to life again ... John fell from his tree like a ripe plum; Yuri heaved his last stone and then abandoned his target; Nikolai lumbered out from the trees clutching his garland and joined us by the car. The spell was broken, the interlude was over, and we drove back through the forest towards the city and the world of party slogans, the exhortatory banners, the phoney statistics, the symbolic jungle of electricity wires and the long wait for beer and borshch. The scent of the forest was left behind us.

from : Douglas Botting, *One Chilly Siberian Morning*

3 Being young in Kiev

Ukraine, U.S.S.R.

The Spring began when the Dnieper overflowed its banks. You had only to climb the Vladimir Hill on the edge of the town for a great expanse of bluish sea to open out before you.

But this was not the only flood in Kiev—the city was inundated with sun, freshness and warm scented winds.

The sticky cone-shaped poplars on Bibikov Boulevard burgeoned, filling the surrounding streets with a smell of incense. The chestnuts put out their first, creased, transparent leaves covered with a reddish down. By the time their yellow and pink candles were in flower, Spring was at its height, and the damp smell of new grass and the whispering of newly unfolded leaves poured over the streets. There were caterpillars on the pavement even in the Kreshchalik. The wind swept fallen petals into drifts. Butterflies and maybugs flew in at the windows of the trams. Nightingales sang at night. The fluff of the poplars eddied on the flagstones like the surf of the Black Sea, and dandelions blossomed in the gutters.

Striped awnings were lowered over the wide-open windows of pastry shops and cafés. Vases of lilac sprinkled with water stood on the tables of restaurants, and young girls searched its clusters for five petalled blooms, their faces shadowed to a creamy ochre by their summer hats.

In Spring, I vanished for whole days into one or other of the Kiev parks. There I played and did my homework and read, coming home only to eat and sleep.

from : Konstantin Paustovsky, *Story of a Life*,
Vol. I, 'Childhood and Schooldays'

4 In tune with the earth

England, 1883

The long-lived summer days dried and warmed the turf in the meadows. I used to lie down in solitary corners at full length on my back, so as to feel the embrace of the earth. The grass stood high above me, and the shadows of the tree-branches danced on my face. I looked up at the sky with half-closed eyes to bear the dazzling light. Bees buzzed over me, sometimes a butterfly passed, there was a hum in the air, greenfinches sang in the hedge. Gradually, entering into the intense life of the summer days—a life which burned around as if every grass blade and leaf were a torch—I came to feel the long-drawn life of the earth back into the dimmest past, while the sun of the moment was warm on me ... I was aware of the grass-blades, the flowers, the leaves on hawthorn and tree. I seemed to live more largely through them, as if each were a pore through which I drank. The grasshoppers called and leaped, the greenfinches sang, the blackbirds happily fluted, all the air hummed with life. I was plunged deep in existence, and with all that existence I prayed.

from : Richard Jefferies, *The Story of my Heart*

5 Freedom

Western Australia

A small exultance grew inside the youth. After all he had got away, into a country that men had not yet clutched into their grip. Where you could do as you liked without being stifled by people ...

It was spring in Western Australia, and a wonder of delicate blueness, of frail unearthly beauty. The earth was full of weird flowers, star shaped, needle pointed, fringed, scarlet, white, blue, a whole world of strange flowers. Like being in a new Paradise from which man had not been cast out.

The trees in the dawn, so ghostly still. The scent of blossoming eucalyptus trees : the scent of burning eucalyptus leaves and sticks in the camp fire. Trailing blossoms wet with dew; the scrub after the rain; the bitter-sweet fragrance of fresh-cut timber.

And the sounds! Magpies calling, parrots chattering, strange birds flitting in the renewed stillness. Then kangaroos calling to one another out of the frail, paradisal distance. And the birr! of crickets in the heat of the day. And the sound of axes, the voices of men, the crash of falling timber. The strange slobbering talk of the blacks! The mysterious night coming round the camp fire.

Red gum everywhere! Fringed leaves dappling, the glowing new sun coming through, the large, feathery, honey sweet blossoms flowering in clumps, the hard, rough-marked, red-bronze trunks rising like pillars of burnt copper, or lying sadly felled, giving up the ghost. Everywhere scattered the red gum, making leaves and herbage underneath seem strewed with blood . . .

And far away, unending, upslope and downslope and rockface, one far unending dimness of these changeless trees, going on and on without variation, open enough to let one see ahead and all around, yet dense enough to form a monotony and a sense of helplessness in the mind, a sense of timelessness. Strongly the gang impressed on Jack that he must not go even for five minutes' walk out of sight of the clearing. The weird silent timelessness of the bush impressed him as nothing else did, in its motionless aloofness. 'What would my father mean, out here?' he said to himself. And it seemed as if his father and his father's world and his father's gods withered and went to dust at the thought of this bush.

from : D. H. Lawrence and M. L. Skinner, *The Boy in the Bush*

6 A new world

New Zealand, 1943

The head of the pass was lost in a blur of rain. The road now hung above a gorge through whose bed hurried a stream, its turbulence seen but not heard at that height. The driver changed down and the engine whined and roared. Pieces of shingle banged violently on the underneath of the car.

'Hallo!' said the passenger. 'Is this the top!' And a moment later. 'Good God, how remarkable!'

The mountain tops had marched away to left and right. The head of the pass was an open square of piercing blue. As they reached it the black cloud drew back like a curtain. In a moment it was behind them and they looked down into another country.

It was a great plateau, high itself, but ringed about with mountains that were crowned in perpetual snow. It was laced with rivers of snow water. Three lakes of a strange milky green lay across its surface. It stretched bare and golden under a sky that was brilliant as a paladin's mantle. Upon the plateau and the foothills, up to the level of perpetual snow, grew giant tussocks, but there were no forests. Many miles apart, touches of *pinus radiata* or lombardy poplars could be seen and these marked the solitary homesteads of the sheep farmers. The air was clear beyond belief, unbreathed, one would have said, newly poured out from the blue chalice of the sky.

The passenger lowered the window, which was still wet but steaming now, in the sun. He looked back. The cloud curtain lolled a little way over the mountain barrier and that was all there was to be seen of it.

'It's a new world,' he said.

from : Ngaio Marsh, *Died in the Wool*

7 Lure of the jungle

Liberia, 1954

It is partly to get back a robust appetite for life that one goes to live among the native people, who devour each small incident of the day, happy or otherwise, with healthy zest. Often when you start out over an unmarked, unmapped trail, you do not care where it goes or the names of the villages along the way, because the place where you are really hoping to go is towards a better understanding of yourself.

Most travellers through the deep forests of tropical Africa have experienced a sense of pilgrimage. The reason for the trip and the excuse for going are often quite different . . .

As you live in the villages under the brim of the forest, you become contemporary with people who have lived in shelters of mud and thatch for centuries, and you get the feeling that this is where you started from many generations ago. You have come the long way back, you have come home. Then you begin to understand truths that you would not know if you had not travelled the long distance away, and what seems the shorter trip, the distance back.

from : Esther Warner, *Trial by Sasswood*

8 Mateando

Paraguay

Few moments so enjoyable, giving one so much awareness of life, as taking maté in the early hours, waiting for the dawn, while one's horse, saddled, waits too, and one's little fire is the only rejoinder to the black immensity round one. No sound, save the snorting of a horse, the cough of an animal hidden by darkness and undergrowth, the low murmuring voices. Nothing visible save the fire, the glow of cigarettes. A stranger might think that all were awaiting some announcement of far-reaching importance, a great event, the beginning of a battle. But the group is just 'mateando'; in a little while, still before light, it will mount and ride away.

from : Gordon Meyer, *The River and the People*

9 Almond blossom and blue skies

Spain

We leave the plantations and climb sharply, on a ridge between fields; the scent of pines and mountain herbs grows stronger.

Still there are small terraces with single carob-trees, the arrangement of their leaves and the bean-pods regular to perfection. Small tidy terraces with not a weed, every stone carried to the border to make it level.

There is a shout from the children who have reached a rock above us. We look up towards the dramatic blue of the sky, the deep royal blue, and we see it too : frail, infinitely graceful, almost transparent and yet absorbing all the light of the sun, a small almond tree, white, tipped with a pink hue somewhere. White, rose, gold and blue—and the humming of bees. The scent of honey—yes, of course.

There is not one almond-tree, there are a dozen—twenty—on a weedless terrace where no one seems to be working. And round the bend, where we now catch sight of Tia Maria, twenty more, no, a hundred, a thousand trees in bloom. White, rose, pink, snow-white almond-trees, the whole mountainside is a shimmering, humming, honey-scented cloud of blossom.

We look down at the valley where no almonds are in bloom, though there are many trees down there. Why here then, Tia Maria, why?

'Ah,' she says lifting her small work-hardened brown hand, a little claw of a hand, towards the sun : 'Ah.'

from : Gunda Lambton, *The Compleat Imbiber*

10 Flying at Night

General

I have flown many times by night. But I have never quite got used to that first moment in the dark when one sits with folded hands, alone, speeding through the air at a pace one cannot feel or adequately imagine. The night looks on steadily, its feet on the earth far below, its head in the stars. It is a solemn moment; sensations you have not felt and thoughts you have not thought since childhood come back to you. You feel yourself then to be really on a journey in the fullest sense of the word; not just a shifting of the body from point to point but a journey that moves through all conceivable dimensions of space and time, and beyond. For a voyage to a destination, wherever it may be, is also a voyage inside oneself; even as a cyclone carries along with it the centre in which it must ultimately come to rest. At these moments I think not only of the places I have been to but also of the distances I have travelled within myself without friend or ship; and of the long way yet to go before I come home within myself and within the journey. And always when the curtains are lifted, the night is without, peering in steadily and constantly, with the light of the stars far beyond.

from : Laurens Van Der Post, *Venture into the Interior*

11 Above the storm

General

Little by little he spiralled up in the well that had opened and which closed again beneath him. As he rose the clouds lost their muddy shadows, they swept against him in ever purer, ever whiter waves. Fabien rose clear.

433

His surprise was extreme. The brightness was such that it dazzled him, and for several seconds he had to close his eyes. He never would have thought that the clouds at night could dazzle. But the full moon and the constellations had changed them into radiant billows.

At a single bound, as it emerged, the plane had attained a calm that seemed wondrous. There was not a wave to rock him, and like a sail-boat passing the jetty he was entering sheltered waters. He had found refuge in some uncharted spot of sky, as hidden as the bay of the Happy Isles. Beneath him, nine thousand feet deep, the storm formed another world, shot through with gusts and cloudbursts and lightning flashes, but towards the stars it turned a surface of snowy crystal.

Fabien felt as though he had reached some strange limbo, for everything now grew luminous—his hands, his flying togs, his wings. For the light did not stream down from the stars : rather it welled up from underneath and around him from these endless white drifts. The clouds beneath reflected back the snow shed on them by the moon, as did those banked up to right and left of him like towers. The two of them were floating through a milky stream of light. Fabien, when he looked round, saw the radio operator smiling.

'We're doing better !' he cried.

But the sound was lost in the roar of the flight, and the smiles alone came through. 'I must be mad to smile,' thought Fabien. 'We're lost !'

A thousand dark arms had relinquished their grip on him. His bonds had been loosened, like those of a prisoner allowed to walk for a while alone among the flowers.

'Too beautiful,' thought Fabien. He was wandering through a dense treasure-hoard of stars, in a world where nothing, absolutely nothing else but he, Fabien, and his companion, were alive.

from : Antoine de Saint-Exupéry, *Night Flight*

12 Sunrise in Africa

Kenya

The mornings are tremendous because the scale is so vast. The sky before sunrise is an immense cauldron of crimson; bands of pink stretch like mighty pennants from one horizon to another. Like a series of gigantic monsters, the mountains crouch in every shade of blue and indigo. All is spread out as if fresh from creation, and yet immemorially old. Man has no part in it at all, he is invisible, nothing shows of him or his works. So it was, you feel, a million years ago and so it will be after another million. This scale, reducing man to insignificance, frightens some people and stimulates others : it is of Africa's essence, at once comforting, because folly and misfortune cannot matter, and crushing, because no human effort can amount to more than a leaf floating in a stream.

The sun came up in a great golden flood in reverse, at first illuminating the mountain sides above a dark plain and then surging downwards into the valley, starting into sudden life every tree and bush and boulder.

from : Elspeth Huxley, *A New Earth*

13 Looking at a waterfall

Victoria Falls, Southern Africa

Wearing oilskins and sou'westers provided by our hotel we walked through the Rain Forest along the edge of the cliff facing the falls. There can hardly be another walk like it in the world. Most waterfalls you view from one end or the other. You see Niagara from the American end or the Canadian. But suppose you could walk through the air in front of the falls from the American side to Canada, close enough to get the full impact of the thunder, the winds and the spray, what a sensation that would be !

That is what one does at Victoria. Facing the waterfall is another cliff equally high with a chasm about 100 feet wide between them. Into this chasm the waterfall thunders. And you walk along the edge of the cliff for a mile, past the various parts of the great spectacle, the Eastern Cataract, the Boiling Pot, the Rainbow Falls, Livingstone Island, Main Falls, Cataract Island and Devil's Cataract, and all of them within a short stone's throw.

It is not an easy walk. A drenching rain is falling, the winds set up by the waterfall seem determined to rip the oilskin from your back, and in many places on the path the water from the everlasting rains is ankle deep, deeper in the mudholes.

But what a sight ! At Niagara or Iguassu, the water crashes into spray which spreads forward down the river and dissipates. Here the action is quite different. The water after crashing on the rocks is backed by the facing cliff. The downrush has made a downdraught of air. There is no place for the air to go except up on the other side.

So up it comes, carrying the spray with it, an upgoing rain. It not only rises some 350 feet to the edge of the cliff but keeps right on going up for another 5,000 feet, making the famous pillar of cloud that is the distinctive feature of Victoria. These lofty columns of rising rain can be seen fifty miles away. Interlaced with them are brilliant rainbows.

At last the uprush loses momentum and down again comes the water on the heads of observers in a torrential tropical downpour of oversized drops, the conflicting winds from the chasm tossing them about. So, at one moment you have rain rising straight into your hat, at the next moment coming down, and at every moment sailing in laterally from any angle.

The perpetual rain makes the Rain Forest, a jungle of matted trees and vines, contrasting sharply with the brown, sunburnt landscape roundabout. The Rain Forest lies along the cliff edge for a mile and is roughly an eighth of a mile wide. The sun is shining brilliantly upon the waterfall and this terrific downpour comes from a perfectly blue sky.

At the end of the memorable mile we stood with thoroughly soaked feet and bodies shaken by the violent winds (though the day was windless) before the statue of Livingstone. It stands on the spot where the exporer first looked upon the phenomenon that he chose to name after the great Queen but which the inhabitants of this land had long before named Mosi-oa-tunya, The Smoke That Thunders. We felt like explorers ourselves, discoverers of a brand-new and never-to-be-forgotten experience.

from : Willard Price, *Incredible Africa*

14 Colour photography

Arctic, Canada

At a lonely weather-station I asked an American weatherman why he had signed on for a third tour of duty in the Arctic. He said that the attraction for him was colour photography! Colour photography in the Arctic! In popular imagination it is just unrelieved white, but, as people like the weatherman discover, the Arctic is rich in colour. In the Arctic night, lasting six months, there is not just a black-out : there is the moon reflected by the white brilliance of the snow. There are the 'moon-dogs', the paraselenae. (The real moon is surrounded by luminous rings due to ice crystals in the atmosphere and in these rings appear mock-moons, repeating the original across the sky.) But even when there is no moon the sky glow in the clear atmosphere makes the night visible. In addition there are the pyrotechnics of the Northern

Lights, flaunting their fantastic coloured draperies in a decor which no producer could ever imitate. In the summer there are the parahelia, the mock-suns. These 'sun-dogs' multiply the images of the sun in the sky as the paraselenae do the moon. When the snow leaves the Arctic Islands, as it does in the summer except in sheltered canyons or on the ice-plateau, the landscape becomes alive with colour. There are Arctic poppies, red saxifrage, purple willow and the innumerable coloured mosses and lichens. The Arctic flowers are all brightly hued—red, blue, orange and white. The sides of the hills in the Arctic summer are often completely covered with saxifrage. There are butterflies in the Arctic, and mosquitoes and tiny black spiders and beetles. There are 200 kinds of birds, including the snow owl and the gyrfalcon, one of the world's most beautiful birds.

'Colours,' said the weatherman, enthusiastically. 'Colours so beautiful that the colour films can't do justice to them.'

from : Ritchie Calder, *The Inheritors*

15 Ice at sea

At sea (40° South), eighteen-thirties

At twelve o'clock we went below, and had just got through dinner when the cook put his head down the scuttle and told us to come on deck and see the finest sight that we had ever seen. 'Where away, Doctor?' asked the first man who was up. 'On the larboard bow.' And there lay, floating in the ocean, several miles off, an immense irregular mass, its top and points covered with snow, and its centre of a deep indigo colour. This was an iceberg, and of the largest size, as one of our men said who had been in the Northern Ocean. As far as the eye could reach, the sea in every direction was of a deep blue colour, the waves running high and fresh, and sparkling in the light, and in the midst lay this immense mountain island, its cavities and valleys thrown into deep shade, and its points and pinnacles glittering in the sun. All hands were soon on deck, looking at it, and admiring in various ways its beauty and grandeur. But no description can give any idea of the strangeness, splendour, and, really the sublimity, of the sight. Its great size—for it must have been from two to three miles in circumference, and several hundred feet in height—its slow motion, as its base rose and sank in the water, and its high points nodded against the clouds; the dashing of the waves upon it, which, breaking high with foam, lined its base with a white crust; and the thundering sound of the cracking of the mass, and the breaking and tumbling

437

down of huge pieces; together with its nearness and approach, which added a slight element of fear—all combined to give to it the character of true sublimity. The main body of the mass was, as I have said, of an indigo colour, its base crusted with frozen foam; and as it grew thin and transparent towards the edges and top, its colour shaded off from a deep blue to the whiteness of snow. It seemed to be drifting slowly towards the north, so that we kept away and avoided it. It was in sight all the afternoon; and when we got to leeward of it the wind died away, so that we lay-to quite near it for a greater part of the night. Unfortunately, there was no moon, but it was a clear night, and we could plainly mark the long regular heaving of the stupendous mass, as its edges moved slowly against the stars, now revealing them, and now shutting them in. Several times in our watch loud cracks were heard, which sounded as though they must have run through the whole length of the iceberg, and several pieces fell down with a thundering crash, plunging heavily into the sea. Toward morning a strong breeze sprang up, and we filled away, and left it astern, and at daylight it was out of sight.

from : R. H. Dana, *Two Years before the Mast*

16 Ice at dawn

New York State, U.S.A.

She raised the sash, and then indeed, a glorious scene met her delighted eye. The lake exchanged its covering of unspotted snow for a face of dark ice that reflected the rays of the rising sun like a polished mirror. The houses were clothed in a dress of the same description, but which, owing to its position, shone like bright steel; while the enormous icicles that were pendent from every roof caught the brilliant light, apparently throwing it from one to the other, as each glittered, on the side next the luminary, with a golden lustre that melted away, on its opposite, into the dusky shades of a background . . . The huge branches of the pines and hemlocks bent with the weight of the ice they supported, while their summits rose above the swelling tops of the oak, beeches, and maples like spires of burnished silver issuing from domes of the same material. The limits of the view in the west, were marked by an undulating outline of bright light, as if, reversing the order of nature, numberless suns might momentarily be expected to heave above the horizon. In the foreground of the picture, along the shores of the lake and near to the village, each tree seemed studded with diamonds. Even the sides of the mountains where the rays of the sun could not yet fall were decorated with a glassy coat that presented every graduation of brilliancy, from the first touch of the luminary to the dark foliage of the hemlock, glistening through its coat of crystal. In short, the whole view was one scene of quivering radiancy, as lake, mountains, village, and woods, each emitted a portion of light, tinged with its peculiar hue, and varied by its position and its magnitude.

from : James Fenimore Cooper, *The Pioneers*

17 At leisure in the tropics

South Pacific

I am sitting comfortably in front of my bamboo palace reading a little, smoking a bit, and occasionally falling into a brief slumber. A coconut falls and I wonder if it would be better for a drinking nut or a milk nut. I hear the roaring of the reef-surf and watch some children, bathing, naked on the beach. A pretty native girl passes and greets me, and as is the custom asks me what I am doing. I tell her 'nothing', and she passes on while I take a puff at my pipe, and returning to my book, perhaps read! 'There is a tear that no philosophy can dry and a pang that will rise when we approach the Gods.' That is enough to think about for the rest of the afternoon so I drop my book and doze again until Terii calls me to eat ... There is something about the tropics, brother, which you do not understand. There is a feeling of rest and comfort and contentment, which after all is one of the greatest things we can wish for, because after all what do we strive for in life if it is not a future chance for rest and comfort and contentment?

from : Johnny Frisbie, *The Frisbies of the South Seas*

18 At work in Katmandu

Nepal, 1962

There are about fifty banking offices scattered around Nepal which I have to visit. Many of them are difficult of access. I have a Land Rover for getting around the five offices in Katmandu Valley and down the one and only road to India which gets me to three more.

Some are served by fair-weather air strips (and are cut off during the monsoon) and quite a lot, which are close to the Indian Border, are reached by rail on the Indian side, which involves travelling on very slow trains on side-lines and constantly crossing and recrossing the border. The most remote can only be reached on horseback or on foot, and trekking around the mountains with porters to carry all our luggage is the best kind of banking I've ever done and I simply can't believe that I get paid for doing it.

We live in a little flat in the only proper office building in Katmandu, right in the bazaar area, with temples and tightly packed little buildings round us with their attendant noises and smells. We are the only foreigners in the neighbourhood. The immediate surroundings are squalid, but framed in our doorway is Langtung, 23,750 feet, and from our roof we can see the whole rim of Katmandu Valley, and permanently snow-capped mountains standing up beyond, from Makalu 27,824 feet in the east, to Ganesh 23,361 feet to the west; this kind of view makes up for a lot.

The stupendous scenery is, of course, one of the great things about being here. It is not only a matter of living with the big snows, but also with deep valleys and noisy streams, with hair-raising bridges and big expanses of terraced hillsides for paddy cultivation, with unsophisticated villages surrounding flamboyant temples. Another good thing is the climate; Katmandu is only 4,500 feet above sea level but that is enough to be sure of cool weather (almost too cool in the winter, as our flat has only oil stoves for heating and the windows don't fit in their frames). The monsoon is lovely because the rain falls mainly in the night and the beautifully vivid green of the hill-sides and paddy fields shines in the sun through most of the day.

Until recently there was no road into Nepal, and everything had to be carried in on porters' backs over mountain tracks (even a few motor cars and one steam roller). Now there is a very spectacular road to Katmandu, but to nowhere else, and everything going elsewhere still goes on porters' backs except where there are airfields. The first wheel ever to be seen in the valley next to ours was on the first aeroplane which landed there. No bullock carts!* This is living in the Middle Ages but I have no wish to be anywhere else at the moment.

A special contribution by Ralph Wyeth

---

* Some planners have been along to make a road building programme, and there has even been some actual road building, but the dominant means of transport for a long time to come will be strictly human

19 Pleasure of travelling by train

U.S.A., nineteen-fifties

I have spent much time in American long-distance trains, and still enjoy them, even though the service and the food in them are not as good as they used to be. East of Chicago I prefer to fly, but in the larger and more promising spaces of the South-West I still like to rumble along, day and night, popping in and out of my metal hutch, thick with the sweet reek of Burleigh tobacco, lurching along the corridors in search of a martini and a magazine or chilled tomato juice and pork chops, pleasantly aware that all the time I am reading, eating, drinking, talking, shaving, brushing my teeth, that unwanted leagues of prairie are vanishing beneath the wheels; I am preparing myself for that moment in the early morning when the bar of the window blind, suddenly released and flying up, seems to work like an enchanter's wand—and we are rolling through a new landscape, far away from the land where the sun went down. A full night's journey on an express, particularly in the South-West, is always long enough to conjure this miraculous transformation. (The aeroplanes, for all their three hundred miles an hour, can never complete the trick, for they show you something like a relief map, and by the time you are down to earth you are in an airport, exactly like the one you left the night before.) This train to Texas, next morning, did not cheat me. My first peep through the window showed me autumn rolled out like a golden-brown carpet, a hundred miles of it ending in a faint blue smudge. I was rolling along, somewhere else.

from : J. B. Priestley and Jaquetta Hawkes, *Journey down a Rainbow*

Acknowledgements

Grateful acknowledgement is made to the following for permission to include copyright material in this book.

The figure in brackets preceding the extract number indicates the section concerned.

George Allen & Unwin Ltd. and the respective authors for (2)5, (4)15, (6)5, (8)11.

W. H. Allen & Co. Ltd. and the respective authors for (5)18, (9)17.

Angus & Robertson (U.K.) Ltd. and the respective authors for (2)14, (2)31, (4)3, (6)42, (9)13.

The Architectural Press Ltd. and the author for (6)31.

Mrs. George Bambridge and Macmillan & Co. Ltd. for (9)24.

Barrie & Jenkins Ltd. and the author for (9)15.

The Beaver and the respective authors for (3)22, (5)4.

Adrian Bell, Esq. for (8)4.

G. Bell & Sons Ltd. and the author for (1)2, (5)3.

The Bodley Head and the author for (2)2.

B.B.C. Publications and the author for (4)24.

Miss Sonia Brownell and Secker & Warburg Ltd. for (9)19.

Professor Sir Colin Buchanan and Mrs. Buchanan for (6)25.

Jonathan Cape Ltd. and the respective authors for (6)11, (7)29, (7)32.

Cassell & Co. Ltd. and the respective authors for (2)22, (3)31, (5)31, (8)18.

Chatto & Windus Ltd. and the respective authors for (1)21, (2)25, (3)7, (3)24, (4)19, (4)35, (6)3, (6)37, (7)7, (7)11, (7)26, (7)28, (8)21, (10)12.

Cedric Chivers Ltd. and the Estate of the Late Upton Sinclair for (9)14.

Jonathan Clowes Ltd. and the author for (7)12.

William Collins Sons & Co. Ltd. and the respective authors for (1)9, (1)10, (1)11, (1)31, (2)15, (2)33, (3)27, (5)30, (6)34, (7)37, (8)14, (9)3, (9)20, (9)22, (10)6.

Collins-Knowlton-Wing, Inc. and the authors for (3)6, (6)2. Copyright © 1960, by Lorus and Margery Milne.

Curtis Brown Ltd. and the respective authors for (1)33, (4)31, (6)23, (7)16, (7)23.

The Daily Telegraph and the respective authors for (1)32, (2)17, (3)17, (3)23, (3)28, (4)32, (5)22, (5)28, (6)13, (6)18, (6)28, (8)20, (8)25, (9)6, (9)7, (9)9, (9)28, (9)30.

Peter Davies Ltd. and the author for (9)23.

J. M. Dent & Sons Ltd. and the author for (1)1, (1)29, (2)18.

André Deutsch Ltd. and the author for (4)9, (7)5, (7)30, (7)36.

Dobson Books Ltd. and the author for (1)20, (2)3, (5)13, (7)10.

Doubleday & Co. Inc. for (8)7 and (10)17 from *The Frisbies of the South Seas* by Johnny Frisbie. Copyright © 1959 by Florence Frisbie Henbenstreig.

Gerald Duckworth & Co. Ltd. and the respective authors for (2)27, (4)11.

Elek Books Ltd. and the author for (1)30, (2)6.

Malcolm Elwin, Literary Executor to the Llewelyn Powys Estate, for (8)26.

Eyre & Spottiswoode (Publishers) Ltd. and the respective authors for (5)1, (5)7.

Faber & Faber Ltd. and the respective authors for (2)4, (6)38, (6)40, (7)34, (7)35, (8)12.

John Farquharson Ltd. and the respective authors for (1)15, (3)8, (6)12, (7)4, (8)29, (10)7.

Miss Vivien Flaxman for (2)10.
Journal of the Franklin Institute and the author for (6)7.
Garnstone Press Ltd. and the respective authors for (1)8, (5)8, (6)4.
The Geographical Magazine and the respective authors for (4)37, (5)16, (5)20.
Victor Gollancz Ltd. and the respective authors for (3)19, (4)22, (4)28, (9)11.
Granada Publishing Ltd. and the author for (7)15.
Nicholas Guppy, Esq. and Francis Huxley, Esq. for (6)10.
Robert Hale & Co. Ltd. and the respective authors for (1)17, (4)10.
Hamish Hamilton Ltd. and the author for (5)26; and for (4)33 and (7)27 from *The Great Hunger: Ireland 1845–9*. Copyright © 1962 by Cecil Woodham-Smith.
Harper & Row, Publishers, Inc. and the author for (4)22 and (4)28; for (4)12, (7)19 and (7)21 from pp. 66–67, 170–2 in *Traditional Cultures and the Impact of Technological Change* by George M. Foster. Copyright © 1962 by George M. Foster; for (5)14 (150 words) from *The Virginian* by Owen Wister; and for (4)1 (130 words) from *World without Want* by Paul G. Hoffman.
George G. Harrap & Co. Ltd. and the respective authors for (4)2, (8)27.
Professor Heinrich Harrer for (3)13, (7)8.
The Harvill Press Ltd. and the author for (10)3.
William Heinemann Ltd. and the respective authors for (1)12, (1)16, (1)26, (2)1, (3)11, (3)21, (4)7, (4)16, (4)29, (5)19, (6)32, (7)2, (8)1, (9)2, (10)5, (10)11, (10)13, (10)14.
Her Majesty's Stationery Office for (8)15.
Hodder & Stoughton Ltd. and the respective authors for (2)19, (2)21, (2)23, (2)31, (3)4, (4)4, (7)6, (8)5, (10)2.
William Hodge & Co. Ltd. and the author for (3)15.
The Hogarth Press Ltd. and the respective authors for (1)23, (1)28, (3)2, (3)16, (4)5, (5)9, (5)23, (7)14, (7)31, (10)10.
Hutchinson Publishing Group Ltd. and the respective authors for (2)16, (3)12, (4)30, (5)10, (6)16, (9)8, (9)16.
The Illustrated London News and the author for (6)30.
Dan Jacobsen, Esq. for (6)24.
Michael Joseph Ltd. and the author for (6)27.
Humphrey Kempe, Esq. for (8)3, (8)10.
William Kimber & Co. Ltd., the author and the Longman Group Ltd. for (5)25.
Herbert Kubly, Esq. for (9)10.
Little, Brown & Co. and the author for (2)20. Copyright © 1956 by Katharine Scherman Rosin.
Douglas Lockwood, Esq. for (3)1, (3)20.
Longman Group Ltd. and the respective authors for (3)5, (4)6, (6)26, (8)6, (8)8, (9)27.
Lutterworth Press Ltd. and the author for (6)35.
Macmillan & Co. Ltd. and the author for (2)11, (6)19, (9)31.
The Macmillan Co. of Canada Ltd. and the author for (1)7.
Patrick McGeown, Esq. for (5)11, (9)1, (9)12.
Methuen & Co. Ltd. and the respective authors for (1)6, (2)13, (2)24, (4)26, (4)34, (8)2, (10)8.
William Morrow & Co. Inc. and the author for (7)13.
Frederick Muller Ltd. and the author for (4)13, (4)27, (7)20, (7)22.
John Murray Publishers Ltd. and the respective authors for (1)14, (1)24, (1)27, (2)8, (3)14, (4)8, (5)2, (5)12, (6)39, (7)25, (8)22, (8)24, (10)1.
National Geographic Magazine and the respective authors for (3)30, (8)28.
New Society and the author for (6)17. This article first appeared in *New Society*, the weekly review of social sciences, 128 Long Acre, London W.C.2.
The Estate of Nevil Shute Norway and William Heinemann Ltd. for (1)22.

The Observer and the respective authors for (4)36, (5)21, (5)27, (7)17, (8)19, (9)21.

Oxford University Press for (3)9 and (7)18 from *East African Childhood: Three Versions*, edited by Lorene K. Fox and published by Oxford University Press, Eastern African Branch.

Pan Books Ltd. and the author for (4)20.

Penguin Books Ltd. for (6)33 and (6)36, 400 words from pp. 276–7 and 400 words from pp. 292–3 of Robert Arvill: *Man and Environment*, © Robert Arvill, 1967; and for (8)17 Gerard Chaliand: *The Peasants of North Vietnam*, pp. 144–7 (1,300 words). Copyright (1969).

A. D. Peters & Co. and the respective authors for (4)33, (6)14, (10)19.

Sir Isaac Pitman (Aust.) Pty. Ltd. and the author for (3)3.

Laurence Pollinger Ltd. and the author for (7)16 and (7)38; and the Estate of the Late Mrs. Frieda Lawrence for (10)5.

The Estate of the Late Marjorie K. Rawlings for (9)29.

The Reader's Digest Association Ltd. and the respective authors for (1)25, (6)21, (6)41.

Marie Rodell and the author for (9)25. Copyright © 1941 by Rachel L. Carson.

Routledge & Kegan Paul Ltd. and the author for (9)26.

Secker & Warburg Ltd. and the respective authors for (7)9, (9)4.

Simon & Schuster Inc. and the author for (2)25.

Studio Vista Publishers, the author and editor for (10)9.

Sungravure Pty. Ltd. and the respective authors for (1)19, (8)23.

Mrs. Muriel Sutherland for (6)6.

Nicholas Thompson and the author for (4)25.

Times Newspapers Ltd. and the respective authors for (1)18, (2)29, (3)18, (3)25, (4)14, (5)24, (5)29, (6)20, (6)29, (7)24, (8)16, (9)18.

The Tweedsmuir Estate for (2)9.

University of California Press and the respective authors for (7)16. Originally published by the University of California Press; reprinted by permission of the Regents of the University of California.

University of Texas Press and the author for (2)34.

Van Nostrand Reinhold Co. for (1)13, (2)26 from Nesbitt, Pond and Allen: *The Survival Book*, copyright 1959.

Weidenfeld (Publishers) Ltd. and the author for (7)33.

Henry Williamson, Esq. for (8)13.

In a very few instances it has not proved possible to trace copyright holders and the publishers would be pleased to rectify any omissions from the above list in subsequent editions of this book.

Index of Topics

The figures indicate page numbers

449